One Nation Underground

American History and Culture

Neil Foley, Kevin Gaines, Martha Hodes, and Scott Sandage
GENERAL EDITORS

Guess Who's Coming to Dinner Now? Multicultural Conservatism in America
Angela D. Dillard

One Nation Underground: The Fallout Shelter in American Culture
Kenneth D. Rose

One Nation Underground

The Fallout Shelter in American Culture

KENNETH D. ROSE

New York University Press

NEW YORK AND LONDON

2001

NEW YORK UNIVERSITY PRESS
New York and London

Library of Congress Cataloging-in-Publication Data
Rose, Kenneth D. (Kenneth David), 1946–
One nation underground : a history of the fallout shelter /
Kenneth D. Rose.
p.   cm. — (American history and culture)
Includes bibliographical references and index.
ISBN 0-8147-7522-5 (acid-free paper)
1. Fallout shelters—Social aspects—United States. 2. Nuclear
warfare—Social aspects—United States. 3. Cold War—Social
aspects—United States. 4. United States—Social conditions—1945–
5. Popular culture—United States—History—20th century.   I. Title.
II. American history and culture (New York University Press)
UA927 .R67 2001
303.6'6—dc21   2001004000

New York University Press books are printed on acid-free paper,
and their binding materials are chosen for strength and durability.

Manufactured in the United States of America

10 9 8 7 6 5 4 3 2 1

To my father, whose selfless devotion to a very dangerous profession continues to inspire me, and to Jeanne, whose encouragement, patience, and good humor made this project possible.

Contents

Acknowledgments

Niko Pfund at New York University Press believed in this project from the very beginning, and I owe him a great debt for his stewardship of *One Nation*. Also much thanks to Niko's successor at NYU Press, Eric Zinner, and to Cecilia Feilla, with whom I worked closely on the final manuscript. As always, Despina Gimbel was diligent in her duties as managing editor, and Rosalie Morales Kearns did a superb job as copy editor.

Bob Harris proved to be an inexhaustible font of knowledge on this subject. Without his guidance and suggestions this book would have been much less than it is. Scott Sandage and Jeanne Lawrence gave my manuscript a close reading, and I am very grateful for their suggestions. Fellow Cold War traveler Laura McEnaney also had a number of observations that helped me a great deal.

Thanks to California State University, Chico Interlibrary Loan staff, especially George Thompson and Jo Ann Bradley. The Summer Scholar Award I received from CSU, Chico enabled me to gather most of the photographs in this book. Early on in this project Gray Fitzsimons directed me to some valuable sources, which I greatly appreciate. My colleagues in the CSU, Chico history department, including Mike Magliari, Mike Gillis, Cliff Minor, Lisa Emmerich, and Joanna Cowden, provided me with invaluable input, and department chair Carl Peterson has been very supportive of this project. The members of the writing group—Larry Bryant, Laird Easton, Weikun Cheng, Jeff Livingston, Tim Sistrunk, Judy Raftery, Jeanne Lawrence, and Steve Lewis—were especially helpful. Jeff Livingston also steered me to the Committee on the Present Danger material, for which I am quite grateful. Tom Parker and Jim Connolly were not only good enough to read one of my chapters, but each helped guide me to Bob Dylan's "Let Me Die in My Footsteps." Many thanks to Kate Transchel for her translations from the Russian, and for trying to gain access to civil defense material in Russia. Alas, as Kate informs me, the Russians are still keeping much of this material classified. Mark Schara was very generous in his hospitality in Washington, D.C., and thanks to Roger Green and Gaby Whiteman for putting me up in Ft. Myers. As always, a special acknowledgment to Kim Hoagland of Hotel Hoagland fame.

Nick Natanson at the National Archives Annex in College Park, Maryland, helped me find the materials I needed, and the rest of the staff was also quite patient and helpful. Thanks to Randolph Langanbach at FEMA, and a special thanks to former OCD spokesperson Russell B. Clanahan for fielding my many phone calls and letters. Ann Seeger at the National Museum of American History went out of her way to assist me on this project. As always, the staff at the Library of Congress was very efficient. I also owe a great debt of gratitude to Mercedes Emperado at the Federal Emergency Management Agency Library for letting me use the library's resources.

Fran and Vernie Wilson very graciously showed me around their Paradise fallout shelter, and I am grateful to Les Lawrence, who helped arrange a fascinating tour of Chico's former Titan missile facility. Thanks to Greg Taylor for the loan of *Level 7* and his observations on nuclear physics, and thanks to Mike Cannon and the rest of the Pub Scouts for helping to keep me sane.

This book deals with controversial issues, and my interpretation is not the only one open to scholars of good will. The people who helped shepherd me through this project represent a variety of points of view, and my book is better for it. Any errors in this book belong to me, and not to my excellent readers and editors.

Introduction

Only once in our history has the question of nuclear war and survival been embraced by an entire nation as a subject of urgent debate. Discussions about the ramifications of nuclear war had, until that time, been almost exclusively the private preserve of policy makers, scientists, and intellectuals such as Herman Kahn, J. Robert Oppenheimer, and Henry Kissinger. But the fallout shelter controversy that began in 1961 (which *Business Week* succinctly described as "to dig, or not to dig") created a startling and unprecedented public involvement in this debate, claiming the passion and energies of citizens from all strata of society.[1] The major media produced a flurry of essays devoted to this subject, but so did the media outside the mainstream. When publications as diverse as *Yale Review, Business Week, Architectural Record, Good Housekeeping, Catholic Nation*, and *Successful Farming* all began producing articles on the fallout shelter issue, it was clear that something significant was happening in American culture. (In 1961 even *Sunset* magazine ran a story on fallout shelters tucked in among such articles as "Transforming Leftovers: The Sauce Is the Secret" and "How to Display and Store Magazines.")[2] As *Time* magazine put it, "At cocktail parties and P.T.A. meetings and family dinners, on buses and commuter trains and around office watercoolers, talk turns to shelters."[3]

The debate touched the lives of people in the smallest and in the largest of communities. In Glendo, Wyoming, residents voted to buy a potato cellar that would house the entire population of 294 in case of nuclear attack—making Glendo the first community to offer shelter for every resident.[4] In America's great cities, where debate was raging over whether *any* kind of shelter could effectively protect urban dwellers, there was a small boom in demand for the canned drinking water that went into fallout shelters. This water, according to city sophisticates, lacked the chemical taste of ordinary tap water, and made an excellent highball mixer.[5] In the suburbs, families agonized over whether or not to make the considerable investment in a fallout shelter, and how they would feel about shooting less-prepared neighbors who might intrude into their shelter during a nuclear emergency.

The flashpoint for this remarkable phenomenon, and the beginning of our story, was a speech given by John F. Kennedy on July 25, 1961. Kennedy's speech concerned Berlin, where Khrushchev was threatening to negotiate a separate peace with East Germany, and to declare Berlin a "neutral" city from which the Western Allies would have to withdraw by the end of the year.[6] Berlin had been a lightning rod for East-West tensions in both the Truman and Eisenhower administrations, and the underlying text in previous Berlin crises had always been whether or not the United States would risk a general war over the defense of Berlin. For the Kennedy administration, the scene had been set at the Vienna summit in June, where Khrushchev had attempted a rhetorical bludgeoning of Kennedy. "We are going to negotiate a new agreement with East Germany, and the access routes to Berlin will be under their control," proclaimed Khrushchev. "If there is any effort by the West to interfere, there will be war." Kennedy responded to this crude assertion by replying, "Then there will be war, Mr. Chairman. It's going to be a very cold winter."[7]

Emphasizing his determination to oppose Soviet designs on Berlin even to the brink of nuclear war, Kennedy said in his July speech that "we do not want to fight—but we have fought before." The seriousness of the situation was underlined by Kennedy's request for a $3.24 billion increase for the military, and for an additional $207 million to fund a civil defense initiative that would "identify and mark space in existing structures—public and private—that could be used for fall-out shelters in case of attack" (fig. 1). Acknowledging that the necessity for fallout shelters was a concept "new to our shores," Kennedy nevertheless insisted that "the lives of those families which are not hit in a nuclear blast and fire can still be saved—*if*

2

FIG. 1. *Washington Post*, 26 July 1961. Collection of the Library of Congress. © 1961 by the Washington Post. Reprinted by permission.

they can be warned to take shelter and *if* that shelter is available. . . . in the coming months I hope to let every citizen know what steps he can take without delay to protect his family in case of attack." At the end of his speech Kennedy issued a grim reminder that "in the thermonuclear age, any misjudgment on either side about the intentions of the other could rain more devastation in several hours than has been wrought in all the wars of human history."[8]

While American anxieties about nuclear threats to their homes had been steadily increasing since 1945—the successful Soviet explosion of an atomic bomb in 1949, the Soviet detonation of a hydrogen bomb in 1953, and the launching of Sputnik in 1957 were signposts along the way— nothing previously had brought nuclear war into the homes of Americans in such a literal sense as Kennedy's speech. Kennedy's speech was an official enunciation of what was already a fait accompli: the American home had been put on the front lines of the Cold War. This development was a logical progression in a trend that had been developing since the beginnings of the twentieth century, as the traditional distinctions between civilian and military became increasingly blurred with each war. Civilian casualties accounted for perhaps 5 percent of the total during World War I, and as much as half of the total during World War II.[9] But in the next, and perhaps final, world war, civilian casualties might account for over 95 percent of the total because the incredible power and crudity of nuclear weapons made it virtually impossible to distinguish between military targets and civilian neighborhoods. As Harold Urey, a Nobel Prize–winning chemist, noted in 1945, "atomic bombs don't land in the next block, leaving survivors to thank their lucky stars and . . . to hope the next bomb will also miss them."[10] Val Peterson, Eisenhower's much maligned chief civil defense administrator, was both dispensing sound advice and belaboring the obvious when he suggested that "the best way to be alive when an atomic bomb goes off in your neighborhood is not to be there."[11]

The ocean barrier that had been a source of comfort and security to Americans since the founding of the republic had been rendered moot by advances in aviation, first by the long-range bomber, then decisively by the intercontinental ballistic missile. Some immediately recognized that a crucial shift had taken place. In a radio address given one day after Hiroshima had been destroyed, General Henry Arnold warned Americans that the next enemy attack might not occur thousands of miles away, but might "be centralized on Michigan Boulevard, Biscayne Boulevard, Sunset Boulevard or on Main Streets in your home town."[12] For most Americans, however, this was an extremely difficult concept to absorb. Writing in 1960, C. Vann Woodward maintained that "the end of the era of free security has overtaken Americans so suddenly and swiftly that they have not brought themselves to face its practical implications, much less its bearing upon their history."[13] The physicist Eugene Wigner also observed that "our population has experienced no war on our own territory, and it is difficult to imagine such an event in the abstract."[14] Americans, according to Val Peterson, had "simply not accepted yet the possibility of an enemy attack on the United States from the skies by intercontinental bombers," and Peterson's agency, the Federal Civil Defense Administration, began to produce posters emphasizing civilian vulnerability to enemy attack (see figs. 2 and 3).[15]

The development of a species of weapons without precedent in human history had mandated a huge strategic shift, and Americans were now called on to make an equally huge psychological shift. In a 1955 article for *Science News Letter* entitled "Backyard Front Lines," Howard Simons proclaimed that "terrifying weapons have moved the fox-hole, bunker and emergency ration from the infantryman's front-line to everybody's backyard. 'Dig or die,' and 'duck and cover,' apply not only to G. I.'s some 10,000 miles away, but are realities for the politician, the housewife, the worker and the schoolboy."[16] Chet Holifield, representative from California and chair of numerous congressional civil defense committees, declared that in the event of nuclear war, "all the people in our country are frontline soldiers" and that "there is no frontline, no backline, the whole world is a battlefield."[17]

Even the farm had become part of this battlefield. The editors of *Successful Farming* lamented, "God forbid, but if World War III erupts, we're all going to be in the front lines—and part of the battleground may be your farm."[18] In a publication titled *Livestock, Fallout and a Plan for Survival*, farmers were told that they "control a valuable, destructible, and essential national resource" and that it was "their duty to defend it to the limits of their ability." The strategically minded farmer understood that "should a nuclear war occur, survival of our country would depend largely upon the survival of a productive agriculture."[19] Livestock no less than human beings would have to be sheltered from the effects of nuclear war. In an acknowledgment of this, the Roberts Dairy company of Omaha, Nebraska, announced plans to build a bomb shelter for two hundred cows, and the Department of Agriculture released a publication called *Bunker-Type Fallout Shelter for Beef Cattle*.[20]

FIG. 2. Federal Civil Defense Administration poster. RG 304-P-2, Still Pictures Branch (NNSP), National Archives at College Park, MD.

The Berlin crisis of 1961 made the backyard battlefield a more immediate possibility. In a series of articles for *Saturday Review* that year, Norman Cousins insisted that "the key fact, the dominant fact, in modern warfare is that the civilian will be the prime target."[21] Gerard Piel, publisher of *Scientific American*, agreed, noting that Kennedy's July 25 speech had made it clear for the first time that the power of the American people was "predicated upon their readiness to accept assault upon their home territory."[22] Putting it in starker terms was Lewis Mumford, who took note of the "sudden radical change-over from war to collective extermination."[23]

Military strategists, no less than ordinary Americans, also had some painful readjustments to make.[24] Assumptions about how and why wars were fought—assumptions that had prevailed for millennia—now had to be reassessed. There were a few, such as the physicist Herman Kahn, who continued to insist that "our military forces exist to protect our people; not vice versa. People are ends, not means."[25] Others, however, concluded

Fig. 3. Federal Civil Defense Administration poster. RG 304-P-6, Still Pictures Branch (NNSP), National Archives at College Park, MD.

that the strategy of nuclear deterrence had transformed each private home into a de facto military target and, according to Hannah Arendt, had "changed the role of the military from that of a protector into that of a belated and essentially futile avenger."[26] Bernard Brodie, a RAND Corporation researcher, concluded that while the purpose of the military before the advent of atomic weapons had been to win wars, "from now on its chief purpose must be to avert them. It can have almost no other useful purpose."[27] "In the next war," said Eugene Rabinowitch, editor of the *Bulletin of the Atomic Scientists*, "civilian casualties will be considered in the same light as military casualties," and the main problem of nuclear war will not be saving the greatest number of lives, but "how to prevent the heartbeat of the nation from stopping."[28]

Berlin represented the most serious crisis of the Cold War to date because there was little doubt that Kennedy would use nuclear weapons to defend that city. When Kennedy's brother and confidant Robert Kennedy was interviewed in September for the *Meet the Press* television show, Kennedy noted that Berlin occupied more of the president's time than any other issue. As to how far the president would go in defense of Berlin, Robert Kennedy replied, "There's no question that he (the President) is prepared to use nuclear weapons if it comes to that."[29] Americans were extremely anxious and fearful over the prospects that the world might be plunged into a nuclear war, but Americans also overwhelmingly supported a strong Allied stand in Berlin and elsewhere. (In the first eighteen hours after Kennedy's speech, the White House received two thousand telegrams, with support for Kennedy's Berlin stand running twenty to one in favor.)[30] In a Gallup poll released on July 30, 1961, 82 percent favored the maintenance of American, British, and French forces in Berlin "even at the risk of war."[31] That risk seemed considerable to Americans, a majority of whom believed that there would be another world war within five years. This pessimism did not result in a grassroots clamoring for peace negotiations with the Soviets, however, and in fact polls consistently revealed an American preference for nuclear annihilation over communism.[32] This grim determination was also widely reflected in American editorials. Dean Pearson of the *Washington Post* commented that the Soviets would not be impressed by the United States sending a few more divisions to Berlin, but that they would be impressed by "American willingness to undergo atomic war."[33] The CBS news analyst Richard C. Hottelet noted that "the Soviets know that if they push in Berlin, they play with world war," and a *Life* magazine editorial was equally blunt: "Khrushchev must be aware that the American people are willing to face nuclear war for Berlin."[34] Making the situation even more tense was the belief on the part of many Soviets that the West was planning a preemptive attack on the Soviet Union. Speaking before the Communist Party congress in the fall of 1961, defense minister Rodion Malinovsky declared that "it is precisely a surprise nuclear attack on the Soviet Union and other socialist countries that the imperialists are preparing."[35]

While the phrase "Better Dead Than Red" has today become synonymous with the political philosophy of the far-right lunatic fringe, there is ample evidence that a broad range of Americans in the late 1950s and early 1960s understood that a nuclear war would bring unprecedented horrors (the media barrage made ignorance of this subject a virtual impossibility), but that a holocaust might be necessary to oppose communist domination.[36] While most Americans found no paradox in the fact that they both greatly feared nuclear war and approved of its use against communist aggression, American allies often maintained a very different perspective. When both Americans and Britons were asked by Gallup pollsters in 1961, "Suppose you had to make the decision between fighting an all-out nuclear war or living under communist rule—how would you decide?" 81 percent of Americans opted for nuclear war, while only 21 percent of the British chose this option.[37] This apparent willingness to move to the extreme of nuclear annihilation both exasperated and horrified observers outside the United States. Bertrand Russell, for instance, complained that when Americans said they "stand for freedom" it meant "you must be quite willing to perish in order to be free in hell."[38]

At the center of national anxieties about confrontation with the Soviets and the possibility of nuclear war was an intense national debate over fallout shelters. Immediately after Kennedy's speech the questions began to multiply—questions not only about how best to protect the home, but also about whether the home *could* be protected against nuclear weapons, or even *should* be protected against nuclear weapons. Scientists, priests, sociologists, and government officials weighed in with a barrage of statistical tables, theoretical models, behavioral studies, and moral assessments. Arguments proliferated over the fallout shelter's role in nuclear strategy, antiballistic missile systems, and numerous other aspects of the Cold War. Would World War III be a "counterforce" war limited to attacks on military targets and not civilian targets? Would nuclear attacks create massive firestorms, rendering all but the most elaborate of shelters useless? Would the building of fallout shelters indicate American resolve and insure the peace, or would this be a provocative action that would move the world closer to war? To what extent had civil defense become a component of military strategy?

Meanwhile, bewildered ordinary citizens faced even more troubling questions as they agonized over whether or not to build a fallout shelter. Could an effective shelter be built inexpensively, or would only the well-to-do be able to provide nuclear protection for their families? If a shelter owner had only enough food and water in his shelter for his family, would he be justified in killing his neighbors if they tried to get in? Was a new morality necessary for the Nuclear Age?

With large numbers of Americans seemingly both willing to fight a war with the Soviets and convinced that such a war would occur in the near future, it seems reasonable that these same Americans would be taking steps to protect themselves from the results of such a war. As we shall see, this did not happen, and the evidence indicates that very few Americans took any steps toward preparing their homes against nuclear attack. While this is an apparent contradiction, most Americans would ultimately reject shelter building for a number of very good reasons. First, shelters were expensive, and represented a considerable outlay for the average American family. Second, while the home shelter might be able to protect its occupants from fallout, it offered little protection from nuclear blast and heat. The urgency to build a shelter also decreased after the Berlin and the Cuban crises had passed and tensions had eased somewhat between the United States and the Soviet Union. But the main reason Americans rejected shelter building had to do with the troubling moral aspects of shelters. These included questions of personal ethics and relationships with one's neighbors, as well as questions of national identity and the ultimate morality of the kind of world that would be created by a nuclear exchange. In order to "preserve" the United States, would its citizens have to burrow in the earth like moles? To survive, would they have to turn America into a garrison state—a Sparta for the Nuclear Age? And even if shelters did preserve the lives of those inside from the immediate ravages of nuclear war, what kind of life could the survivors expect when the bombs quit falling? Would such a life be worth living?

This book examines the social, cultural, political, and scientific aspects of this remarkable debate from its origins after World War II to its peak in the early 1960s. Chapter 1 will examine the slow dawning of the Nuclear Age and the early troubled history of civil defense. In chapter 2 the distinctive, apocalyptic writing produced during this era—and the urgency it added to the fallout shelter debate—will be scrutinized. The controversy over the moral aspects of fallout shelters and the way this issue was played out nationally and locally will be analyzed in chapter 3. Businesses, government bureaucracies, and schools were also preparing to go underground during this era, and chapter 4 will examine these preparations. There was a scientific as well as a moral controversy over fallout shelters, and the way scientists and others with technical expertise engaged this issue is the subject of chapter 5. Finally, chapter 6 will look at the "shelters that were not built" and summarize the many reasons that Americans turned away from shelters. A postscript will delve into the brief renewal of interest in civil defense during the Reagan administration.

After 1963 the public's involvement with the issues of fallout shelters and nuclear arms rapidly fell off. Public concern over nuclear arms would be revived during the Reagan years, but such concerns never approached the intensity witnessed in the early 1960s. Today, with the breakup of the Soviet Union and the end of the Cold War, the fallout shelter controversy of the early 1960s has assumed a droll, fantastical quality. Now that the threat of world annihilation has subsided, it has become easier to view that earlier era in an indulgent, bemused manner. Once ominous icons of the Nuclear Age have even become tourist attractions. In Albuquerque one can visit the National Atomic Museum and inspect Minuteman and Polaris missiles as well as replicas of the Hiroshima and Nagasaki atomic bombs. The museum also features a gift shop, which, until recently, sold silver earring replicas of the "Little Boy" and "Fat Man" atomic bombs.[39] In Green Valley, Arizona, a Titan II missile installation has been preserved at the Titan Missile Museum. In this interactive facility, visitors are given red folders marked "Top Secret," as the guide starts the launch countdown in the control room. Finally, in the words of a writer from *Travel & Leisure*, we "thrill ourselves silly turning a pair of keys (placed far enough apart so as to require two people) and watching the board light up. Not long ago, this would have spelled the end for a mysterious place still known as Target No. 2."[40]

The fallout shelter and its accoutrements have also become the object of Cold War nostalgia. The once secret facility at the Greenbriar resort that was designed to provide nuclear shelter to fleeing members of Congress is now open to the public with regularly scheduled tours.[41] Emergency water canned by a Florida firm during the Cuban Missile Crisis is currently being offered at fifteen dollars per can to raise money for the Cold War Museum in Virginia.[42] And in a clear indication that the fallout shelter has become a relic of the past, a complete home shelter is on permanent display at the National Museum of American History in Washington, D.C. (see fig. 4). The fallout shelter, like other Cold War artifacts, now seems quaint, even amusing (indeed, a fallout shelter was the central motif in the 1999 romantic comedy *Blast from the Past*). As Bruce Watson has observed, "nothing seems more darkly comic than Dad out in the yard digging for his family's survival under the shadow of a mushroom cloud."[43]

But there was nothing very comic at the time about the threat of nuclear war. It was a bipolar world, a world of intense ideological and economic competition, a world of overheated rhetoric and precious few opportunities for compromise or accommodation. The dilemma, posed by Henry Kissinger, was that "mankind has at its disposal the means to destroy itself at the precise moment when schisms among nations have never been deeper."[44] In these traumatic few years, climaxing with the Cuban Missile Crisis of 1962, humanity came as close as it has ever come to exterminating all life on the planet. The threat seemed so dire at the time

Fig. 4. Fallout shelter display, installed 1994. National Museum of American History, Smithsonian Institution. Photo no. 94-9115.

FIG. 5. The author's father, far left, and his crew in front of their B-47, ca. 1960.

that Margaret Mead suggested that an international program be developed that would continually rotate through blastproof shelters society's most productive members as well as a certain number of recently married couples. Thus the continuance of the human race would be preserved against the threat of nuclear annihilation.[45]

Some modern readers might be tempted to dismiss 1960s talk about nuclear holocaust as exaggerated and hysterical. While scholarly works seldom benefit from the personal revelations of the author, a brief anecdote from my own life might add some perspective on the times. I grew up in a military family, and in the mid-1950s we were transferred to Lincoln Air Force Base in Lincoln, Nebraska. The base at Lincoln was a large Strategic Air Command (SAC) facility with two wings of B-47 bombers, and my father, Howard Rose, was a B-47 pilot (see fig. 5). When the Cuban Missile Crisis reached its last, crucial stage, my father disappeared out to the base and was gone for a week. Rumor reached us that SAC bombers had been dispersed around the country. When we asked my father later what he had been doing during that week, he said that he had spent a good deal of the time sitting in his plane with his crew, with the engines running and a full load of nuclear weapons.

Waiting for the word to go.

CHAPTER I

A New Age Dawning

Often forgotten in the post-Hiroshima world is that the most common first reaction to the dropping of atomic weapons on Japan, at least among Americans and their allies, was not universal horror but unalloyed joy and relief. By the summer of 1945 preparations were under way for a November invasion of the Japanese home islands, an operation that had the potential to become a military nightmare. The use of atomic bombs on Hiroshima and Nagasaki would make that invasion unnecessary. Paul Fussell, an infantryman during the war, remembered that

> when the atom bombs were dropped and news began to circulate that "Operation Olympic" would not, after all, be necessary, when we learned to our astonishment that we would not be obliged in a few months to rush up the beaches near Tokyo assault-firing while being machine-gunned, mortared, and shelled, for all the practiced phlegm of our tough facades we broke down and cried with relief and joy. We were going to live.[1]

Freeman Dyson, who worked for the Royal Air Force Bomber Command during World War II, was scheduled to be sent to Okinawa in the summer of

1945, where three hundred British bombers (called Tiger Force) would take up the bombing of Japan. As Dyson noted, "I found this continuing slaughter of defenseless Japanese even more sickening than the slaughter of well-defended Germans." Dyson was at home when he heard of the Hiroshima explosion: "I was sitting at home, eating a quiet breakfast with my mother, when the morning paper arrived with the news of Hiroshima. I understood at once what it meant. 'Thank God for that,' I said. I knew that Tiger Force would not fly, and I would never have to kill anybody again."[2]

As nuclear weapons have increased in strength and number since 1945, the enormity of Truman's decision to use these weapons has grown to the point that it is now widely considered to be the most controversial act of the twentieth century. If nothing else, it has spawned a bitter debate among historians, some of whom believe that Japanese surrender was imminent, and that therefore use of atomic weapons was totally unjustified, while others maintain that the Japanese were prepared to continue fighting indefinitely.[3] Truman himself expressed no regrets about the use of atomic weapons on Hiroshima and Nagasaki, and in a 1961 speech he responded to his critics in his inimitable fashion by observing, "I haven't heard any of them crying about those boys in those upside-down battleships at Pearl Harbor."[4]

Regardless of one's opinion on whether or not the use of atom bombs was necessary to end the war, the fact that they *were* used has assumed a prominent place in modern history. Indeed, the importance of this event is now universally acknowledged (a group of sixty-seven of the nation's leading historians and journalists in 1999 called this the most important news story of the twentieth century), but in the immediate aftermath the transformational implications of what had been wrought at Hiroshima were absorbed by Americans only slowly.[5] As late as 1960 Arthur Koestler argued that humanity had found it difficult to come to terms with the Nuclear Age because "from now onward mankind will have to live with the idea of its death as a species." Koestler compared the reluctance to accept the post-Hiroshima world to the slow, difficult acceptance of the Copernican system over the Ptolemaic.[6] Vincent Wilson, Jr., also found little evidence that this much heralded new era had taken root, and even argued that "it would seem more to the point to label these past years the T. V. Age—considering the apparent impact of television on the population as a whole."[7]

Even military strategists at first refused to believe that the bomb had changed anything. That a single airplane had visited such destruction on Hiroshima was impressive, but the quantity of destruction was still on a recognizable scale, such as had been seen in earlier Allied bombings. Referring to

FIG. 6. The caption attached to this photograph was "Baker day—Bikini—The cauliflower aftercloud, after dumping two million tons of water, which had been sucked up by the underwater explosion, rises in breath taking wrath, July 25, 1946." RG 304-NT-AEC-48-3721 (folder 1A), Still Pictures Branch (NNSP), National Archives at College Park, MD.

atomic weapons in the fall of 1945, James V. Forrestal, secretary of the navy, cautioned that it was "dangerous to depend on documents or gadgets, as these instruments do not win wars."[8] A few months later the Pentagon issued its first assessment of the impact of atomic weapons, and concluded that the bomb's destructiveness, limited availability, and great expense "profoundly affect the employment of this new weapon and consequently its influence on the future conduct of war."[9]

The views of the atomic pessimists seemed to be vindicated by the results of the "Able" atomic test at Bikini Atoll on July 1, 1946. The bomb was some two miles off target and sank only a few of the assembled ships. The Bikini "Baker" test of July 25, 1946, was a different story, however, and proved to be sufficiently destructive to restore the bomb's tarnished image (see figs. 6 and 7). By June 1947 the Joint Chiefs had concluded that "atomic bombs not only can nullify any nation's military effort, but can demolish its social and economic structures and prevent their reestablishment for long periods of time."[10]

Certainly the public itself seemed initially impressed. Paul Boyer has called the first reaction to the atomic bomb "a psychic event of almost unprecedented proportions," but has also characterized the public opinion data on the bomb for this period as "confusing and to some extent contradictory."[11] A survey conducted by the Social Science Research Council (SSRC) in 1946 found that 98 percent of Americans had heard of the atomic bomb, but of course this meant that 2 percent of Americans (some two million) remained ignorant of this revolutionary new weapon.[12] The survey was also remarkable in the depth of pessimism it revealed. Two-thirds of the respondents expected another war, but three-fourths claimed not to worry about the bomb because ordinary people were powerless to address such problems.[13] As the Soviets developed their own atomic weapons, American fears began to increase that U.S. cities would be subject to attack by nuclear weapons in a conflict with the Soviet Union. By

FIG. 7. The Baker mushroom cloud, as it begins to flatten out. RG 304-NT (folder 1A, fig. 2.42), Still Pictures Branch (NNSP), National Archives at College Park, MD.

1953 the Soviet Union had successfully exploded a hydrogen bomb, and as the decade of the 1950s wore on polls registered increasing anxieties that this terrible new weapon would be used against the United States.[14]

Still, the expectation of another war within a generation and the conviction that nuclear and thermonuclear weapons would be used against American cities did not result in increased preparations against such a calamity. By 1960, in fact, Americans by overwhelming margins had not only made no preparations for nuclear war, they had not even *thought* about making such preparations. In part this was because Americans believed that civil defense was properly a government responsibility rather than a private one.[15] Government officials, however, often had a very different opinion. In a famous 1961 Columbia Broadcasting System program on civil defense, secretary of defense Robert McNamara proclaimed that "certainly the Federal Government, the State, and local governments all have parts to play, but most importantly, it's the responsibility of each individual to prepare himself and his family for that (thermonuclear) strike."[16] McNamara's statement was less callous than it might appear, given the woeful history of civil defense programs during the previous decade. During the two world wars civil defense had generally meant the marshaling of resources for the war effort rather than protection of the civilian population from attack, but by the end of World War II the development of long-range bombers and nuclear weapons had added a new urgency to civil defense in the United States. In 1948 the Office of Civil Defense Planning had characterized civil defense as the "missing link" in America's defenses, and had called for civil defense training for a cadre of fifteen million Americans.[17] This vision was not to be realized, and in succeeding years civil defense would be eschewed by the military as a civilian responsibility, shunned by state and municipal governments as too expensive, and largely ignored and chronically underfunded at the federal level. Civil defense consistently fell victim to what Thomas J. Kerr, in his authoritative work *Civil Defense in the U.S.*, has called "the politics of futility."[18]

Strategy during the 1950s

By necessity, civil defense issues were closely linked to nuclear strategy, and an understanding of overall nuclear strategy during this era will shed some light on the fallout shelter debate of the 1950s and 1960s. With the emergence of a bipolar world after World War II, the chief element in

American foreign policy became the "containment" of the Soviet Union. George Kennan, head of the State Department's Policy Planning Staff, had emphasized a nonmilitary approach to containment, and President Truman himself was initially resistant to large outlays for defense. Truman also had difficulty, according to David Alan Rosenberg, in seeing the atomic bomb as "anything other than an apocalyptic terror weapon," and one of Truman's legacies to subsequent presidents was to establish civilian control of nuclear weapons and to make sure that the ultimate decision to use such weapons would rest with the chief executive.[19]

The most important strategic document produced during the Truman administration was NSC 68, a secret National Security Council study. Under the direction of Paul Nitze, who took George Kennan's place as director of the Policy Planning Staff in 1950, NSC 68 portrayed the competition between the United States and the Soviet Union as a bleak struggle for survival. NSC 68 insisted that "the cold war is in fact a real war in which the survival of the free world is at stake," and endorsed "building up our military strength in order that it may not have to be used."[20] NSC 68 suggested that nuclear weapons alone could not do the job, and advocated a buildup of conventional forces for an "increased flexibility" that would enable Americans to "attain our objectives without war, or, in the event of war, without recourse to the use of atomic weapons for strategic or tactical purposes."[21] While the idea of flexible response suggested by NSC 68 would largely be ignored by the Eisenhower administration, this doctrine would be revived in 1960 under Kennedy.[22]

During the Eisenhower era, the president and secretary of state, John Foster Dulles, sought to limit both Soviet ambitions and American defense spending. They believed that they could accomplish these goals through the strategy of "massive retaliation," of responding with nuclear weapons to a wide range of potential international problems. While defense spending in the Eisenhower administration would remain relatively high, especially for "peacetime," it was considerably less than many were calling for.[23] Emphasized by Eisenhower throughout his administration was a buildup of nuclear forces and a reduction of conventional forces (the so-called New Look). This philosophy was reflected in America's growing nuclear arsenal, which increased from about a thousand weapons in 1953 to nearly eighteen thousand by 1960.[24] The crucial psychological aspect of massive retaliation was to convince potential enemies of America's willingness to avail itself of the nuclear option to defend its interests. This approach was emphasized in NSC 162/2, a secret 1953 document in which strategic planners were urged to "consider nuclear weapons to be as available for use as other munitions."[25] To this end Eisenhower insisted that "the United States cannot afford to preclude itself from using nuclear weapons even in a local situation," while Dulles observed that "the ability to get to the verge without getting into the war is the necessary art."[26]

In the event of war, it would be the Strategic Air Command (SAC) that would be delivering the weapons. Actual target selection seems to have been left largely to the discretion of Curtis LeMay, commander of SAC (fig. 8). LeMay was blunt in expressing his views, and his general theory of warfare was never in doubt. In 1953 LeMay told Sam Cohen (who would later achieve fame as the inventor of the neutron bomb), "I'll tell you what war is all about—you've got to kill people, and when you've killed enough they stop fighting."[27] In another discussion, LeMay was asked whether the SAC war plan during the 1950s had come from Washington. LeMay claimed, "We had a war plan of how we were going to fight the war. . . . It was ours. There wasn't anything that came out of Washington."[28] While nominally subject to the approval of the Joint Chiefs of Staff (JCS), SAC's target selection was rarely questioned in part because SAC analyzed target information on its own IBM 704 computer, a capability that none of the other services could match.[29] The targets themselves were largely military strategic assets (what would later be called "counterforce" targeting) and industrial centers, rather than urban populations. As David Burchinal, chief of staff of SAC's Eighth Air Force until 1958, makes clear, "We were not trying to hold cities hostage by means of a terror threat, or anything like that. We were targeting, if push came to shove, what was important militarily and what was important economically to him in supporting his military."[30]

By 1956 there was a widening rift between Eisenhower and Dulles, with Dulles moving more toward the ideas of flexible response and limited nuclear war, while Eisenhower more firmly insisted that any war between the United States and the Soviet Union would quickly become an all-out nuclear war. Campbell Craig has recently argued in *Destroying the Village* that Eisenhower's strategy to avoid war with the Soviets "was to make American military policy so dangerous that his advisers would find it impossible to push Eisenhower toward war and away from compromise."[31] Others have a different perspective on Eisenhower and nuclear weapons. Samuel F. Wells, Jr., has observed that massive retaliation still evokes "images of SAC on the rampage" and "retains its reputation as almost a caricature of intelligent strategic doctrine—inflexible, incredible, and very dangerous." In fact, Wells believes that Eisenhower nurtured these images and

Fig. 8. Curtis LeMay, 1958. Photograph by Thomas J. O'Halloran. Library of Congress, Prints and Photographs Division, *U.S. News & World Report* Magazine Collection, LC-U9-7275, frame 36.

that "the administration's strategy was more subtle than its spokesmen were willing to admit."[32] The circumstances under which the Eisenhower administration *would* resort to nuclear weapons thankfully never materialized, and the extent to which he was willing—or unwilling—to resort to the nuclear option remains a subject of debate.[33]

Another troubling question that lingered throughout the Cold War was whether the United States would be the first to use nuclear weapons against an enemy. While attacking first was often lumped under the single term "preemptive attack," there was, in fact, a difference between a preemptive attack in which an enemy would be attacked because the enemy gave every indication that it was preparing to attack the United States, and a "preventive attack," in which an enemy would be attacked not because of overt, hostile military moves but because of concern over the enemy's increasing nuclear capacity and dangerous potential. The distinction was a fine one, and each carried a burden of unsettling moral questions that persisted throughout the Cold War.[34]

While Eisenhower had been willing to spend the money to build up the nation's nuclear arms, he was *not* willing to spend the money on a shelter system to *protect* against nuclear arms. As we shall see, Eisenhower and Dulles, having kept overall defense spending in check by emphasizing nuclear armaments, clearly had no enthusiasm for spending the savings on a $20 billion to $30 billion shelter program. The rejection by the Eisenhower administration of the shelter programs recommended by the Holifield committee, the Gaither Report, the Rockefeller Report, and the administration's own civil defense director would make this clear.

When the Kennedy administration was installed in 1960, a new phrase was adopted to describe America's deterrent strategy: "assured destruction." Coined by secretary of defense Robert McNamara, assured destruction rested on the premise that even after absorbing a nuclear attack, the United States would still have sufficient military assets (a "second strike" nuclear capability) to "inflict an unacceptable degree of damage upon any aggressor."[35] A balance of terror would prevail between the United States and the USSR, each massively armed and each capable of visiting annihilation on the other—like "two scorpions in a bottle," in J. Robert Oppenheimer's famous simile.[36] If deterrence and other options under a more flexible defensive philosophy failed (and the outbreak of nuclear war would be a clear sign of such a failure), then the Kennedy administration believed that fallout shelters and "active" defensive systems, such as antiballistic missiles (ABMs), would reduce casualties.

Civil Defense in the 1950s

Facing the consequences of a possible nuclear war was not something that most Americans cared to do, and civil defense agencies in the decades after

World War II grappled with the difficult task of educating a resistant public. Initially, a period of optimism prevailed that nuclear weapons had not greatly changed the basics of protecting the civilian population, and until the mid-1950s civil defense planners spent a great deal of time preparing for a type of war that was closer to World War II than any future thermonuclear war. An army study issued in 1946, for instance, maintained that the "same passive defense measures that were employed in defense against conventional air raids can be adopted to atomic attack, no matter how intensive."[37] Also reflecting this optimism was *Survival under Atomic Attack*, one of the first attempts by the Civil Defense Office to educate a large swath of the American public about the perils of nuclear warfare. Issued in 1950, *Survival* maintains a reassuring tone, insisting, "You can survive. You can live through an atom bomb raid and you won't have to have a Geiger counter, protective clothing, or special training in order to do it." Often fatally glib, *Survival* offers such insights as "atom-splitting is just another way of causing an explosion" and "your chances of making a complete recovery [from radiation exposure] are much the same as for every day accidents."[38] The pamphlet also advises that "there is one important thing you can do to lessen your chances of injury by blast: Fall flat on your face."

This publication takes especially great pains to soothe anxieties about radioactivity, noting that people are continually bombarded by radiation from cosmic rays, and claiming that "in spite of the huge quantities of lingering radioactivity loosed by atomic explosions, people fortunately are not very likely to be exposed to dangerous amounts of it in most atomic raids."[39] *Survival* suggested that a "'cyclone cellar' or something similar" would "give excellent protection against atomic bombs."[40] Written before the hydrogen bomb tests of the mid-1950s, much of the advice found in this booklet would quickly become misguided or even dangerous.

Responsibility for civil defense was under the aegis of the National Security Resources Board (NSRB) after World War II, and this agency produced a series of bulletins offering civil defense guidance to individual states. The vague suggestions made by these bulletins, however, often frustrated local officials. San Francisco mayor Elmer E. Robinson complained that this literature contained no "instruction for planning for civilian defense, except to lick your wounds, nurse your injuries, and die."[41] The creation of the Federal Civil Defense Administration (FCDA) by executive action in 1950, and passage of the Federal Civil Defense Act by the legislature in the same year, seemingly reflected a response to such criticisms, and an interest in developing a coherent, national civil defense policy. The

FCDA administrator Millard Caldwell began to lobby for a program that would provide federal matching grants for state shelter programs. While the construction of large, underground shelters was being contemplated, Caldwell promoted the "shoring up" of existing buildings for shelter use. (It should be emphasized that what the FCDA was contemplating at this point were *bomb* shelters, not fallout shelters. The full extent of the fallout problem associated with atomic weapons would not be made public until 1955.) Congress responded by totally rejecting all shelter funding in 1951, 1952, and again in 1953.[42] Philip Funigiello has argued that this resounding rejection occurred because there was no political support for a serious civil defense effort, that "neither the military, the Congress, the Truman administration, nor the public ever fully accepted civil defense as a viable, important, and essential federal responsibility." Instead, it was the "proactive" defense represented by SAC that "fired the congressional and popular imagination" in a way that civil defense planning could not do.[43]

Also lurking behind the failure of proposed shelter programs in the early 1950s was their considerable expense. States and municipalities would have had difficulty producing the matching funds the programs required, and as the New York architect and defense consultant Ellery Husted claimed in 1953, a nationwide public shelter program "if done right" would cost nearly as much as "the total of all the country's personal income tax collections for one year."[44] As for private home shelters, despite the many appeals to the homeowner's sense of duty (in his 1951 book on civil defense Augustin Prentiss insisted that it was "the duty of each householder to protect his home and family to the full extent of his ability"), this period witnessed little enthusiasm for the construction of home shelters.[45] Clearly lacking in the equation was what Ellery Husted called "times of more imminent (or at least more apparent) danger to stir home owners out of their indifference."[46]

With the installation of an economically minded Eisenhower administration in 1952, the new FCDA chief, former Nebraska governor Frederick "Val" Peterson, switched his agency's emphasis from shelters to evacuation (fig. 9). In the budget proposal for 1954, in fact, Peterson had claimed that the increased power of nuclear weapons "could turn such public shelters into death traps in our large cities."[47] Pleasing to both the administration and congressional critics (evacuation was cheap, shelters were not), evacuation now became the cornerstone of FCDA policy. The first hints that this policy might be dangerously inadequate began surfacing shortly after the 1954 Bravo test of a hydrogen bomb at Bikini Atoll. Best remem-

FIG. 9. Civil defense director Val Peterson. RG 304-NT ("Operation Ivy" folder, #19), Still Pictures Branch (NNSP), National Archives at College Park, MD.

bered for the *Lucky Dragon* incident in which twenty-three Japanese fishermen were contaminated while sailing through the test area, the Bravo detonation was a startling event because of the unexpectedly high levels of radioactive fallout that were produced. While official test data were not made public until 1955, a number of scientists had been able to piece together information sufficient to make surmises about both the quantity of Bravo's radioactive fallout and the extent of its distribution.

One of these scientists was Ralph Lapp, civil defense editor of the *Bulletin of the Atomic Scientists*. In November 1954 Lapp published a piece in the *Bulletin* that described the unexpectedly large quantity of radioactive debris (mostly pulverized coral) from this test and the great distance that this debris had been carried. Lapp cautioned that "the new peril from radioactive fall-out is more than just a threat to civil defense—it is a peril to humanity."[48] In the next issue of the *Bulletin* Lapp ambushed Val Peterson in an interview. First Lapp asked Peterson point-blank whether evacuation of cities was the official policy of the FCDA, to which Peterson replied in the affirmative. Pressing Peterson on the large quantities of fallout from the Bravo test that had apparently been distributed over thousands of square miles, Lapp asked, "Does this strike you as an underestimate or exaggeration of the hazard?" Peterson answered that he hoped to be in a position to discuss the problem "in the reasonable future." Lapp persisted:

Q: It would seem that if a man 70 to 80 miles downwind of an H-bomb detonation can be killed by radioactive fall-out that civil defense faces a radical new threat.

A: Well, that isn't a question. That is just a plain statement.[49]

Civil defense did indeed face a new threat. By February 1955 the suspicions of Lapp and others about the radioactivity produced by the Bravo test were officially confirmed, and in congressional hearings that year Atomic Energy Commission (AEC) officials admitted that the explosion had produced radioactive fallout over a seven-thousand-square-mile area.[50] This new awareness of the dangers of fallout placed Peterson's evacuation policy in considerable doubt, and in the Holifield hearings of 1956 and 1957, chaired by Chet Holifield (D-Calif.) (fig. 10), Peterson was subjected to considerable criticism. General Otto L. Nelson, who had headed the Project East River civil defense study, called Peterson's program "worse than no program at all," while Merle Tuve, chair of the National Academy of Sciences civil defense committee, described it as "fumbling and inconsistent."[51]

It was oddly the case that Peterson himself was among the most pessimistic that meaningful preparations might be made for surviving a nuclear war. Life after such a war, according to Peterson, "is going to be stark, elemental, brutal, filthy, and miserable." As Peterson put it, "We just are not going to be prepared for that kind of a hell."[52] Continuing to cling to the evacuation idea, Peterson insisted that "evacuation is the only tool that we have" to counter the effects of a nuclear attack.[53] Even Peterson conceded, however, that at least three hours' warning would be needed to evacuate successfully a city, and witnesses before the Holifield committee emphasized the difficulties involved in urban evacuation even under the best of conditions.[54] When questioned about the coming of the inter-

FIG. 10. Congressman Chet Holifield, 1961. Photograph by Marion S. Trikosko. Library of Congress, Prints and Photographs Division, *U.S. News & World Report* Magazine Collection, LC-U9-6404, frame 10.

continental ballistic missile (ICBM) era and drastically reduced warning times, Peterson replied, "The evil of today is sufficient in this business."[55]

Beginning in 1954, the FCDA staged yearly "Operation Alert" exercises, which simulated nuclear attacks on American cities and which were supposed to determine how well civil defense plans would work under attacks.[56] Certainly, the response of the general public to Operation Alert was tepid at best.[57] In the 1955 Operation Alert, Eisenhower and fifteen thousand federal employees were scheduled to evacuate the capital to spend three days at thirty-one "secret sites." The route of the presidential motorcade was supposedly classified, but along the way "schoolchildren and parents with cameras were waiting for a glimpse of Ike." A number of federal employees seemed equally unimpressed with the gravity of the occasion. Health and education secretary Oveta Culp Hobby was a late arrival at the government-in-exile's headquarters because, she confessed, she had stopped for lunch on the way.[58] Washington civil defense official John Garrett Underhill called Operation Alert "so inadequate it couldn't cope with a brush fire threatening a doghouse in the backyard." Underhill was promptly relieved of his duties.[59] Ralph Lapp called Operation Alert's planning assumptions "obsolete" for its failure to "treat radioactive fall out seriously."[60]

After viewing the results of the 1957 Operation Alert in Chicago, civil defense officials concluded that insufficient warning time and the unpredictable dispersion of fallout "do not support the policy of pre-attack evacuation." If Chicago had been evacuated during an actual attack, "hundreds of thousands of people from the heart of Chicago might have been moving through the areas of impact when the bombs fell."[61] The New York urban planner Robert Moses also had some choice words about evacuation, noting that the breakdown of a single car could clog a major artery for hours, and that "any thought that you can evacuate a large population in a short time from any large city, even if you have a place to move them to, is so much moonshine."[62]

The largest practical test of evacuation took place in Mobile, Alabama, in 1955. Called "Operation Kids" by local officials, this exercise was designed to move some 37,300 Mobile schoolchildren away from a simulated nuclear attack. The results were not encouraging. There were heavy traffic jams, radio stations failed to broadcast crucial information, and children whose parents did not own cars were evacuated late. Commenting on this problem, one civil defense official suggested that in the future parents might be prevailed on "to take the first children waiting to be loaded, even though their own children are not among them."[63]

The evacuation idea was finally put out of its misery when its only remaining virtue, its cheapness, was called into question by the Bureau of Public Roads. The bureau estimated in 1957 that some $23 billion in improved highways and bridges would have to be spent to move efficiently people out of 147 target areas. Such a cost, noted Chet Holifield, was roughly the same as a national shelter program.[64] But civil defense was still a hard sell, and the House slashed the FCDA budget from a requested $130 million to $39.3 million in 1957.[65] Much of the blame for the failure of federal civil defense programs during this era has been connected to congressional impatience with Val Peterson. While disenchantment with Peterson was certainly a factor, neither Peterson's predecessor, Millard Caldwell, nor his successor, Leo Hoegh, fared better at the hands of Congress, and throughout its life the FCDA received only about 20 percent of the funding suggested by the chief executives.[66]

With the dangers of fallout now conclusively demonstrated and the specter of an operational Soviet ICBM lurking in the background, the Holifield subcommittee early in 1957 recommended a national shelter program that would cost between $20 and $40 billion.[67] Holifield called a shelter program "the acid test of a national will to build an effective civil defense."[68] In truth, the FCDA and the Holifield subcommittee were not far apart on the shelter issue. In December 1956 Peterson and the FCDA had submitted their own $30 billion shelter program to the National Security Council.[69] Eisenhower was clearly unenthused at the prospect of having to come up with the billions needed to finance such a scheme, and Peterson's many confusing statements made during these days reflect a clear tension between his advocacy of a shelter program and his loyalty to the administration. In March 1957, for instance, Peterson observed, "we believe in shelters but we don't want to mislead the people."[70] When questioned before a congressional committee that year on the status of his fallout shelter program, a clearly uncomfortable Peterson could only reply that the FCDA had submitted to the executive branch a proposal for a national shelter system "involving tremendous sums of money."[71] Eisenhower marked time by creating a committee under H. Rowan Gaither, Jr., to further study the problem of civil defense. By August 1957 Leo Hoegh had replaced Peterson as head of the FCDA, and Hoegh also argued before the National Security Council that a $20 billion-plus program for fallout shelters would be a good investment that "might save fifty million American lives."[72]

If Eisenhower had expected a different recommendation from the Gaither committee, he was destined to be disappointed. Completed late in 1957, the Gaither Report recommended a $25 billion system of shelters that would be stocked with about $10 billion worth of equipment and supplies. The Gaither committee members also suggested that it might be necessary in the future to build shelters that could protect the population from blast as well as fallout, at a cost of an additional $20 to $30 billion. Shelters, according to the Gaither Report, would not only protect the population, but would also permit "our own air defense to use nuclear warheads with greater freedom."[73]

Fueling the anxieties of the civil defense debate of 1957 was the successful testing of a Soviet ICBM, followed by the launch of the Sputnik satellite in October.[74] The Rockefeller Report on international security, issued the following year, took note of the "U.S. lag in missiles and space machines" and worried that the United States was "rapidly losing its lead in the race of military technology." Like the Gaither Report, the Rockefeller Report called for a national fallout shelter program, insisting that "in the age of the ballistic missile" a society's ability to withstand attack "will become an increasingly important deterrent."[75] When he was questioned on *Face the Nation* about the report, Nelson Rockefeller reiterated the deterrent value of shelters, claiming that shelters could enhance "the will to resist on the part of the people" and make the enemy hesitate before attacking.[76]

One final key report on shelters was issued by the RAND Corporation in 1958. Under the direction of Herman Kahn, *Report on a Study of Non-Military Defense* provided a three-tiered estimate of costs for shelters, depending on the level of protection the shelters provided. "Light shelters," built mainly for fallout protection, would cost about $150 per person, "medium shelters" geared for a ninety-day occupancy would cost $300 to $400 per person, and heavy "deep rock" shelters would cost $500 to $700 per person. As an example of the latter, the RAND report posited "a system of deep rock shelters under Manhattan Island for 4 million people." Located some eight hundred feet below the surface, this shelter would be powered by diesel generators, and the air would be purified and enriched with oxygen. There would be some ninety-one entrances to this shelter, so that everyone in Manhattan would be within five to ten minutes' walk of an entrance. According to the RAND report, "occupants would be assigned berths in a large dormitory, would receive two cold meals and one hot meal per day, and would draw fresh clothing, take showers, and exercise on a rotational basis." Funding a national shelter program would, according to the RAND researchers, cost between $20 billion and $150 billion, depending on the scale.[77]

In 1958 Benjamin Taylor, director of engineering research for the FCDA, appeared before the Holifield hearings and presented a version of the RAND Manhattan Island shelter idea. Committee member William E. Minshall of Ohio described such a shelter as a "gold-plated job," and Chet Holifield was furious. Holifield called it a "fantastic scheme" that would "kill serious consideration of an economically and technically feasible shelter program." Holifield worried that because of its huge costs, the Manhattan Island shelter idea would "give to the newspapers a motif for ridiculing and discouraging the whole consideration of shelter."[78]

Cost estimates of shelter building programs varied wildly. At the low end was Willard Libby of the AEC. On *Face the Nation* in 1958, Libby claimed that if Americans followed his advice of "fixing up your cellar so you have a place to hide for 48 hours or so," it would save ten million lives in the event of nuclear attack.[79] Also on the cheap side was Val Peterson. Still loath to abandon the evacuation idea, Peterson regaled dubious representatives at the Holifield hearings with a plan for digging ditches along evacuation routes (at a cost of only twenty-five cents per foot). These ditches would be covered by tar paper, and would provide shelter for fleeing Americans caught out in the open during an attack.[80] Elaborating on this scheme in a magazine article, Peterson suggested a relatively simple way for persons huddled in tar paper–covered trenches to dispose of accumulations of radioactive fallout: "persons down in the trench could, every few minutes, give that paper a flip and flip the stuff off."[81]

Opting for a more expensive solution was Edward Teller, who rejected urban evacuation as "self defeating." Teller insisted that the best way to protect the population was with "an adequate system of shelters," and he estimated that such a system could be built for $7.5 billion.[82] At the high cost end was Lieutenant General Samuel B. Sturgis, chief of the Army Corps of Engineers, who claimed that an effective national shelter system would cost about $240 billion.[83]

Regional and local differences could also have an impact on the cost of shelter building. For instance, Willard Libby's suggestion that Americans build shelters in their cellars and basements (the least expensive option) made some sense in the North, where 80 percent of homes had basements, but in the South only 10 percent of homes included basements.[84] Local demographics could also have an impact on costs. Paul G. Steinbicker, civil defense executive of the St. Louis Civil Defense Office, criticized the Holifield testimony because he believed that both shelter costs and the numbers of shelters needed had been substantially underestimated. According to Steinbicker, costs of shelters built in central St. Louis would be closer to $500 per person than it would be to the $100 per person FCDA estimate. In addition, Steinbicker claimed that Edward Teller's formula for determining how many shelters would be necessary for an urban area (calculated by the total population divided by 1,000) was flawed because of the way urban populations shifted every day. With the population of downtown St. Louis fluctuating from 225,000 during the day to 30,000 at night, Steinbicker believed that to assure protection of the population at all hours of the day St. Louis would need 2,000 shelters rather than 1,500.[85]

Part of the problem of arriving at a cost estimate for shelters lay in how the FCDA itself defined a "fallout shelter." Following the lead of the Atomic Energy Commission, the FCDA in 1955 classified a fallout shelter as a structure with a "protection factor" (PF) of 5,000 or greater (meaning radiation levels inside the shelter would be 1/5,000th of outside levels). The 5,000 PF was still the standard when the FCDA announced its fallout shelter policy in 1958. This was an extremely high protection factor that entailed considerable construction costs (the guidelines for installing such a structure in a federal building called for concrete walls with a thickness of twenty-six inches). The PF standard would be progressively lowered to 1,000 by the end of 1958, to 100 by 1960, and finally to 40 during the Cuban Missile Crisis.[86] But to a great extent the damage had already been done, and public perceptions of what constituted a fallout shelter continued to be extremely thick walls and costly single-purpose construction long after these standards had been abandoned.[87]

There were plenty of shelter skeptics, and prominent among them was Robert Moses. Moses declared that among the "stupidest" of the claims made by shelter supporters was that "abandoning our way of life and crawling into cellars will terrify the enemy and thus prevent war."[88] Despite the advocacy of various committees and the support of a large portion of the press, Moses did not believe that a shelter system would ever be built because of the "ambivalence of the executive branch."[89]

Ambivalence is perhaps too mild a word to describe the Eisenhower administration's opposition to a shelter system. The high cost estimates were disturbing enough, but Eisenhower also saw embodied in a national shelter system grave social and geopolitical implications. The president saw it as a step toward turning America into a "garrison state," and secretary of state John Foster Dulles believed that embarking on a massive shelter program would "just write off our friends in Europe."[90] Eisenhower remembered the following exchange between Dulles and himself:

> "If a wave of a hand could create those shelters," he [Dulles] said, "we'd of course be better off with them than without them. But it's hard to sustain simultaneously an offensive and defensive mood in a population. For our security, we have been relying above all on our capacity for retaliation. From this policy we should not deviate now. To do so would imply we are turning to a 'fortress America' concept."
>
> "You *are* a militant Presbyterian, aren't you?" I remarked. A little laughter around the table helped to lighten the air.[91]

Eisenhower "decided that we would not embark on an all-out shelter program," and shelved the Gaither Report.[92]

In 1958 the FCDA and the Office of Defense Mobilization were combined into the Office of Civil and Defense Mobilization (OCDM). Leo Hoegh, director of this new entity, announced that there would be "no mas-

FIG. 11. Office of Civil and Defense Mobilization poster. RG 304-P-52, Still Pictures Branch (NNSP), National Archives at College Park, MD.

sive federally financed shelter construction program" and instead proposed a "national shelter plan," the essential feature of which was an emphasis on private shelter construction and government "stimulation" and "guidance."[93] OCDM posters now began to emphasize the danger of fallout and encourage the home remedy of building a family shelter (see figs. 11, 12, and 13). Hoegh put his own spin on the "fortress America" concept at a speaking engagement that year. Linking dual-purpose home shelters with the pioneer

Fig. 12. Office of Civil and Defense Mobilization poster. RG 304-P-59, Still Pictures Branch (NNSP), National Archives at College Park, MD.

past, Hoegh proclaimed, "Every home a fortress! That can well be our watchword as we strive to attain the freedom won so dearly by our pioneer forebears."[94] What was dubbed the "do-it-yourself" shelter policy of the Eisenhower administration attracted a host of critics.[95] Especially outraged was Chet Holifield, who compared the idea of getting everyone to build their own shelter to building "an army, or a navy or an air force by advising each one to buy himself a jetplane."[96] Holifield was in a bitter mood when he was interviewed by Ralph Lapp in April 1958. Holifield had been informed by Eisenhower that the Gaither Report would not be made available to Holifield's committee, and Holifield confided to Lapp his hope that "the executive branch might wake up to its responsibilities before it's too late. I'm not sure that it is not already too late." Holifield insisted that a strong shelter system would also have a great deterrent value, and claimed that "unless we show our determination to survive a massive attack ourselves, we can hardly expect the Russians to believe that we really mean what we say about massive retaliation." Without shelters, the United States was presenting a "glass chin" to the enemy.[97]

While congressional committees continued to press for a shelter program (hearings in 1959 claimed that shelters could reduce fatalities from a nuclear war to 3 percent, while serving to resist Soviet "nuclear blackmail"), for the rest of Eisenhower's tenure in office there was little change in the administration's shelter policy, and Congress as a whole showed lit-

FIG. 13. Office of Civil and Defense Mobilization poster. RG 304-P-60, Still Pictures Branch (NNSP), National Archives at College Park, MD.

tle inclination to appropriate huge sums of money for shelter building.[98] A key to congressional malaise on civil defense was a lack of interest on the part of the constituents.[99] By 1960 Holifield's subcommittee had concluded that a national shelter plan could claim little in the way of tangible results, and that "few shelters of any description have been constructed in the United States."[100] As the Eisenhower era drew to a close, Holifield and other civil defense prophets were left to wander in the desert of public indifference.

The Kennedy Administration and Flexible Response

When the Kennedy administration assumed power, it was immediately apparent that there would be crucial differences between this regime and its predecessor on the subject of American nuclear strategy and civil defense. In the last year of the Eisenhower presidency, the executive branch had drawn up a master plan for nuclear war that called for a massed attack of the entire U.S. strategic force against a mix of military and industrial targets in the Soviet Union.[101] McGeorge Bundy, Kennedy's assistant to the president for national security affairs, complained that this plan was "dangerously rigid" because it called "for shooting off everything we have in one shot, and so is constructed to make any more flexible course very difficult."[102] Other critics of massive retaliation included the RAND researcher Albert Wohlstetter and the army chief of staff Maxwell Taylor, who penned the influential book *The Uncertain Trumpet*.[103] In a significant departure from the Eisenhower era, Kennedy would begin to move toward a "flexible response" strategy in which the president would not be limited to the nuclear option in responding to an act of aggression, but would have a number of options to choose from. Such options would include diplomacy, the use of conventional forces, covert action, counterinsurgency, and the use of nuclear weapons.[104]

It should be emphasized, however, that the Eisenhower administration was never as "inflexible" in its determination to use nuclear weapons as it was reputed to be, nor was the Kennedy administration as "flexible" as one might wish in considering options other than nuclear. Eisenhower, for instance, firmly refused to consider the nuclear option during the Quemoy-Matsu crisis, and had rejected the idea of using nuclear weapons to help the French under siege at Dien Bien Phu. According to Eisenhower, he told his advisers, "You must be crazy. We can't use those awful things against Asians for the second time in less than ten years. My God."[105]

Meanwhile, under the supposed flexible response doctrine of the Kennedy administration, the country came perilously close to waging nuclear war with the Soviet Union. Just six months after Kennedy took office, the new administration was faced with the Berlin crisis and found itself compelled to adopt the Eisenhower nuclear strategy simply because there were not sufficient conventional forces available with which to be "flexible." And while flexible response had been fully implemented as the cornerstone of the administration's Cold War strategy by 1962, it cannot be said that flexible response was notably successful in preventing the United States and the Soviet Union from skittering toward the abyss of nuclear war during the Cuban Missile Crisis. Certainly Soviet belligerence was at a peak in the early 1960s, but the Kennedy administration indulged in some of its own belligerence. While it is John Foster Dulles whom we most closely associate with "nuclear brinkmanship," Walt Rostow, Kennedy's chairman of the Policy Planning Council in the State Department, was not above a bit of brinkmanship himself. Rostow insisted that Americans must be ready and willing to go to war with nuclear weapons because "there is no posture which is more likely to lead to nuclear war than the notion that nuclear war is unthinkable. . . . the heart of a credible deterrent in a nuclear age lies in being prepared to face the consequences, should deterrence fail."[106]

If the adoption of flexible response by the Kennedy administration represented a significant departure from the Eisenhower years, there would be an even greater difference between the two administrations on the shelter issue. It was Kennedy's July 25 speech on the Berlin crisis and his call for a shelter system that changed everything. Kennedy had already suggested a strengthened civil defense program with an emphasis on fallout shelters in a May 25 address to Congress, calling civil defense "insurance for the civilian population in case of an enemy miscalculation."[107] But his Berlin speech two months later was made in an atmosphere of crisis and produced an immediate public clamoring for information on how citizens could protect themselves and their families. Congress also caught the mood, and within sixteen days had authorized every penny of the $207 million that the administration had requested to identify, mark, and stock buildings that could serve as fallout shelters. Neal Fitzsimons, who had been on the staff of the FCDA and the OCDM since 1956 and who did pioneering engineering work on design applications for fallout shelters, described the effect of Kennedy's speech on civil defense as "staggering."[108]

Civil defense, which had hobbled along for more than a decade under a burden of neglect and indifference, now began to bask in the warmth of a totally unexpected reversal of fortune. The civil defense office was reorganized, with Kennedy splitting responsibility for civil defense between the OCDM, which was charged with the stockpiling of materials and coordinating local and state planning, and the Office of Civil Defense (OCD), which was placed under the Department of Defense, and which assumed directorship of the fallout shelter program.[109] The able Steuart L. Pittman was placed at the helm of the OCD, and with executive and legislative support and adequate resources for the new agency, the future seemed bright. The *Christian Science Monitor* proclaimed that the "lean years are over: Now Civil Defense today is the success story of Washington."[110] These halcyon days would be short-lived, however, and rather than marking the beginning of an era of broad public support and steadily increasing appropriations, 1961 would prove to be the apex for civil defense in this country.[111]

The coming years would be chaotic ones, with the Kennedy administration seemingly unable to formulate and promote a coherent shelter program and the experts themselves deeply divided over the worth of shelters. An overwhelming number of ordinary Americans also became involved, and before the fallout shelter controversy was over Americans would be forced to face agonizing questions of individual survival, personal morality, and how they defined themselves as a people.

And the third angel sounded, and there fell a great star from heaven, burning as it were a lamp, and it fell upon the third part of the rivers, and upon the fountains of waters;

And the name of the star is called Wormwood: and the third part of the waters became wormwood; and many men died of the waters, because they were made bitter. —*Revelation 8:10–11*

CHAPTER 2

The Nuclear Apocalyptic

Before examining the political, moral, and scientific aspects of the fallout shelter, it is important to understand that there would not have *been* a fallout shelter debate without the flowering of a distinctive subgenre of speculative literature, what might be called the nuclear apocalyptic. Based on anxieties about nuclear war and its aftermath, the nuclear apocalyptic was based on the widespread belief during the 1950s and early 1960s that nuclear weapons had brought humanity near the final apocalypse. Philosophers, intellectuals, and ordinary individuals insisted that such an event was possible, even likely. As Karl Jaspers observed in 1958, "now, mankind as a whole can be wiped out by men. It has not merely become possible for this to happen; on purely rational reflection it is probable that it will happen."[1] The pervasiveness of this view was part of the zeitgeist of this era, and the nuclear apocalyptic would fuse with the fallout shelter issue and would endow the debate over shelters with a distinctive millenarian urgency.

Among the first to express his anxieties about a world with nuclear weapons was Bertrand Russell. Just weeks after the explosion at Hiroshima Russell, who would go on to become the best-known antinuclear activist of his era, predicted that the Soviets would develop their own nuclear weapons and that the world would be plunged into nuclear war: "One must expect a war between U.S.A. and U.S.S.R. which will begin with the total destruction of London. I think the war will last 30 years, and leave a world without civilised people, from which everything will have to build afresh—a process taking (say) 500 years."[2] Russell's views on the subject had not become more hopeful by 1963, when he was interviewed by *Playboy* magazine: "But I don't see any reason to be optimistic. I still feel that the human race may well become extinct before the end of the present century. Speaking as a mathematician, I should say that the odds are about three to one against survival."[3]

Others sharing this view included C. Wright Mills, who claimed that "doctrinaire incompetence is leading mankind into the great trap," and Erich Fromm, who insisted that "we are threatened with extinction or a new barbarism." "The policy of the deterrent will not ensure peace," said Fromm, "it will most likely destroy civilization, and it will certainly destroy democracy even if it preserves peace."[4] To Reinhold Niebuhr, "war by miscalculation or misadventure [is] more and more a probability rather than a possibility."[5]

A number of Nobel laureates publicly expressed their anxieties about the implications of nuclear weapons, including the chemist Harold Urey and the physicist Leo Szilard. Urey claimed that such weapons had created "the most dangerous situation that humanity has faced in all history," while Szilard, who made key contributions to the development of the atomic bomb, expressed his belief in 1962 that "our chances of getting through the next ten years without war are slim."[6] W. Warren Wagar, writing in 1963, declared that humanity was faced "with the most radical crisis in history.... The wolves are not howling outside the ramparts of civilization: they have broken in. Their breath is hot on our cheeks."[7]

The penetration of nuclear anxiety into the culture could also be seen at the other end of the intellectual spectrum, where comic book writers and B-movie producers enthusiastically incorporated nuclear themes into their creations. Spiderman and the Incredible Hulk, for instance, were both created for the Marvel comic group in 1962, and each gain their super powers when exposed to some form of radioactivity. When Peter Parker, nebbish lab assistant and future Spiderman, is bitten by an irradiated spider, he exclaims, "A—A spider! It bit me! But why is it *burning* so? Why is it *glowing* that way?? . . . It's the *spider!* It *has* to be! Somehow—in some miraculous way, his bite has transferred his own power—to *me!*"[8] In another part of the comic book world, Bruce Banner, atomic scientist and genius creator of the "G-bomb," is nervously waiting for the first test of this awesome new weapon when a motorist drives on to the test range. Banner rushes out to rescue him, but before they can get back to safety Banner's scientific rival sets off the bomb and Banner "is bathed in the full force of the mysterious gamma rays!" This exposure has an interesting effect on Banner, who henceforward will occasionally put on three hundred pounds, turn green, and be transformed into the Incredible Hulk:

"What is happening??? Arghh"
"*Hey! Look* at you! You *changed!*"
"Get out of my way, insect!"[9]

The B-movies in which nuclear tests play a role in spawning hideous monsters are almost too numerous to mention, but include two classics from 1954: the Japanese film *Godzilla*, featuring a fire-breathing monster awakened by nuclear tests, and the American film *Them!* which brought forth menacing ants grown giant due to radiation exposure.[10] In an interesting variation on this theme, the protagonist of the 1957 film *The Incredible Shrinking Man* grows *tiny* rather than huge after a dose of radiation.

Wagar's wolves of nuclear war were also anxiously contemplated by practitioners in other fields. Writers in the late 1950s and early 1960s would produce a flood of nuclear apocalyptic literature, and Paul Brians, author of *Nuclear Holocausts: Atomic War in Fiction, 1895–1984*, counts 169 short stories and novels written on the subject of nuclear war between 1957 and 1964.[11] Perhaps of even greater significance were the numerous nuclear apocalyptic scenarios that appeared in mainstream magazines and newspapers, often incorporated as part of a feature story on the fallout shelter controversy. Because of the circulations of these periodicals, these descriptions would reach a very wide swath of the public.

Like other genres, the nuclear apocalyptic, whether found in a specialty or mainstream publication, had certain conventions that were observed by its practitioners. Typically, a nuclear apocalyptic begins with a description of a town or city, and the ordinary daily activities of its residents. The mundane quality of such activities will stand in sharp contrast to—and help dramatize—what follows. Next the focus shifts to the international arena, where tensions between East and West will precipitate a nuclear war, or alternatively, a nuclear war will start by accident. The town is now attacked by nuclear weapons, and there are vivid descriptions of the devastation wrought on the city's physical features as the fierce blast and heat combust buildings and topple skyscrapers. The authors also record the effect of the attack on the residents, both in macro detail to create an impression of the holocaust on the general population, and in micro detail to personalize the horror of this event by focusing on the ordeals of a few families or individuals. Descriptions of radiation sickness, blindness, terrible burns, gaping wounds, and missing limbs proliferate, and the authors conjure up gruesome images of corpses strewn about homes, workplaces, and sidewalks. When the bombs finally stop falling, the nuclear apocalyptic will emphasize how life has been reduced to a low, primitive state in which each day is a grim struggle for survival. Disease, dementia, lawlessness, and hunger are constant companions. In many nuclear apocalyptics, an occasional artifact from the past will surface to remind survivors of all that they have lost. Finally, depending on the author's view of nuclear war, the survivors will either begin building a new tomorrow, rising phoenix-like from the ashes, or hopelessly resign themselves to an endless era of darkness and barbarity. The basic question of the survivability of nuclear war and the efficacy of civil defense is a recurrent theme in these works, mirroring the same debate on the fallout shelter issue that was taking place around the country.

The anxiety-producing potential of this form of literature is obvious. But there was also a sense in which this was a genre of thrills, with both author and reader *exulting* in the terrible maiming and devastation visited by nuclear weapons. There is often an unmistakable pride in the raw power that produces such carnage, and a supernatural awe as author and reader contemplate the effects of such a force. The nuclear apocalyptic was ubiquitous during this era, and some version of a nuclear disaster scenario had to be running through the individual's mind as he or she contemplated whether to build a fallout shelter.

Science Fiction and the Nuclear Apocalyptic

Science fiction magazines, of course, had been the first to mine this vein, and since the end of World War II these publications had been inundated with stories dealing with nuclear war and its aftermath.[12] Defining the genre of science fiction presents certain problems (for instance, do the speculative works of top-flight writers such as Jules Verne, H. G. Wells, or even Mary Shelley and Edward Bellamy constitute science fiction?), but it is clear that the prospect of nuclear war often brought out the best in writers who regularly produced science fiction, and proved to be sufficiently compelling to prompt science fiction pieces from many writers who ordinarily did not work in this field.[13] As with any genre of literature, however, the good science fiction pieces were less numerous than the mediocre and the bad, and before we look at the good, a look at the not-so-good might prove instructive.

An outstanding example of bad science fiction (and one in which a shelter plays a prominent role) is Robert A. Heinlein's 1964 novel *Farnham's Freehold*. Much of the action in the early pages of this potboiler takes place inside a shelter that one Hugh Farnham has built for his family. While nuclear war rages overhead, Farnham regales his captive audience, which includes a nubile dinner guest named Barbara that Hugh has his eye on, with his social theories:

> This may be the first war in history which kills the stupid rather than the bright and able. . . . And of civilians those who used their heads and made preparations stand a far better chance. Not every case, but on the average, and that will improve the breed. When it's over, things will be tough, and that will improve the breed still more.[14]

A firestorm gives Hugh the opportunity to order everyone to take off their clothes ("Now you girls peel down, panties and bra or such . . ."), and there are a number of other scenes designed to appeal to the reader's libidinal interests. One of these is a sexual encounter between Hugh and Barbara that takes place inside the shelter while the rest of the family, including Hugh's intoxicated wife, is sleeping.[15] When they are able to emerge from their shelter Farnham's group finds itself not in a world of radioactive rubble, but rather in the middle of a green, pristine wilderness. The nuclear weapons, it seems, have transported them to a different time and place. As Hugh Farnham puts it, "Call it the fourth dimension. That last big one nudged us through the fourth dimension."[16] It cannot be said that the rest of *Farnham's Freehold* is an improvement on this unfortunate beginning.

While the consequences of radiation and nuclear war often received similar trivial treatments, many science fiction writers attempted to deal seriously with the issues raised by these themes. Of the countless science fiction pieces produced during this era that addressed nuclear holocaust, clearly the one that had the greatest impact on the public was Nevil

Shute's *On the Beach*, published in 1957. Shute, a British author who ordinarily did not write science fiction, produced in *On the Beach* a frightening story in which a nuclear war has desolated the Northern Hemisphere. The war apparently starts by mistake, after an incident in the Balkans, and "it just didn't stop, till all the bombs were gone and all the aircraft were unserviceable. And by that time, of course, they'd gone too far."[17] Set in Australia, *On the Beach* describes the lives of individuals helplessly awaiting their own extinction, as radiation slowly drifts southward. The hopelessness of this novel profoundly affected readers, making *On the Beach* a publishing sensation (and displacing *Peyton Place* from the top of the bestseller list).[18] The release of the film version in 1959 had an even more powerful effect on movie audiences, some of whom wept during intermission.[19] The *New York Times* critic Bosley Crowther made *On the Beach* one of the top films of 1959, claiming that "the shock and shame of the possible annihilation of many by fallout from a nuclear war are brought home with strong and personal feeling in this graphic drama about the last people on earth."[20] The Eisenhower administration was forced to counter the bleak message of *On the Beach* by insisting that such a scenario could never happen. Civil defense director Leo Hoegh complained that "if you read 'On the Beach,' and took that thing as being the truth, everyone would give up."[21] The negative publicity of this novel and film even prompted the U.S. Information Agency to create a special file called "Possible Questions and Suggested Answers on the Film 'On the Beach.'"[22]

If *On the Beach* had described civilization's last days, Walter M. Miller, Jr.'s novel *A Canticle for Leibowitz* detailed the years that followed, as the world degenerates into madness and a postnuclear Dark Ages. In *Canticle*, what has not been demolished by war is destroyed by angry mobs, who blame intellectuals for the nuclear holocaust:

> So it was that, after the Deluge, the Fallout, the plagues, the madness, the confusion of tongues, the rage, there began the bloodletting of the Simplification, when remnants of mankind had torn other remnants limb from limb, killing rulers, scientists, leaders, technicians, teachers, and whatever persons the leaders of the maddened mobs said deserved death for having helped to make the Earth what it had become.[23]

As one savage generation follows another, it is only in monasteries that the faint light of civilization is kept alive, as monks painstakingly illuminate circuit designs and other relics from the past. At one point one of these monks, a novice named Francis, comes across an ancient fallout shelter: "He had never seen a 'Fallout,' and he hoped he'd never see one. A consistent description of the monster had not survived, but Francis had heard the legends. He crossed himself and backed away from the hole."[24]

Pat Frank, another writer who ordinarily did not dabble in science fiction (Frank had served as a consultant for both the Department of Defense and NASA), published *Alas, Babylon* in 1959. By 1964 it had gone through nineteen printings. Focusing on the fortunes of a small central Florida town called Fort Repose after a nuclear war, *Alas, Babylon* emphasizes the breakdown in the infrastructure of civilization, followed shortly thereafter by the breakdown in law and order. While the crisis that fuels this novel is sparked by events in the Middle East, Frank implies that the real source of the crisis is the missile gap that supposedly existed between the Soviet Union and the United States at the end of the 1950s:

> "Can they [the Soviets] get away with it?"
> "Three years ago they couldn't. Three years hence, when we have our own ICBM batteries emplaced, a big fleet of missile-toting subs, and Nike-Zeus and some other stuff perfected, they couldn't. But right now we're in what we call 'the gap.'"[25]

Along the way Frank also takes some swipes at lackadaisical civil defense officials (the local Fort Repose official refuses to distribute booklets on nuclear fallout because they are "too gruesome"), and one of Frank's characters claims that children had become inured to the idea of nuclear annihilation because they've always "lived under the shadow of war—atomic war. For them the abnormal has become normal."[26]

While Fort Repose receives no direct missile attack, the rest of Florida is not so fortunate:

> What had jolted Randy from sleep—he would not learn all the facts for a long, a very long time after—were two nuclear explosions, both in the megaton range, the warheads of missiles lobbed in by submarines. The first obliterated the SAC base at Homestead, and incidentally sank and returned to the sea a considerable area of Florida's tip. Ground Zero of the second missile was Miami's International Airport, not far from the heart of the city. . . . Gazing at the glow to the south, Randy was witnessing, from a distance of almost two hundred miles, the incineration of a million people.[27]

Shortages develop immediately in Fort Repose, and life becomes a grim struggle for survival. As the rule of law breaks down, highwaymen reappear and an armed citizenry restores order. Communication with the outside world is sporadic, and shortwave radio broadcasts reveal that vast areas of the United States are contaminated by nuclear fallout. Residents of Fort Repose also learn that Josephine Vanbruuker-Brown, secretary of health, education, and welfare and the highest-ranking government official to survive, has become acting president of the United States. At the end of *Alas, Babylon*, Fort Repose is finally visited by military officials from the outside, and the following conversation takes place:

> Randy said, "Paul, there's one thing more. Who won the war?"
>
> Paul put his fists on his hips and his eyes narrowed. "You're kidding! You mean you really don't know?"
>
> "No. I don't know. Nobody knows. Nobody's told us."
>
> "We won it. We really clobbered 'em!" Hart's eyes lowered and his arms drooped. He said, "Not that it matters."
>
> The engine started and Randy turned away to face the thousand-year night.[28]

Two works by Philip Wylie are also notable: *Tomorrow!* published in 1954, and *Triumph*, published in 1963. Both have frightening depictions of nuclear war; as Wylie once said to a group of writers, "We have taught the people to be afraid, because most of *us* are afraid."[29] But there is a decided difference in tone between these two novels that mirror Wylie's evolving views on the survivability of nuclear conflict. In the early 1950s Wylie was a civil defense optimist. Wylie believed that American cities must not be evacuated in the event of nuclear attack because it was logistically impractical ("Conceive of the drivers as being moved by the hysteria and panic which always accompanies flight. For every stalled car, every car out of gas, and every wreck, imagine fifty") and because cities could take practical steps toward preparing for a nuclear attack ("It is practical to arrange for the best possible air or other raid warning and the best possible shelters. . . . It is practical to organize the environs of every city—the schoolhouses, hospitals, and other public places—for emergency uses"). A prepared urban population would make the difference between "rout and utter disaster" and "a brave and orderly dealing with the facts."[30]

Tomorrow! is a novel reflecting Wylie's optimism. At base it is a tale of two neighboring cities, Green Prairie and River City, each with a differing outlook toward preparing for nuclear attack. Green Prairie has chosen to develop an effective civil defense, while the residents of River City scorn civil defense as a waste of money and as a dangerous government intrusion. In one notable debate, a River City socialite condemns civil defense efforts as "sabotage left over from the imbecilities of Harry Truman's administration" that "squanders billions of man-hours" and diverts efforts from apprehending "dangerous radicals at home." A newspaper editor responds by asking,

> Doesn't the failure of the American people to get ready for atomic warfare reflect *lack* of realism and guts? Isn't Green Prairie rather exceptional—because it *is* sort of ready, after all these years? If *you* were the Soviets, wouldn't you rather America *neglected* atomic defense and wasted its muscle chasing college professors and persecuting a few writers? You *bet* you would![31]

As the Soviet Union launches an attack against the United States, Wylie describes the complete disorganization of civil defense in the country: "When, in the space of a dozen hours, the actual onslaught took place, this disorganized, decentralized, variable whole soon lost every tenuous relationship. Wires went, tunnels blew, power stations became vapor in the sky, nothing worked that should have; the people at Pearl were paragons of preparedness by comparison."[32] Wylie spends some three pages describing the effect of a nuclear weapon dropped on the Green Prairie/River City area ("on sidewalks boiling like forgotten tea, were dark stains that had been people, tens of thousands of people"), and even includes a map of the two cities showing ground zero (located just south of River City's "Negro District") and the rings of destruction radiating out from it.[33]

In the meantime, the U.S. military has not remained idle. American nuclear weapons have destroyed Moscow, Leningrad, and other cities in the Soviet Union. When the Soviets demand that the U.S. government surrender, the American president declares, "We know his philosophy. We bleed now under his treachery. Disarmed, we shall surely soon be enslaved."[34] Instead, the United States sends a submarine to the Baltic Sea. The submarine contains "the largest hydrogen bomb ever assembled" wrapped in layers of cobalt. When this fearsome weapon is detonated, the resulting blanket of radiation wipes out virtually all life in the Soviet Union. Without a hint of irony, Wylie observes, "The last great obstacle to freedom had been removed from the human path."[35] At the end of *Tomorrow!* Green Prairie has fared better than River City, thanks to Green

Prairie's civil defense program. Green Prairie and the rest of America begin to emerge from the ashes of nuclear holocaust, and "those [cities] that had been bombed provided people with a surge of exhilaration, for the bombing had proved an ultimate blessing furnishing a brand-new chance to build a world brand-new—and infinitely better."[36]

In Wylie's 1963 novel *Triumph* we have some of the most graphic depictions of nuclear war in the entire genre, and in contrast to his earlier novel, Wylie insists on the uselessness of civil defense in general and fallout shelters in particular. First is the problem of getting into the shelters. As nuclear war breaks out between the Soviet Union and the United States a mad scramble for shelter space ensues. There is a crush at the door of a public shelter that has been closed, and

> the people nearest the entrance, which was barred and boarded, were being literally squeezed to death. Many, already limp and motionless, were being supported by the press of those around them. From the mouths and nostrils of some—both the dead and the living—blood trickled redly. . . . Rib cages cracked with suddenness, like crates under triphammers, and people thus slaughtered were lucky, for they died quickly, in gouting blood-vomits or a last explosive belch of red-frothed air.[37]

A similar scene takes place in front of a private shelter, which has a machine gun mounted at its entrance:

> The machine gun's jumpy bursts began, and went on. And the camera tilted up to catch a series of objects hurtling through the air, then tilted back to watch them explode: grenades. They left, with the machine gun, a gory havoc that set the unhurt attackers running in all directions: a wriggling, tottering, yowling scrabble of people, of women without clothes, of a child crawling as its knees pulled out its own intestines, of a mother hugging a headless baby to a shot-off breast.[38]

Wylie's protagonist in *Triumph* observes, "I remember how, years back, arguments flared up over whether or not people in shelters should let outsiders in, even if they overcrowded the shelters. And now the answer is plain: anyone, apparently, would kill, if it required killing to save those he had arranged for and held dear!"[39] Monstrous firestorms sweep across the landscape, and Wylie insists that "people in shelters under these holocausts, people in subways, even miners, if their mines run beneath these H-hit areas in firestorm will soon die hideously, deprived of oxygen, as every breath of underground air is pulled out to hotten every Everest-tall blaze."[40] In a notable contribution to the nuclear-destruction-of-New-York motif, Wylie describes a river of melted glass that has been produced by the superheating of windows blown out of skyscrapers.[41]

Even those taking shelter in communities well removed from urban targets are doomed because the Soviet Union has detonated nuclear mines along both coasts of the United States, producing enormously high quantities of radioactive sodium that can only be survived in the most elaborate, sealed shelters. In "Zanesville," a town similar to *Tomorrow!*'s Green Prairie in its civil defense preparedness, citizens take to their shelters, but "so great and swift was the penetration of the radiation that here—as everywhere with the sodium assault that night—all civilian life was exterminated. For the people of North America had not, anywhere, prepared shelters against fallout of such high levels."[42] There is no rebuilding a better America in *Triumph* because a certain number of nuclear weapons have been held in reserve by both the United States and the Soviet Union, and these are unleashed some months after the initial attack against the few survivors who have emerged from their shelters. By the time of *Triumph's* publication, Wylie's personal statements on fallout shelters had become as outspoken, even as violent, as his fiction. Calling the building of shelters a "preposterous and useless effort," Wylie insisted that the public should think carefully "before it lays a block or spends a dime or invests idiot feelings of security of possessing little, sham shelters that won't save it in an H-war anymore than a paper sack would spare a mouse floating into it, in the middle of a gasoline pool on fire!"[43]

Another treatment of a nuclear theme that was both a best-seller and a popular film was *Fail-Safe*, written by Eugene Burdick and Harvey Wheeler and published in 1962. *Fail-Safe* thoughtfully engages many of the nuclear issues of the early 1960s, including nuclear strategy, the "Doomsday Machine," and the shape of a post–nuclear war world. One of the characters, Walter Groteschele, has written a Herman Kahn–style book called *Counter-Escalation*, and Groteschele has become the pet of the Washington, D.C., cocktail circuit:

> Looking coolly at a room full of people he would tell them how many decades it would take the survivors of a thermonuclear war to regain the standard of living of medieval days. He could see the audience stiffen,

tongues licking at the corners of their mouths, the signs of nervousness and fascination multiply.[44]

Groteschele predicts that the likeliest survivors of nuclear war would be hardened convicts locked away in solitary confinement and insurance file clerks locked away in fireproof rooms. Fighting for supremacy, one group would have "a monopoly of violence" while the other would enjoy "a monopoly of organization."[45] Along the way Groteschele even discovers the erotic possibilities of nuclear annihilation ("when he described the Doomsday system, hinting that it was semiclassified, she closed her eyes for a moment and a slight smile started at the corners of her mouth").[46] At a cocktail party debate Groteschele asks his opponent, the editor of "*Liberal Magazine*," "But would you not grant that the culture which is the best armed, has the best bomb shelters, the best retaliatory capacity, the strongest defense, would have an ancient and classical advantage?" The editor responds by describing such a culture as one "with most of its people dead, the rotting smell of death in the air for years, its vegetation burned off, the germ plasm of survivors contaminated."[47] The two adversaries are brought to a halt when a woman at the party breaks in and condemns both men for being caught up in a "fantasy world of logic and reason," and expresses the hope that if her children must die from nuclear war that she will be there "to ease their last pain with morphine."[48] Even more astounding, an air force general attending the party offers the opinion that the United States and the Soviets were both reconciled to mutual destruction, and "in that case, morphine *is* more important than a bomb shelter."[49]

At this point, *Fail-Safe* becomes a story of technology gone awry, as a system that is designed to prevent accidental war fails.[50] A group of American bombers, believing that it has been ordered to attack the Soviet Union, proceeds to its target, Moscow. While clearly this nightmarish situation is an accident, the American president realizes that he must offer compensation to the Soviet Union or a global nuclear war will follow. A conference call is hurriedly arranged between the president, Khrushchev, the American ambassador in Moscow, and the Soviet ambassador in New York. What the president offers Khrushchev to atone for a demolished Moscow is New York:

"No, no, Mr. Premier. That is not what I had in mind. You must listen to me, *listen to me*. At the moment that we hear the shriek of the melting telephone in Moscow, I will order a SAC squadron which is at this moment flying over New York City to drop four 20-megaton bombs on that city in precisely the pattern and altitude in which our planes have been ordered to bomb Moscow. They will use the Empire State Building for ground zero. When we hear the second shriek over the conference line we will know that your delegate to the United Nations is gone and along with him, New York."

"Holy Mother of God," Khrushchev said. His voice seemed almost like a pant.[51]

As they wait for Moscow and New York to be obliterated, a bond develops between the president and Khrushchev, and a good deal of one chapter is devoted to philosophical ruminations between the two leaders on the state of humanity and the modern world:

> The President was still talking. "Today what we had was a machine-made calamity. And I'm thinking that today you and I got a preview of the future. We damn well better learn carefully from it. More and more of our lives will be determined by these computerized systems."
>
> "It is true," Khrushchev said simply. "I wonder what role will be left to man in the future. Maybe we must think of man differently: 'The computer proposes; man disposes.'"[52]

Thoughtful and serious in tone with complex portrayals of both American and Soviet characters, *Fail-Safe* is, as Paul Brians puts it, "clearly a post–cold war novel."[53]

In *Level 7* (1959), written by Polish-born University of Minnesota professor Mordecai Roshwald, all the action takes place underground in an elaborate seven-level shelter system. Widely praised by Bertrand Russell, J. B. Priestley, Linus Pauling, and others, *Level 7* creates a nightmarish scenario in which shelter space has been prepared for virtually the entire population. The shelter system is hierarchical, with military personnel assigned to levels 6 and 7, politicians level 5, various elite classes on levels 3 and 4, and the rest of the nation on the first two levels. It is never made clear which "nation" has created this system, though apparently the nation's adversary, referred to throughout as the "enemy," has created a similar system.

The primary occupation of those on the seventh level is to push the buttons that will launch strategic nuclear weapons should war break out.

The novel is narrated by an occupant of level 7 who, like the others, is known only by a number and who has been chosen for his lack of social and emotional attachments. Because the outbreak of war could be swift and unexpected, the personnel on levels 7 and 6 (air defense specialists) have been moved permanently underground and have no contact with the surface. A support staff (including a large contingent of psychiatrists) maintains these button pushers.

Level 7 succeeds as both a political and social satire. For instance, when the residents of level 7 are initially moved underground, they are not told that the move is permanent. The news is broken to the new occupants of level 7 via loudspeaker:

> You have been brought here today to serve as the advance guard of our country, our creed, our way of life. To you men and women on Level 7 is entrusted the operation of the offensive branch of the military machine of our country and its allies.
>
> You are the defenders of truth and justice. Our infamous and treacherous enemy has gone too far in developing his striking-power. In order to make ourselves safe from surprise attack and capable of retaliation, it is imperative that we protect our protectors, that we secure for our security forces the best possible shelter.

The loudspeaker reassures level 7 occupants that "You need not worry about your friends and relatives outside. They will be notified that you have been killed in a painless accident and that you left no remains."[54]

Eventually, of course, war does break out, and the button pushers begin by launching a limited counterforce attack against the enemy as the enemy does the same. Up above, there is a mad scramble for shelter space with "bloody battles which became even more ferocious as distant explosions were heard. Entrances to shelters were blocked by people fighting in the most primitive and cruel way with the nearest weapons that came to hand—kitchen knives, clubs made from broken-up furniture, and bare fists if they could not find anything better."[55] Soon this "limited" nuclear war gets out of hand, and in the end both sides launch everything they have, including bombs rigged for maximum radiation. By the time the two sides are out of weapons, much of the world has been destroyed or rendered uninhabitable for hundreds of years by radiation. "Needless to say," comments the narrator of *Level 7*, "we are the victors."[56] *Level 7* ends as the carefully prepared protective features of the shelters begin breaking down, and inexorably, level by level, the residents sicken, then die of radiation poisoning.

The Mainstream and the Nuclear Apocalyptic

Isaac Asimov may have been right to claim that "with the coming of the atom bomb, society could no longer look upon science fiction as childish escape-literature," and indeed, one of the salient features of the fallout shelter debate is the degree to which the literary and journalistic mainstream co-opted science fiction's nuclear apocalypse scenario.[57] A nuclear attack was not only possible, but it had happened in recent memory at Hiroshima and Nagasaki, and as the descriptions of what had occurred in those two cities began to emerge after World War II, all speculative accounts of nuclear war paled before the real thing. One eyewitness was the photographer Yoshito Matsushige, who was in Hiroshima on August 6, 1945, when the bomb was dropped. As a stunned Matsushige staggers through Hiroshima he finds that his town has become a chamber of horrors. Walking past the university swimming pool, he notices that the pool is empty when it had been full the day before. Several people had apparently jumped into the pool to save themselves when the bomb went off, but the terrific heat of the bomb had evaporated the water, and these people now lay "like boiled fish at the bottom of the pool." Next Matsushige encounters a streetcar stopped in the middle of the street, and he steps aboard. The streetcar is jammed with people, "all in normal positions, holding onto streetcar straps, sitting down or standing still, just the way they would have been before the bomb went off. Except that all of them were leaning in the same direction—away from the center of the blast. And they were all burned black, a reddish black, and they were stiff."[58]

Such nonfiction accounts would help bring nuclear war into the literary mainstream, with John Hersey's *Hiroshima* having the greatest impact on the public. A narrative re-creation of the nuclear attack on Hiroshima gleaned from testimony of the survivors, *Hiroshima* was first published in 1946 in the *NewYorker* and had gone through numerous printings by the mid-1960s. Because they are factually based, Hersey's descriptions produce in the reader a resonance and a horror that fictional works found difficult to replicate:

He was the only person making his way into the city; he met hundreds and hundreds who were fleeing, and every one of them seemed to be hurt in some way. The eyebrows of some were burned off and skin hung from their faces and hands. Others, because of pain, held their arms up as if carrying something in both hands. Some were vomiting as they walked. Many were naked or in shreds of clothing. On some undressed bodies, the burns had made patterns—of undershirt straps and suspenders and, on the skin of some women (since white repelled the heat from the bomb and dark clothes absorbed it and conducted it to the skin), the shapes of flowers they had had on their kimonos.[59]

Inspired by such ghastly narratives, mainstream writers now began to produce speculative accounts of what might happen if *America* were subjected to nuclear attack. In 1948 the atomic scientist Ralph Lapp described what might be the impact of an atomic bomb dropped on "city X." Under the blast "the evanescent flash of heat has seared pedestrians into unidentifiable charred, grotesque forms," said Lapp. Soon "the air is thick with dust from pulverized buildings," then a "firewind" of gale proportions sweeps across the city and finishes off what is left.[60] In contrast to Lapp, most writers preferred using recognizable cities rather than anonymous ones. New York, with its many well-known landmarks, was a favorite target of writers, who destroyed Gotham countless times (fig. 14). As early as 1950, *Time* magazine targeted that city for destruction as "a Russian bomber carrying an atomic bomb, the equivalent of 50,000 tons of high explosives, swept through the stratosphere above New York and dropped its missile":

Within a radius of one mile of Union Square (Ground Zero), the city would appear to have been struck by a giant fist. Within that radius would be the lofty Empire State Building; the teeming cliff dwellings of Peter Cooper Village and Stuyvesant Town; Klein's department store; 14th Street's subway complex; a labyrinth of gas mains, water lines, telephone cables, electric wires; 55 elementary schools, high schools and trade schools; 17 universities and private schools; twelve of the city's hospitals. Whole sections would be obliterated.

Time estimated that 100,000 casualties would require 600,000 pints of blood over a six-week period, and that it would take seventeen freight cars to hold that number of pint bottles.[61]

By far the most lavish treatment of the nuclear apocalyptic by the periodic press during the 1950s was produced by *Collier's* magazine. The October 27,

FIG. 14. The "Mike" thermonuclear device was detonated in the Marshall Islands in the fall of 1952. This illustration, which was widely released, shows Mike's nuclear fireball, some three and a quarter miles in diameter, superimposed over the New York skyline. RG 304-NT ("Operation Ivy" folder, #10), Still Pictures Branch (NNSP), National Archives at College Park, MD.

1951, issue was titled "Preview of the War We Do Not Want," and was devoted to describing the causes and impact of World War III. A stunning array of writers contributed to this issue, including Hanson W. Baldwin, Lowell Thomas, Arthur Koestler, Walter Winchell, Allan Nevins, Edward R. Murrow, J. B. Priestley, Walter Reuther, and Senator Margaret Chase Smith. Bill Mauldin was even recruited to draw his cartoon characters Willie and Joe wandering through a nuclear battlefield. The purpose of the issue, according to *Collier's*, was to warn the Soviets that their design for world domination would lead to World War III, and that the Western powers would win such a war.[62] The editors of *Collier's* modestly described this as "the most important single issue that any magazine has ever published."[63]

There were a number of eyebrow-raising aspects of the *Collier's* extravaganza. First, there was the blurring of the boundaries between journalism and speculative fiction. Two of the most respected journalists of the day,

Edward R. Murrow and Walter Winchell, each contributed fictional pieces. Murrow's article is "A-Bomb Mission to Moscow," in which he relates what happens when he accompanies a bomber crew that drops a nuclear weapon on Moscow. For his contribution Walter Winchell produced a column in which he reports on conditions in the Soviet capital after World War III ("Walter Winchell in Moscow").[64] The lead *Collier's* article is "The Third World War," written by Robert E. Sherwood. It starts by describing how the war began (a 1952 Soviet assassination attempt on the life of Marshal Tito in Yugoslavia), then narrates in imaginative detail the course of this conflict as the United States and its allies (which will eventually include United Nations forces) oppose Soviet advances. As Soviet forces swarm across the German plains, American bombers hit Soviet targets with nuclear weapons. Sherwood is careful to emphasize that these are strategic counterforce targets, and not population centers, but the Soviets are less scrupulous.[65] In the first year of the war London is attacked by nuclear weapons, as well as Detroit, New York, and Hanford, Washington. The following year Chicago, New York, Washington, Philadelphia, Los Angeles, and San Francisco all receive nuclear hits. (Sherwood declares that "casualties were immeasurably greater than they should have been because of the failure of civil defense.")[66] While Sherwood details the damage caused by these attacks, the most vivid descriptions are to be found in a *Collier's* "eyewitness" account. In "Washington under the Bomb," Hal Boyle describes the nuclear devastation in the District of Columbia: "The heat seared. The entire business district raged in bonfire. It crackled like a million cattle stampeding in a field of potato chips. Shriveled corpses lay where they had fallen. They looked small and lonely." In addition, "most of the shrines that unite the American people are casualties," with the Jefferson and Lincoln memorials in ruins and the top of the Washington Monument "sheared off."[67] Sherwood adds a nice touch in his account of the attack on Washington, noting that "the statue of Abraham Lincoln catapulted forward so that Lincoln's stone face was lying on the crumpled steps of the Lincoln Memorial and, in the shattered background, were legible the remnants of an inscription: '. . . for the people, shall not perish from the earth.'"[68] After many twists and turns, the American/UN forces triumph in the end, destroying the communist regime, occupying the Soviet Union, and restoring freedom to the Russian people. Meanwhile, in the United States, the grim work of restoring cities rav-aged by war begins, and *Collier's* includes a piece by Philip Wylie that describes the rebuilding of a nuclear-shattered Philadelphia, and the budding romance between an American in charge of reconstruction and a female Soviet locomotive engineer.[69]

While *Collier's* may not have produced "the most important single issue that any magazine has ever published," certainly this was a remarkable publishing event. In addition to the formidable array of writing talent that *Collier's* drew upon, there were lavish illustrations that accompanied each story. Publishing expenses were considerable, and for *Collier's* to calculate that this would be a commercially viable enterprise the editors had to believe that this issue would resonate with the public. Clearly the Korean War cast a shadow over the proceedings, and in fact the editors themselves noted that work on this issue had begun in the preceding January in the midst of "the creeping pessimism of the free world as it faced the threat of an unending series of Koreas."[70] The premise that underlay the *Collier's* issue—that nuclear conflict with the Soviet Union was virtually inevitable—reflected the public's own views as revealed in opinion polls. It must also be acknowledged that early on the public had seemingly developed a perverse taste for descriptions of nuclear holocaust, and the kinds of descriptions featured in the *Collier's* articles would find their way into other publications in increasingly more elaborate and more graphic forms as the Cold War progressed toward its most dangerous stage.

The degree to which the nuclear annihilation scenario was becoming part of the culture could be seen in the surprisingly diverse publications that presented such scenarios.[71] In 1958 *Good Housekeeping*, in a radical departure from its usual fare, published an article called "A Frightening Message for a Thanksgiving Issue." Better known for its domestic advice than for analyses of defense issues, *Good Housekeeping* warned readers that "very likely you won't finish this article, because it's about death. You probably don't like to think about death, especially violent death." *Good Housekeeping* then destroys St. Louis:

> The story begins when the first atomic bomb falls in the United States. Let's say it's ten o'clock on a January Tuesday in St Louis, Missouri.
>
> Workers are at work, children are at school, housewives are at home or at the market. The weather is cold and clear—no rain or snow predicted for the next few days. The winds in the upper air are from the southwest.
>
> At exactly 10 a.m., an atomic bomb explodes a few hundred feet above the heart of the city. There is a searing flash of light; the earth itself shivers; the day seems to darken. In a split second, millions of dollars

worth of buildings crumble to the ground; thousands of fires are instantly ignited; and between one breath and the next, a quarter of a million lives are snuffed out. Everybody you know may be dead.

The survivors—and there will be some survivors—open their eyes to a holocaust. Against a scene of incredible destruction and chaos, a scene of smoke and flame and heavy, choking dust, will be the wounded, the disfigured, the terribly burned, and the horribly bleeding. If, by some miracle, a survivor escapes unharmed, he will seem to be the only wholly, uninjured person in the world.

But the bomb has only begun its business.[72]

One year after *Good Housekeeping* destroyed St. Louis, that unlucky city was attacked once again in the pages of *Nuclear Information*. Published by the Committee for Nuclear Information (CNI), an influential organization concerned with nuclear issues, *Nuclear Information* made its first appearance in 1958. Throughout its history, CNI took great pains to ground its articles in scientific evidence (which made them widely cited), and nearly every *Nuclear Information* article included notes that referred the reader to the current literature.[73] In 1959 Florence Moog, a professor of zoology at Washington University, wrote an article for *Nuclear Information* called "Nuclear War in St. Louis: One Year Later." While obviously fictional, the newsletter emphasized that this story was "not to be regarded as a work of imagination," but was based on testimony from the Holifield hearings. A physicist, a doctor, and a housewife, all three of whom are living in a World War III survivors' camp, take turns narrating this story. Their lives, as one of them puts it, had been reduced "to an elemental struggle against hunger, sickness, grief and despair." More than half a million St. Louis residents had been killed that first day, as a firestorm engulfed the city. Doctors quickly exhausted their supplies of opiates, after which "we could do nothing to quiet the screams of the burned and mangled patients who lay all around us. We didn't even have dressings to cover their torn and seared flesh." Following this initial horror "there was starvation, and there was typhus, and then there were a lot of people who just went out of their minds and either killed themselves or died because they couldn't make the effort to survive." As the weather became colder and sanitary conditions declined, more and more people became ill. "New and troublesome insects" appeared, and "before long we are fighting off rats too." Camp life was bearable, "if you can forget your hunger and don't think about the past or future":

But there are times when you wake up at night, and you can't help thinking. You wonder if there will ever be anything to life again beyond this struggle to exist. You try to recall what a piece of fresh meat looked like. You ask yourself what your children will do when they grow up—if they'll grow up—or if they will ever have children of their own. You wonder if you've fought your way this far, only to be cut down by cancer. You ask if the landscape will ever be clothed in green fields and forests again. There's a biologist here who claims to know the answer to that one. He says the fields and forests will come back. Only it will take hundreds of years.[74]

Los Angeles was not destroyed by writers as often as other cities, perhaps because its lack of a city center with tall buildings restricted the writer to fewer dramatic opportunities.[75] In March 1961, however, the *Los Angeles Times* produced an extensive article, replete with lavish illustrations, called "Red Alert! What If H-Bomb Hits Los Angeles?" (figs. 15 and 16). This piece contains most of the classic elements of the nuclear apocalyptic. It is noon, and Angelenos break for lunch, oblivious to the impending disaster: "The noon whistle has released industrial workers for an hour's rest and in thousands of homes housewives put aside their regular Monday chores to feed a 4-year-old perhaps, and then sit down with a sandwich and a cup of coffee." But there is also tension abroad, and at 12:13 P.M. American early warning systems pick up "the incredible in tiny flecks of light—a series of radar blips rising high over the ice-locked top of the world. . . . High over the Arctic Ocean the warheads streak on at 15,000 m.p.h., vaulting through the black vacuum of space, one of them on perfect trajectory for Los Angeles and the city's noontime millions." Sirens sound, citizens are told to tune to Conelrad stations, which inform listeners there is a red alert, and that they must seek shelter. Angelenos "crowd into the basements of stores and business buildings . . . jam into shops, run deep into tunnels, duck into culverts, jump into ditches." In schools, "children obey automatically, march into basements, curl under desks, their arms across pale faces and tight-closed eyes." Thousands of others remain in the open, "running, crying, clawing, fighting."

A ten-megaton warhead ignites over the city, flattening everything within a three-mile radius and "killing or hideously injuring every living thing within the central circle of horror encompassing more than 28 square miles." There are elaborate descriptions of the effects of this "vast cipher of death" as downtown buildings are "burned by the searing heat of

FIG. 15. A page from "Red Alert! What If H–Bomb Hits Los Angeles?" *Los Angeles Times*, 12 March 1961. At top is a panorama of destruction; at bottom a couple waits it out in their shelter. Illustration by Harlan Kirby. Collection of the Library of Congress. © 1961 by the Los Angeles Times. Reprinted by permission.

FIG. 16. Illustration from "Red Alert! What If H-Bomb Hits Los Angeles?" *Los Angeles Times*, 12 March 1961. Illustration by Oliver French. Collection of the Library of Congress. © 1961 by the Los Angeles Times. Reprinted by permission.

the flash, then heaved by the tormented earth in a rolling quake and finally slammed by the shock wave." In the immediate aftermath massive fires burn out of control and "death is everywhere in grotesque, shapeless horror. Pain and blood shroud the living in the macabre, fire-lighted hell under a greasy pall of smoke" as the city burns to death. Half of the city's doctors and nurses have been killed or seriously injured, and three-fourths of the city's hospitals are now useless. The ones that are still functioning are totally overwhelmed by victims of the blast. Meanwhile, a cloud of radioactive fallout is drifting down to Los Angeles from Vandenberg Air Force Base, which has been hit with a large, ground-level nuclear weapon. This is a grim scenario indeed, and while the article includes descriptions of the efforts of various civil defense officials and others to address this disaster, clearly the emphasis is on the overwhelming, catastrophic nature of this event.[76]

Another notable depiction of an H-bombed Los Angeles appeared in *Community of Fear* (1960). Here coauthors Harrison Brown and James Real creatively exploited Los Angeles's concentration of automobiles to produce a memorable literary conflagration in which "a good proportion of the metropolitan area's three-and-a-half million cars and trucks would be lifted and thrown like grotesque Molotov cocktails, to spew flaming gasoline, oil, and automotive shrapnel onto and into everything in their paths."[77] Underground gasoline and oil tanks would also rupture, feeding "a suffocating firestorm" at least twenty-five miles in radius. Only those in deep shelters with adequate oxygen supplies and cooling systems would survive, and after "clambering for dozens of miles over huge, smoking piles of radioactive rubble," the survivor would probably have accumulated a fatal dose of radiation, "which would shortly claim what was left of his life."[78]

By 1962 the relatively modest fifty-kiloton weapon used in *Time's* fictional attack against New York in 1950 had been upgraded to a twenty-megaton monster. (At this point both the United States and the Soviet Union had added twenty-megaton weapons to their arsenals, and in October 1961 the Soviets tested a fifty-megaton bomb.)[79] *Science Digest* declared that when a weapon this powerful was detonated, "a man standing 60 miles away would see a fireball 30 times brighter than the noonday sun . . . the heat would ignite a man's clothing 21 miles away and seriously burn exposed skin at 31 miles." The blast would create a hole 240 feet deep and a half mile across, and a firestorm fanned by winds of more than 1,000 miles an hour would engulf an area of 30 to 50 miles, "destroying all that will burn—structures and living things." Out of eight million New Yorkers, according to *Science Digest*, five to six million would die within the first few days.[80]

The nuclear apocalyptic was even encouraged by the Federal Civil Defense Administration (FCDA) during its yearly "Operation Alert" exercises during the mid-1950s. These were simulated nuclear attacks on American cities designed to test civil defense preparedness and to educate the public, but some believed that *terrifying*, rather than educating, the public was the only accomplishment of the various versions of Operation Alert. Secretary of defense Charles Wilson, for instance, worried that the 1956 Operation Alert would "scare a lot of people without purpose," and in the newspaper special editions created for this event it is easy to see his point.[81] The Operation Alert edition created by the *Buffalo Evening News* ran a headline that read, "125,000 Known Dead, Downtown in Ruins," and included an illustration of Buffalo's city hall collapsing into rubble (fig. 17). The story informed readers that "Buffalo's entire downtown area is completely leveled—a smoldering, blazing ruin. Unknown thousands of Buffalonians are presumed dead and many more thousands injured."[82] Readers of the *Grand Rapids Herald* received similarly distressing news under the headline "16,200 Die as H-Bomb Levels Grand Rapids" (fig. 18). An illustration showed the direction in which fallout was drifting from a nuclear mushroom cloud. It should be noted that the FCDA was not above using the nuclear disaster scenarios created under Operation Alert to promote its own agendas. For instance, the *Grand Rapids Herald* story told readers that a "Civil Defense evacuation" of Grand Rapids had saved 136,000 lives.[83]

Portrayals of nuclear war during this era run the gamut from the thoughtful to the lurid, and appeared in an extraordinary variety of forums. In a 1951 article written for the *Journal of Social Hygiene*, the Harvard physician Charles Walter Clarke worried that a nuclear war might bring on a sexual apocalypse, with a meltdown in moral standards and an increase in promiscuity.[84] What would follow, according to Clarke, might be an increase in venereal disease of "1,000% or more."[85] Against such a possibility, Clarke urged public health officials to lay in generous supplies of penicillin, and called for strict policing of bombed areas that would include "vigorous repression of prostitution and measures to discourage promiscuity, drunkenness, and disorder."[86]

A group of Harvard School of Business graduate students that supported a national shelter building program produced an account called "Effective Civil Defense," which they read into their congressional testimony. In this

Warning: This Didn't Happen ... But It Could!

Emergency Edition	BUFFALO EVENING NEWS	Emergency Edition

FRIDAY, JULY 20, 1956

125,000 KNOWN DEAD, DOWNTOWN IN RUINS

City Hall Tower Crumbles as Fire Rages Uncontrolled

News photographer, airlifted by Bell helicopter over Buffalo's devastated downtown section, risked fallout dangers of nuclear blast to get this graphic photo of fire-weakened City Hall crumbling into ruins. Lamp globe, right foreground, survived.

2 NUCLEAR BOMBS HIT BUFFALO AND NORTHERN SUBURBS; DAMAGE HEAVY

State of Emergency Declared as Civil Defense Teams Swing Into Action on Wide Front

The heart of Buffalo is gone. The Twin Cities of the Tonawandas are heavily damaged.

Buffalo's entire downtown area is completely leveled—a smoldering, blazing ruin. Unknown thousands of Buffalonians are presumed dead and many more thousands injured.

No accurate count is obtainable—and won't be for many days—but CD officials state that at least 125,000 area residents have been killed and a minimum of 150,000 injured.

The Buffalo skyline has disappeared. City Hall, the Liberty Bank Building, Rand Building, Ellicott Square, all the familiar landmarks of the downtown area are gone. Nothing distinguishable remains within a one-mile radius of what used to be McKinley Monument. The entire Niagara Frontier is under a state of emergency.

Scoring a bull's-eye, the enemy.

Scoring a bull's-eye, the enemy plane dropped its bomb with a direct hit on the McKinley Monument. Then the plane went on to drop even a more powerful bomb on the City of North Tonawanda, just over the Erie County border in Niagara County.

Help on the Way

Enemy planes struck else where in the state and nation, Rochester, Binghamton, Syracuse and New York have been hit. The sneak attack by the enemy aircraft made targets on many more cities across the nation.

Local, state and national Civil Defense forces and the military are coordinating rescue efforts.

Help is on the way. Doctors and nurses, medical supplies, food, water, clothing and other emergency supplies are being sped to the stricken areas.

Support areas garnered forces to assist in the rescue work and are preparing to house and feed evacuees and the injured.

Two Bombs Hit Area

In areas throughout the nation which escaped attack, industries have closed their plants and businesses have shut down in order to make manpower available in stricken areas.

From the type of devastation wrought, the bomb which hit Buffalo evidently was a 100-kiloton bomb, equivalent to 100,000 tons of TNT, and the one which severely damaged the Tonawandas is evidently a one-megaton hydrogen bomb equivalent to 1,000,000 tons of TNT. Both were surface bursts, detonating on impact.

Almost unbelievable conditions prevail. The areas of complete destruction encompass more than 2 square miles of downtown Buffalo but the area damaged by the Tonawanda bomb is much larger.

Everything within the Buffalo area extending north to Allen St., west to the Coast Guard Station is reduced to rubble. The same is true of the entire city of North Tonawanda.

Only part of the Buffalo Skyway is standing—the south approach. The rest is twisted steel and broken concrete.

Warning Saved Many

Warning is in operation, keeping the surviving public informed and instructed.

Fortunately, there was enough time between the first warning of the approaching enemy planes and the bomb burst to get most

of the thousands in downtown Buffalo to their homes before the enemy struck. CD officials presumed the bomb—if it came—would fall in the heart of the city and their guess was accurate.

Coast Guard vessels, the Buffalo fireboat, and lake vessels in the harbor were warned—and had sufficient time—to head out into the lake to escape the blast. After the all-clear, they returned to join in the firefighting and rescue work.

Damage from the Buffalo blast extended north to Soldier's Pl., east to the New York Central Terminal, south to about one-fourth mile south of the Ford Plant and west across the Niagara in Garrison Rd. and King St., in Ft. Erie South.

Fires rage and are being fought by regular and auxiliary forces on a one-mile front encircling the damaged areas.

Fallout Path Wide

The area damaged by the Tonawanda bomb was wider in scope —75 square miles—encompassing much of Grand Island and the greater portion of the northwest section of Erie County, extending into Buffalo and the Town of Amherst to the East.

Moving northeastward from the stricken zones are massive smoke palls laden with radio-active material, carried by a moderate wind. The dangerous fallout path widens as it moves along with the wind. Civil Defense forces are being directed from the Lancaster control station, which is in communication with support areas and state CD officials.

Radiological experts, equipped with scientific instruments, have entered contaminated areas.

There's a Reason for This

Ever wonder about the importance of a newspaper in the face of a major emergency? The National Fire Protection Association included this excerpt in a compilation about the atom-bombing of Hiroshima:

"To prevent the spread of rumors and brace morale, 210,000 copies of out-of-town newspapers were brought in daily to replace the destroyed local press...."

Volunteers Badly Needed

Emergency appeals have been issued by Civil Defense officials for blood donors, volunteer medical aides, and stretcher bearers. All able-bodied men and women are urged to help.

CD Chief OK's Special Edition

"Operation Alert," the massive nation-wide Civil Defense training exercise is now under way. This special "emergency" edition

Help Spike Rumors—Listen to Conelrad

Stay tuned to your Conelrad station during this emergency. Radio Stations WBEN and WGR will continue to broadcast on the special 640 and 1240 frequencies during this emergency condition.

Don't repeat rumors. Don't believe rumors. Stay tuned to your Civil Defense leaders and authoritative information.

of The Buffalo Evening News, which helps to lend a touch of realism to the deadly serious business of preparing for nuclear warfare, has the complete endorsement of Civil Defense officials.

"The News is to be commended for this further expression of leadership in publishing a special edition in conjunction with 'Operation Alert,'" declared Maj. Edwin G. Ziegler, director of the Erie County Civil Defense program.

"It is the type of unstinting public service that we in the Civil Defense organization hope for but seldom get," he added.

Copies of this emergency edition were distributed to Civil Defense workers by dispatch riders operating out of the central control headquarters in Lancaster.

Emergency Facilities Used to Publish News

This emergency edition of The Buffalo Evening News was compiled by a small number of News employees who escaped being wiped out along with their co-workers only because they were off-duty or vacationing.

By a pre-arranged plan, all made their way over refugee-clogged highways to a Niagara County publishing plant, one of several in the Buffalo area especially selected for just such emergency conditions.

The News will continue to publish a daily emergency edition pending completion of arrangements to resume regular publication. Tomorrow's edition will include a 16-page supplement listing the dead and badly injured.

Kilotons vs. Megatons

Nuclear weapons are measured in terms of kilotons or megatons and instructed. A kiloton is the equivalent to the power of 1000 tons of TNT; a megaton is the equivalent to 1,000,000 tons of TNT.

Heed These Instructions and Live

Beware broken wires. Boil all water before drinking. Keep your car off the streets. Use your telephone only for emergency calls.	Looters will be shot on sight. Don't pay black market prices for food. If forced to evacuate your home, be sure to take ample blankets and clothing.

FIG. 17. Operation Alert edition of *Buffalo Evening News*, 20 July 1956. RG 397-MA 2-N-4 (box 13), Still Pictures Branch (NNSP), National Archives at College Park, MD.

SUNDAY, JULY 22, 1956   Three

AS PAGE ONE OF THE HERALD MIGHT LOOK AFTER H-BOMB ATTACK

The Grand Rapids Herald

SEVENTY-SECOND YEAR   SATURDAY, JULY 21, 1956   PUBLISHED IN BATTLE CREEK

16,200 DIE AS H-BOMB LEVELS GRAND RAPIDS

DEADLY PATH OF H-BOMB FALLOUT

So far as is now known, no photographer who might have snapped the H-bomb cloud over Grand Rapids survived the blast, if he was still that near the blast. But Staff Artist Charles Albright, from his place near Cutlerville, on a hill about 10 miles South of Grand Rapids, got a good view of the mushroom cloud and sketched it. The cloud is still hovering over Kent County but thinned out, and is drifting eastward. The cloud itself as it Friday evening was no longer visible but radioactive dust which is dispersed over hapless populations is still potent enough to cause death or permanent injuries.

Stay out of the path of the downwind fallout drift until you receive Civil Defense instructions that the danger is past.

25,500 Injured; Fast Evacuation Saves 136,000

City's Business District Is Wiped Out; Heavy Damage Extends Outward a Mile

Doomsday for Grand Rapids came at 12:45 p. m. on Friday, July 20, 1956.

At that moment, an enemy bomber dropped a nuclear bomb carrying the equivalent explosive force of 100,000 tons of TNT on the City known throughout the world as the "Furniture Capital of America."

Seconds later, Grand Rapids was a shambles, with more than 16,200 of her 178,515 citizens dead and an estimated 25,500 more injured.

The heart of the City's business district has been wiped out. A ring of complete destruction extends outward for almost a mile from Campau Square. Extremely heavy damage extends outward for almost another mile, while rings of moderate to light damage encompasses almost all of the territory within the city limits.

In addition to the 16,200 estimated dead and injured from the blast effects of Friday's explosion, thousands more persons were exposed to dangerous radioactive fallout resulting from the blast. It is feared that the eventual total of dead and injured may exceed 100,000.

Thousands of lives were saved by a Civil Defense evacuation which was ordered at 10:16 a. m. It is estimated that more than 136,000 residents were able to escape the rings of complete and heavy destruction between the sounding of the evacuation signals and the attack on the City at 12:45 p. m.

Grand Rapids was one of the 78 targets in the Black Friday attack on the United States and its territories, which resulted in an estimated 10,000,000 deaths and 10,500,000 injuries.

ONLY MICHIGAN CITY

(No other Michigan city was hit in the attack which included guided missile attacks, launched from submarines, on Hawaii, Puerto Rico, the Canal Zone and Alaska. Mainland targets hit by nuclear bombs included Washington, D. C., New York, San Francisco, Chicago, Seattle, Portland, Ore.; Minneapolis, St. Paul, Milwaukee, Philadelphia, Baltimore, Denver, Los Angeles, New Orleans and other important cities as well as Air Force bases and Atomic Energy Commission installations.

(President Eisenhower and top Government officials evacuated Washington before the attack and are conducting the affairs of Government from secret relocation sites outside the Capital.

(Many enemy bombers are be-

Continued on Page 21

Radioactive Dust Imperils West State

Residents of a 1,000 square-mile area in Kent, Montcalm and Ionia Counties are now being threatened by dangerous radioactive fallout resulting from Friday's nuclear bomb attack on Grand Rapids.

The fallout area extends approximately 50 miles eastward from Grand Rapids to Muir, Lyons and Ionia.

The southern edge of the fallout area is believed to roughly parallel the route of U. S. Highway 16, with the northern edge extending as far as Greenville.

Heaviest concentration of the fallout is in the destroyed metropolitan area of Grand Rapids. However, the amount of radiation, even on the outer fringes of the fallout pattern, may be sufficient to be extremely dangerous.

Civil Defense experts, on the basis of Weather Bureau plotting of the fallout pattern, the known facts about the size of the bomb and the type of explosion, estimate that the fallout would be sufficiently radioactive to result in a possible 30,000 deaths in this area if no protective measures had been taken. These estimates indicated that an additional 22,000 persons would receive a sufficient dose of radiation to make them ill, without proper precautions.

How many fallout victims will be added to the 16,200 killed and 25,500 injured by the blast effects of the Grand Rapids bombing will not be known for some time.   Continued on Page 21

Explanation of how Herald Staff might prepare emergency edition following H-bomb attack appears on opposite page.

Avoid Panic — Listen Only to Official CD Bulletins

Among the survivors are many families which were separated at the start of the evacuation. Don't let panic get the upperhand. Your missing loved ones may be safe in one of the many scattered reception areas. Registration of all survivors is being speeded by Civil Defense authorities and their names will be broadcast over West Michigan's radio stations as they become available. This will require several days but the lists will be broadcast and posted in public parks as soon as they are available.

It is imperative that you avoid rumors and pay heed only to the official Civil Defense instructions and announcements that will come to you over local radio stations, two of which have made prompt emergency portable transmitter installations to the north and west. Emergency editions of The Herald will continue to be published as promptly as possible, but be patient if these editions are late or consist of only a few pages.

Aid to essential local industries is being rushed from Lansing, Detroit and many distant cities. If the fallout drift to the east did not persist, it might be possible to say: "The worst is over!" But survival is a big job, an uncertain test of our will and patriotism. Help is being rushed to us, so let us help ourselves and help each other and somehow piece things together again.

FIG. 18. Operation Alert edition of *Grand Rapids Herald*, 21 July 1956. RG 397-MA 2-N-2 (box 13), Still Pictures Branch (NNSP), National Archives at College Park, MD.

64

tale, Ed Baker, an employee at a publishing firm in Garden City, is at his desk when he is "startled by a flash of blue-white light." An atomic bomb has been dropped on New York City, and while Ed's reflexes as a former soldier enable him to save himself, his secretary is not so lucky ("a flying sliver had caught her in the neck, slicing open the arteries"). The window washer is equally unfortunate ("his dark blue shirt was smoldering and his skin was burning red where the direct light from the blast had touched it"). Ed is able to make his way home through the chaos of a disintegrating civilization to his wife and child, but the Bakers have no fallout protection. As he and his family become sicker and sicker with radiation poisoning, Ed is forced to make a grim decision:

> Ed walked upstairs. The dust didn't bother him now. The nausea was part of the past. He took his Smith and Wesson .38 and painstakingly loaded all six chambers. Tears were rolling down his cheeks. He went down into the basement again, just as he had gone to war, with a slow and deliberate step as if the enemy was around the next corner. Ed knew what he must do.[87]

Providing a forum that was much different from a congressional hearing was *Playboy* magazine, which in 1962 published one of the most sordid examples of the nuclear apocalyptic. In Vance Aandahl's story of a post–nuclear war society, one of the disconcerting effects of radiation is that the survivors progressively lose parts of their anatomy. As one of the companions of Adam Frost, the protagonist of this story, observes, "Every day, something goes putrid. One day, it's an eye. The next, it's a foot."[88] As Frost's own deterioration accelerates, he becomes relatively unconscious of his condition until he meets a girl at a garbage dump who has not been irradiated:

> "Your arms!" The girl shuddered. Frost looked downward.
> Clusters of sores had almost reached his shoulders. The skin on his hands was peeling away; it hung in greenish-gray ribbons about his wrists. His fingernails had fallen out. One of his fingers was gone.

The story ends when Frost seizes the girl and "sprawling on a heap of refuse, Frost madly gave life to mankind's first new child."[89]

There *were* a few brave souls who insisted that nuclear holocaust was not all it was cracked up to be. Chief among those who believed that most

FIG. 19. Herman Kahn, 1959. Photograph by Warren K. Leffler. Library of Congress, Prints and Photographs Division, *U.S. News & World Report* Magazine Collection, LC-U9-3508, frame 16.

scenarios of a post–nuclear war world were overly grim was Herman Kahn, principal author of a RAND Corporation report on nuclear shelters published in 1958 (fig. 19). Kahn emphasized that "we should not underestimate the strength in an emergency of a decentralized private-enterprise economy and of widespread ingenuity among the people," and predicted that "extensive reorganization" of the economy could be accomplished within six months after a nuclear war.[90]

In 1960 Kahn published *On Thermonuclear War,* easily one of the most controversial books produced during the Cold War era. Kahn was one of those public figures who seemingly delighted in stirring up public opinion. Sharon Mindel Helsel, who wrote a doctoral dissertation on Kahn, observes that in Kahn's briefings "he sometimes seemed to deliberately impersonate a mad scientist with his jokes, giggles, slurred and stuttered speech, waggish examples" and that Kahn "spoofed his dignified audiences in the grotesque-science Enlightenment tradition."[91] In Kahn's writings too there is an over-the-top quality in his willingness—even compulsion—to take controversial stands that he knew would infuriate many readers. In *On Thermonuclear War* and other works that would follow, Kahn would display a genius for inciting critics, especially with his suggestion that it was possible to stage-manage nuclear war to "limit" its effects, and that recovery from nuclear war would not only be possible but even probable—if the right preparations were made beforehand. The reviews of this book were apoplectic, and tended to veer into ad hominem attacks on Kahn himself. In *New World Review*, Jessica Smith proclaimed, "I cannot stomach more than a few chapters of this inhuman document," and identified Kahn as one of those "who have prostituted their brains to the service of death and destruction."[92] George Kirstein ended his review of *On Thermonuclear War* by saying of Kahn, "To be blunt, his book made me ashamed that we are fellow countrymen."[93] Perhaps the most vituperative was James R. Newman, who began his review in *Scientific American* by wondering, "Is there really a Herman Kahn? It is hard to believe. Doubts cross one's mind almost from the first page of this deplorable book: no one could write like this; no one could think like this. Perhaps the whole thing is a staff hoax in bad taste."[94]

Much of the hostility directed against Kahn comes from his approach to the subject. In *On Thermonuclear War*, Kahn looks at the problems of nuclear war from the perspective of the systems analyst, adopting a dispassionate prose style and regaling the reader with some seventy-five tables. The overall effect is disturbing, even cold-blooded. In one table, for instance, Kahn estimates genetic damage from nuclear war under the categories of "major defects," "minor defects," "early mortality," and "decreased fertility."[95] In table 3, under the heading "Tragic but Distinguishable Postwar States," Kahn has a column for the number of dead in a nuclear attack, and a column for "economic recuperation." Thus Kahn estimates that if there were 2 million dead, economic recuperation would take one year; 20 million dead would take ten years; 160 million dead would take a hundred years.[96] There is a chart for how radioactive the world would be a hundred years after an attack, and a chart of the types of wars that might be fought (titled the "Eight World Wars").[97] In this huge volume (weighing in at over 650 pages), Kahn poses the question, "Will the survivors envy the dead?" after a nuclear war, and answers in the negative. Kahn notes, for instance, that if thousands of Americans died prematurely because of radioisotopes created by a nuclear war,

> simple arithmetic shows that such deaths would be of small significance *compared to the war itself.* Few would call it a "total catastrophe" if *all* survivors of a thermonuclear war lost a few years of life expectancy and even ten or twenty million of the survivors lost an average of ten or fifteen years of life expectancy. To repeat: I think that any individual who survived the war should be willing to accept, almost with equanimity, somewhat larger risks than those to which we subject our industrial workers in peacetime. (emphasis in original)[98]

Kahn insists that while "the amount of human tragedy would be greatly increased in the postwar world," such an increase "would not preclude normal and happy lives for the majority of survivors and their descendants."[99] Kahn's emotional distance was frequently criticized, and Kahn himself admitted, "My wife, Jane, insists that I am unpleasantly detached on this subject."[100]

Later, in *Thinking about the Unthinkable* (1962), Kahn reiterated his claim that while a "postwar environment might be more hostile to human life for many years," such an environment would not preclude "decent and useful lives for the survivors and their descendants" and that "relatively normal and happy lives would not be impossible even under the harsh conditions that might prevail after a nuclear war." In fact, Kahn believed that after the first year or two of a nuclear war, the standard of living "would be higher than the standards prevalent in the U.S. between 1900 and 1930."[101]

Sidney Winter, Jr., another RAND researcher, thought it possible that once recovery got under way after a nuclear war, industrial output could be restored to present per capita levels in about a decade, and Marshall K. Wood of the National Planning Association believed that if an effective shelter program could be established, it would be possible "within a few months" to "support a standard of living equal to or better than that of the thirties."[102] The physicist Ralph E. Lapp, who had alerted the public to the unexpectedly large amounts of radioactive fallout from the 1954 Bikini Atoll hydrogen bomb test, also claimed in 1960 that estimates of long-term radiation had been overstated.[103]

Time magazine joined those who insisted that nuclear war was over-rated, claiming in 1961 that "95% of the nation's land would still be green" and that people could start emerging from their shelters for brief periods only two days after the bombs stopped dropping. *Time* predicted that within two weeks "civil defense, military police and fire authorities should be back at work with fair effectiveness," and industries "that have taken precautions" could be back in business. The can-do American, with "trousers tucked into sock tops and sleeves tied around wrists, with hats, mufflers, gloves and boots" would venture forth from his shelter "to start ensuring his today and building for his tomorrow."[104] Richard F. Dempe-wolff, writing in *Popular Mechanics*, claimed that 96 percent of the land area of the United States "would be virtually unchanged" following a nu-clear war: "You would emerge to find your town looking about the same as ever." While some things would be different, "it would be far from the silent world of hot rubble often conjured up. In most places there would be considerable human activity."[105]

Taking issue with these optimistic views was the chemist Gordon S. Christiansen, who concluded that "more probable than the arrival of teams of saviors would be the arrival of roving bands of marauders— frightened, injured, maddened, short-term survivors of other similarly devastated areas."[106] *U.S. News and World Report* also expressed doubts about the normality of life following a nuclear war, insisting that a postapocalyptic world would indeed be a silent one: "Most of the famil-iar sounds would be missing. Birds and insects would be dead, so you wouldn't hear them. Traffic would be dead, too—or very nearly so. And the factories, of course, would be out of operation. It would be a silent world to which you emerged."[107] In *Saturday Review*, Norman Cousins made a similarly grim prediction. Cousins promised that when the sur-vivors emerged from their holes after the apocalypse, they would "embark upon an ordeal unlike anything the human race" had ever known. The earth itself would be "burned and clotted" and anything standing would be "charred and skeletonized." All human institutions would be gone. "This is what nuclear war is. No deodorizing can change the fact."[108]

In "The Biology of Nuclear War," the geneticist Bentley Glass predicted that birds, because of their sensitivity to radiation, would quickly die, leaving the world to radiation-resistant insects. These insects, "unchecked in their ravages, may quickly destroy every green thing left by fire and blast." This might not be much, however, because Glass claimed that firestorms would engulf thousands of miles of forest land. Massive erosion of the topsoil would follow, and "unless the fires did a very thorough clean-up job the millions of unburied corpses of human beings and animals would provide a hotbed for the growth of the organisms of death and decay." Glass's conclusion? "Life will be very primitive for the survivors for a long time to come."[109]

Apocalypse Now

These many descriptions of the end of our civilization, in both their vividness and quantity, cannot be found in any other era of American history. While previous generations have occasionally raised millenarian alarms, it is only in the Cold War era that we see such a large cross section of the population, from renowned philosophers to the editors of *Good Housekeeping*, producing such a large quantity of apocalyptic literature. In effect, a genre of literature that had originally been the purview of clerics and social critics was now being embraced by virtually everyone. In his book *Fictions of Nuclear Disaster*, David Dowling defends the extreme, apocalyptic language that dominated much of the literature of nuclear war, noting that the "Biblical imagery remains tenaciously appropriate since what is contemplated is not so much the end of the physical world as proof of man's degeneracy and the end of the Christian era."[110] Joseph Dewey contends that with the Hiroshima blast "there seemed born into the world a most supernatural presence, one that commanded a religious response. . . . the fiery sweep of the mushroom cloud would precede the world's consummation like John's thundering horsemen."[111]

Just as mainstream writers co-opted the nuclear disaster scenario from the genre of science fiction, so too did they embrace the language of the apocalypse from popular religious writers. Nuclear weapons were now being described in apocalyptic terms. In *Disaster and the Millennium*, Michael Barkun observes that millenarian movements have historically been rural in origin and that the "disaster events" that have driven the apocalypse have been natural occurrences, such as floods, famines, and earthquakes. But as the impact of natural events lessened in the twentieth century, manmade disasters took their place.[112] Nuclear weapons especially have become, in Barkun's phrase, "a surrogate for natural disasters":

> The danger and imminence of nuclear war promises precisely the finality that premillennial doctrine requires, for unlike past conflicts, war may

now occur with no credible opportunity for victory or reconstruction. No matter how stable the international environment may be in other respects, the presence of nuclear weapons insures that predictions of a climactic battle between good and evil will appear inevitable.[113]

The German scholar Klaus Koch noted in 1970 that "Apocalyptic is one of the few theological terms which has been absorbed into the jargon of the mass media."[114] A great deal of the credit for this phenomenon can be ascribed to the creation of nuclear weapons.

Paul Boyer observes that "at the level of popular religious belief, the bomb's impact was immediate and dramatic."[115] In the wake of Hiroshima, evangelical writers rushed in to demonstrate that the advent of nuclear weapons had been foretold in the Bible, and that in the words of one enthusiast, "The holocaust of atomic war would fulfill the prophecies. . . . The Bible and science go right down the line together on the forecasting of future events for earth."[116] In this formulation the nuclear bomb was the instrument of God, a weapon unleashed on sinful nations.[117] Wilbur M. Smith, a Presbyterian minister and prophecy writer, postulated that Sodom and Gomorrah may have been destroyed by nuclear weapons.[118] While the wicked would perish in nuclear fire, the faithful would be spared, lifted up by the Rapture to witness Armageddon from a safe distance. In his novel *Cat's Cradle* (1963), one of Kurt Vonnegut's characters describes the plot of a novel containing all the important elements of the nuclear weapons/Final Judgment scenario: "It told about how mad scientists made a terrific bomb that wiped out the whole world. There was a big sex orgy when everybody knew that the world was going to end, and then Jesus Christ Himself appeared ten seconds before the bomb went off."[119]

As to the fallout shelter issue, there was some difference of opinion as to where, exactly, God stood on the matter. The radio evangelist M. R. De-Haan declared in 1962, "No shelter . . . can protect us from the bombs being produced today. The only way *out* is *up*."[120] Johnny Bob Harrell, the leader of a religious anticommunist movement called the Christian Conservative Church, believed the contrary, claiming that God himself told him to build fallout shelters. On an estate that Harrell established for his group in Clay County, Illinois, Harrell managed to construct two fallout shelters by October 4, 1961—the construction deadline set by God. "We just made it," declared Harrell, who went on to predict that a nuclear attack on the United States would take place by the end of the year. "In fact we will be fighting Russian troops on American soil by Christmas."[121]

Mainstream writers were also often tempted to put an apocalyptic spin on Cold War politics—a struggle between good and evil with the Soviet Union standing in for the Antichrist. Arthur Waskow worried that nuclear war might hold a "dark attraction" for those desiring a "world wiped clean of complications, ambiguities and dissension."[122] Philip Wylie, according to Spencer Weart, was one of those who "thought all would be well if only the evils of Communism could be erased. . . . he wanted to attack evil itself, passing through Armageddon to world rebirth."[123] Even Bertrand Russell at various points in his career found this idea seductive. Russell stated in 1950 that the advent of nuclear war would be "the greatest disaster that will have befallen the human race," but he also believed that "the extension of the Kremlin's power over the whole world" would be an even greater catastrophe. In Russell's view "a war would do less harm than world-wide tyranny." Several times in the years immediately following World War II Russell even suggested that the United States might be justified in launching a preemptive nuclear strike against the Soviet Union.[124]

The Soviets themselves, because their state was officially atheistic, did not frame the possibility of nuclear war in apocalyptic terms. But nuclear war was frequently portrayed as an event that would be unprecedented in human history. A 1962 *Pravda* article described such a war as an occurrence before which "the horrors of the invasions of the Vandals and the Crusades, the Thirty-Years' and One Hundred-Year's [*sic*] Wars, the Napoleonic Battles, and Hitler's 'blitzkrieg'" would pale into "insignificance." The same year defense minister Rodion Malinovsky called nuclear war a disaster that would "far exceed anything which history has so far known."[125]

Without discounting the urgency that motivated the apocalyptic literature of this era, it must be observed that the Nuclear Age helped laypersons rediscover the peculiar pleasures of the Jeremiad. Indeed, there even seemed to be a perverse pride in the awesome destructive power now possessed by humanity, and the fact that the twentieth century's unique contribution to the end of the world was that divine intervention was now no longer required. As Paul Brians has observed, in our largely secular culture, "nuclear war is the nearest thing we have to Armageddon."[126] Writing in 1961, Paul Tillich of Harvard University raised "the possibility that it is the destiny of historical man to be annihilated not by a cosmic event but by the tensions of his own being and in his own history."[127] This connection between nuclear disaster and biblical disaster, and the overwhelming destructiveness of the former, was alluded to by the biologist Tom Stonier in 1963, who posited a post–nuclear war insect assault "which would make the locust plagues of Biblical times look like tea parties."[128] Indeed, running through the literature is a certain satisfaction in humanity's newfound ability to destroy itself. As Arthur Koestler put it, "the voluble phrases about the possibility of blowing the whole planet to glory sounded at first both frightening and subtly flattering to our vanity."[129]

But it was Thomas Merton who was most eloquent in drawing a parallel between the apocalypse prophesied by the Bible and the state of affairs of modern humanity:

> It is no exaggeration to say that our times are Apocalyptic, in the sense that we seem to have come to a point at which all the hidden, mysterious dynamism of the "history of salvation" revealed in the Bible has flowered into final and decisive crisis. The term "end of the world" may or may not be one that we are capable of understanding. But at any rate we seem to be assisting at the unwrapping of the mysteriously vivid symbols of the last book of the New Testament.[130]

Merton called the urge to wipe out Bolshevism "one of the apocalyptic temptations of twentieth-century Christendom," and he described the idea of Christianity defending itself with nuclear weapons "pure madness."[131] Merton detected a "moral passivity" on both sides of the Iron Curtain, as well as a technological "demonic activism" that had moved beyond the control of political leaders and was plunging the world toward disaster.[132] To Merton, the most important issue of the time was "the moral responsibility of global suicide," which, if chosen by humanity, "would be a moral evil second only to the crucifixion."[133]

Scientists, no less than theologians and novelists, were transfixed by the possibility of apocalypse, and one of the most interesting theoretical creations of the day—a construct that combined science with Armageddon—was the Doomsday Machine. It was Herman Kahn who had first brought public attention to the Doomsday Machine, which Kahn described as a "device whose only function is to destroy all human life." Consisting of a bomb in the gigaton range buried thousands of feet underground to protect it from enemy attack, the Doomsday Machine would be connected to a computer, which in turn would be connected to sensory devices all over the country. "The computer," according to Kahn, "would then be programmed so that if, say, five nuclear bombs exploded over the United States, the device would be triggered and the earth destroyed."[134] In one of Kahn's infamous tables (this one called "Desirable Characteristics of a Deterrent"), Kahn evaluates the qualities of the Doomsday Machine under the categories "frightening," "inexorable," "persuasive," "cheap," "nonaccident prone," and "controllable." Kahn awards the Doomsday Machine high marks in every category except "controllable" because "a failure kills too many people and kills them too automatically."[135] Kahn estimated that such a machine could be built for about $10 billion.[136] While frequently described as cold and overly rational in his discussions of nuclear war, Kahn adopts a language that draws more heavily on theology than physics to describe the triggering of a Doomsday Machine. It would be, in Kahn's words, "Armageddon—a final battle between 'good' and 'evil' in which civilization itself will receive an enormous setback no matter who wins the battle or, even more finally, a battle in which human life will be wiped out."[137]

While Kahn did not believe that the Doomsday Machine would or should be built, the fact that he was willing to discuss the possibility of such a monstrous device contributed to Kahn's increasing notoriety.[138] This idea would be parodied, and would become the concluding dramatic device, in one of the great icons of Cold War culture, Stanley Kubrick's 1964 film *Dr. Strangelove*. In this masterpiece of dark humor, a rogue American air force general launches an attack on the Soviet Union.[139] The American president is able to recall all planes but one, and as the lone B-52 bomber speeds toward its target, its commander, Major Kong (referred to as "King" by his associates), has a talk with the crew:

> When King spoke, it was with quiet dignity. "Well, boys, I reckon this is it."
> "What?" Ace Owens said.
> "*Com*-bat."
> "But we're carrying hydrogen bombs," Lothar Zogg muttered.
> King nodded gravely in assent. "That's right, *nuclear com*-bat! Toe-to-toe with the Russkies."[140]

Meanwhile, the American president and his top advisers (including former Nazi scientist Dr. Strangelove) have assembled in the "War Room," and it is here that a drunken Soviet premier informs his ambassador (De Sadeski) via telephone that the Soviet Union has put in place a device that will automatically detonate and destroy the world if that country is attacked.

> De Sadeski slowly took his hand away from the telephone. Slowly he raised his head until he was looking right at the President. He said softly but bitterly, "The fools! The mad, crazy insane fools!"

The President said quickly, "What are you talking about?"
"The Doomsday Machine."

De Sadeski then describes the Doomsday Machine as "a device which will destroy all human and animal life on earth."[141] When an incredulous president turns to Dr. Strangelove and asks him whether such a weapon is possible, Strangelove replies that he had recently commissioned a study by the "Bland Corporation" on the Doomsday Machine. Strangelove then describes the technical aspects of the Doomsday Machine in perfect Herman Kahn–style language, and concludes that the Doomsday Machine is "terrifying, simple to understand and completely credible and convincing."[142] Despite frantic efforts to shoot down the American bomber, it reaches and destroys its target. It is now obvious that the Doomsday Machine will be set in motion, but before the final apocalypse is unleashed, *Dr. Strangelove* manages to parody one last symbol of the Cold War, the fallout shelter. As the occupants of the War Room try to decide what to do next, Dr. Strangelove suggests that Americans take shelter in deep mine shafts.[143] As to who would be chosen to occupy the limited available space, the doctor demonstrates that he has already worked out the details:

> Strangelove said, "Offhand, I should say that in addition to the factors of youth, health, sexual fertility, intelligence, and a cross section of necessary skills, it would be *absolutely vital that our top government and military men* be included, to foster and impart the required principles of leadership and tradition."[144]

Strangelove has now gained the attention of the War Room, and enthusiasm for his plan increases after he suggests that shelters contain a gender ratio of "ten women to each man":

> General Turgidson looked at Strangelove. He said, "You mentioned the ratio of ten women to each man. Wouldn't that necessitate abandoning the so-called monogamous form of sexual relationship—at least as far as men are concerned?"
>
> "Regrettably, yes. But it is a sacrifice required for the future of the human race. I hasten to add that since each man will be required to perform prodigious service along these lines, the women will have to be selected for their sexual characteristics, which will have to be of a highly stimulating order."[145]

In a clear swipe at Herman Kahn and other RAND researchers, Strange-love suggests that after a hundred-year stay in their mine shafts, occupants could emerge and "work their way back to our present gross national product within twenty years."[146] As the credits roll in the film version of *Dr. Strangelove*, there is a montage of nuclear explosions as a big band singer croons, "We'll meet again, don't know where, don't know when."[147]

It is useful to speculate to what degree the nuclear apocalyptic of this era corresponds to what Richard Slotkin has called "the myth of regen-eration through violence . . . the structuring metaphor of the American experience."[148] As we have seen, the evidence for such a mythic element in this genre is mixed, varying from work to work and even varying within the oeuvre of a single author. In *On the Beach*, for instance, the violence of World War III leaves no opportunities for regeneration, but allows only for the death of the entire human race. In *Alas, Babylon*, the human race does not entirely perish after a nuclear war, but the ending is hardly optimistic as survivors gird themselves for "the thousand-year night." There is a regeneration of sorts after the nuclear holocaust in *A Canticle for Leibowitz*, but it is painfully slow renewal gained over hun-dreds of years of darkness, violence, and ignorance. In Philip Wylie's nov-els we have both: *Tomorrow!* reflects an optimism that humanity can both survive a nuclear war and build a better world in its aftermath, while *Tri-umph* is closer to the despair of *On the Beach* in which humanity has suc-ceeded in annihilating itself.

Almost always missing from the nuclear apocalyptic is a political cri-tique suggesting how such a disaster could have been avoided.[149] Accord-ing to Paul Brians, the reason authors alerted readers to the perils of nu-clear war while offering little in the way of a solution might be related to the fact that nuclear war may be "the symbol of our common death," and that folk wisdom instructs us to accept death as inevitable. "Indeed," says Brians, "it is much easier to resign oneself to extinction than to engage in the complicated and exhausting task of staving off an atomic Armaged-don. The mesmerizing power of the threatened end of civilization, if not of all life on earth, seems to cast a pall over the human will."[150]

While the nuclear apocalyptic may not have offered a political solution, clearly a political *critique* was embedded in these tales of atomic disaster. Did the nuclear apocalyptic, then, represent a populist attack on a political establishment that insisted on maintaining a dangerous, even insane, strat-egy of mutual assured destruction? And did this form of literature have any effect on overall nuclear policy? With the exception of *On the Beach*, there is little indication that these works had sufficient impact to penetrate to the highest levels of government. Allan Winkler observes that while novels, stories, films, and other cultural expressions "served as something of a safety valve" for the fears that artists were feeling, it was "government officials rather than scientists or cultural critics [who] seized the initiative in shaping the public agenda."[151] While it is difficult to quantify such things, it is possible that a more modest claim can be made for the nuclear apocalyptic. This genre may not have affected overall nuclear policy, but in the many depictions of the uselessness of civil defense in general and shelters in particular, and in the grim descriptions of life after nuclear war, the nuclear apocalyptic may have helped turn public opinion against a national shelter system.

Regardless of its political impact, the flowering of the nuclear apocalyptic in literature was a remarkable development in the history of the Cold War. It flourished when tensions between East and West were at their peak, and attracted a wide range of writers that included science fiction authors, mainstream novelists, journalists, students, scientists, screenplay writers, and even editors of women's magazines. Perhaps at its source was a *fin-de-siècle* impulse—a pervasive feeling that an era was coming to an end (and nothing ends an era quite as decisively as a nuclear war). It was contemporaneous with the fallout shelter debate, and shelters themselves were frequently the subjects of these works. These descriptions of nuclear war and its aftermath were inventive, imaginative, and lavish. And while writers defended the nuclear apocalyptic by insisting that they were only trying to awaken their readers to the dangers of nuclear war, the obvious gusto with which writers "destroyed" America with nuclear fire, and the lingering attention to the details that made up the horror of life following a nuclear war, frequently produced an impression that was both unsettling and oddly prurient. Thomas Mann's character Settembrini in *The Magic Mountain* took note of the horrible, erotic magnetism of death, observing that it is a "lustful power, whose vicious attraction is strong indeed; to feel drawn to it, to feel sympathy with it, is without any doubt at all the most ghastly aberration to which the spirit of man is prone."[152] Even more ghastly is an attraction to the death of the entire human species, which was often the disturbing subtext of the nuclear apocalyptic. Sometimes pornographic in its violence, often Wagnerian in its fiery, nihilistic grandeur, and frequently millenarian in its moral message, the nuclear apocalyptic spoke to a generation that saw the Final Days not as a biblical abstraction, but as a concrete, immediate, even probable reality.[153]

CHAPTER 3

Morality and National Identity at the Shelter Door

The first indication that there would be problems ahead for shelters and civil defense was that the Kennedy administration seemed both surprised at and unprepared for the tremendous public reaction to Kennedy's Berlin speech. Frightened Americans, who previously had tried to ignore the possibility of nuclear war, now besieged their government for information on surviving such a catastrophe. The Office of Civil Defense hurriedly began work on a civil defense pamphlet, and the result was finally released to the public in December 1961 under the title *Fallout Protection: What to Know and Do about Nuclear Attack.* In many ways a peculiar document, *Fallout Protection* was uneasily poised between impressing its readers with the serious consequences of a nuclear attack and reassuring them that everything would somehow work out. Predicting that nuclear war would be "terrible beyond imagination and description," the authors of *Fallout Protection* then seemed to argue the contrary: "If effective precautions have been taken in advance, it need not be a time of despair."[1] The main argument presented in *Fallout Protection*, which was premised on the effects of a five-megaton bomb detonated at ground level, was that shelters "could greatly reduce the number of casualties."[2]

Fallout Protection did not have a kindly reception, prompting instead a chorus of jeers from the critics. The Washington Association of Scientists (WAS), a local chapter of the Federation of American Scientists, derided the pamphlet for understating the dangers of nuclear fallout, and for its assumption that the enemy would restrict its attack to a five-megaton ground blast. The scientists maintained that the circumstances in which fallout shelters would save lives were extremely limited, and that in truth "no individual can by his own efforts insure his survival in a nuclear war." The best long-term security, according to WAS, rested in a recognition that "nuclear war is not a feasible means of resolving international conflicts."[3] A *Commonweal* article also excoriated *Fallout Protection*, describing the five-megaton premise as "either scandalous ignorance or scandalous deception." Another supposition of the pamphlet, that nuclear attack would be directed solely at military targets and would consist only of groundbursts (both were preconditions for fallout shelters to be effective), was described by *Commonweal* as "almost pathetically unlikely." *Commonweal* concluded that the shelter debate could be reduced to the following formula:

> under certain (improbable) conditions—involving one particular (unlikely) pattern of nuclear attack, by means of a certain (minimal) number of bombs, exploded in a certain (relatively inefficient) way, on certain (extremely limited) targets—some kind of fallout shelter program, if not the present confused efforts, might indeed save millions of lives that otherwise would be lost.[4]

Even *Time* magazine, which claimed that "cheap fallout shelters are a modest insurance for everyone," acknowledged that the government pamphlet "offers far too rosy advice on how Americans can protect themselves, at cut rates, against nuclear onslaught."[5]

Before Kennedy's Berlin speech, the number of fallout shelters that had been built in the country was relatively small. As late as March 1960, the Holifield committee reported a total number of 1,565 home fallout shelters in thirty-five states. As Chet Holifield put it, "very little has been accomplished."[6] A little more than a year later the Berlin crisis had produced an explosion of public interest in fallout shelters, encouraging many to believe that the business of building shelters would be a guaranteed success. There were expectations that annual sales could run between $2 billion and $20 billion, and that shelter building would achieve the magnitude of other federally promoted programs such as highway building and urban renewal.[7]

Fear of nuclear war was certainly on many people's minds, and the shelter business was quick to capitalize on such apprehensions, nurturing customers with what *Newsweek* called "equal parts of show biz., peep show, and hard sell." In a Prince Georges County shopping center outside Washington, D.C., shoppers were treated to a recording of air raid sirens, exploding bombs, and an anguished male voice that cried out, "My wife, my children . . ." The moral of this drama? "If I'd only listened to Civil Defense . . . I'd be in that shelter now."[8] At least one Virginia realtor placed advertisements in Washington, D.C., papers promoting "life and peace of mind outside the Washington target area."[9] Frank F. Norton, owner of the Chicago-based Atomic Shelter Corporation (and president of the National Shelter Association), boasted that "my best salesmen are named Khrushchev and Kennedy." Indeed, there was a flurry of shelter building following Kennedy's 1961 speech, and Norton and others in the business were swamped with orders.[10]

Leo Hoegh, former director of civil defense under Eisenhower, proclaimed that "fallout shelters are needed everywhere," and to emphasize the severity of the situation Hoegh was sending out pamphlets filled with quotations from communist leaders who threatened to bury the West. Hoegh was not a completely disinterested patriot, as he was also Frank Norton's crosstown rival and vice president of the Wonder Building Corporation, which was selling two hundred shelters a week by the fall of 1961.[11] *Newsweek* reported that in Atlanta thirty shelter firms had been created, and that three small advertisements in local papers had resulted in five thousand inquiries.[12] At the 1961 Texas State Fair in Dallas 350 people per hour made their way through an exhibitor's shelter.[13] James Reston of the *New York Times* noted sardonically that "no group of citizens is showing more solicitude for the future well-being of the Nation" than the builders of fallout shelters.[14]

One sign of the popularity of any new product launch is the degree to which it attracts fraud, and almost immediately the unscrupulous and the incompetent began moving into the shelter building business. In one case, a woman in Mt. Vernon, New York, was given an $850 estimate for a shelter that civil defense officials said should cost $180. In California, a contractor charged $5,000 for a shelter that inspectors described as "a potential tomb."[15] *Consumer Reports* observed that "the swimming pool contractor suddenly has become an authority on bomb shelters," and in at least one instance the resemblance between shelters and pools was striking.[16] James Raisin, proprietor of Family Shelters, built eighteen shelters in the Detroit area, and all of them leaked. Raisin protested that "even with water in them they're better than no shelters at all."[17] There were reports out of New York that shelter salesmen were posing as civil defense officials, and in Los Angeles Roy Hoover, that city's assistant civil defense director, asked for help to eliminate what he called "the suede-shoe boys" (shady shelter contractors).[18] Paul Rand Dixon, chairman of the Federal Trade Commission, declared that "ideologically, we're at war with communism," and therefore promoting worthless shelters "comes pretty close to being treason."[19]

The Kennedy administration had initially found a key ally in its promotion of home fallout shelters and a national fallout shelter system in *Life* magazine. In September 1961, as the Kennedy shelter program was just getting under way, *Life* published a cover story (replete with photographs, illustrations, and elaborate plans) lauding the home fallout shelter (figs. 20 and 21). Also included in this issue was a message from Kennedy reminding Americans that "the ability to survive coupled with the will to do" were "essential to our country" (fig. 22). In this issue *Life* would make a number of claims that would attract criticism, including the assertion that fallout posed the greatest danger from a nuclear attack, that "every family shelter will contribute to the nation's deterrent." *Life* declared that ninety-seven out of a hundred Americans could be saved in a nuclear attack if they built fallout shelters.[20]

Shelters very quickly produced their own fallout, attracting a torrent of criticism and making them popular objects of vilification. It was apparent how quickly the tide against shelters had changed when just four months after *Life*'s initial cover story it published another cover story in which the editors were furiously backpedaling (fig. 23). Now *Life* was saying that there was "unwisdom, if not added danger, in an over-ambitious shelter program." The 97 percent claim had also been abandoned, and now the editors were saying that "shelters would somewhat increase the chances of survival" and "under certain ghastly circumstances they *might* save millions of lives—and the nation" (emphasis in original).[21] This was hardly the ringing endorsement of just a few months previous, and an examination of how this issue played out both locally and nationally will demonstrate why this arbiter of middle-brow opinion executed such a brisk about-face.

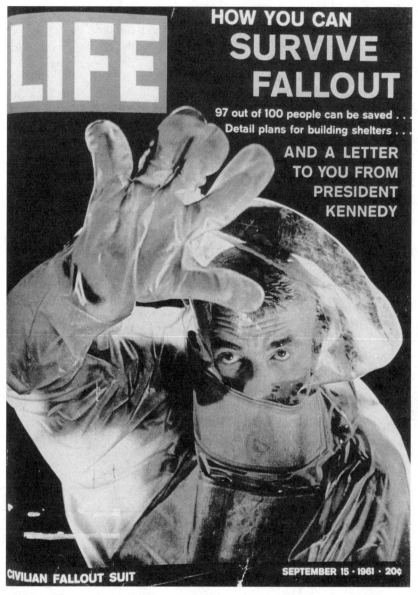

Fig. 20. *Life*, 15 September 1961. Cover photograph by Ralph Morse. Library Collection of California State University, Chico.

Big Pipe in the Backyard under Three Feet of Earth

If you have no basement—or decide not to use it—you can dig in outside and construct a reinforced concrete bunker in the ground, then cover it up with earth. But reinforced concrete requires the services of a contractor since it must be mixed, poured and cured with precision to make it safe. An easier and less expensive backyard shelter is shown here. It consists of a section of galvanized corrugated steel which almost any steel distributor can provide because it is of a standard type used in road underpasses. The pieces for the hatchway would cut to order. The shelter should be closed in at both ends bulkheads and fitted with the entrance before being buried cement blocks jutting more than halfway across the width of serves as a shield against any radiation which might get in entrance hatch.

Although you can do much of the work on this shelter you will probably want to hire a contractor to dig out the yard with a bulldozer and to cover up the shelter when you You will also need the services of a welder to seal up the help construct the entrance. Materials for this shelter cost app $700. The fees for the welder and the bulldozer might run $150. The completed shelter would reduce radiation to less th

FIG. 21. *Life*, 15 September 1961. Illustration by Elmer Wexler. Library Collection of California State University, Chico.

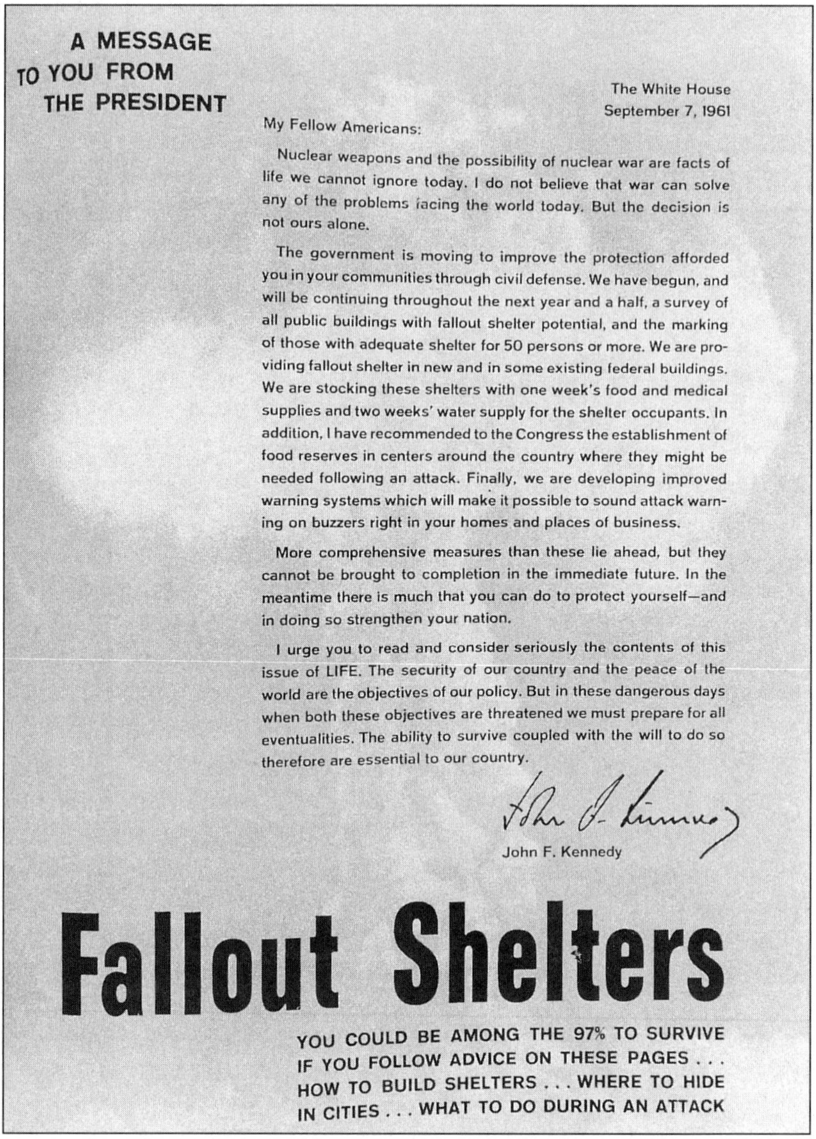

A MESSAGE TO YOU FROM THE PRESIDENT

The White House
September 7, 1961

My Fellow Americans:

Nuclear weapons and the possibility of nuclear war are facts of life we cannot ignore today. I do not believe that war can solve any of the problems facing the world today. But the decision is not ours alone.

The government is moving to improve the protection afforded you in your communities through civil defense. We have begun, and will be continuing throughout the next year and a half, a survey of all public buildings with fallout shelter potential, and the marking of those with adequate shelter for 50 persons or more. We are providing fallout shelter in new and in some existing federal buildings. We are stocking these shelters with one week's food and medical supplies and two weeks' water supply for the shelter occupants. In addition, I have recommended to the Congress the establishment of food reserves in centers around the country where they might be needed following an attack. Finally, we are developing improved warning systems which will make it possible to sound attack warning on buzzers right in your homes and places of business.

More comprehensive measures than these lie ahead, but they cannot be brought to completion in the immediate future. In the meantime there is much that you can do to protect yourself—and in doing so strengthen your nation.

I urge you to read and consider seriously the contents of this issue of LIFE. The security of our country and the peace of the world are the objectives of our policy. But in these dangerous days when both these objectives are threatened we must prepare for all eventualities. The ability to survive coupled with the will to do so therefore are essential to our country.

John F. Kennedy

John F. Kennedy

Fallout Shelters

YOU COULD BE AMONG THE 97% TO SURVIVE
IF YOU FOLLOW ADVICE ON THESE PAGES . . .
HOW TO BUILD SHELTERS . . . WHERE TO HIDE
IN CITIES . . . WHAT TO DO DURING AN ATTACK

FIG. 22. Kennedy's message on fallout shelters. *Life*, 15 September 1961. Library Collection of California State University, Chico.

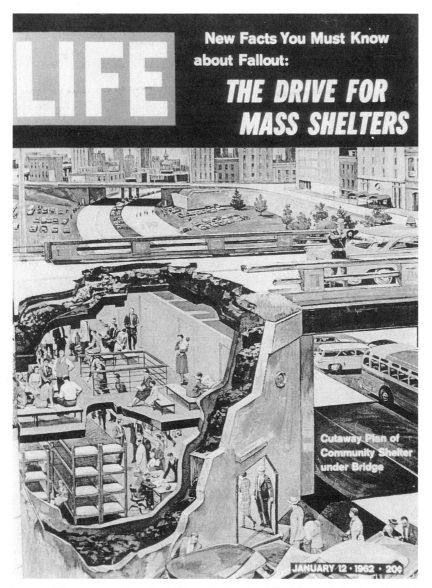

FIG. 23. *Life*, 12 January 1962. Cover illustration by Ken Riley. Library Collection of California State University, Chico.

The National Reaction: The Nation at the Crossroads

It was immediately apparent that the fallout shelter debate would move into realms far removed from questions of mere technological feasibility. Many believed that this issue had brought the nation to a crossroads in its historical destiny. As *Newsweek* observed, the initiation of an enhanced civil defense program "may well involve a monumental change in the very quality of American life, the consequences of which cannot be fore-seen."[22] Clarence Huebner, director of the New York State Civil Defense Commission, believed that by the mid-1960s Americans might be dwelling permanently in fallout shelters, emerging into the sunshine only as a calculated risk.[23] A report published in 1960 by the Center for the Study of Democratic Institutions predicted the development of 1,000-megaton bombs and the necessity of placing factories and homes in bombproof shelters until "eventually, most human life will be underground."[24] Herman Kahn insisted that civil defense could save millions of lives, and "also prove crucial to the continued survival of Western ideals and institutions," but many others believed that if the nation adopted shelter building on a massive scale it would be a betrayal of America's errand to the world.[25]

Charles Newman in the *Yale Review* asked, "What would John Winthrop have thought if the hill upon which he was to build his city was honey-combed with cells for omnipresent defeat? Why should he have left Europe at all? It is difficult to construct a Heavenly City, when the contractor's plans, of necessity, allot a space for Hell."[26] In an article written for *Christian Century*, Ronald E. Sleeth found it repugnant that the inheritors of the spirit of the American Revolution would be found cowering in their underground shelters: "We are advised to hoard, to store up for ourselves treasures under the earth where moth, rust and radiation will not consume them. Where will the fearless, red-blooded Americans be whose ancestors fought and died at Valley Forge? Again, presumably hiding in their basements, huddled in a cor-ner."[27] Thomas E. Murray, for seven years a member of the Atomic Energy Commission, found something sad "about the sight of a great nation falling back upon sheer survival as its all-consuming purpose in history," and George Kennan wondered,

> Are we to flee like haunted creatures from one defensive device to an-other, each more costly and humiliating than the one before, cowering underground one day, breaking up our cities the next, attempting to sur-round ourselves with elaborate electronic shields on the third, concerned

only to prolong the length of our lives while sacrificing all the values for which it might be worth while to live at all?[28]

Gerard Piel, publisher of *Scientific American*, observed that "the firestorms of a thermonuclear war would work an irreversible disruption of the social and moral fabric of Western Civilization. The kind of society that would emerge from the shelters may be guessed from the kind of society that is preparing to go into the shelters now."[29] A few suggested that, on the contrary, a nuclear war might invigorate the race by purging society of its effete intellectuals. The psychologist H. B. Hurt of Oak Ridge, Tennessee, proclaimed that "the goodie-goodies and the fancy pants—the brains minus the brawn are apt most to fall by the wayside when war comes." Hurt suggested laying in a good supply of guns and ammunition because "the main thing we have to fear is people out of control—more even than the atom out of control."[30]

Such comments poorly served the cause of fallout shelters, and promoters of the shelter program were repeatedly put on the defensive by critics who said fallout shelters were immoral because they encouraged cowardly or selfish behavior. No one had worked harder to establish a national shelter program in the United States than Chet Holifield, and he believed that the public's lukewarm reception to such a program was rooted in its "psychological approach" to warfare. Like Ronald Sleeth, Holifield saw the public as stubbornly oriented toward "the traditional modes of warfare, such as when the men stood and fought at Concord and Lexington." According to Holifield, "that concept of warfare no longer obtains."[31] Steuart L. Pittman, assistant secretary of defense and the Kennedy administration's point man on civil defense, claimed that the real moral issue was whether Americans had "the courage to face a disaster far enough ahead to have a chance in the crisis to do all they can to take care of the people or children they look out for."[32]

There was heated debate over what "deterrent" value a shelter program might have. Rogers S. Cannell of the Stanford Research Institute observed that without fallout protection, the United States must "either invite an attack or give in to the Kremlin without a struggle." An effective shelter system would enable the United States to "rebuild our civilization" and to "justify the faith placed in us by our own families and by the peoples of the free world."[33] Edward Teller agreed, and claimed that with adequate military preparation and a shelter system, "we shall avoid wholesale destruction and we shall avoid all-out atomic war." Teller also put the moral shoe on the other foot by referring to "a determined enemy who is not inhibited by moral considerations."[34] A group of 183 university professors from the Boston area argued the opposite. In an open letter to President Kennedy printed in the *New York Times*, these intellectuals insisted that a shelter program would prepare Americans "for the acceptance of thermonuclear war as an instrument of national policy," and that such a preparation "would substantially increase the likelihood of war."[35]

Questioning the quality of the civilization that could be rebuilt was Bentley Glass. Glass believed that "life would be very primitive for the survivors for a long time to come," and was dubious as to how much sympathy the peoples of the world might extend to the United States after a nuclear war: "If America survived at all, could it be as more than a tenth-rate power? Would the more fortunate lands take pity on the country that first produced and used the atom bomb, and later engaged in the accelerating arms race?"[36] Ralph Lapp also maintained that the extent of assistance that Americans might receive after a nuclear war was "highly debatable." "Fear of radioactivity," noted Lapp, "might discourage many a good Samaritan."[37]

The Metaphor War

Shelter advocates may have had reasonable arguments, but what they did *not* have, for the most part, was metaphor. It proved to be extremely difficult to put an admirable (much less heroic) spin on burrowing into the earth to save one's hide, regardless of the reasonableness of such an action in the face of a nuclear explosion. On the other hand, vesting fallout shelters with negative connotations was virtually effortless, so plentiful were the available metaphors. One of the most obvious, and ubiquitous, of these was the "mole" metaphor. When the Holifield committee proposed a national shelter program in 1957, Robert Moses asked, "Why not go all the way? Let's draw up new laws, codes, and a constitution to organize for the good rabbit-and-mole life of the future."[38] Commenting on reports that some suburbanites were constructing shelters at night to keep knowledge of them from their neighbors, William L. Shirer asked, "Are we to become a nation of sneaks, doing things furtively that we are ashamed for our neighbors to see?" Shelter dwellers were "groveling under the ground like moles" on the off chance they might survive "to eke out a miserable, degrading, inhuman existence on the burnt-out crust of the earth."[39] Rabbi

Maurice N. Eisendrath, president of the Union of American Hebrew Congregations, also referred derisively to "the morality of moles or other underground creatures, slithering in storm cellars," and Charles Newman expressed concern with what he called "the metaphor of tunneling . . . how the American Mind will work in the cellar."[40]

Another theme frequently developed in this debate was that the building of fallout shelters represented a devolution of the human species, and that humanity's long climb out of the dark caves was now being reversed. With the building of fallout shelters, and the possibility that in the future people might have to dwell permanently in underground cities, humanity was returning to the origins of its primitive ancestors. "Is this troglodytic life the fulfillment of the American Dream?" asked Erich Fromm and Michael Maccoby, and Governor Edmund G. Brown of California referred to a "reversion to cave-man barbarism."[41] In "Some Psychiatric Considerations in Planning for Defense Shelters," P. Herbert Leiderman and Jack H. Mendelson mused on this devolutionary development, finding in the construction of shelters an "atavistic return of man and his tribe to the recesses of the earth":

> It is one matter for man to have evolved from living deep in a Paleolithic cave to the city apartment or the garden home in the suburb, but an entirely different matter to consider whether he can successfully return to the cave. The question of whether an abrupt return along this evolutionary path is psychologically possible will hopefully remain a metaphysical issue.[42]

In *Community of Fear* (1960), Harrison Brown and James Real also foresaw the creation of an American subtopia in which factories, stores, and apartment houses would be built in caves. Eventually, predicted Brown and Real, "most human life will be underground," and a new pattern will have been accepted, "that of adjusting ourselves to the idea of living in holes. From that time onward it will be simple to adjust ourselves to living in *deeper* holes," and with the era of the cave dweller reinstated, "the epic of man's journey upward into the light will have ended."[43] Robert B. Meyner, governor of New Jersey, also found this a resonant theme, calling fallout shelters "primordial caves" that a nuclear attack would turn into "mass burial vaults."[44] Warning against a future that consisted of "a cringing subsistence underground," Meyner claimed that "when primitive man left his cave and began to live in the light, he was meant to travel onward and upward; not to circle back."[45]

The supposed parallel between shelters and the Maginot Line also proved to be a popular historical analogy. In his 1962 article "The Case against Fallout Shelters," Hanson W. Baldwin worried that a fallout shelter program might "create a false sense of security," and that "this Maginot Line psychology could cost us dearly, as it did France."[46] Air force general Curtis E. LeMay sneeringly referred to fallout shelters as "holes in the ground to crawl into," and called expenditures for civil defense "a Maginot Line concept" that was "doomed to failure."[47] Such vivid metaphors, calling up the woeful shortsightedness of the past, were extremely hard to counter. Typically, shelter promoters were reduced to weak assertions that such comparisons were not valid, without producing equally vivid metaphors of their own. In her questioning of LeMay, for instance, Representative Martha W. Griffiths took issue with his Maginot Line comparison, insisting, "I don't think the shelter system is really the Maginot line.... The shelter system is your last best chance of surviving."[48]

Those opposed to a shelter system knew that the Maginot Line metaphor was compelling, and they continued to employ it in wholesale fashion. Claiming that the military advances of the twentieth century had obliterated boundaries and barriers, Kenneth Boulding observed that "the ancient concept of defense symbolized by the wall, whether the walled city, the Great Wall of China, the Maginot line, or even DEW line, has crumbled in ruins."[49] Also worried that a shelter program might be "analogous to building another Maginot Line" was Tom Stonier, a biology professor at Manhattan College. The *National Review*, which defended shelter building, produced the feeble response that "a shelter program is not a Maginot Line" because "the existence of shelters at home will facilitate the will to stand firm abroad."[50]

The "garrison state" metaphor was also widely used as an argument against shelter building. In this formulation, a fallout shelter system would reduce the United States to a "garrison state"—a nuclear Sparta dominated by the military. Eisenhower himself employed this metaphor. In his rejection of the Gaither Report's recommendation for an ambitious national defense buildup that would include an expensive fallout shelter program, Eisenhower concluded that "we could not turn the nation into a garrison state."[51] Hanson W. Baldwin believed that a massive government program of fallout shelters had the potential to be "a gigantic boondoggle" that might "blaze the trail to the much-feared garrison state."[52] Gerard Piel agreed, and warned that "The social cost of going underground would require nothing less than the suspension of civil institutions, the habituation of our people to violence and the ultimate militarization of our society. By that time it would surely be difficult to define the ideological conflict that the war is supposed to be fought about."[53]

An elaborate civil defense bureaucracy might also be a step toward militarizing the society. In Chet Holifield's advocacy for a "universal system of training for civilian defense" and a "full-time [civil defense] corps," Arthur Waskow, who served on the staff of the Peace Research Institute and was legislative assistant to Congressman Robert W. Kastenmeier of Wisconsin, saw a civil liberties nightmare.[54] Waskow mused that "the training of a large cadre of men and women to a fine pitch of elaborate knowledge and total dedication" in the realm of civil defense would require the rest of the population to be trained in "unquestioning obedience. . . . The demand for disciplined obedience to authority extended to the entire population would be entirely new in U.S. life."[55] Writing for the *Bulletin of the Atomic Scientists*, David R. Inglis argued that an extensive civil defense program would "increase military dominance of civilian thought" and lead to the "psychology of the garrison state."[56]

Chet Holifield proved to be as inept in dealing with the garrison state metaphor as he had with the Maginot Line metaphor. While acknowledging that one factor in the American reluctance to build shelters was "a fear we might go in the direction of the 'Fortress America' concept," Holifield insisted that "a shelter program does not mean moving cities underground or becoming 'cave dwellers.'" Shelter building, said Holifield, was a prudent precaution "so that if the missiles start raining upon us we shall have some place to go."[57] Much more forceful was the argument of Harvard University professor David Cavers, who claimed that if there were enough crises to advance a national fallout shelter program, people would soon realize that such a program was "either obsolete or obsolescent" and there would be agitation for shelters with blast and fire protection. This would "put the Nation underground" and would signal the "start of the garrison state in America." "Once it started rolling," observed Cavers, "I suspect only the unconditional surrender of the Russians and the Chinese could stop it."[58]

There was also the apprehension that support of civil defense might become linked to patriotism, and opposition to it a form of communist subversion. Roger Hagan quotes a pamphlet issued by the Civilian Defense Organization of Nutley, New Jersey:

Every loyal, true American should stand at the side of his neighbor wearing an arm band of the Civilian Defense Corps, pledged to support and to uphold the Constitution and the principles upon which our defense rests. There can be no equivocation. Either you belong now—committed to your nation's defense—or you do not belong, and so stand "uncommitted." Today, no commitment in this matter is an open invitation to party-line Communist penetration.[59]

While critics of fallout shelters seemed more adept than their opponents at creating the telling metaphor, in at least one case (a letter published in the Harvard *Crimson* in October 1961), the authors produced an extremely clever parody of opposition to fallout shelters by drawing an analogy to lifeboats:

To the Editors of the *Crimson*:

It has been brought to our attention that certain elements among the passengers and crew favor the installation of "life" boats on this ship. These elements have advanced the excuse that such action would save lives in the event of a maritime disaster such as the ship striking an iceberg. Although we share their concern, we remain unalterably opposed to any consideration of their course of action for the following reasons:

1. This program would lull you into a false sense of security.
2. It would cause undue alarm and destroy your desire to continue your voyage in this ship.
3. It demonstrates a lack of faith in our Captain.
4. The apparent security which "life" boats offer will make our Navigators reckless.
5. These proposals will distract our attention from more important things, i.e., building unsinkable ships. They may even lead our builders to false economies and the building of ships that are actually unsafe.
6. In the event of being struck by an iceberg (we will never strike first) the "life" boats would certainly sink along with the ship.
7. If they do not sink, you will only be saved for a worse fate, inevitable death on the open seas.
8. If you should be washed ashore on a desert island, you will be unaccustomed to the hostile environment and will surely die of exposure.
9. If you should be rescued by a passing vessel, you would spend a life of remorse mourning over your lost loved ones.

10. The panic engendered by a collision with an iceberg would destroy all vestiges of civilized human behavior. We shudder at the vision of one man shooting another for the possession of a "life" boat.

11. Such a catastrophe is too horrible to contemplate. Anyone who does contemplate it obviously advocates it.

Committee for a Sane Navigational Policy,
Stephen A. Khinoy, '62, Robert Fresco, '63
Richard W. Buillet, '62, Donald M. Scott, '62

Herman Kahn added, "To make the satire more complete: the added weight of lifeboats will no doubt increase the risk that the ship might sink of its own accord."[60]

Gun Thy Neighbor

As strategists worried about the Maginot Line and social critics warned of the garrison state, ordinary Americans were finding that the most disturbing aspects of fallout shelters were the most personal ones, especially when they were distilled down to the relationship between a shelter owner and his neighbors. Even before the rush of shelter building that occurred in 1961, there was already some inkling of what would eventually become one of the most troubling moral quandaries of the fallout shelter. In 1959 the director of civil defense for Los Angeles complained that one of the difficulties in knowing the exact number of fallout shelters built in the city was that people were building shelters but were not designating them as such through building permits. Some people did not want it known that they had a fallout shelter, he said, "because they do not want their neighbors to know it exists." Also taking note of this phenomenon was Eisenhower's civil defense director Leo Hoegh, who testified in 1960 that many shelter owners had told his office that they did not want to make the presence of their shelters "public knowledge and, therefore, have everyone in the neighborhood rush in and take over."[61]

By 1961 "shelter morality" had become an intensely debated topic. At issue was controlling entry to one's personal or community fallout shelter. Such control would be necessary, according to one architectural guide, not only to keep out radioactive fallout, but also "to prevent exceeding the maximum capacity of the shelter" and the "uncontrolled entry of persons requiring decontamination."[62] One of the most frequently cited articles dealing with this issue was a piece called "Gun Thy Neighbor," published by *Time* magazine in August 1961. In this story a Chicago suburbanite proclaimed,

> When I get my shelter finished, I'm going to mount a machine gun at the hatch to keep the neighbors out if the bomb falls. I'm deadly serious about this. If the stupid American public will not do what they have to to save themselves, I'm not going to run the risk of not being able to use the shelter I've taken the trouble to provide to save my own family.[63]

Pat Frank, who in 1959 published the best-seller *Alas, Babylon*, a depiction of the bleak aftermath of nuclear war (see chapter 2), had prepared his Florida home against the possibility of nuclear war, and warned that he would shoot anyone found rummaging about in his emergency supplies. Frank confided that he had put away some cigarettes and liquor as trade items because "after the outbreak of nuclear war a pound of tobacco will be worth more than a pound of gold." As for protecting one's home, Frank recommended "the Remington 66, a .22-caliber automatic rifle with nylon stock, so light that your wife can easily handle it. And if there is no war, it is a fun gun."[64] Charles Davis, of Austin, Texas, was prepared to defend his shelter premises with four rifles and a .357 magnum handgun. Pointing to the shelter's four-inch-thick wooden door, Davis said, "This isn't to keep radiation out, it's to keep people out." Davis was also prepared if his neighbors got into the shelter before he did: "I've got a .38 tear-gas gun, and if I fire six or seven tear-gas bullets into the shelter, they'll either come out or the gas will get them."[65]

There were other chilling pronouncements along these lines. In a meeting of local residents in Hartford, Connecticut, convened to discuss civil defense, one person warned that since his fallout shelter contained only enough water and food for his immediate family, he would be forced to shoot any neighbors seeking entry into his shelter during a nuclear attack. The following exchange took place between the shelter owner and his next-door neighbor:

> "John," she said, "you and your family have been our closest friends for ten years. Do you mean to say that if this city was bombed and my baby and I were caught in the open, and we were hurt, and came to your shelter you would turn us away?"
> John nodded in the affirmative. His neighbor pressed the point.

"But suppose we wouldn't turn away and begged to get in?"

"It would be too bad," John said. "You should have built a shelter of your own. I've got to look out for my own family."

"But suppose we had built a shelter of our own, yet were caught by surprise, being out in the open at the time of an attack, and we discovered that the entrance to our shelter was covered with rubble and we had no place to turn except to you. Would you still turn us back?"

The answer was still yes.

"But suppose I wouldn't go away and kept trying to get in. Would you shoot us?"

John said that if the only way he could keep his friend out would be by shooting her and her baby, he would have to do it.[66]

A similar exchange took place between two doctors, one of whom had built a shelter and was determined to defend it against all comers. The pseudonymous Dr. G. C. Chalmers claimed that "a sick or dead doctor is of no value to his country," and that he had accordingly built a shelter beneath his yard. Chalmers declared, "There are two precautions I've taken in case a nuclear catastrophe interrupts the normal enforcement of law and order. I've taught my family a special knock code as a signal for opening the shelter's thick, steel-plated door. And I've stocked the shelter with firearms and ammunition." Responding to Chalmers was Dr. Eugene V. Parsonnett:

> I suppose Dr. Chalmers plans to remain in his secure little shelter, having morally protected himself and his immediate family, having probably had to shoot to death some stray friends and acquaintances who may have wished to invade his sanctuary. . . . I find it inconceivable that people who proudly bear the name of doctor can isolate themselves from family, friends, and society in this immoral kind of seclusion.[67]

At the minimum, the gun-thy-neighbor attitudes expressed by Chalmers and others seemed to be at odds with traditional Christian teachings, and the clerical community might reasonably have been expected to help Americans gain some understanding of the moral implications of fallout shelters. But even among clerics, the fallout shelter issue became a source of controversy. In the same *Time* article in which shelter owners expressed a willingness to gun down their neighbors if necessary, the Reverend Hugh Saussy of Holy Innocents Episcopal Church in Atlanta stated, "If someone wanted to use the shelter, then you yourself should get out and let him use it. That's not what would happen, but that's the strict Christian application."[68]

Father L. C. McHugh, S.J., took issue with Saussy's statement in an article called "Ethics at the Shelter Doorway," which appeared in the Jesuit publication *America* in September 1961. McHugh said that he couldn't accept Saussy's argument as it stood, and in words that would make this article among the most controversial penned by a clergyman during the 1960s, McHugh expounded on his own concept of fallout shelter morality:

> It [Saussy's statement] argues that we must love our neighbor, not as ourselves, but more than ourselves. It implies that the Christian law runs counter to the instinct of self-preservation that is written in the human frame. If I am right, then the American people need more than blueprints for shelter construction. They also need a little instruction in the grim guidelines of essential morality at the shelter hatchway. Are there any moral constants that apply when unprepared or merely luckless neighbors and strangers start milling around the sanctuary where you and your family have built a refuge against atomic fire, blast and fallout?

McHugh claimed "moralists agree" that "a man under grave attack may take those emergency measures which will effectively terminate the assault, even if they include the death of the assailant." According to McHugh, it was "the height of nonsense" to claim that Christian ethics demanded that a man "thrust his family into the rain of fallout when unsheltered neighbors plead for entrance." A man responsible for a family "may not idly stand by while his brood is robbed of what is necessary for life and then explain that his cowardice is actually a wholehearted obedience to the Biblical injunction to overcome evil by good."

McHugh offered what he called "a partial code of essential shelter morality." First, shelter owners should "think twice before you rashly give your family shelter space to friends and neighbors or to the passing stranger." Second, those who tried to break into your shelter may be "repelled with whatever means will effectively deter their assault." "Does prudence also dictate that you have some 'protective devices' in your survival kit, e.g. a revolver for breaking up traffic jams at your shelter door?" asked McHugh. "That's for you to decide, in the light of your personal circumstances."[69]

While there were a few who were willing to defend McHugh's remarks (Karl Kalland, dean of Denver's Baptist Seminary, insisted that "if you allow a tramp to take the place of your children in your shelter, you are in error"), the overall reaction to McHugh was resoundingly negative.[70] Episcopal Bishop Angus Dun of Washington professed that he failed to see "how any Christian conscience" could condone "saving your own skin" without regard for your neighbor. "Justice, mercy and brotherly love," according to Dun, "do not cease to operate even in the final apocalypse." Condemning the man who would "dig himself a private mole hole," Dun proclaimed that "only community shelters will insure the survival of the kind of people who will be needed to rebuild a world that has been devastated by nuclear war."[71] The nondenominational *Christian Century* editorialized that "men and women who manage to survive a nuclear attack by locking doors on imperiled neighbors or shooting them down to save themselves might conceivably survive. But who would want to live in the kind of social order such people would create out of the shambles?"[72]

Others condemning McHugh's brand of shelter morality included Billy Graham, who stated, "I feel a primary responsibility for my family but I don't believe I myself could stay in a shelter while my neighbor had no protection," and Edward L. R. Elson of the National Presbyterian Church claimed that "some very sturdy Christians will decide to live dangerously, to ignore preparation of shelters and to die with dignity as part of the brightly colored cloud."[73] Episcopal clergyman Frederick Jessett questioned whether "our interest is so much in survival as in the fascinating possibility we might be legitimately able to get rid of our neighbors."[74] Even the Soviets got into the act, with a *Pravda* columnist commenting, "If only we could open the eyes of these moles armed with machine guns. . . . But moles, as we know, are unseeing creatures, and moles of bourgeois origin, moreover, suffer from class blindness."[75]

The gun-thy-neighbor issue was a gold mine for editorialists, who worked themselves into a froth of moral indignation on the subject, and in the process badly damaged the reputation of the home shelter. According to Norman Cousins, shelter enthusiasts had already created some of the "worst horrors" of nuclear war by prescribing "the circumstances under which it is spiritually permissible to kill one's neighbors."[76] Eugene Rabinowitch, editor of the *Bulletin of the Atomic Scientists*, called home fallout shelters "pathetic," and condemned gun-thy-neighbor discussions as "demonstrations of human depravity."[77] Richard Horchler, writing in *Commonweal*, claimed that the fallout shelter debate had produced "a reversion to the selfishness and cruelty of the savage. Already we have invented a grim term for what we expect of one another—the phrase 'shelter morality.'"[78] Noting that the Office of Civil Defense had not taken a position on the gun-thy-neighbor issue, Harvard professor Gabriel Kolko expressed confidence that this federal agency would "not complain when shelterless neighbors remove their armed neighbors' shelter filters, or slip a plastic bag over the air intake."[79]

Dismayed by the controversy, President Kennedy suggested that we "concentrate more on keeping enemy bombers and missiles away from our shores, and concentrate less on keeping neighbors away from our shelters."[80] When the issue came up at a meeting of the president and his advisers on Thanksgiving 1961, Robert Kennedy quipped, "There's no problem here—we can just station Father McHugh with a machine gun at every shelter." But because of the tremendous controversy, the president shifted the administration's emphasis from private to public shelters.[81]

Playboy magazine tried to lighten the tone a bit in a humorous 1962 piece called "How to Stop Worrying about the Bomb." In one cartoon, a family is shown huddled in a fallout shelter viewing a mushroom cloud through a tiny window in the door. The caption reads, "Inasmuch as fallout may continue for several years, it is not advisable to open your shelter door for newspaper or milk deliveries. Defending yourself from shelterless freeloaders may provide some unpleasant moments for the sensitive."[82] The cartoonist Jules Feiffer also took on the fallout shelter issue on a number of occasions. In figure 24, Feiffer expresses his views on civil defense through a neurotic shelter inmate.[83]

At the same time that the treatment of one's immediate neighbors in the wake of nuclear war was becoming an issue, there was the parallel issue of how communities spared from nuclear destruction might treat persons from less fortunate cities. Val Peterson reported that he had received a visit from a farmer from Weld County, Colorado, in 1954 who told Peterson that the farmers in his county had made arrangements to feed and shelter—at their own expense—some 200,000 refugees from the Denver metropolitan area in the event of nuclear war.[84] It was a different story further west. In Las Vegas, J. Carlton Adair, head of the city's civil defense agency, was anticipating an invasion after a nuclear war—an invasion of Angelenos. Drawing on a biblical metaphor, Adair postulated that a tattered horde of Los Angeles residents "could come into Nevada like a swarm of locusts" after a nuclear war. "A million or more persons might stream into this area from Southern California," said Adair, "and pick the valley clean of food, medical supplies, and other goods." Adair advocated the creation of a 5,000-person militia to protect Las Vegas against such a possibility.[85]

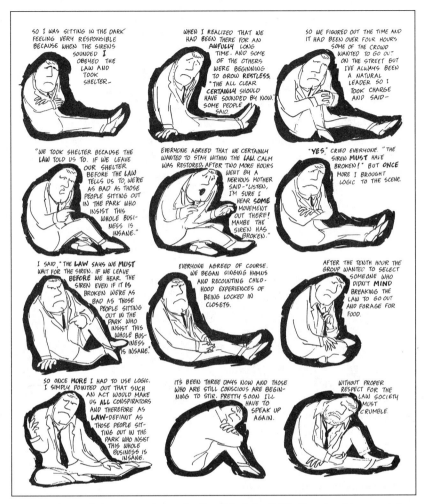

FIG. 24. Jules Feiffer's neurotic shelter dweller. © by Jules Feiffer. Reprinted by permission of Universal Press Syndicate. All rights reserved.

It was not only Las Vegas that feared the predations of an uprooted Los Angeles population. Indeed, this scenario captured the imagination of several civil defense coordinators. Keith Dwyer, civil defense coordinator of Riverside County, also suggested that the county arm itself against the onslaught of a ragged stream of refugees fleeing an H-bombed Los Angeles. In a speech to police reservists in Beaumont, California, Dwyer brandished a pistol above his head and counseled, "Get one of these and learn how to use it."[86] In Bakersfield, chief of police Horace V. Grayson (who also served as civil defense coordinator for Kern County) claimed that "the greatest danger to Bakersfield would not be from an atomic bomb or its fallout, but from hundreds of thousands of displaced residents from the Los Angeles area." Grayson expected that up to one million would approach Bakersfield from the south after a nuclear attack on Los Angeles. "They must not come here," said Grayson. "They must be stopped south of town and shown a route to some kind of refuge on the desert." Doing the stopping would be local law enforcement officers, who could not have drawn much comfort from Grayson's speech: "We have plenty of them, and they are expendable," said Grayson.[87]

The Local Reaction

The fallout shelter issue commanded the same attention on the local level as it did on the national level. Local papers ran editorials and political cartoons on the subject, examined the possible impact of a nuclear bomb on the home town, and joined in the gathering debate on the social, political, and moral aspects of shelters. It was also frequently the case that these same papers would publish elaborate, often multipart, articles on the fallout shelter issue. While regional interests often put a slightly different spin on the discussion, to a remarkable degree the basic concerns that were expressed were similar throughout the country.

The *New York Times* provided extensive local and national coverage on the fallout shelter issue. The *Times*, in a September 1961 survey of the fallout shelter debate, concluded that the country was infected with a curious combination of heightened interest in civil defense and apathy and fatalism.[88] A month later the *Times'* Peter Braestrup wrote an article describing the gathering controversy concerning fallout shelters, and finally in November the *Times* ran an illustrated, full-page spread on the fallout shelter issue with contributions from Braestrup and others.[89] James Reston's editorial comments issuing from the *Times* were especially acerbic, and Reston's status as a syndicated columnist meant that his opinions circulated far beyond New York. In a piece called "How to Be Evaporated in Style," Reston complained of Kennedy's Berlin speech that "if you start with speeches that scare the daylights out of people before you have a clear policy and the means of carrying it out, you are asking for trouble." Reston predicted that the "political fall-out will be ghastly" if the administration did not deal with the fallout shelter question more effectively.[90] Reston's mood had not improved a month later. "The situation, to state it mildly, is a mess," said Reston, who noted that while a person could be thrown in jail for shouting "fire" in a crowded theater, the government was doing the same thing by "shouting for months about the biggest fire in the history of the world without coming up with a plan to deal with it."[91] Finally Reston tallied the damage that had been done by the Kennedy administration's initial emphasis on the do-it-yourself home shelter, arguing that it had revealed disturbing class inequities while creating "a war psychology," and had loosed on the public a breed of builders eager to exploit public fears. The whole fiasco had "weakened the confidence abroad in Kennedy's judgment."[92]

The *New York Times* also followed the feud between New York governor Nelson Rockefeller and New Jersey governor Robert B. Meyner over fallout shelters. For several years Rockefeller had been trying to convince the state legislature to make it mandatory for New York homeowners and owners of commercial properties to build fallout shelters, but Meyner called the promotion of fallout shelters a "cruel deception on the American people."[93] Rockefeller's mandatory shelter idea was not overwhelmingly popular with New York legislators either, and in March 1960 Rockefeller was forced to withdraw his bill from consideration.[94] Rockefeller did practice what he preached, however, and by 1961 he had built shelters at all four of his residences.[95] In contrast to Rockefeller, only five governors had shelters at their official residences, and only one member of Kennedy's cabinet, postmaster general Edward Day, had a home fallout shelter.[96] By November 1961, with the Berlin crisis as a backdrop, the mood of the New York legislature had changed, and Rockefeller succeeded in gaining legislative approval for a $100 million program that would provide state matching funds for school and college shelters.[97]

New Yorkers, like other urban residents, were concerned with the effects of a hydrogen weapon on their city, and when the Soviets tested a monstrous fifty-megaton bomb in October 1961, the *New York Times* ran a story describing the possible impact of such a bomb on New York. The *Times* predicted that the bomb, "with its hurricane-like blast wave and intense burst of radiation," would totally destroy buildings within a five-mile radius and ignite fires up to thirty-five miles away.[98] It was this fear—that New York might be devastated by nuclear attack—that prompted twelve families in the New York area to begin making plans in the fall of 1961 to leave en masse and move to Chico, California. This story was sufficiently intriguing to be picked up by the wire services, and was reprinted in papers around the country. The band of refugees included artists, actors, teachers, and businessmen, and according to the group's leader, Alvin Bauman of Smithtown, Long Island, the motivation for this diverse group's exodus was simply the increasing danger of war. Chico, a town of fifteen thousand in 1961, was chosen because its topography and wind patterns supposedly created a favorable environment for protection from the ravages of nuclear war. A group member named Jane Andrews declared, "I feel we are going to a much safer place." The choice of Chico befuddled most observers, however, as a Titan missile base was being installed seven miles north of town. Alvin Bauman seemed unfazed ("we knew we couldn't escape every possible danger"), and Chico city manager Fred Davis professed that while Chico would welcome its new residents, "we're not convinced that we live in the safest place in the world."[99]

Kennedy's speech stimulated an interest in civil defense that was as keen in the American West as it was in the East. In Denver the civil defense office began operating on an "emergency basis" to supply the many requests for literature on fallout shelters.[100] At Denver's Lakeside Shopping Center a model shelter was put on display that was erected by the brick manufacturing companies of Colorado. Not surprisingly, the shelter was of brick construction.[101] Those doing their shopping at the Cherry Creek Shopping Center could view a rival shelter design—this one made of wood. Supervising construction of this particular shelter was Wood, Inc., an organization that promoted Colorado timber products. When he was interviewed by the *Denver Post*, company president Clark Gittings seemed a bit defensive about the viability of a wooden shelter against nuclear attack (perhaps because of the widespread public perception that wood burns). "There is a general misconception," said Gittings, "that only concrete and steel shelters work."[102] Meanwhile, Denver city officials were reviewing plans for a neighborhood fallout shelter to be built under city streets. The shelter would hold twenty families of five persons each plus a fifty-person overload, and would be financed by each family buying stock at a cost of $1,200 to $1,500. According to a spokesman, Robert Behrent, a single community shelter would be cheaper than numerous individual shelters, and would have the added moral benefit of eliminating armed shelter owners.[103]

The fallout shelter issue had an editorial evolution in the pages of the *Denver Post* that was similar to what we have seen at *Life*. The initial reaction of the *Post* to Kennedy's call for a beefed-up civil defense program was positive: the *Post* called it "an eminently sensible beginning for a revitalized civil defense program." The paper chided individuals with a "fatalistic" attitude toward civil defense, condemning them for their "profound irresponsibility" toward family, fellow citizens, and country.[104] But a little more than a month later, as some of the uglier aspects of shelter morality were beginning to surface, the same *Denver Post* was considerably less generous toward the federal program, and now called for "some plain talk about the problem of bomb shelters." Especially disturbing to the *Post* were the gun-thy-neighbor aspects of private shelters. Taking note of the fact that Denver's Jefferson County civil defense director had equipped his personal shelter with an arsenal to keep out unwanted visitors, the *Post* asked, "Are we, then, to be turned into a nation of animals by the presence of shelters for those who can afford to build them, and the absence of shelters for those who cannot?"[105] Political cartoons in the *Post* also would reflect this growing unease with the shelter program. In one example titled "The Epic of Man," a cave dweller is shown emerging from his cave above, while below a more modern citizen is shown fleeing back into a cave-like fallout shelter.[106] In another cartoon children have built a play fallout shelter and a little boy is shown at the door of the shelter pointing a gun at a little girl. The girl is crying, "How come I always have to be the neighbor . . !"[107]

Especially revealing was an editorial by Lawrence G. Weiss entitled "Moral Dilemma at the Shelter Door" (fig. 25). Occupying an entire page, this piece voices the fear of many that the fallout shelter issue was leading to a "morality of wolves." Probing and remarkably erudite, Weiss draws on the Bible, the Talmud, and the writings of Francis Bacon as well as maritime court cases to shed light on the difficult question of when it is permissible to take life to assure one's personal survival. Weiss found the answer to be elusive, and concluded that shelter owners might have to face "a choice of horror," and that "the moral dilemma will continue to haunt the shelter door."[108]

In St. Louis there was also heavy coverage of the fallout shelter issue in the *St. Louis Post-Dispatch*. In October the *Post-Dispatch* writer Marquis Childs produced a long article on the condition of the world following a nuclear war. Drawing on the work of the biologist John Wolfe of the AEC, the article paints a bleak picture of the aftermath of a nuclear attack. Childs observes that even those able to survive a nuclear war in a fallout shelter would emerge to an "uninhabitable desert" in which civil order

FIG. 25. Editorial by Lawrence G. Weiss, *Denver Post*, 15 October 1961. Collection of the Library of Congress. Reprinted by permission.

had totally broken down and in which the means to sustain life would be "virtually non-existent."[109]

The *Post-Dispatch* also ran an extensive, six-part series on civil defense with the stated goal of helping the reader understand what he could do to "protect himself and family in a war, which in its direst terror could end civilization." The series offered little in the way of encouragement. In his contribution to the series, Raymond Brandt took the national leadership to task for creating "confusion, apathy and resignation," while Richard Dudman produced a more evenhanded analysis that incorporated the views of both pessimists and optimists. Dudman quotes extensively from Willard Libby, who claimed that 95 percent of the population could survive a nuclear attack with fallout shelter protection, and that such shelters could be built extremely cheaply. But the Dudman article also includes a photograph of Libby surveying the ruins of his own inexpensive shelter after it was destroyed by a Los Angeles brushfire.[110] Perhaps the most hard-hitting editorial emanating from the *Post-Dispatch* was a piece entitled "The Shelter Illusion." Here the editor attacked the counterforce premise that the fallout shelter program was based on, as well as the argument that shelters would serve as a "deterrent" to nuclear attack. The conclusion was blunt: "The basic fact about nuclear warfare is that organized society cannot survive it."[111] *Post-Dispatch* cartoonist Bill Mauldin created a cartoon that was widely reprinted of a dog with its own personal fallout shelter (fig. 26).[112]

In Chicago, residents discovered that their city was even further behind on civil defense than other U.S. cities. In a series of articles on Chicago civil defense, *Chicago Tribune* reporter Howard James found that the Chicago "plan" for responding to a nuclear attack was evacuation, a concept that even the city's acting civil defense director, Robert J. Quinn, called "impossible" and "outdated." "With the speed and devastating power of the weapons today, there would be little time to evacuate," said Quinn, who added that when the sirens went off in Chicago, the residents of that city would be "on their own."[113] Among Chicago's other civil defense problems was the absence of any community fallout shelters.[114] Making things even worse was that until late in 1961, building a private fallout shelter was illegal in Chicago because such structures were in violation of local building code requirements. (An emergency meeting of the city council in August 1961 finally enacted an ordinance that allowed for shelter construction.)[115] As was the case in other urban newspapers, the *Tribune* series included an illustrated article on the effects of a nuclear bomb, this one dropped on downtown Chicago.[116]

October 18, 1961

FIG. 26. The prepared canine, 1961. Reprinted by permission of Bill Mauldin and the Watkins/Loomis Agency.

The way this issue was reported in Denver, St. Louis, Chicago, and New York was similar to reporting in other parts of the country. Virtually no newspaper of any size was without elaborate features devoted to the question of fallout shelters and the local impact of nuclear war. In Atlanta the number of callers to the local civil defense office had jumped from fifty to over four hundred a day as the *Atlanta Journal* began a series of civil defense articles written by Pat Watters. While Watters acknowledged the instinct for self-preservation that was behind the fallout shelter boom, he also asked, "Who can accept, really, in his heart the me-first, jungle-ethic code of survival implicit in the home shelters, as the final word on the situation?"[117] The *San Francisco Chronicle* produced a very telling story on what happened when an ambulance attendant named John Gunning tried to build a fallout shelter to the specifications provided by the government.

After digging a large hole in his backyard, Gunning discovered that the main structural piece called for in the plans (a supposedly common item) was not available locally.[118]

Interest was also keen in Los Angeles, where the civil defense office was flooded with both inquiries and suggestions.[119] The *Los Angeles Times* produced one of the largest single pieces on the consequences of a nuclear attack printed in an American newspaper. Like so many other nuclear attack scenarios produced by the press, "Red Alert! What If H-Bomb Hits Los Angeles?" was factually based but presented in fictional form. While the evacuation idea had been abandoned in Los Angeles because of estimates that it would take sixty-eight hours to evacuate the city, Los Angeles had only a few public shelters, and as "Red Alert!" declared, "few will be able to sustain life for more than a few hours." Notable for its lavish illustrations, "Red Alert!" includes a cutaway of a family in a fallout shelter, a depiction of an accident that stalls motorists trying to escape the city, and a spectacular full-page rendering of a nuclear bomb igniting a firestorm in Los Angeles (see figs. 15 and 16 in chapter 2).[120]

Fictional Shelters

Writers of fiction, no less than editorialists, employed the fallout shelter as a symbol of America's moral and ethical decay. One of the best examples is John Cheever's short story "The Brigadier and the Golf Widow," in which Cheever incorporates some of the enduring themes of the shelter controversy. The Pasterns, a suburban couple who have decided to build a shelter, try to keep it a secret from their neighbors, but "the trucks and bulldozers going in and out of their driveway had informed everyone."[121] Once it is built, the Pasterns must decide who will have access to their shelter when the bombs start falling. Many years later the Pasterns were still troubled by their "night of judgment," when they "had agreed to let Aunt Ida and Uncle Ralph burn, when she had sacrificed her three-year-old niece and he his five-year-old nephew; when they had conspired like murderers and had decided to deny mercy even to his old mother."[122] When Mr. Pastern has an affair with a neighbor woman, the shelter becomes a symbol of his infidelity when she asks him for a key. Pastern hesitates, then takes this "genuine talisman of salvation, a defense against the end of the world—and dropped it into the neck of her dress."[123] Meanwhile, Mrs. Pastern is visited by the local bishop, but she soon begins to suspect that he has more on his mind than praising her for her charitable work. In fact, the bishop is single-minded in his interest in the Pasterns' fallout shelter, and even insists on being shown the inside. Mrs. Pastern is shaken by the visit, ruminating, "Was it impious of her to suspect that he was traveling around his domain picking and choosing sanctuaries? Was it possible that he meant to exploit his holiness in this way? The burden of modern life, even if it smelled of plastics—as it seemed to—bore down cruelly on the supports of God, the Family, and the Nation."[124] In his journal Cheever observed of the shelter debate that "this has never been seen before—the population of this mighty nation in utter confusion about the enduring nature of their sense of good and evil, about whether they should be prepared to live underground."[125]

Even the issues of race and civil rights became entangled with the issues of nuclear weapons and fallout shelters. Jules Feiffer published a short play in 1961 called *Crawling Arnold*, in which the fallout shelter is once again subjected to rough treatment. The play features Barry and Grace Enterprise, who have called in Miss Sympathy, a social worker, to examine their son Arnold. Arnold has reverted back to crawling after the arrival of a new baby, Little Will. Arnold is thirty-five.

As Miss Sympathy enters the Enterprise home, she is greeted by Barry and Grace, who are both wearing tin air raid hats in preparation for the upcoming civil defense drill. Barry immediately begins bragging about the accoutrements of their fallout shelter, including slides with the titles of their favorite television shows, which are projected on a screen at the time that they would normally be seen:

GRACE: Lassie—Bachelor Father—Danny Thomas—
BARRY: And during the half hours those shows normally run we sit and reminisce about our favorite episodes. It's very important under crisis conditions to simulate normal conditions of living.[126]

The Enterprises' enthusiasm for civil defense is, it seems, boundless, and at one point Barry rhapsodizes, "A nationwide alert! All the American people mobilized as one, sitting it out in shelters all over the country. That's what I'd like Little Will to grow up to see. I guess it's just an old man's dream."[127]

In the meantime, cocktails are served by the Enterprises' surly black maid, Millie. Arnold, crawling around on the floor, sends his martini back because it contains an olive rather than a lemon peel. As Millie coolly removes the offending cocktail, Miss Sympathy whispers to her, "I have great regard for the aspirations of your people!" Millie, it seems, has been a problem in regard to the fallout shelter. Barry reveals that when he started work on the shelter, he was going to build one exactly like it for Millie, but that Millie rejected the separate shelter:

MISS SYMPATHY: I sympathize with her aspirations. She wanted to share *your* shelter, of course.

BARRY: (*outraged*). *Yes!*

MISS SYMPATHY: You see, while on the surface it would seem that the two shelters are alike in every way, the simple fact that Millie is excluded from one of them can have a devastating psychological effect on her. I have always been opposed to separate but equal air-raid shelters.[128]

As the civil defense drill begins, Arnold refuses to remove himself to the basement, where the shelter is, despite the insistence of his parents that "it's the law." Miss Sympathy stays with Arnold, and as the parents descend to the basement they discover that Millie has commandeered the shelter and has locked them out. Unable to persuade Millie to open the door, Barry and Grace decide to stay in the basement until the "all clear" signal has been given. Upstairs, Arnold and Miss Sympathy are chatting, and Miss Sympathy unexpectedly begins to find Arnold extraordinarily attractive. By the end of the play Barry and Grace are still waiting for the "all clear" signal in the basement, while upstairs romance has blossomed and Miss Sympathy has taken to crawling like her new amour.[129]

Few writers could combine the themes of white liberal guilt, Jim Crow facilities, and civil defense hysteria in a single parody, and Feiffer's observations are amusing because they are so accurately drawn. Langston Hughes also explored this territory, especially through his "Simple" stories. "Simple" was a black resident of Harlem who was funny and outspoken, and who acted as a sort of alter ego for Hughes (Hughes described Simple as "just myself talking to me").[130] In these stories Hughes explores various Nuclear Age controversies through Simple's commentaries. For instance, in "Serious Talk about the Atomic Bomb," Simple asks his friend, "And how come we did not try them atomic bombs on Germany?" Then Simple proceeds to answer his own question: "They just did not want to use them on white folks. Germans is white. So they wait until the war is all over in Europe to try them out on colored folks. Japs is colored."[131] In "Bones, Bombs, Chicken Necks," Simple critiques the bombs that had been used to "singe them Marshall Islanders all up, like them pictures that they showed after that big bomb test they had out in the Pacific. Them folks will never have no more hair on their heads, and them atomized Japanese fishermen will have no more children. . . . Atom bombs is lowering the tone of the whole world."[132]

An obvious issue for civil defense in the South was whether public fallout shelters would be segregated. In "Radioactive Red Caps," Simple simultaneously takes on segregationist Mississippi and fallout shelters. Simple is convinced that blacks in the South will be deprived of the right to enter a fallout shelter in much the same way that their social and political rights had been curtailed:

> "If I was in Mississippi, I would be Jim Crowed out of bomb shelters, so I would need some form of protection. By the time I got the N.A.A.C.P. to take my case to the Supreme Court, the war would be over, else I would be atomized."
>
> "Absurd!" I said. "Bomb shelters will be for everybody."
>
> "Not in Mississippi," said Simple. "Down there they will have some kind of voting test, else loyalty test, in which they will find some way of flunking Negroes out. You can't tell me them Dixiecrats are going to give Negroes free rein of bomb shelters."[133]

Simple's suspicions of what a segregationist white South might do were echoed in a notorious incident in Mobile, Alabama. During a scheduled civil defense drill in Mobile, a group of black residents became convinced that nuclear weapons were going to be dropped on the black sections of town. According to the rumor, this act was to be consummated as a way to avoid school desegregation. A large number of frightened Mobile blacks gathered up their belongings and took to the highways.[134]

One of the most interesting responses to the McHugh controversy, and a prime example of how the question of "shelter morality" was embraced by popular culture as well as high culture, was aired on the immensely popular television show *The Twilight Zone*. Clearly disturbed by McHugh's comments, Rod Serling, creator of *The Twilight Zone*, wrote an episode called "The Shelter," which aired on September 29, 1961.[135] "The Shelter" opens with a birthday party for the neighborhood doctor, Bill Stockton. The party turns into a sort of testimonial as one neighbor after another praises Stockton for his devotion to their health at all hours of the day or night, and his willingness to let his patients' bills slide. Stockton is also teased about the noise the construction of his fallout shelter has made in the neighborhood. In the midst of the celebration, there is a radio announcement that radar has picked up unidentified flying objects approaching the United States. Civil defense authorities declare a "Yellow Alert" and advise Americans to go to their shelters. Stockton's friends immediately realize that he has the only shelter in the neighborhood. Jerry Harlowe, one of Stockton's best friends, is the first to plead with Stockton:

He stared at Stockton's impassive face. "Bill, we've got to use your shelter!" he cried. "I've got to keep my family alive! And we won't use any of your stuff. Don't you understand? We'll bring our own."

"What about your own air? Will you bring your own air? That's a ten-by-ten room, Jerry." . . .

"When that door gets closed, Jerry, it stays closed. Closed and locked. There'll be radiation—and God knows what else." He felt an anguish rising deep inside him. "I'm sorry, Jerry. As God is my witness—I'm sorry. But I built that for *my* family."

He turned and started for the basement.

Jerry's voice followed him. "What about *mine*? What do *we* do? Just rock on the front porch until we get burned to cinders!"[136]

Stockton seals his family in the shelter and a procession of neighbors are now pounding at the door, begging to be let in. A fight breaks out between two of the neighbors, and Harlowe intercedes. "Just keep it up—we won't need a bomb. We can slaughter each other."[137] Finally, the neighbors become a mob and decide to batter their way into Stockton's shelter. At the moment they break into the shelter the radio announces that there has been a false alarm, and that no enemy planes are approaching. The subdued neighbors offer to pay Stockton for the damages, and Stockton replies, "Do any of you have any remote idea just what the 'damages' are?" "The damages I'm talking about," he explains, "are the pieces of our selves that we've pulled apart tonight. The veneer—the thin veneer that we ripped aside with our own hands." Finally, Stockton expresses the hope that if a real bomb ever falls to destroy and maim, "the victims will be human beings—not naked, wild beasts who put such a premium on staying alive that they claw their neighbors to death just for the privilege."[138]

At least one serious song emerged out of the shelter controversy, and that was Bob Dylan's "Let Me Die in My Footsteps." Originally recorded in 1962 for the *Freewheelin' Bob Dylan* session, the song was not released on the *Freewheelin'* album but later turned up as a bootleg. The genesis of "Let

Me Die in My Footsteps," according to Dylan, emerged out of a trip to Kansas, where he came across a fallout shelter being constructed. "As I watched them building," said Dylan, "it struck me sort of funny that they would concentrate so much on digging a hole underground when there were so many other things they should do in life. If nothing else, they could look at the sky and walk around and live a little bit instead of doing this immoral thing." The first verse of the song reflects the misgivings that many others besides Dylan had developed about fallout shelters:

I will not go down under the ground
'Cause somebody tells me that death's coming 'round.
And I will not carry my self down to die
When I go to my grave my head will be high.

The chorus is, "Let me die in my footsteps / Before I go down under the ground." Dylan obviously attached a great deal of importance to this song, noting that "here is one song I am really glad I made a record of."[139]

There was no pro-shelter equivalent to Dylan's "Let Me Die in My Footsteps" or to Serling's *Twilight Zone* episode. Proponents of an American fallout shelter system were never able to gain the moral high ground or capture the sympathies of the American public. To a great extent shelterists lost the political war because they lost the metaphor war. They were incapable of summoning images as brilliant as those commanded by their adversaries. In this cultural struggle, critics of shelters were aided greatly by a general unease in regard to fallout shelters. To many Americans, there was something inherently shameful about burying themselves under the earth to save their lives, despite the excellent utility of such a move in the wake of a nuclear attack. Compounding the shame was the barbarism of threatening to kill one's neighbor to protect one's shelter, what Walter Lippmann called the "evil" of "each family for itself, and the devil take the hindmost."[140] In Arthur Waskow's words, the shelter issue "strained the web of community." By "excluding neighbors, or people from the next block, or strangers from the next county, or casual visitors to town. . . . Suburbia has been pitted against city, one state against another."[141] The "mole," the "caveman," and the "barbarian" thus became metaphors for the shelter owner, while the "Maginot Line" and the "garrison state" were used to describe a national shelter system. Perhaps more than any other factor, the images that these metaphors called forth—of a militarized nation and a fearful people huddled beneath the ground in dank shelters—would spell doom for a national shelter system.

CHAPTER 4

Taking Government, Business, and Schools Underground

The survivability of nuclear war was not only an issue for individual Americans, it was also widely debated by those in government, business, and education. The question could be reduced to a simple proposition: Would there be enough left after a nuclear war that would still be recognizable as "America"? While many maintained that any belief in a "recovery" from a nuclear war was illusory, nuclear survival and restoration was official Cold War doctrine for much of this era, and the rest of America was encouraged to adopt a similar view. The argument that with the proper preparations American institutions could both survive a nuclear attack and resume their ordinary functions at its conclusion appears on the surface to be a curious denial of the nuclear facts of life. But a number of elements were at work here, not least of which was the incomprehensibility of nuclear war itself. Without precedent on which to draw, civil defense officials in effect did what the military is often accused of doing—they prepared for the *last* war rather than the next one. Civil defense planners had seen the British taking shelter and surviving the Blitz during World War II, and the Germans digging out from under the rubble at the war's conclusion and producing an economic miracle. Surely hearty, determined Americans could do the same in the next war. While many civil defense officials might privately admit that World War II would bear the same resemblance to a thermonuclear war as World War I did to the Seven Years' War, they might also insist that making some preparations, however inadequate in the face of nuclear war, was preferable to the feeling of helplessness and despair that was the alternative.

From an early date, the federal government calculated that one of the essentials of surviving a nuclear war would be military and industrial dispersal, and in 1947 the joint Munitions Board of the Army and Navy asked amateur explorers to identify caves that might be useful for dispersal purposes.[1] The Truman administration also expressed concerns about the survival of the government should Washington be subject to nuclear attack, and in 1950 asked Congress for money "to insure the continuity of essential functions of Government in event of emergency." In an era of congressional wrangling with the executive branch, the request died in committee.[2] The increasing power of nuclear weapons also complicated dispersal plans. A 1952 Department of Defense plan to disperse some essential activities from Washington to nearby Andrews Field and other local facilities was criticized by Tracy B. Augur of the National Security Resources Board as a proposal to "enlarge the Washington target rather than to disperse it."[3]

By the mid-1950s plans were well under way to assure American political continuity, and by 1961 *U.S. News* was reporting that "an alternate structure of Government has been organized—and actually set up in skeleton form—to carry on if Washington is wiped out." The article reported the existence of "94 secret centers" in a "federal arc" extending three hundred miles west of Washington, D.C., that were being readied to serve as government offices should Washington be destroyed.[4] Perhaps the most spectacular of these "secret centers" was a bunker hidden under the Greenbrier resort in White Sulphur Springs, West Virginia, built between 1956 and 1962. The existence of this shelter was classified until 1992, when *Washington Post* reporter Ted Gup investigated what by then had become a very poorly kept secret. Designed to house the 535 members of Congress and 565 staff members and to "permit the continuation of the American form of constitutional government in the event of nuclear war," the facility at Greenbrier had separate chambers for the House and the Senate, and a hall large enough for joint sessions.[5]

Constructing such an elaborate facility was a massive undertaking, and those who built it were not told what it was they were building. Randy

Wickline, for instance, who hauled an estimated fifty thousand tons of concrete to the site, was never told the purpose of this large quantity of concrete. But with walls two feet thick and a concrete roof buried under twenty feet of dirt, there was little doubt as to the function of this facility: "Nobody came out and said it was a bomb shelter, but you could pretty well look and see the way they was setting it up there that they wasn't building it to keep the rain off of them." Another contractor who was hired to work on an "exhibit hall" observed, "We've got 110 urinals we just installed. What in the hell are you going to exhibit?"[6] Managers of the facility, former and present, were unwilling to talk to Gup, but others were more amenable. Former House Speaker Thomas P. "Tip" O'Neill, who had visited Greenbrier some six times, recalled that his interest in Greenbrier waned when he was told that members of Congress would not be allowed to bring family members to the shelter. "I said, 'Jesus, you don't think I'm going to run away and leave my wife? That's the craziest thing I ever heard of.'"[7] Gup's article merely confirmed what was already widely known, and shortly thereafter House Speaker Thomas S. Foley recommended that the Department of Defense close the facility.[8]

Greenbrier has been decommissioned since 1995, and today much more is known about the formerly secret facility. Guided tours have become popular among visitors, who learn that the shelter contained its own power plant, food for sixty days, and a staff of sixty who worked in the bunker and were sworn to secrecy. Fleeing solons were to pass through a decontamination room with showers, then be issued army fatigues, shoes, and a bag with a toothbrush, toothpaste, hair tonic, and two kinds of deodorant. Among the features at Greenbrier are a 25-ton blast door with 1,500-pound hinges, an operating room, and an incinerator large enough to cremate bodies. There is also a television studio with the U.S. Capitol as a backdrop, "for broadcasting to anyone who might be left on the outside."[9] Currently the Greenbrier management is trying to gain voter approval to turn the bunker into a casino.[10] Another facility, Mount Weather, was built to house the president, cabinet officials, and Supreme Court justices. Located fifty miles northwest of Washington in the Blue Ridge mountains, Mount Weather is a self-contained facility that also has its own television studio.[11]

While most federal employees would not be able to avail themselves of the comfortable digs at Greenbrier during any nuclear unpleasantness, they nevertheless were expected to resume their duties following an attack. By 1957 the Office of Defense Mobilization was sponsoring what it called the "Nation-Wide Post-Attack Registration of Federal Employees," under which federal employees who survived an attack would inform the Civil Service Commission whether or not they would be reporting for work.[12] Four years later construction began on a $2.5 million shelter near Denton, Texas, which was designed for up to five hundred federal employees. This installation would control federal agencies in the Southwest, and if need be in the entire nation, after a nuclear war. The Denton center was to serve as a model for seven other federal regional centers.[13] Twenty-six state governments were taking similar steps to develop "protected" emergency capitals, and at least one city, Kalamazoo, Michigan, had already signed contracts with thirty private firms "to work for the city if a big war should come" on a "cost-plus basis."[14] Such preparations impressed the eternally ebullient *Popular Mechanics*, which predicted that following the apocalypse "probably one of the first things you'll see in your town will be a government interview trailer fom [sic] one of 2,000 state employment services set up to put people back to work."[15]

The federal government also took steps to preserve the monetary system from nuclear destruction. The Treasury put aside an eight-month supply of one-dollar bills and a two-year supply of fives, tens, and twenties, and urged "all banks to keep duplicate records in bombproof places and name other banks to take over if they should be destroyed." Nuclear war or no, such a plan would "enable you to write checks on your bank account—even if the bank itself were destroyed."[16] Treasury officials were also planning to pay for World War III in the same manner that it had financed World War II—through war bonds. Treasury officials assured Eisenhower in 1954 that even if Washington were destroyed, the Treasury Department could quickly be reestablished elsewhere and a bond issue floated in short order.[17] The Federal Reserve maintained its own underground facility near Culpeper, Virginia, and promoted a plan under which each bank would have its own civil defense program and provide shelter for its employees. This plan was voluntary, however, and as of November 1961 only a thousand out of eighteen thousand commercial banks had made any civil defense preparations.[18] James L. Robertson, governor of the Federal Reserve, observed that "victory, if one can speak of victory in connection with a holocaust, might go to the nation which recovered most swiftly from the effects of attack."[19]

The military too was positioning itself to survive the war, with a number of "little Pentagons" ready to pick up the nuclear slack if need be. Site R, along the Maryland-Pennsylvania border, is probably the best known.

Maintained by nearby Fort Ritchie, Site R was blasted into Raven Rock Mountain in 1953 and was designed to house the Alternate Joint Communications Center and the Alternate National Military Command Center. Encompassing some 265,000 square feet, the underground buildings at Site R would be the primary relocation site for the Joint Chiefs of Staff, who would conduct operations here during a nuclear war if the Pentagon was destroyed.[20]

Missile silos were being "hardened" against nuclear attack, as was Strategic Air Command headquarters in Omaha. SAC also maintained a plane in the air at all times with a general officer who could assume command should SAC commanders on the ground be killed.[21] By 1966 the North American Air Defense Command had also dug in, carving itself into Cheyenne Mountain near Colorado Springs. Covering some five acres and built behind a series of twenty-five-ton blast doors, the Cheyenne Mountain facility was built to monitor a Soviet attack on the United States, and to serve as a military nerve center during a nuclear war.[22]

Stockpiles and Industrial Survival

Part of the national scheme for survival was to stockpile strategic materials. Established in 1946, the bulk of the National Stockpile was taken up with some seventy-three materials, mainly metals. When the Office of Civil and Defense Mobilization announced its intention in 1958 of disposing of almost one-fourth of the $8 billion stockpile, it was widely interpreted as an admission that the stockpile no longer represented present-day realities. As Edward Ziegler in the *Nation* magazine put it, the OCDM's decision was a realization that "a stockpile that would see us through a five-year war had very little utility in a two-week atomic war." Holman Pettibone, the Chicago banker who wrote the appraisal of the stockpile, recommended building up stores of food, clothing, and drugs for use after a nuclear war.[23] By 1961 the U.S. government had cached $200 million worth of medical supplies throughout the country, including 1,930 "civil defense emergency hospitals" packed in wooden crates that contained everything necessary to establish two-hundred-bed emergency units (fig. 27).[24]

There was also the question of preserving America's industrial capacity. Edward Teller recommended sheltering people, machine tools, and power plants in deep underground mines in order to assure that "at least a

FIG. 27. Stockpiled medical supplies, San Jose, California, November 1955. FCDA photo. RG 397-MA 5-S-3 (box 18), Still Pictures Branch (NNSP), National Archives at College Park, MD.

reasonable fraction of our economic potential should be rebuilt within a year."[25] This was similar to the "sub-economy" idea that Oskar Morgenstern had proposed in 1959. Under this plan a portion of American industry, including machine-tool plants, nuclear power facilities, and pharmaceutical industries, as well as hospitals and refineries, would be installed permanently underground. While these operations would function normally in peacetime (except for their underground siting), after a nuclear war they would provide the core that would enable the economy to "once more in some fashion arise from the shambles."[26]

In 1958 a report issued by the Rockefeller Brothers Fund recommended "stockpiling food reserves and industrial reserves" against nuclear attack.[27] In the same year the RAND Corporation made an even more ambitious proposal. RAND researchers suggested the sheltering of "complete plants in the durable goods sector of the economy," and estimated that about one-fifth of American manufacturing could be sheltered at a cost of $30 billion.[28] One of the RAND report's most unusual recommendations was for the establishment of a War Damage Equalization Corporation that would "prefinance" economic recovery after a nuclear war. The corporation would essentially be selling nuclear insurance to businesses, individuals, and financial institutions, with the money from the premiums being used to accumulate industrial stockpiles and shelters. After the war, claims on the corporation "could serve as a basis for restoring postattack operations of financial institutions and business firms."[29]

Certainly the vulnerability of American industry to nuclear attack seemed real. The Moreel Report of 1954, for instance, concluded that two nuclear bombs could eliminate one-third of American steel capacity. To counter this geographical concentration, the report called for the eventual establishment of eighteen new steel plants dispersed around the country, at a cost of some $9 billion.[30] Without dispersal, Eugene Rabinowitch, editor of the *Bulletin of the Atomic Scientists*, feared that "on the day after the mutual holocaust, we will face an enemy still pouring steel, building planes, and weaving textiles, while we will be disabled for a long period of time."[31]

While the federal government encouraged dispersal (the Defense Production Act of 1956 granted rapid tax amortization for dispersing industries), there were political as well as practical reasons that made dispersal a hard sell in Washington. Dispersal, as one writer noted, "is still regarded by the industrialized states . . . as a 'dagger pointed at the heart of every industrial region.'" In Connecticut Senator McMahon's view, what dispersal meant to New England residents was "the move to Nevada."[32] Other critics included the Holifield subcommittee, which found "little promise in dispersal as a civil defense measure."[33] Even RAND researcher Bernard Brodie had his doubts, noting that "costly dispersion could to a large extent be countered by the very cheap expedient of delivering a vastly more powerful bomb."[34] By 1960 industrial dispersal was virtually dead as a national policy. The tax amortization benefit had expired in the previous year, and as Eisenhower's civil defense chief Leo Hoegh put it, "dispersion now occurs when it is of business advantage to the corporation without regard to tax benefit."[35]

Many private enterprises were developing their own programs to assure that at least their bureaucracies would be ready to do business after the bombs quit falling. As *American Business* magazine declared in 1950, "More and more businessmen are wondering what would happen to their investments tomorrow if an atomic bomb landed on their city today."[36] One of the first companies to perceive a business need for nuclear protection was the Iron Mountain Atomic Storage Corporation, which was established in 1951. Iron Mountain acquired an abandoned iron mine near Hudson, New York, and installed four hundred vaults that could withstand fire, water, and (allegedly) a nuclear blast. New York City banks, insurance companies, and manufacturing concerns began storing records at the Iron Mountain facility.[37]

To protect its employees from nuclear attack, Rohm and Haas, a chemical manufacturing firm, built at all five of its factories shelters that could withstand the blast and fallout from a twenty-megaton thermonuclear device at five miles' distance. At a cost of about $250 per employee, Rohm and Haas had spent about 1 percent of its total assets on the shelters.[38] Other companies that were making preparations for nuclear war included the First National Bank of Boston, which built a concrete and steel bunker in Pepperell, Massachusetts, to hold microfilms of its own records as well as the records of nine other banks leasing space. Entry to the vault at Pepperell was through a 16,000-ton door. In addition to storage space, the vault also contained a double filter to eliminate radioactive particles, and a shower where bankers could decontaminate themselves.[39] In 1963 congressional testimony, executives from the Jones and Laughlin steel company and Chase Manhattan Bank described the "emergency corporate headquarters" that they had established away from the target area. As Chase's Frank Keeler put it, the banking industry was determined "to survive—to be alive—after a nuclear attack on this Nation."[40]

Standard Oil's alternate headquarters in Morristown, New Jersey, had its own electric generator, artesian well, and a sprinkling system on the roof "to wash down accumulations of fallout in time of H-bomb attack."[41] Numerous companies took the precaution of storing microfilmed records at alternate locations, including Minnesota Mining and Manufacturing, International Harvester, Bell and Howell, International Business Machines, and the Ford Motor Company. The New York Stock Exchange was storing records in the Adirondacks, and even the McGraw-Hill Publishing Company was renting a vault to store its vital records in a mine 125 miles outside New York.[42]

The energetic efforts of businesses to assure that the inconvenience of a nuclear war need not impede their operations were brilliantly illustrated by First Federal Savings and Loan of Atlanta. A company of only fifty employees, First Federal had put its records on microfilm and had maintained a company shelter program for ten years. In addition, First Federal's four cars carried water, blankets, tools, and transistor radios. Bank president George W.

West, Jr., served notice to other savings and loans that come hell, high water, or nuclear attack, "We are going to be here, we are going to survive."[43]

Finally, to accommodate the business traveler who might find himself or herself on the road when the Big One dropped, a number of hotels were offering fallout shelter protection for their guests. Chicago's O'Hare Inn near the airport began construction in 1961 on a $45,000 fallout shelter capable of protecting five hundred guests.[44] In Danvers, Massachusetts, a motel developer announced that the motel he was building would be equipped with a fallout shelter that could accommodate guests for up to six months. Also allotted shelter at the motel were fifty persons from various professions that included a lawyer, an estate planner, civil defense officials, twenty municipal officers, and a machine gunner.[45]

The efforts made by businesses to survive a nuclear war should not be overly exaggerated. A survey of one thousand companies made by the McGraw-Hill Publishing Company revealed that only one in four businesses were making plans to construct shelters for their employees, and only 2.5 percent actually had shelters.[46] Still, one in four is considerably above the percentage of individual Americans making plans for their personal survival, and one has to wonder under what assumptions these preparations were made. Companies that managed to survive a nuclear attack would not only have to contend with disruptions of supplies, transportation, and labor resources on an unprecedented scale, but would somehow have to conduct business without the basic infrastructure required by modern industry. The economic problems would also be staggering. As Jack Hirshleifer noted in 1957, one of the consequences of a nuclear war would be a "chain reaction of bankruptcies."[47] Despite the grim prognosis, hundreds of firms, at a considerable financial outlay, did make preparations for surviving a nuclear war. As in the case of individuals building home shelters, these companies were expressing the faith that if they made certain preparations the familiar forms of life could somehow be renewed after a calamity without parallel in human history. Whether these preparations were grounded in prudence or a ludicrous optimism was very much in the eye of the beholder.

The Broken-Backed War and the Minutemen

The American businesses and individuals who were making plans to assure their survival were operating for the most part on the assumption that

World War III would be the last war, and that in the war's aftermath citizens on both sides would be too absorbed with survival and recovery to put any energy into geopolitics. There were others, however, who urged Americans to make preparations to fight World War IV. Colonel Virgil Ney, a history instructor at George Washington University, argued that America's retaliatory strike against the Soviet Union's initial attack might not be enough, and that the United States might have to continue to fight a "broken-backed" war with a badly fractured infrastructure and economy. Ney advocated more stockpiles, underground factories, and the training of military personnel to run factories. *Fortune* magazine reassured readers that if they took precautions, "the economy can go on making war and survive with victory," and Donald Robinson, writing in the *Saturday Evening Post*, also tried to rally Americans who might succumb to discouragement following a nuclear war: "How would the American people take the blow? Would we crumble mentally amid the heaps of blackened corpses? Would we have panic, looting, chaos? Or would we rise from the ruins and start rebuilding our civilization? Would we ignominiously surrender to the Communists or fight on to preserve our freedoms?"[48]

One group dedicated to fighting on was the Minutemen. In an era in which some Americans were preparing themselves for armed struggle in front of their fallout shelters against their fellow citizens, members of the Minutemen were arming to oppose what they believed would be an inevitable Soviet invasion following nuclear war. According to Minuteman lore, the idea for the group emerged while Missouri resident Robert DePugh and several of his friends were on a hunting trip. One of the hunters remarked that if the communists ever invaded America, hunting groups could easily be turned into guerrilla groups, and that day the Minutemen were created. With DePugh as Minutemen national coordinator, the group began in 1960 to study guerrilla tactics, to stage maneuvers, and to stash supplies and weapons around the country.[49] Like other Americans, DePugh had come to the conclusion by the early 1960s that a nuclear war between the United States and the Soviet Union was imminent. DePugh, in fact, was concerned enough to move his home and business from Independence, Missouri (which is in close proximity to Kansas City, an obvious target city) to Norborne, seventy miles to the north. Once in Norborne, DePugh built two shelters, even though he and other Minutemen held the national fallout shelter program of the Kennedy administration in contempt. A 1961 Minuteman pamphlet called *Join the Minutemen* makes this clear:

It is easy to see why most Americans have shied away from the government's civil-defense program. It is the American tradition to stand up and fight. It is not in keeping with this tradition to ask Americans to dig holes to hide in or to abandon their homes and flee helter-skelter to nowhere.

What was different about Minutemen shelters, according to this pamphlet, was that these were "not merely holes to hide in" but were "well camouflaged, stocked and fortified to serve as a 'center of resistance' for a future underground army."[50]

In October 1961 DePugh assembled a group of Minutemen and an arsenal near Shiloh, Illinois. The group was there to practice guerrilla warfare "as a last line of defense against Communism." "We must stop wondering if and when World War III will start," proclaimed DePugh. "It's already started. We are in it up to our ears." Shortly after the meeting broke up, Rich Lauchli, the supplier of Minutemen weapons, was arrested for possession of illegal firearms.[51] Lauchli darkly hinted that his arrest at Shiloh had been "Communist-inspired."[52]

The Minutemen claimed a membership of twelve thousand in 1961 (although actual membership was more likely in the hundreds than the thousands), and by this date the emphasis in Minutemen circles was already shifting from the Soviet invasion scenario to a preoccupation with communist fifth columnists intent on undermining the government.[53] That the Minutemen are the spiritual ancestors of today's militia groups can be quickly established by the similarities of their conspiratorial fantasies. In one example, Robert DePugh referred to the possibility that Americans might be "sold out to their enemies. . . . If the United States, for instance, should turn over all its military power, including its nuclear weapons, to the UN."[54] The Minutemen also shared another trait with contemporary militia groups, and that is their high estimation of their own importance. Rich Lauchli declared that the reason the Minutemen did not like their photographs taken was that "we are the first ones the Communists will want to kill" and that "any picture of our members that appears in a newspaper tomorrow will be in Moscow next week."[55]

In a 1961 *Time* magazine interview with California Minutemen leader William F. Colley, Colley described the buried medicine, supplies, and ten thousand rounds of ammunition that his group had hidden throughout the state. Colley declared, "We hope we never have to use that gear up in the mountains. But it's not hurting us to put it there. And if we ever do need it, we'll be better off than those folks buried under radioactive ash in their concrete coffins."[56]

The Nuclear City

Rather than establishing alternate urban headquarters or dispersing vital industries, many with an interest in urban planning believed that it made more sense to change the very idea of the modern industrial city. As early as 1949 Ralph Lapp suggested that there were at least three possible design approaches that would make cities less vulnerable to nuclear attack: the "satellite city," with the business district in the center and industrial, residential, and airport districts on the perimeter; the "doughnut city," with the airport in the center, a business area a few miles further out, and residential and industrial areas forming an outside ring around the whole; and the "rodlike city," with a long, narrow business district in the center and industrial and residential centers running parallel on either side.[57]

There were a number of variations on these basic concepts. In 1950 Norbert Wiener of the Massachusetts Institute of Technology suggested that planners could lessen the effects of a nuclear attack on American cities by building additional roads radiating out of the cities like spokes, and by establishing express highways and railroad lines that would ring the cities beyond the areas of congestion. Along these highway "life belts" there would be warehouses, hospitals, and power stations as well as parkland "made ready for large tent cities which could quickly be erected to shelter the refugees." Such a plan, said Wiener, "would bolster the nation's civilian defenses" in time of war, and in peacetime "accelerate the current trend of many city dwellers toward the suburbs."[58]

In *Total Atomic Defense* (1952), Sylvian Kindall claimed that the factors that had previously been important in the growth of cities had "shrunken in importance before the terrible power and danger of the atomic bomb." Reducing the vulnerability of cities to nuclear attack had now become the most important consideration in urban planning, and to this end Kindall suggested that cities have factory zones at their perimeter (and a buffer zone free of buildings between this part of the city and the rest), and zoning laws limiting population density to under one thousand per square mile. Kindall also recommended that the capital of the United States be relocated near Rocky Mountain National Park: "Into the solid rock of the buttes and ridges that abound about the area would be tunneled caverns for the storage of permanent records, and chambers where personnel could work and hold assembly during times of great peril, safe against the most powerful atomic bomb that might be projected into the area."[59]

In 1956 Lawrence R. Hafstad of the Atomic Energy Commission described an "annular city" that would "be essentially turned inside out." In such a city parks and airports would be located in the center, residential areas partway out, and industries on the outer fringe. This was similar to other proposals that essentially reversed the ordinary configuration of urban areas. Hafstad promised that if these new cities were built future generations might view the development of the atom bomb as "Nature's slum clearance program."[60] This notion was also found in Philip Wylie's 1954 novel *Tomorrow!* in which nuclear annihilation has become an opportunity for cities to reinvent themselves, with "room for broad streets with underpasses at intersections, room for vast parking areas, room for gardens, for parks, for picnic grounds right in the center of the city, room for swimming pools and dance floors and everything else that added to life's enjoyment."[61]

Others suggested that the best way to make cities nuclear-proof was to put them underground. By 1958 considerable work had already been done in this area in Sweden, which now maintained some of the world's most elaborate shelter facilities. A seven-story shelter had been constructed beneath Göteborg, and Stockholm boasted the world's largest shelter, capable of holding twenty thousand people and equipped with its own oxygen supply. Sweden was also concerned with industrial survival, and *Time* magazine reported that "all over Sweden factories are going underground . . . airplanes, precision instruments, munitions, radios are also made in below-ground factories; hydroelectric power is generated in stations tucked inside mountains; cavernous hospitals are complete with X-ray rooms, operating theaters, fully equipped wards." In cave factories the air was changed four times an hour, and worker claustrophobia was avoided "through the use of windows that look out on painted landscapes and cloud-filled skies."[62]

More ambitious plans that would place both people and factories permanently underground were on the drawing boards. In 1959 a Cornell University graduate school project under the direction of F. W. Edmondson, Jr., created a design for a city of nine thousand that would be self-contained and sheltered from nuclear attack. As Edmondson observed, "our cities and our civilization are threatened, really for the first time, with massive destruction," and such a threat must inevitably inspire "new city forms." At the heart of the model city created by the Cornell students was an elaborate shelter system with "seatway tunnels" connecting outlying suburban shelters to a large central shelter beneath the business district. Underground shelter space included cafeterias, clinics, gymnasiums, and headquarters for police and public officials. The central shelter was designed to be the town's "cultural center," with a library, museum, and auditorium. Also placed underground to protect it from nuclear attack was an electronic manufacturing facility, which was expected to be the city's main employer.[63]

Edmondson believed that it was possible to design and build nuclear-proof cities much larger than this one, and he offered as an example an imaginary city called NEUS (an acronym derived from northeastern United States, where this city would be located) that could house a population of 150,000. NEUS would be "completely enclosed, a controlled environment," and all strata of government would be represented here. Communications at NEUS would be routed by satellite, while transportation would be handled via "VTOL [vertical takeoff and landing] airborne mass transit." One-third of this city would be built underground, "hardened against overpressures and screened against all nuclear, chemical and bacterial assault." NEUS residents would be able to draw on a twenty-five-year food supply.[64] In both NEUS and the Cornell student-designed city, the energy needed by residents would be provided by nuclear power.

There was no lack of doubters who claimed that all the planning and scheming to make cities nuclear-proof was misdirected. One of the earliest was the atomic scientist Harold Urey, who in 1946 called the dispersal of American cities a "retreat"—a "fantastic flight from the consequences of our evil genius."[65] Others, however, saw these weapons as challenges to scientific and architectural ingenuity. The bomb had a stimulating effect on this group, who now began calling into question the basic forms of human habitation that had prevailed for centuries.

Children, Schools, and the Shelter Question

Redesigning the American school—and indoctrinating the American student—was also being urged by civil defenders to accommodate what they saw as the grim realities of the Nuclear Age. Indeed, with the introduction of school shelters and classroom civil defense instruction, the Cold War began to intrude into American education just as it had into other segments of American society.

Those who did not live through this era find it hard to imagine the atmosphere of fear and anxiety created by the constant threat of nuclear war. The Conelrad tests, which beginning in 1953 periodically interrupted radio programs to inform listeners that they would be given instructions in the event of nuclear attack, along with the periodic testing of air raid sirens, were often more frightening than reassuring. Even those most knowledgeable about the subject often described the situation in apocalyptic terms. The editors of the *Bulletin of the Atomic Scientists*, for instance, observed in 1954 that "an untoward event tomorrow may trigger a tense world to erupt in flames of atomic or thermonuclear warfare, [and] that there will be 'no place to hide' for the great masses of civilized mankind."[66]

For children, the specter of atomic peril was especially bewildering, and from an early date attempts were made to calm their fears. In 1956 the Disney company released *The Walt Disney Story of Our Friend the Atom*. The atom in this tale is compared to a genie in a bottle, whom one must finesse to bring out his good side. If done successfully, "the atomic Genie will not throw his energy at us in a torrent of heat and radiation; rather he will give us energy as a gently flowing spring gives us water."[67] In addition to "an almost endless source of energy," the atomic Genie "will grant the gifts of modern technology to even the most remote areas. It will give more food, better health—the many benefits of science—to everyone."[68]

There were certain scenarios, however, in which the atom was considerably less than friendly. In the years following Hiroshima educators struggled with the extremely difficult problem of how to prepare children for the possibility of nuclear war. Eventually what evolved, according to JoAnne Brown, was a "symbiotic relationship" between civil defense professionals and teachers that determined "what kind of information about nuclear war reached an entire generation of schoolchildren."[69] Under fire during the early 1950s from both anticommunist reformers and critics of "life adjustment education," teachers eagerly embraced nuclear education as a way to demonstrate both their patriotism and their serious practicality.[70] As Michael J. Carey notes, this would inaugurate a "special chapter in American education's history, special because this generation had a formal bomb-threat education."[71] Publications and films designed to educate children about what to do in case of nuclear attack would constitute a large proportion of FCDA printed materials.[72] The purpose of such materials was laid out by the comic book *The H-Bomb and You*: "We Americans must get used to the threat of war as a new way of life. It is not our choice but it IS our duty to be constantly prepared if our country is to survive."[73]

Of all the school materials created by the FCDA, perhaps the best known was *Duck and Cover*, which was produced as both an animated film and a booklet in 1951. In *Duck and Cover* the cartoon character Bert the Turtle instructed schoolchildren in the rudiments of survival in the event of an atomic explosion (fig. 28). The creators of Bert the Turtle were forced to pick their way delicately through overly glib depictions of nu-clear war on one hand, and terrifying descriptions prescribing hysteria and panic on the other. The use of a friendly cartoon character helped to de-fang the nuclear menace, and *Duck and Cover* tried to bolster the confi-dence of children by implying that they already knew what to do in cer-tain dangerous situations: "You have learned how to take care of yourself in many ways—to cross streets safely. And you know what to do in case of fire—but . . ." The "but," of course, is the atomic bomb, which "explodes with a flash brighter than any you've ever seen. Things will be knocked down all over town and, as in a big wind, they are blown through the air." Children were reassured that various authority figures would probably have the situation under control ("your city and its civil defense will try to warn you with a special alarm"), and were enjoined to obey instructions

FIG. 28. Federal Civil Defense Administration, *Bert the Turtle Says Duck and Cover*, 1951.

FIG. 29. Federal Civil Defense Administration, *Bert the Turtle Says Duck and Cover*, 1951.

("you must go quickly and quietly to the special shelter as the block warden, your teacher or your parents tell you"). However, it was possible that "the bomb might explode and the bright flash come . . . without any warning!" In such a situation children, like Bert, must duck and cover. The last panels of *Duck and Cover* show children taking cover as glass and other objects fly through their homes and classrooms (fig. 29). Children caught outdoors are shown taking cover behind walls and trees. A brilliant flash illuminates the distance.[74]

The Department of Education also published a number of school-oriented civil defense pamphlets through its Civil Defense Education Project. The principal author of these pamphlets, Janice M. Johnson, produced in one of these publications a playlet that elementary school children were encouraged to perform called *Skit for Planning a Home Shelter Area*. In this drama Judy, a sixth-grader, and Tommy, a fifth-grader, return home from school to tell their father about the shelter drill they had had that day:

DADDY: A drill, what are you talking about Judy? You mean you had another fire drill today? You had one yesterday.

129

JUDY: No, Daddy, it wasn't a fire drill, but it was just as important. This was a shelter drill.

DADDY: A shelter drill—what is that?

After explaining to their blockhead dad about shelter drills, the children clue their dad into the Nuclear Age facts of life:

JUDY: Oh Daddy! In our town we have 2 civil defense signals. One is the alert signal which is a steady blast of 3 to 5 minutes. This means that enemy planes are headed our way and that we should turn on our radios to 640 or 1240 on the AM dial to find out what to do.

TOMMY: In some towns people will be asked to evacuate their homes and schools and go to a safer place, but in our town we're supposed to turn on our radios to the CONELRAD stations for information and when we hear the signal of short blasts lasting for 3 minutes, we're supposed to take shelter.

At this point it has already become extremely difficult to imagine primary school children performing such a stultifying piece, and the skit mercifully draws to a close when Judy delicately hints that it is time to prepare a shelter. Dad has finally caught on ("Well, we have a basement we could use as a shelter"), and after Judy and Tommy instruct their dad in what they'll need in this shelter, Judy becomes ecstatic:

JUDY: I can hardly wait to tell my teacher what we're going to do. We're going to have the best shelter in town![75]

If a single theme ran through civil defense education in the 1950s, it was the insistence that discussions of nuclear war be presented in terms as mundane as possible, with only muted references to death, destruction, and dismemberment. L. J. Mauth in the *Journal of Education* observed that "panic is contagious and in times of emergency the teacher must be emotionally prepared to assume a confident air." Emotionalizing headlines "would only augment student fears." Instead, Mauth suggested "a matter-of-fact consideration" of such issues as atomic war.[76] The Parent-Teachers' Association advised its members to "maintain calmness and transmit a feeling of assuredness" in the face of emergency.[77] Such calmness, it was hoped, would be transmitted to children, who would approach the end of the world with a certain aplomb.[78]

FIG. 30. Schoolchildren covering up in Marshall, Michigan. RG 397-MA 9-E-6 (box 9), Still Pictures Branch (NNSP), National Archives at College Park, MD.

The degree to which teachers were successful in inculcating such cool confidence in their charges is debatable. The "duck and cover" school drills, in which students crawled under their desks and assumed the "atomic clutch" position with hands to the back of the neck, were often run without students knowing whether this was an exercise or an actual atomic attack (fig. 30).[79] One person recalled that during these drills "You could feel the tension in the air, fear. The kids are fidgety and jumpy and talking—whispering—but then there would be absolute silence. You never knew if it was a drill—a test—or the real thing."[80] Todd Gitlin notes that "under the desks and crouched in the hallways, terrors were ignited, existentialists were made. . . . we could never quite take for granted that the world we had been born into was destined to endure."[81] Annie Dillard, who grew up in Pittsburgh, recalled that during air raid drills the teachers would take their students to the basement, where "we tucked against the walls and lockers: dozens of clean girls wearing green jumpers, green knee socks, and pink-soled white bucks. We folded our skinny arms over our heads, and raised to the enemy a clatter of gold scarab bracelets and gold bangle bracelets."[82]

In his novel *The Nuclear Age*, Tim O'Brien's protagonist William Cowling begins digging up his backyard one night after succumbing to a life-time of anxiety about the bomb. Recalling his youth during the 1950s, Cowling remembered that he

> converted my Ping-Pong table into a fallout shelter. Funny? Poignant? A nifty comment on the modern age? Well, let me tell you something. The year was 1958 and I was scared. Who knows how it started? Maybe it was all that CONELRAD stuff on the radio, tests of the Emergency Broadcast System, pictures of H-bombs in *Life* magazine, strontium 90 in the milk, the times in school when we'd crawl under our desks and cover our heads in practice for the real thing. Or maybe it was rooted deep inside me. In my own inherited fears, in the genes, in a coded conviction that the world wasn't safe for human life.[83]

In *Born on the Fourth of July*, Ron Kovic observes of his childhood that, "We joined the cub scouts and marched in parades on Memorial Day. We made contingency plans for the cold war and built fallout shelters out of milk cartons."[84]

Doris Kearns Goodwin, who grew up in the New York suburb of Rockville Centre, notes that "To us, the Cold War was not an abstraction. It was the air-raid drills in school, the call for bomb shelters, and exposure to the deliberately unsettling horror of civil-defense films."[85] Like so many other schoolchildren, Goodwin dutifully practiced the duck and cover drill, crouching under her desk with elbows over her head (although Goodwin confesses, "I could never figure out how my flimsy desk, with its worn inkwell and its years of name-scratching, could protect me from the atomic bomb").[86]

Interestingly, children on the other side of the Cold War divide were receiving civil defense instruction that was much the same as in American schools. Vladislav Zubok and Constantine Pleshakov, the Russian authors of *Inside the Kremlin's Cold War*, remembered that

> We learned to look for an *Enola Gay* in the skies even before we learned to brush our own teeth. Soviet middle schools would hold civil defense classes in which ludicrous survival skills were taught in preparation for

all-out war. Although still half believing in Santa Claus, we were already very skeptical of gas masks and bomb shelters.[87]

One especially telling detail that indicated the extent to which the Nuclear Age had begun to blur the distinctions between military and civilian (and which conjured up images of the "garrison state") was the campaign to provide schoolchildren with dog tags. Designed to assist officials in identifying lost, dead, or wounded children, identification tags were issued to schoolchildren in New York, San Francisco, Seattle, and other American cities. The tattooing of children for identification purposes was also considered, but rejected. According to the assistant superintendent of Milwaukee schools, tattooing was not administered to children "because of its associations and impermanence in the case of severe burns."[88]

If the relationship between the FCDA and teachers had been cozy during much of the 1950s, by the early 1960s that relationship had begun to cool as the government began to press both for civil defense training in schools and the construction of community fallout shelters in schools. In essence, teachers were now being asked to accept responsibility not only for the welfare of their students during a nuclear war, but for the welfare of the entire community. The questions proliferated. Was this a burden that could rightly be placed on the schools? Should school shelters be built to withstand the blast, heat, and fire of a nuclear explosion, or only the fallout? Should local school districts or the federal government pay for the construction of such shelters? With many local school budgets already stretched to the limit, this latter consideration was especially pressing. The American Association of School Administrators, at its annual meeting in February 1962, declared that providing protection against nuclear attack was "a total public responsibility," and that if there was indeed a consensus that the school building was the proper place for a shelter, "then it should be financed by appropriations outside the school budget."[89]

Not building school shelters also presented teachers and school administrators with potential nightmare scenarios. As W. Gayle Starnes, an FCDA official, noted in 1957,

If we send our youngsters en masse to safety areas, it may be days, even weeks before they can be reunited with their families. . . . On the other hand, if the children are dismissed from school, we can only hope that they will arrive home safely and in time to join the family before it is swept up in the evacuation traffic or movement to community shelters. They will have to fight their own way through streams of people pouring down every street.[90]

In fact, a uniform civil defense policy among American schools never developed, and the result was a patchwork of widely differing school policies—or no policy at all. A 1962 survey of school superintendents conducted by *Scholastic Teacher* revealed the wide range of variations. Schools in Little Rock, Arkansas, established three plans for their students in the event of nuclear attack (staying in school, walking home, or riding home in a private car), one of which would be chosen by the parents. Helena, Montana, schools had a civil defense program that identified students with dog tags and fingerprints, and in El Paso, Texas, every teacher was required to take the Adult Civil Defense Survival Course. While all El Paso students were to remain at the school in the event of a nuclear attack, in San Antonio evacuation was still the official policy. A superintendent in Maine and one in Kentucky confessed to having no policy at all, pending "further instructions" from civil defense officials.[91]

From an early date, federal officials and other civil defense enthusiasts saw schools as the obvious providers for local shelters because students in primary and secondary schools comprised nearly one-fourth of the American population. In addition, the schools themselves were typically among the best equipped buildings in the community, their locations were closely related to population density, and, as the OCD put it, schools were maintained by "responsible leaders and orderly procedures."[92] Writing in the *American School Board Journal* in 1956, Walter Rein claimed that a modern school "could readily be converted into an almost ideal emergency hospital" and that schools "cry out to be adapted to the immediate purpose of civil defense."[93] Don E. Carleton, civil defense director of Milwaukee, contended that the only things schools would lose by incorporating shelters would be windows, which "with modern lighting and ventilation, are not needed. You could have schoolrooms which would constitute efficient shelters."[94]

This was a claim that generated a great deal of debate. Certainly the architectural profession was generally optimistic that effective fallout shelters could be built into new school construction and retrofitted to existing school facilities. The architectural firm Caudill, Rowlett and Scott, for instance, which drew up plans in 1961 for adapting Boswell High School in Saginaw, Texas, for fallout shelter use, concluded that it was economically and functionally feasible "to provide fallout protection to a school building without sacrificing conventional design features of teaching space."[95] Pearce and Pearce, a St. Louis architectural firm that produced drawings for a high school fallout shelter in Lemay, Missouri, insisted that fallout shelters could be built in schools "at a very reasonable cost and without impairing the intended use of the building."[96]

School fallout shelter construction presented a number of problems, however. For maximum effectiveness, a school shelter would not have any windows (ideally, such a shelter would be built below grade, in school basements) and would be surrounded by enough mass to protect the inhabitants from radiation. Shelters would also require permanent load-bearing walls and short spans between walls. These requirements were diametrically opposed to prevailing school construction philosophy, which put a premium on flexible interior space and abundant natural light. There were also sometimes conflicts with state laws, as many building codes forbade the use of basements for educational purposes (in part because of the hazard presented should fire break out in a basement facility).

Especially upsetting to some educators would be the absence of windows in school/shelter configurations. Many schools in America had been built so that each classroom would have a bank of windows—a "wall of light" to provide better ventilation and light.[97] The architect Lyndon Welch acknowledged that standard shelter design "conflicts with current educational and architectural thinking directed toward achieving spaces as open as possible, with maximum natural light."[98] In the context of a nuclear attack, however, the glass that conveyed the natural light was the worst possible material for the classroom. Chet Holifield called such school construction "glass deathtraps . . . any kind of blast would cause the glass to fly and cut the children all to pieces."[99]

By the summer of 1963, congressional committee hearings were being held on a proposed national fallout shelter program, and the issue of shelters in the schools was creating a lot of friction. Under the program being contemplated, shelters would be constructed in federal buildings, and "incentive" money would be provided to build shelters in other public and private buildings, especially schools. The reaction of educators to this proposed additional burden was ambivalent at best. In his congressional testimony, David Cavers, professor of law at Harvard, claimed that under the proposed federal plan "a school would have to take a nice, airy basement, brick up the windows, impair the adequacy of the exits by erecting baffles at the door, and contract not to use this space for any permanent arrangement inconsistent with shelter use by the general public for 5 years."[100]

The nation's largest school system was in California, and that state's department of education stated flatly that "shelters are not compatible with schools," and that it was "cheaper to build a good school and a good shelter as separate units." The department believed that the flexibility of space so highly prized by schools, including the easy removal of interior walls or partitions, was diametrically opposed to shelter design requirements. Providing light and climate controls would also be problematic in an underground school, and such schools "would be less safe for normal everyday hazards such as fire and earthquake."

Finally, the California Department of Education characterized the many school shelter plans submitted to it as "virtually worthless" because of the low protection factor of such plans.[101] The Pearce and Pearce plan to which we have alluded was based on a radiation protection factor of 100 (meaning radiation levels inside the shelter would be 1/100th of outside levels).[102] California's Department of Education, however, claimed that "a protection factor of 100 is not considered safe," and instead insisted on a protection factor of 1,000.[103] The differences between providing a protection factor of 100 and one of 1,000 were huge in terms of building requirements and costs, and here as elsewhere in this debate there was little in the way of consensus. Finding funding for shelters was also a problem at the college level. As one college president put it, "It practically means a choice between plans for expansion for growing attendance over the next five years—or shelter plans."[104]

In addition to the problems of cost and the physical requirements of school shelters was the issue of community responsibility during a nuclear attack. The handbooks and guides created for teachers and administrators put the responsibility squarely on the school staff. The pleasing notion that teachers could easily deal with the problems of children and anyone else who took shelter during the pandemonium of a nuclear war is encapsulated in a 1960 "manual" produced by the Eberle Smith architectural firm for the OCDM. The *Technical Guide Manual: Fallout-Radiation Protection in Schools* is stunningly optimistic in its views of the effects of a nuclear attack. The manual asserts that "children are more psychologically resilient than adults" and would "suffer less initial trauma in an attack," and that "most persons entering fallout shelters will not have suffered either physical hurt or any initial trauma in an attack." The guide admits that "some means of control or confinement" would be necessary to deal with the "few individuals" whose emotional traumas threatened to become contagious. In addition, an infirmary would have to be established in the shelter to deal with the sick and injured. And who would be responsible for the doctoring, social work, food preparation, and law enforcement of the shelter? "It is assumed that school faculty will staff the shelter."[105]

Another OCD publication designed to serve as a guide to school administrators in the event of nuclear attack stated unequivocally that "responsibility for this planned protection rests clearly with the school administrator."[106] Burden shifting such as this often left school officials seething with resentment. Lawrence H. Shepoiser, superintendent of the Wichita, Kansas, schools, denied that the schools had any responsibility whatsoever for the community's safety during a nuclear attack, and declared that his school system was "in no position to guarantee physical protection to adults or pupils from a thermonuclear explosion or radioactive fallout." "If survival is of national concern," added Shepoiser, "it is the responsibility of the President of the United States and Congress to make public shelters available."[107]

One approach to the funding problem, the so-called Norwalk Plan of 1962, avoided the problem of federal participation altogether. The Norwalk Plan was the brainchild of Norman Heap, business manager for the public schools of Norwalk, Connecticut. Heap recommended that shelter building originate at the local level because "shelter programs can be devised, financed, and constructed by *local* governments in the time it takes the *federal* government to make a survey."[108] The Norwalk Plan called for the construction of about twenty-five shelters underneath the city's school playgrounds. Each shelter would accommodate about three thousand persons (including residents of the community as well as students) and would cost about $125 per person. Heap believed that there was an urgent need for such shelters because "the threat of nuclear war, the possible annihilation of 50 million children, is not a future problem."

Among those opposed to Heap was Nolan Kerschner, a builder and chairman of the Fairfield County branch of the Committee for a Sane Nuclear Policy. Kerschner objected to Heap's plan because Kerschner was convinced that "there's no such thing as any protection for my family other than peace." Kerschner also believed that shelters were delusive and impractical, and would "bring on a psychology that leads people to think of the inevitability of war—and the concept of striking first."[109] The *NEA Journal*, official organ of the National Education Association, invited its readers to comment on the Norwalk Plan in 1962. Reactions were mostly negative, with commentators criticizing shelters for their adverse psychological impact and because they acted as a diversion from searching for a peaceful solution to East-West tensions.[110]

The debate that raged in Norwalk was also played out in other cities. When plans were being drawn up in 1961 for the new high school in Greece, New York (a suburb of Rochester), they included a provision for a fallout shelter. When some locals objected, voters were allowed to decide directly if they wanted the school to include a shelter. Opposition to the shelter coalesced around a group called the Independent Political Forum, which argued that shelters "encourage a war psychology, intensify the arms race and promote the idea that nuclear war is necessary or inevitable."[111] Voters approved the school bond issue, but rejected the shelter by better than two to one.[112]

One school that became a unique laboratory for both shelter design and student behavior in a shelter environment was the Abo Public Elementary School. Located in Artesia, New Mexico, 40 miles south of Roswell and 110 miles east of Alamogordo, the Abo school took the Norwalk Plan a step further by turning the school itself into a fallout shelter. It was built entirely underground (the only one of its kind in the country), and doubled as a fully equipped fallout shelter.[113] The school contained two deep wells for an uncontaminated water source, air filters, bedding, survival food, an emergency power system, decontamination showers, and a morgue. If an attack occurred during school hours, Abo would shelter its own students and those from other schools. Otherwise it would accommodate the first 2,160 people to show up. Those arriving too late would find entry to the school blocked by two 1,800-pound steel doors (fig. 31).[114]

The experience of teaching school in a windowless, underground environment left most teachers favorably impressed. Gertrude McCaw found the students at Abo to be "less rambunctious. You spend more time teaching and less time disciplining." McCaw attributed this to the quiet and the lack of distracting windows. The students themselves seemed proud of their school, and several verified McCaw's impressions, noting that the lack of windows helped keep them from getting in trouble with their teachers.[115]

The unique architecture of the school, however, did make several students anxiously aware of the possibilities of nuclear war. Sixth-grader Martha Terpening worried that while her mother was a teacher and would be safe, "my daddy works at the post office and he wouldn't have any place to go." Nine-year-old Rusty Heckel also worried about his parents, and explained that "being underground gives you a funny feeling—but you know you're safe." Russ Baldwin added, "You think a lot about the danger while you're here. Sometimes I have the feeling that

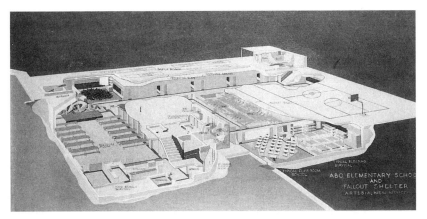

FIG. 31. Abo Elementary School and fallout shelter, Artesia, New Mexico. Note the morgue at front center. Frank M. Standhardt, architect, Roswell, NM. RG 397-MA 2-S-271 (box 18), Still Pictures Branch (NNSP), National Archives at College Park, MD.

fallout is coming now—that it is out there now—and then I go out and it isn't." The Abo school model, however, tended to attract hostility rather than enthusiasm at the national level. The National Council on Schoolhouse Construction at its annual meeting flatly rejected underground schools, insisting that "shelter provisions are not compatible with educational requirements."[116]

While the school fallout shelter issue was raging among educators and public officials, questions were also being raised as to the psychological effect this high-profile debate was having on children themselves. In 1962 Marquis Childs posed this educational problem in the following way:

> So let us imagine that Catherine is already grown a bit older, say six or seven, and she comes home from school one day and says, "All the kids are talking about fallout shelters and whether there's going to be a war or not and Sally Brown's father is building a fallout shelter in their basement. Aren't we going to have a fallout shelter? Is there really going to be a war, and will everybody be killed?" How do you answer such questions?[117]

Childs believed that the first obligation of the parent to the child was to tell the truth—that those within ten miles of a city center "have little chance of survival from a direct hit."[118]

In a 1961 *Newsweek* article on the effect of nuclear survival discussions on children, an art teacher named Nancy Lawson estimated that half of her class was preoccupied with nuclear fallout. Displaying a batch of student watercolors with "brilliantly colored versions of mushroom clouds, flaming cities, running children, and fallout-flaked skyscrapers," Lawson observed that "a child just naturally uses brilliant colors in painting. But we are having an awful lot of trouble getting them to paint a *clear* sky."[119]

The psychiatrist Lester Grinspoon compared the building of school fallout shelters to the father who tells his child "that there may be some savage beasts at large in the community" and that therefore they must build a high fence with barbed wire and broken glass: "Does this make the child feel more secure? It may not. For the child the fence may be an ever-present, anxiety provoking reminder of the hostile and insecure nature of the world he lives in."[120] David Cavers condemned school environments "poisoned by the continuing threat of extermination, a threat made obvious by shelter posters, shelter stockpiles and shelter drills."[121]

In 1962 and 1963 a study was conducted on the psychological effects of the threat of nuclear war on New York schoolchildren. Sibylle Escalona found that such a threat exerted "a corrosive and malignant influence" on both normal and more vulnerable schoolchildren.[122] According to Escalona, 70 percent of the 311 children that were studied mentioned the issue of war and peace when asked about their concerns for the future.[123] One child worried that "if there is a world ten years from now, it will be horrible and full of fear from war," while another predicted that China will "find the atom bomb and bomb the world." The statements of several children clearly showed that the issues of the fallout shelter debate had filtered down to the primary school. "The people will be living underground, and they would have to have a lot of light," was the opinion of one concerned child. Another foresaw a world in which "there wouldn't be any schools or houses and they would live in the ground."[124]

Parents themselves had equivocal feelings about leaving their children in even the safest schools in the event of a nuclear war. When parents in Northampton, Massachusetts, were asked what they would do if an attack occurred while their children were in school, 80 percent responded that they would retrieve their children from school, "whether they felt them safe there or not."[125] Zeldine Golden of Trenton, New Jersey, wrote a letter to *Newsweek* asking, "What is the use of any form of shelter? Would you go into one knowing your children were in school and your husband at work? We all feel a deep despair, especially for our children. My 10-year-old boy speaks of dying from radiation. What do you tell him?"[126]

The Gendered Holocaust

While publications such as *Duck and Cover* tried to "domesticate" nuclear war in the general sense of housebreaking an unruly pet, civil defense pamphlets and spokespersons also turned to domesticity in its more specific, gendered meaning, and invoked civil defense as an extension of the domestic arts. Civil defense during the 1950s and 1960s would be "feminized" to the extent that links would be suggested between a woman's home and her fallout shelter, and between her domestic responsibilities and civil defense preparedness. An early promoter of the idea of woman as civil defender was Katherine Howard, who was deputy administrator of the FCDA in 1953. Downplaying the threat posed by the hydrogen bomb (she described it as "a bigger A-bomb" and "the same problem, only more so"), Howard emphasized that it would be "feminine courage, and strength of mind and heart" and "motherhood qualities" that would pull the country through in a nuclear attack.[127] Later, Leo A. Hoegh, director of the OCDM, stated before a congressional committee that "the Nation's homemakers are the traditional custodians of the family. This responsibility goes hand in hand with the aims of civil defense." According to Hoegh, the OCDM's "home-protection work-shop program" had been attended by sixty thousand women over a nine-month period, and a civil defense newsletter was reaching some forty thousand women. The emphasis of such efforts, said Hoegh, was "shelter—the shelter which can assure survival for the families these women represent."[128]

The Department of Education also found connections between women's traditional roles and civil defense preparation. In one pamphlet, Janice Johnson suggests that "home economics teachers and supervisors" could help prepare their students for civil defense emergencies. Life in the postwar world chillingly takes shape in the exercises suggested by Johnson:

Develop ability to prepare simple, nutritious meals from emergency supplies.

Acquaint students with methods of emergency sanitation such as disposal of garbage and human refuse.

Discuss radioactive fallout, and household decontamination methods.

Familiarize students with home nursing procedures and care of sick and injured people.

Conduct study of fear, panic and human conduct in emergency situations.[129]

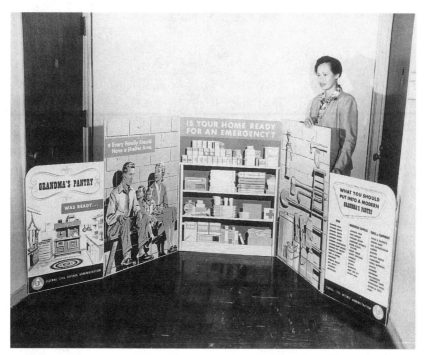

Fig. 32. "Grandma's Pantry" display, RG 397-MA 3-G-1. Still Pictures Branch (NNSP), National Archives at College Park, MD.

Clearly home economics students, the vast majority of whom were female during the 1950s, were being called on to perform the traditional nurturing roles. An outstanding example was the FCDA's "grandma's pantry" campaign.[130] Here women are encouraged to make ready for the possibility of nuclear war, with such preparations compared to the traditional "grandma's pantry" (fig. 32). "Grandma's pantry was ready, is your 'pantry' ready in event of emergency?" asks the FCDA pamphlet. Readers are warned of the possibility of damaged water systems, broken sewer lines, mounting heaps of garbage, and a lack of food and fresh water after an attack, and a list is provided of emergency items that should be stocked in each individual's "grandma's pantry."[131] *Science News Letter* in 1960 also added "nuclear blasts" to the list of disasters against which the "ordinary housewife" would want to guard her family: "Here are some simple but life-saving steps that the ordinary housewife can take to protect her family from major destruction by nuclear blasts, floods or tornadoes."[132]

"Even in the ultimate chaos of an atomic attack," observes Elaine Tyler

May, "appropriate gender roles would need to prevail," with women serving as child nurturers, food preparers, and hospital workers.[133] Indeed, when Philip Wylie described the aftermath of an atomic explosion in his 1954 novel *Tomorrow!* he noted, "They were—the women—tending the hurt, the shocked, the frightened, helping the surgeons, assisting the nurses, corralling the hundreds of lost children, making out tickets of identification, making out cards for withdrawals of food, clothes, shoes, whatever was required."[134] In *The Feminine Mystique* (1963), Betty Friedan discusses the kinds of magazine stories that were tailored for a female audience, and cites an article called "How to Have a Baby in an Atom Bomb Shelter" that had been submitted to a women's magazine. "According to the mystique," said a caustic Friedan, "women, in their mysterious femininity, might be interested in the concrete biological details of having a baby in a bomb shelter, but never in the abstract idea of the bomb's power to destroy the human race."[135]

Women's magazines, it is probably fair to say, were challenged in an unprecedented way by the issues of the Nuclear Age. Clearly these publications did not want to lose their core readers by becoming too heavily involved in discussions of nuclear war and fallout, but the crisis atmosphere of the late 1950s and early 1960s could hardly be ignored. The fallout shelter controversy in particular produced a great deal of concern. As the editors of *Good Housekeeping* noted, "in an atmosphere fraught with bewilderment, frustration, fear and deep concern for the future, the fall-out shelter issue has aroused many motions and emotions. If there are any simple answers to the shelter dilemma, none seems to have been forthcoming, from either side."[136] *Better Homes and Gardens* concurred, and in a 1962 article on one man's construction of a fallout shelter ("Mr. Babcock's Folly") commented that "never before in America has so much dirt been excavated, by so many, so feverishly. The fear of radioactive fallout from an atomic war has itself settled on our land like a deadly fog."[137]

Redbook magazine, journal of the young, harried mother, published a number of articles during this era dealing with nuclear issues, with the emphasis ordinarily, but not always, on their impact on children. In 1959, for instance, *Redbook* editor Walter Goodman published "Fallout and Your Family's Health," which underscored the effects of nuclear testing on the health of children. The presence of strontium-90 drew special attention, and Goodman cites studies showing increased concentrations of strontium-90 in the milk supply of several major cities, and in wheat fields in the upper Midwest.[138] The lack of reliable government information on

FIG. 33. The Powners go underground, 1960. Princeton University photograph. RG 397-MA 21-S-3 (box 19), Still Pictures Branch (NNSP), National Archives at College Park, MD.

radioactive fallout prompted another *Redbook* article titled "What We Are Not Being Told about Fallout Hazards."[139]

In 1960 a New Jersey couple, Tom and Madge Powner, and their three children (ages two, three, and five), volunteered to spend two weeks in a fallout shelter for an OCDM study (fig. 33). An article on the Powners' experiences was published in *Redbook* under the title "The Testing of a

Family." Madge had at first been skeptical ("It's insane even to think of putting three small children in such a place for two whole weeks"), but had been won over partly by the pioneering nature of the experiment. It was also probably the case that Madge succumbed to the domestic imperatives of this era, noting that "if a mother couldn't live for two weeks in a room with her own husband and children, she wasn't much of a person."[140] Not surprisingly, there were some tense moments. A microphone in the shelter recorded all conversations, and at one point the OCDM scientist listening in to these conversations believed that the experiment was endangered:

It would appear now that Madge is brooding. This will probably make Tom angry again and all will be lost. At the moment there seems to be an armed silence. Tom has demonstrated his ability to say he was wrong. Now can Madge do the same? I think Tom offered her a little drink. Judging from Madge's tone, the air is still charged. Boy, this is really touch and go.[141]

The Powners had the option of hitting a "panic button" that would end their stay in the fallout shelter, but were finally able to resolve their differences. While the Powners experienced a number of other difficulties in the course of this experiment, including heat and humidity, odors from the chemical toilet, and difficulties in heating the food, overall this family revealed itself to be remarkably well adjusted. Madge declared at the end of the two weeks that "we've all learned a good deal about one another, and all of it is reassuring . . . more families ought to try to plan vacations where they are really alone together."[142]

Not all *Redbook* articles on nuclear issues were as family-specific. In December 1959, for instance, *Redbook* made *On the Beach* its Picture of the Month, and in August 1961 *Redbook* published Robert Jungk's "Survivors of Hiroshima."[143] Another *Redbook* article, "Are We Powerless to Prevent War?" assembled a group of commentators that included Leo Szilard, Adlai Stevenson, Reinhold Niebuhr, and Walter Lippmann.[144] Fallout shelters generally got negative treatment in *Redbook*. In a Margaret Mead article that appeared in this magazine, Mead claimed that "human beings who can think of nothing better to do than to build individual shelters to crawl into in case of an attack are a hazard to everyone around them."[145] Walter Goodman wrote a sobering *Redbook* article in 1962 called "The Truth about Fallout Shelters," which began by deflating the notion that a cozy domesticity would prevail inside a fallout shelter during a nuclear emergency: "The happy image of father, mother and all the children sitting snugly together in their new convertible gameroom-shelter, first-aid kit ready but unused, is based on several assumptions that may be grossly inaccurate." This included the assumption that "the family would be at home together when the warning came."[146] During the course of this article Goodman discusses the differing scientific opinion on fallout shelters, and describes what the world might look like after a nuclear attack ("the sun will shine through a dust-laden atmosphere; the landscape would be blackened by fire").[147] "The hard truth," said Goodman, "is that no one can assure any family that it would be saved in a nuclear attack, no matter how substantial its shelter," and that each family would have to decide for itself whether "there will be enough left that is worth coming out of the shelter for."[148]

Another magazine with a predominantly female readership was *Good Housekeeping*. This magazine had told its readers in 1958 that "if you recognize the possibility of war between major powers, you must go further and acknowledge that atomic bombs will be dropped. On *us*. . . . if and when a single bomb falls within 200 to 500 miles of you, your survival depends on a shelter—and the shelter depends on you."[149] By 1962, however, it appeared that *Good Housekeeping* no longer had the same enthusiasm for shelters, and the William L. Shirer piece that it ran that year ("Let's Stop the Fall-Out Shelter Folly") was even more hostile to fallout shelters than the Goodman article that appeared in *Redbook*. Shirer emphasized the class aspects of fallout shelters ("Are only the well-to-do among us to have a chance to survive?"), and was especially critical of the hucksters of the shelter building industry, who "threaten to make a racket out of the fears and bewilderment of the American people." Shirer worried that fallout shelter hysteria had brought out the worst in Americans, and declared that Americans should dedicate themselves to finding peace, rather than "to building flimsy shelters of uncertain worth to cower in if we should lose the peace."[150]

Among the most interesting articles published by *Good Housekeeping* was a contribution from Rada Adzhubei, the wife of the editor of *Izvestiya* and the daughter of Nikita Khrushchev. Asked by the editors to write an article on topics that would supposedly be of universal concern to women, Adzhubei initially snubbed *Good Housekeeping* by declaring that she had "never been particularly concerned with women's problems," that she did not like to cook, and that she "had no particular desire to write specially for a woman's magazine." Adzhubei's reluctance was happily overcome after she was told that *Good Housekeeping* had a circulation of ten million.[151]

Adzhubei's article is filled with touching accounts of conversations with her children on the subject of international peace, and declarations of how in the Soviet Union "we bring up our children for peace, not for war." It quickly becomes obvious that Adzhubei has crafted a propaganda piece, as she contrasts peace-loving Russia ("the Soviet Government passed a special law making war propaganda a criminal offense") with the state of things she encountered in her recent visit to New York ("I was astounded to hear so much talk of war"). Adzhubei was especially critical of American fallout shelters:

> Now and then you saw inconspicuous signs on New York streets announcing "bomb shelter entrance." People walked by unperturbed, paying no attention to them. I was overwhelmed. I hadn't seen them since my childhood, since the war against fascist Germany.
>
> As for my children—they have never seen anything so horrible. There are no signs like that in Moscow nor in any other Soviet town.
>
> Various advertisements of shelters are quite usual in American papers and magazines. The same thing is true of television.[152]

Adzhubei did not mention that the Soviet shelter building program was both more developed and more ambitious than its American counterpart, and that civil defense training was mandatory in the Soviet Union.

A similar article (from a different perspective) resulted from an interview that the editors of seven women's magazines had with President Kennedy. Ray Robinson of *Good Housekeeping* noted that the editors agreed that "their readers have shown an increasing awareness and sophistication about the problems of peace and the threat of mutual incineration." The emphasis was once again on the impact on children and the family, and the interview seemed to have been conducted in a congenial atmosphere until someone raised the fear expressed by many that reminders of Cold War tensions (and here the questioner seemed to have had shelters in mind) were having an adverse effect on the mental health and well-being of children. Kennedy bristled at the suggestion, claiming that the problem had been "overstated." "The amount of civil-defense activity in any child's life is quite limited," insisted Kennedy. "In fact there is probably not enough of it, so I do not think it has a measurable effect upon very many children."[153]

The threat of nuclear war put considerable stress on American society, but that stress did not always translate into civil defense involvement. While the government and the military made elaborate contingency plans for weathering a nuclear catastrophe, there was more ambivalence in the private sector. The businesses willing to make serious preparations for surviving nuclear war were a distinct minority, and the troubling question of whether a nuclear war would leave anything left to survive *for* worked against most businesses making a substantial financial commitment to civil defense preparations. While the difficult task of maintaining a business is itself an exercise in optimism, there are limits to the optimism of even the most ardent of capitalists, and nothing drains away optimism quite so thoroughly as the prospect of nuclear war. (Not surprisingly, the one segment of society that seemed both convinced of the survivability of nuclear war and eager for its onset was the far Right, especially the Minutemen.)

Just as businesses often balked at making ready for World War III, so too were there limits to the willingness of teachers to acquiesce to the wishes of civil defense officials. In the decade after World War II patriotic teachers had been willing enough to institute civil defense training in large part because such training did not compromise the primary mission of teaching. The school shelter, or even more radically the school *as* shelter, was a different proposition. Here the perceived needs of teaching—abundant light, flexible open spaces—were in diametric opposition to the requirements of fallout shelter construction. There were few teachers willing to teach in an Abo-style school facility, where bunker classrooms would be a constant reminder of the possibility of nuclear holocaust. There was also the issue of cost, with already strapped school districts being asked to shoulder an additional financial burden for shelter construction. Finally, the blithe assumption that teachers would naturally assume responsibility for the entire community during a nuclear attack did not sit well with teachers themselves, who felt that they were already laboring under enough responsibilities.

Civil defense appeals to female domesticity were also severely undermined by the frightening realities of nuclear war. Women were being called on by the government to perform their traditional, nurturing roles in the extremities of an unprecedented cataclysm, and despite the homey analogies used by government publications to enlist women in this effort—the shelter as old-fashioned storm cellar or the idea of "grandma's pantry"—it was obvious to most that a nuclear attack would present problems far beyond the resources of poor grandma's pantry. While child welfare and home protectionism were still the dominant concerns of women during this era, women had to ask themselves to what degree *could* they assure the welfare of their children or the protection of their homes in an age of nuclear weapons. The women's magazines of this era, as well as the public statements of both prominent and ordinary women, clearly reflect these concerns.

There was also a great deal of discussion over the impact of civil defense preparations on the psychological health of children. Were civil defense publications, films, and especially drills instilling in children the confidence that they could deal with an emergency, or were they frightening them needlessly? Children may have found civil defense creations such as Bert the Turtle both funny and accessible, but they also understood that a very grim, frightening specter lurked behind Bert's friendly banter. Whether fallout shelters would make students feel more secure or less secure was also an open question. Was it better to supply a ray of hope that a child might survive a nuclear emergency, or honestly inform the child that his or her chances of surviving a nuclear war were slim? These are considerations that were also relevant to adults, but questions generated by the shelter issue were seemingly resistant to definitive answers. Instead they had a tendency to drift toward the enigmatic, slipping beyond the grasp of laypersons and experts alike and into the realm of the metaphysical.

CHAPTER 5

The Theory and Practice of Armageddon

Just as the debate over fallout shelters seemed to create endless conflicts in the political and social realms, so too did it engender friction in the scientific community. Indeed, a lack of consensus among experts on even the most basic premises was one of the hallmarks of the fallout shelter controversy. The issues were extremely technical, hard data were frequently lacking, and the conclusions to be drawn highly speculative. Since an all-out nuclear war obviously had no precedent, the consequences of a nuclear exchange between the Soviet Union and the United States were in many ways imponderable (although that did not stop people from pondering them).

It was one of the cold comforts of the thermonuclear era that the Soviets seemed as bewildered as the Americans. The Soviets were making their own preparations for surviving a nuclear war, but the ramifications of such a war were perhaps even more disturbing to Soviet ideologues than they were to Western theorists. As early as 1954, Soviet premier Georgi Malenkov called for a reduction of tension with Western powers as the only alternative to "preparing for a new world war." Such a war, said Malenkov, "given modern weapons, would mean the destruction of world civilization."[1] Also in 1954 Vyacheslav Malyshev, head of the Soviet atomic ministry, and a number of important Soviet atomic scientists sent a letter to Central Committee members calling attention to the "limitless potential for increasing the explosive power of the [atomic] Bomb, which makes defense from this weapon virtually impossible." Malyshev further warned that "the use of atomic arms on a massive scale will lead to the devastation of combatant countries."[2] Such statements were problematic in the context of Marxist-Leninist ideology and, in the words of Vladislav Zubok and Constantine Pleshakov, represented "a startling blow" to the claim that "any war would lead to a crisis in the capitalist world and to the expansion of socialism."[3] Indeed, Khrushchev called Malenkov's warnings "theoretically mistaken and politically harmful" because they encouraged "feelings of hopelessness about the efforts of the peoples to frustrate the plans of the aggressors." Soviet foreign minister Vyacheslav Molotov declared that "a communist should not speak about the 'destruction of world civilization,' but about the need to prepare and mobilize . . . for the destruction of the bourgeoisie."[4] The Soviet leadership suppressed Malyshev's letter and Malenkov's political career suffered as a result of his views. By January 1955 Malenkov had lost his position as prime minister, and by 1957 he had been expelled from the Party and forced into exile.[5]

There was also a debate between the military and civilian leadership in the Soviet Union on the viability of nuclear war as an element of strategy in its competition with the West. By 1962 the awesome destructive potential of nuclear war had become so obvious that the idea of using it as a state instrument of policy was enough to give pause to even the most ardent promoters of Soviet-style socialism. In his doctoral dissertation, "Soviet Attitudes towards Nuclear War Survival (1962–1977)," Robert Lee Arnett concluded that while the military leadership was more likely to defend the use of nuclear war than the civilian leadership, neither had "illusions about the possibility of obtaining a meaningful victory or of avoiding unacceptable damage in a nuclear war."[6] Soviet defense minister Rodion Malinovsky predicted in 1961 that a nuclear war would "lead to the deaths of hundreds of millions of people, and whole countries will be turned into lifeless deserts covered with ashes."[7] Khrushchev described nuclear war as a "catastrophe" that would "spare neither right, nor left, neither those who champion the cause of peace nor those who want to stay aloof," and a commentator for *Izvestiya* claimed that nuclear war was "a direct road to the same heavenly kingdom which is praised by everyone but where no one wants to go."[8] Retired General-Major Nikolay Talensky observed in 1962 that "a modern war could clearly be so devastating that it cannot and must not serve as an instrument of politics."[9] But the idea that there would be no victors in a nuclear war was disturbing to other Soviet military men because they believed it would contribute to the same fatalism that seemed to be plaguing the United States. Lieutenant-Colonel Ye. Rybkin claimed that the dismissal of the possibility of victory in nuclear war "leads to moral disarmament, to a disbelief in victory, to fatalism and passivity," while Lieutenant-Colonel N. Tabunov warned that such attitudes were "sowing seeds of pessimism among the fighting men."[10]

The very form this war might take, whether it would indeed be an "all-out" war against both civilian and military targets, or whether nuclear war might be limited to military "counterforce" targets, was one of the unknowables. This was a question with obvious relevance to the shelter issue because if Soviet attacks were aimed primarily at military installations, then a great number of Americans might survive in their fallout shelters. But if cities were also to be targeted, then the number of sheltered Americans who might expect to survive would be drastically reduced, and a national shelter system would amount to little more than a civil defense white elephant for which the taxpayers would pay dearly. In fact, Soviet targeting philosophy was unclear. While Khrushchev consistently emphasized that the Soviet Union could defeat its enemies by destroying their cities, some among the Soviet military seemed to lean toward a counterforce strategy. In a speech before the Communist Party congress in the fall of 1961, Soviet defense minister Rodion Malinovsky proclaimed that "the targets of crushing nuclear strikes, together with the groupings of enemy armed forces, will be industrial and vital centers, communications junctions, everything that feeds war."[11]

Counterforce

The counterforce idea, that nuclear war could be controlled if the belligerents restricted their strikes to the enemy's strategic military forces (its counterforce), and secondarily to industrial assets, was an element of the flexible response strategy installed by the Kennedy administration. But the suggestion that nuclear war and total annihilation were not necessarily convertible terms had already attracted considerable attention by the late 1950s. In *Nuclear Weapons and Foreign Policy* (1957), Henry Kissinger insisted that the United States should leave no doubt that communist aggression might be resisted by nuclear weapons, but that "we should make every effort to limit their effect and to spare the civilian population as much as possible." Kissinger suggested that the United States should announce to the Soviets that in the event of war, the United States would not use more than five hundred kilotons of explosives and that the bombs would be "clean," with "minimal fall-out effects." In addition, the United States would pledge not to attack Soviet forces or cities more than a certain distance behind a demarcated battle zone, and "would not use nuclear weapons against cities declared open and so verified by inspection." All of the above would be predicated on the enemy's own compliance with what Kissinger called "the understanding."[12] Expanding on his ideas on *Face the Nation*, Kissinger stated that "it is possible to fight a limited war even with nuclear weapons," and that "both sides will be looking for excuses to limit the war, and not to expand it."[13]

Several of the leading proponents of counterforce strategy were researchers for the RAND Corporation (an acronym for research and development). A think tank that was, and is, composed of top scientists and theorists, the RAND Corporation was established after World War II by high-ranking air force officers and others with an interest in national security issues. The mission of RAND, in the words of air force general Henry Arnold, was to "assist in avoiding future national peril and winning the next war."[14] While the RAND Corporation had a number of clients, most of its work was done for the air force, and most of that was secret. Headquartered in Santa Monica, RAND was described by one writer in 1959 as "a university without students—a university in which the whole faculty decided to come in on its day off. Men in garish sport shirts stroll casually about; nobody seems to hurry." Interestingly, the RAND Corporation's chairman of the board was H. Rowan Gaither, Jr., whose committee had produced the suppressed civil defense report that bore his name.[15]

One of the prominent RAND researchers was Bernard Brodie. Brodie had not always been a counterforce advocate, and in fact his thinking on nuclear issues evolved in an interesting way as the Cold War matured. Before he became associated with RAND, Brodie served as both editor and contributor to an influential collection of essays published in 1946 called *The Absolute Weapon: Atomic Power and World Order*. While others at this early date were pondering what significance this new weapon might have, Brodie did not hesitate to call the atomic bomb a "weapon of incalculable horror."[16] Brodie believed that for many years to come "the primary targets for the atomic bomb will be cities," and that such an attack would come on "a gigantic scale," with the attacker employing "hundreds of the bombs, more likely thousands of them" in order to reduce reprisals.[17] That effective shelters might be devised against such weapons was, according to Brodie, "more than dubious." Brodie argued that "the only way of safeguarding the lives of city dwellers is to evacuate them from their cities entirely in periods of crisis."[18] In this groundbreaking work Brodie also dismissed the notion that the United States would be able to retain a monopoly on atomic weapons, addressed the issue of military and government dispersal, and raised the possibility that "the bomb may act as a powerful deterrent to direct aggression against great powers."[19]

By the time he published *Strategy in the Missile Age* in 1959, Brodie's thinking on nuclear attack had shifted significantly, and he had abandoned a number of his previous positions, including the notion that any nuclear attack would be an "all-out" attack directed against cities, and that shelters against such an attack would be relatively worthless. Like other RAND researchers, Brodie was influenced by "game theory" and the supposition that geopolitical behavior proceeded according to rules of rational behavior and self-interest. Now Brodie argued that attacking the civilian population simply did not make sense militarily, and in fact the enemy could gain a greater military advantage by "burdening the opposing government with masses of dispossessed and panic-stricken citizens rather than in killing them." Indeed, Brodie advanced the idea that each side could agree to forgo attacks on enemy populations by reaching "written or unwritten understandings concerning reciprocity."[20] For "limited war" to have any meaning, observed Brodie, "strategic bombing of cities with nuclear weapons must be avoided."[21]

Brodie also believed that shelters could play a key role in restricting the scope of war. Acknowledging that the passions released after the start of even a "limited" nuclear war might make containment of that war difficult, Brodie contended that a sheltered civilian population could help facilitate sound political decisions in the face of such a war. For instance, if "the enemy hits us hard at our air and missile bases but takes care to minimize injury to our cities," angry decision makers might still be "insensitive to whatever discrimination he is practicing." But a sheltered population would make a more measured response possible.[22]

Another important work published in 1959 was Oskar Morgenstern's *The Question of National Defense*. A leading games theorist (he had coauthored the classic *Theory of Games and Economic Behavior*), Morgenstern was pessimistic about the future of the world. Like many observers of the day, Morgenstern had concluded that "the probability of a large thermonuclear war occurring appears to be significantly larger than the probability of its not occurring."[23] Morgenstern argued for the use of small-yield nuclear weapons as a way for the United States to compensate for its smaller conventional forces, and insisted that the use of such weapons would not necessarily escalate because of the "fundamental self-interest of the contestants."[24] Morgenstern described the notion that *any* atomic explosion would be a disaster as a piece of "unmitigated nonsense" that had been "nurtured by Communist propaganda."[25] Indeed, to accept a policy in which the United States renounced the "limited" use of nuclear weapons would mean the loss of the "free Western world to the Communist Moloch."[26]

With his belief in the probability of a major nuclear war, and in his promotion of the viability of limited nuclear war, it is not surprising that Morgenstern promoted a national shelter system. Morgenstern was highly critical of what he saw as the woeful state of civil defense in America. He condemned "absurd, ludicrous civil defense 'exercises'" and "sirens that no one hears or knows how to interpret," and called evacuation a "pathetic scheme" because of shrinking warning times.[27] Instead, the United States should build shelters for its population. Morgenstern acknowledged the difficulties inherent in such a massive undertaking. The demand for cement would be so huge that the U.S. highway building program would have to be curtailed, but Morgenstern argued that surely it was more important to protect the population "rather than have them careen around more swiftly in gaudy motorcars before their premature death by radiation."[28] There was also the difficulty and expense of constructing deep blast shelters in large urban centers. The problems here were so profound that Morgenstern did not believe that such shelters would ever be built ("whole cities will not go underground"); instead he thought that cities would have to depend on the "deterrent" that a largely suburban fallout shelter system would provide.[29] However, Morgenstern was skeptical that the value of such a system would be recognized, and concluded that "nothing decisive will be done."[30]

Bringing the idea of nuclear flexible response and counterforce to its fullest flower was RAND physicist Herman Kahn. Beginning with the publication of *On Thermonuclear War* in 1960, Kahn produced a series of works that examined deterrence, nuclear strategy, and the survivability of nuclear war, and created along the way a vocabulary to describe the forms that future nuclear conflicts might take. Kahn outlined five scenarios for nuclear attacks: (1) "countervalue," in which the attacker tries to inflict maximum damage on that which is most valuable to the defender—"usually people and property"; (2) "straight counterforce," an attack that concentrates on the defender's strategic forces (such as Strategic Air Command bases, missile installations, and Polaris submarines) in order to lessen the strength of the defender's retaliatory strikes; (3) "countervalue and counterforce," an attack on both strategic and nonstrategic targets; (4) "counterforce plus 'bonus,'" a concentration on the defender's strategic forces with some compromise in tactics "in order to obtain bonus damage to countervalue targets"; and (5) "counterforce plus 'avoidance,'" an attack that emphasizes strategic targets but that sacrifices military efficiency in some degree in order to avoid countervalue targets. The latter strategy might be adopted, according to Kahn, "either for moral reasons or because such targets may be more valuable to the attacker as hostages to be threatened."[31]

The relevance of these scenarios to civil defense was made clear in Kahn's 1962 work *Thinking about the Unthinkable*. Here Kahn concedes that a surprise nuclear attack against population centers "presents a virtually impossible problem of protecting those in target areas," but insists that this was "one of the least likely possibilities."[32] The most likely scenario, according to Kahn, would be a counterforce or a counterforce plus avoidance attack, enabling the attacker "to use the cities and the survivors as hostages to deter retaliation or to negotiate a favorable cease-fire."[33] For this reason, Kahn defended the Kennedy administration's fallout shelter program "as a relatively inexpensive form of insurance against a Soviet attack concentrated upon our strategic military force."[34]

It should be emphasized that counterforce targeting was predominantly an air force strategy, and was not necessarily embraced by the rest of the military establishment. General Lauris Norstad, U.S. commander of NATO forces, insisted that a limited war "would immediately mushroom, explode into a larger situation."[35] The navy also never endorsed the counterforce idea, in large part because the navy's strategic forces, chiefly the submarine-launched Polaris missiles that were put into service in 1959, were not effective counterforce weapons. Because of their smaller size, Polaris missiles carried smaller warheads that would not be capable of destroying hardened military sites. As the physicist Ralph Lapp observed in 1960, "Obviously, the thing that Polaris was going to hit in the Soviet Union was the cities. With a 1-megaton or less warhead, they cannot hit hardened targets, and this brings into focus now a really fundamental difference of deterrence."[36] Instead of counterforce, the navy emphasized what Admiral Arleigh Burke called "finite deterrence." Stressing the increasing vulnerability of SAC facilities and the potential for an endless arms race as each side hardened its land-based strategic forces while developing ever more powerful missiles that could destroy hardened sites, Burke advocated developing an invulnerable strategic force, such as the Polaris. This force could remain small and still meet the "objective of generous *adequacy for deterrence alone* (i.e., for an ability to destroy major urban areas, not by the false goal of adequacy for 'winning')."[37]

By 1961 the Kennedy administration had seemingly adopted the counterforce plus avoidance strategy that Kahn had described. In a draft memorandum to the president in September 1961, defense secretary Robert McNamara declared that the American strategic object should be "to strike back against Soviet bomber bases, missile sites, and other installations associated with long-range nuclear forces" while "holding in protected reserve forces capable of destroying the Soviet urban society, if necessary, in a controlled and deliberate way."[38] In a discussion of the defense arrangements for the NATO alliance in 1962, McNamara expanded on these comments, stating that the primary military objective "should be the destruction of the enemy's military forces, not of his civilian population." By adopting such a strategy, and by maintaining "sufficient reserve striking power to destroy an enemy society if driven to it," McNamara believed, "we are giving a possible opponent the strongest imaginable incentive to refrain from striking our own cities."[39]

The idea that military targets should have priority over civilian population centers was not a concept unique to counterforce theory. This had been the strategy of SAC since the 1950s, and as McGeorge Bundy observed, "The strategic targeting of SAC, from Eisenhower's time through Johnson's, was governed by the standards inherited by strategic air commanders from World War II. First came the destruction of enemy offensive strength, now primarily nuclear, and then the destruction of urban-industrial targets as well to ensure defeat." Bundy also notes that beginning with McNamara there was a "fully planned option not to attack targets in cities."[40] What *was* new about the counterforce idea in the early 1960s— and profoundly disturbing to its critics—was the notion that the worst excesses of nuclear war (namely, the killing of civilians on a massive scale) could be eliminated by fine-tuning.[41]

This idea, that careful strategic planning could keep nuclear war from getting out of control, would, according to critics, make the nuclear option more attractive and less "unthinkable." Harrison Brown and James

Real commented, "we are asked to consider that even all-out thermonuclear war is by no means unthinkable—provided it is not too all-out."[42] Counterforce strategy was predicated on rational behavior, but Gerard Piel insisted in an article for the *Bulletin of the Atomic Scientists* that it was unlikely that a real war would be conducted according to "the rational strategies of game theory." Instead, according to Piel, history suggested that even "rational" first exchanges proceeded on to "an unlimited escalation of violence."[43] Indeed, there was no shortage of counterforce critics, and to a great extent it was the fallout shelter debate that mobilized them.

The legislative assistant Arthur I. Waskow also rejected the counterforce assumption that nuclear war would be characterized by "intense self-control from both sides . . . based on a coldly rationalistic analysis of self-interest."[44] Waskow predicted that as communications collapsed under the onslaught of nuclear weapons, so too would control, and then "the counterforce war would degenerate into a completely disordered thermonuclear disaster."[45]

Waskow also expressed doubts that the civilian population could somehow be separated from the military population, and emphasized the enormous cost to the nation—monetarily, politically, and psychologically—of creating a shelter system to protect the civilian population. Waskow claimed that "present choices for missile sites actually unite rather than separate American atomic forces from American populations."[46] The alternative to in-place city shelters—the evacuation of urban populations to rural shelters—also presented problems. First there was the daunting logistical nightmare of uprooting and moving large numbers of people, and the fact that such an evacuation might be interpreted by the enemy as a provocative act. The problems did not end even after the population had been placed in shelters. The luxury of a long stay was not an option for most of the population (a two-week stay was the typical length suggested by civil defense officials), after which the food and water would be gone and shelter occupants would have to move aboveground. Should an enemy wish to destroy this population, it would need only to reserve a certain number of weapons to be fired at the end of two weeks. Thus, according to Waskow, "a difficult and expensive program of civil defense" as an element of counterforce strategy could be nullified by "relatively easy and inexpensive actions on the part of the enemy."[47]

To avoid the problems inherent in evacuating a city, planners could build urban shelters with blast and thermal protection, but the expense would be considerable, amounting to "several hundred billion dollars," according to Waskow.[48] Here, at least, the anti-shelterist Waskow and the shelterist Herman Kahn were in agreement. (In *On Thermonuclear War*, Kahn estimated that "an adequate civil defense program" would cost $200 billion.)[49] Finally, Waskow worried about the "social orientation" aspect of shelters, that Americans might become accustomed "to the notion of cowering in shelters."[50] The civil defense dilemma, as Waskow saw it, was this: A "half-hearted" effort would leave American cities unprotected, while "an effective civil defense would result in an authoritarian state."[51]

One of the most interesting critiques of the game theory rationale employed by Kahn, Brodie, and others was made by Thomas C. Schelling, a Harvard professor of economics who himself had done research at the RAND Corporation. In *The Strategy of Conflict* (1963), Schelling attempts to restore the "irrational" as a component of strategy. In Schelling's formulation, "the threat that leaves something to chance" was an effective deterrent because it held out the possibility that "we might *not* act according to the dictates of reason, that we might in fact act irrationally." What Schelling appeared to have in mind was a Dulles-style "brinkmanship," in which the enemy is deterred from aggressive actions by the idea that the United States might "slip over the brink whether we want to or not, carrying him with us."[52] Schelling also parted with RAND theorists on the limited use of nuclear weapons, arguing that "what makes atomic weapons different is a powerful tradition that they *are* different," and that it would be extremely difficult to "limit" a war once such weapons were introduced.[53]

A fact of life that haunted advocates of a national shelter program (and which made counterforce theory so appealing to this group) was the vulnerability of American urban areas to nuclear attack—Herman Kahn's "virtually impossible problem." Shelter promoters understood that in order to get any shelter program at all, they would have to settle for something in the relatively modest $20 to $30 billion range. To accomplish even as much as this would be a political struggle, and there was certainly not the support for a program in the $200 billion range that would supply blast and thermal protection for urban dwellers.[54]

Even if prohibitively expensive urban shelters were built, there was no guarantee that such shelters would be able to protect a city population against nuclear weapons. First was the obvious problem of urban residents getting to their shelters in time. Ellis A. Johnson, a research scientist at Johns Hopkins, testified in 1958 that only a "marginal" case could be made for building expensive urban shelters not because they would fail to do the job, but "because we won't be able to get a big fraction of the population into them in time." Using New York as an example, Johnson noted that some 1.5 million people in that city lived or worked above the sixth floor, which would greatly increase evacuation time. Also, if New York or any other coastal city were attacked by submarine-launched missiles, warning time would be reduced to three to ten minutes.[55] A further complication faced by coastal cities under attack would be flooding, not only because of the destruction of man-made water barriers, but also because nuclear weapons might be detonated offshore with the intention of swamping cities with tidal waves and radioactive sodium.[56] While the OCD argued that only 28 percent of the American population lived in cities with populations over 100,000, critics countered that if the criterion used was metropolitan area rather than city limits, some 60 to 75 percent of the population would be subjected to the blast and thermal effects from an urban nuclear attack.[57] As Ralph Lapp lamented, "The sad fact is that there isn't much that can be done for the vulnerable central cores of our cities."[58]

Thus, because of its expense and questionable viability, an effective urban shelter program was a political nonstarter. Instead, the program that eventually was created carried with it, according to one observer, "the built-in notice to millions of city dwellers that they are expendable."[59] Oskar Morgenstern claimed that if policy makers built only suburban fallout shelters without urban blast protection, "people living in the large cities will know that they are to be sacrificed in case of large-scale war. . . . This would cause social stratification, privileges and advantages, which cut across all existing ones."[60] That nuclear survival was enhanced by residency in the suburbs was noted by others, including John Kenneth Galbraith. In a letter to Kennedy, Galbraith called the suburban bias of the fallout shelter program "a design for saving Republicans and sacrificing Democrats."[61]

Nuclear War and Civil Defense in the Soviet Union

The extent of the Soviet Union's civil defense program was the subject of considerable speculation, and because of the secrecy of the Soviet state, there was little in the way of reliable information. There was much discussion on whether the Soviets could employ the Moscow subway system as a shelter, and indeed, the Soviets had raised this possibility when construction of the metro was being planned during the 1930s. The manager of metro construction was none other than Nikita Khrushchev, who success-

Fig. 34. Soviet slide presentation on civil defense, 1973. "Nuclear Weapon: This is the most effective means of mass destruction: it has the capacity to cause tremendous destruction, fires, and widespread devastation to people, animals, and plants." Translation by Kate Transchel. RG 397-RS 1-14, Still Pictures Branch (NNSP), National Archives at College Park, MD.

fully argued before Stalin that the added expense of a deeper tunnel was worth the price because of its utility as a possible shelter. The first stage of the subway was completed in 1935, and during World War II the tunnels were indeed used as bomb shelters.[62] Civil defense, of course, would become more problematic for the Soviets and everyone else with the advent of nuclear weaponry.

In 1962 Leon Gouré published *Civil Defense in the Soviet Union*, the most complete work written on the subject. Gouré, a RAND researcher, concluded that over a ten-year period the Soviets had been "engaged in an extensive and expanding civil defense program, which has already resulted in a significant capability."[63] Training in civil defense, which by 1960 consisted of an eighteen-hour course, was theoretically mandatory for the entire Soviet population (figs. 34 and 35). Gouré estimated that somewhere between 50 and 100 million citizens of the Soviet Union had received civil defense training by 1962.[64] There was no public-versus-private shelter debate in the Soviet Union. Virtually all shelters were public, either

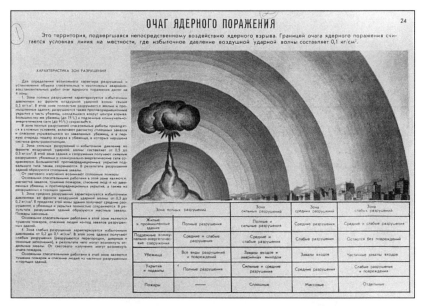

FIG. 35. Soviet slide presentation on civil defense, 1973. "Zone of Nuclear Destruction: This territory is likely to experience the immediate effects of a nuclear explosion. The zone of destruction is calculated to be an area where the air pressure of the shock waves constitute .01 kg/cm². " Translation by Kate Transchel. RG 397-RS 1-23, Still Pictures Branch (NNSP), National Archives at College Park, MD.

built into the basements of apartment buildings or utilizing the large sub-way tunnels in cities such as Moscow and Kiev.[65]

How seriously the Soviet citizen took civil defense is another matter. Gouré recounts one Soviet newspaper article that referred to "an insignif-icant part of the population" that had not "overcome the backward atti-tude that there is supposedly no escape from the atom bomb, and that al-legedly there is therefore no point in studying in civil defense circles." There were other reports that some Soviet citizens came to meetings and then left after attendance was taken, while others at the meetings wore "bored expressions and sat close to the exit."[66] Even some leaders were skeptical that shelters could provide any real protection. The Soviet Union's minister of defense, Marshal Rodion Malinovsky, was blunt in his declaration that "shelters against atomic and hydrogen bombs are nothing but coffins and tombs prepared in advance. There is no bunker, not even hermetically sealed, where one could sit quietly through explosions of atomic and hydrogen bombs."[67] Others believed that there was a great deal of hyperbole in the many reports concerning the Soviet shelter system. Commenting on the congressional testimony of a RAND witness who suggested that Moscow subways could shelter two million people, J. David Singer noted that if such a number crowded into these subways there would be an average of 3.75 square feet of floor space per capita. "Apparently," marveled Singer, "the sturdy Muscovites are capable of standing (sitting would require six square feet) in the same position, motionless, for two weeks or so, while engaging in all of those basic processes essential to human survival!" Singer concluded that "most of the evidence suggests that Soviet civil defense efforts have been little more successful than those of the U.S. in getting shelter and evacuation programs off the ground."[68]

While Soviet newspapers derided American "moles" who were digging fallout shelters, and while Nina Khrushchev was assuring American peace marchers that no shelters were being built in the Soviet Union, the Soviets began quietly planning the construction of what may be the most elaborate shelter ever built.[69] Secretly constructed under the Moscow suburb of Ramenki and completed in the early 1970s, this facility was capable of sheltering thirty thousand Russian elites for several months. The Ramenki complex was served by an underground railroad and was maintained by a section of the KGB known as Directorate 15. The original Ramenki complex had movie theaters and a swimming pool that were designed, as the journalist Carey Scott put it, "to keep the politburo amused as the rest of the population was being irradiated above them."[70]

The Sheltered Life

If having a fallout shelter to go to was one issue, surviving the ordeal of being cooped up in such a shelter was another. To determine how people might react to life in a fallout shelter, researchers conducted numerous studies during the 1960s. In 1963 a Houston family of four, consisting of two adults and two grown boys, volunteered to spend two weeks in an eight-by-ten-foot fallout shelter (similar to the one shown in fig. 36). This family was given a battery of psychological tests before and after its confinement, and each member was charged with keeping a diary during the two weeks. Family members combated boredom by eating frequently, and during the early stage of the test they often slept for up to sixteen hours at a stretch.[71] With the lights turned out, a total darkness prevailed in the

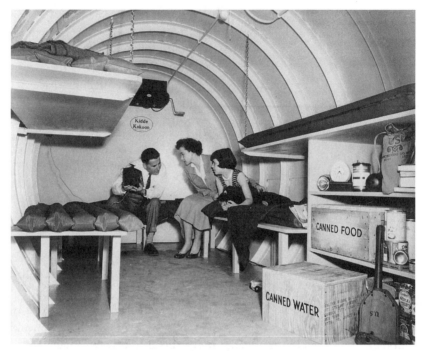

Fig. 36. An idea of the cramped confines of many shelters can be seen in this example, installed in Garden City, Long Island, 1955. Library of Congress, Prints and Photographs Division, LC-US262-89684.

shelter. The mother especially found this to be disturbing, and described this condition as "blindness . . . as though the outside world had stopped and we were like Pharaohs in a tomb."[72] Crises inside the shelter included the threat of the younger son to leave the shelter on day three, and a fight between the two brothers on day nine.[73] The family emerged from the shelter in a mood characterized by researchers as "a depressive bleakness and a diminution of vitality." Tests also revealed spatial disorientation among family members, and in the weeks following his stay in the shelter the father was involved in two automobile accidents.[74]

Among the most thorough of the fallout shelter tests were the twelve studies conducted under the auspices of the Civil Defense Research Staff at the University of Georgia between 1962 and 1967. Participants in these studies included men, women, and children ranging in age from six months to seventy-nine years, and group sizes from thirty to a thousand persons.[75] Researchers found that sometime during the two weeks of their time in a shelter, group members arrived at a crisis. This crisis was usually brought about by a participant who refused to accommodate himself or herself to the group consensus. Indeed, the "ability to move from a position of self-orientation to one of group-orientation" was cited by those studying the data as a "key to withstanding confinement." Persons unable to acquire this group orientation usually left the study during the first week. Of course there would be no early exit from the shelter during an actual nuclear attack, and recalcitrant individuals during such an attack "would likely require the special attention of the Shelter Manager and others in the group." Adding to the stress of confinement during a real emergency would be "anxiety about one's post-attack survival" as well as worries about one's friends and families.[76] In fact, as one article noted, "only under the most fortuitous circumstances would an entire urban family be expected to be in the shelter together" during an attack.[77]

Most participants in shelter tests experienced both physical and mental discomforts during their stays in fallout shelters. Because caloric intake was often reduced to approximate conditions of an actual attack, many lost weight. By 1960 General Mills had created a processed food cracker that, taken in conjunction with daily vitamin C tablets, was supposed to see an individual through two weeks in a fallout shelter. Civil defense director Leo Hoegh described it as "palatable . . . a cross between good Iowa corn and soybeans." Losing weight was no problem with such a cuisine. Hoegh cites a case in which a man "went in with a flabby 213 pounds and came out a very healthy specimen at 198 pounds 2 weeks later."[78] Participants complained of stuffiness (in one navy study, scientists "were surprised at how quickly the men's body heat raised the temperature from a chilly 50 degrees to an uncomfortable 83"), while others took note of the deleterious effect of foul odors on the health of shelter occupants.[79] Such odors could include cigarette smoke. *Science News Letter* observed that shelter occupants could greatly benefit from "smokeless atmospheric conditions," but cautioned that during nonsmoking tests aboard the nuclear submarine U.S.S. *Triton*, "deprived smokers showed overt feelings of hostility and irritability."[80] In another navy study using volunteer servicemen at a Bethesda shelter, the navy wisely did not underestimate the savage potential of a deprived smoker. This time planners allowed the participants all the cigarettes they wanted "to avoid enmity over a dwindling supply." While these men were generally able to "squelch unsociable feelings," they were able to do so in part because they had a seventy-two-hour liberty to look forward to at the end of the experiment. As *Time* magazine noted, this was a "considerably different prospect than emerging into an atomic wasteland."[81]

It was the unknowable psychological impact of an actual nuclear war that could never be replicated in shelter tests. As Otto Friedrich observed, "Whether the people jammed into such pestilential places for days on end would help each other or attack each other is impossible to predict." It depended, said Friedrich, "on whether Rousseau's view of life was truer than that of Hobbes, on whether men are animals."[82] The Harvard psychiatrist Lester Grinspoon postulated that once those who had survived a real nuclear war realized that "they had been reduced to a primitive, chaotic way of life for an indefinite period of time," there would be many who "would be unable to cope."[83]

Hardening

The proposed fallout shelter system became further entangled in military strategy as the air force proceeded to "harden" its ICBM installations. By the early 1960s Atlas and Titan sites were being hardened with concrete and steel to make them less vulnerable to attack. In congressional testimony in 1960 Curtis LeMay, now air force vice chief of staff, claimed that while it would take the enemy two missiles to knock out a conventional ICBM site, the enemy would have to expend "between 10 and 30 [missiles] for one of our hardened sites." LeMay insisted that the location of these future hardened installations would be in "the less densely populated part of the United States," and that hardened sites in a nuclear war would "serve to reduce the total casualties" in the United States because they would draw away enemy ICBMs from population centers.[84]

Chet Holifield was dubious that the proposed hardened sites *were* situated to maximize protection for the civilian population. At the same hearings at which LeMay testified, Holifield displayed a map showing nine hardened Atlas missile bases and five hardened Titan missile bases, all of which were located in what Holifield called the "breadbasket of America," Nebraska, Kansas, and Iowa. These sites would be subject to intense concentrations of radioactivity because the enemy would have to expend "many times more megatonnage" on such hard targets than on a soft base. The result, according to Holifield, would be "the contamination of soil and food supplies" as well as contaminated surpluses in grain silos.[85] When questioning LeMay, Holifield pressed the point that some hardened sites were "upwind from cities, such as Kansas City and Omaha, to mention two, rather than downwind." LeMay replied, "You are upwind and downwind from some place wherever you go."[86]

Holifield continued to press this point at the hearings, and in his introduction to Admiral Arleigh Burke, chief of naval operations, Holifield expressed concerns "over the civil defense implications of hardened bases." "A concentrated enemy assault against those bases," said Holifield, "would subject possibly our entire population and much of our food resources to the deadly effects of radioactive fallout."[87] Holifield had a sympathetic witness in Burke, who declared, "hardening is not practical as a means of protecting air bases," and that with improvements in missile accuracy and "with presently feasible missile yields, the benefits of hardening are degraded." Burke believed that a better solution was mobile land-based missiles and, not surprisingly, sea-launched missiles from navy Polaris submarines.[88]

Gerard Piel maintained that if the enemy did indeed adopt the counterforce strategy that theorists claimed was the most logical, it would have to expend a huge weight of nuclear weapons to destroy hardened military targets. (Piel cited one study showing that nuclear weapons totaling three hundred megatons would have to strike within a few minutes of each other in order to eliminate the eighteen hardened Titan missile bases ringing Tucson, Arizona.) Other communities with missile installations, such as Wichita and Salina, Kansas; Lincoln, Nebraska; Plattsburgh, New York; Abilene, Texas, and others, would receive similarly heavy groundbursts. The consequence, according to Piel, was that "nearby communities would come under fallout of intensities far above those against which the do-it-yourself basement shelter, supplied for two weeks of refuge, could afford protection."[89]

Roger Hagan also maintained that the "insurance" that fallout shelters would supposedly provide would prove to be of little value even for small communities with no military assets if those communities lay within sixty miles of a counterforce target. Hagan made his point by observing that if a single base—Beale Air Force Base in northern California—were hit with such an attack,

> the citizens of not just Marysville but also of Yuba City, Olivehurst, Wheatland, Grass Valley, Nevada City, Emigrant Gap, Auburn, Placerville, Folsom, Roseville, Newcastle, Lincoln, Elk Grove, Ione, Davis, Dixon, Woodland, Esparto, Arbuckle, Colusa, Maxwell, Princeton, Willows,

Williams, Knights Lodge, Butte City, Durham, Chico, Paradise, Feather Falls, La Porte, Downieville, Alleghany, Biggs, Gridley, and even Mr. Nixon's new frontier, Sacramento, will have cause to wonder just what "insurance" involves.[90]

Ralph Lapp was both skeptical of the value of hardening missile sites and disturbed that the location of such sites near the population centers of the northeastern United States seemed to reflect "a lack of coordination, if not of sanity, in national security planning."[91] Lapp was especially concerned that an Atlas base was to be located in Plattsburgh, New York—"very close to very dense population."[92] LeMay had once referred to the building of fallout shelters as a "Maginot Line," and Lapp returned the favor, noting that with Soviet ICBMs soon capable of hitting their targets within the radius of a mile—a virtual direct hit in nuclear weapons terms—"the hardened Atlas-Titan complex assumes a Maginot character." To underscore his point, Lapp called hardened missile sites "Maginot magnets."[93]

Ironically, while LeMay was hardening SAC missile installations to protect them from enemy missile attack, he had taken no steps to provide shelter protection for the dependents and nonoperational personnel at these bases. Instead, SAC planned to evacuate these persons to sites without any fallout protection. Since evacuation had already been thoroughly discredited by 1960 (especially evacuation to areas without fallout protection), an appalled Chet Holifield asked LeMay the following questions:

MR. HOLIFIELD: General, may I ask you if there have been any steps taken at any of your missile sites to provide shelter protection for nonoperational personnel and civilian dependents at these bases?

GENERAL LEMAY: No.

MR. HOLIFIELD: There has been no program to place them in underground shelters? They are considered as expendable as the rest of the population?

GENERAL LEMAY: I wouldn't put it that bluntly; no.[94]

Like Holifield, Ralph Lapp also expressed shock at SAC's evacuation policy, and found it "paradoxical" that SAC would move personnel away from the base to areas that would be exposed to fallout. "That policy of evacuation in time of attack," said Lapp, "seems to me to be playing tag with fallout, which is playing tag with death."[95]

Firestorm

While military strategists argued about counterforce theory, physicists debated the thermal effects of nuclear weapons. Whether or not nuclear weapons would start massive firestorms—and in the process render all but the most elaborate shelters worthless—was one of the key areas of contention. The phenomenon of the firestorm was first seen in a week-long incendiary bombing raid on Hamburg in July 1943, an operation that Arthur Harris, commander of the Royal Air Force Bomber Command, code named "Gomorrah." How firestorms are created is poorly understood, and the physicist Freeman Dyson, who served with the RAF Bomber Command during the war, noted that while "in every big raid we tried to raise a fire storm," they had failed until the Hamburg raid. The Hamburg firestorm may have been what Dyson called a "technological accident," but the phenomenon itself resembled a force of nature.[96]

Bomb blasts at Hamburg created low pressure areas into which the surrounding air rushed. The wind reached speeds of 150 miles per hour, fanning fires that reached temperatures of 1400°F.[97] German officials called what happened at Hamburg a "fire typhoon such as was never before witnessed." Feeding the fire were severed gas lines and the coal and coke that homeowners had stored inside their homes. The storm burned with such violence and the suction was so strong that trees were pulled up by their roots.[98] Conventional shelters provided no protection from this catastrophe, and many of those who took to their shelters during the Hamburg raid died from heat stroke, dehydration, and carbon monoxide poisoning as the storm sucked all oxygen out of the air. Michael Sherry notes that when fires burst through shelters they melted people into "a thick, greasy black mass," or "left behind what the Germans called *Bombenbrand-schrumpfleichen* (incendiary-bomb-shrunken bodies)."[99] Days after the raid, some Hamburg shelters were still so hot that when they were opened the sudden infusion of oxygen caused them to burst into flame.[100]

Would nuclear weapons replicate or even exceed what had happened at Hamburg?[101] The viability of the fallout shelter program depended on the answer, because if nuclear blasts created firestorms only rarely and within a limited radius, then fallout shelters on the periphery of target areas would provide significant protection for those within. But if the side effects of a nuclear attack included huge firestorms spreading out in a wide radius from the center of the blast, then ordinary fallout shelters would serve as little more than burial vaults for those inside. The only applied use of nuclear weapons—at Hiroshima and Nagasaki—had shed little light on the issue. There was no firestorm at Nagasaki. At Hiroshima, the relatively small nuclear weapon (rated at about fifteen kilotons, or the energy released by fifteen thousand tons of TNT) did create a firestorm, but as the physicist Eugene Wigner observed, this firestorm was limited to a radius of two-thirds of a mile from the center of the explosion.[102]

By the time of the fallout shelter debate, nuclear weapons in the *megaton* range were common (a megaton is rated as the energy released by one *million* tons of TNT), and scientists opposed to fallout shelters argued that this quantum leap in destructive power would greatly enhance the possibility of firestorms.[103] Some scientists, in fact, contended that as bombs increased in power, the incendiary radius increased at a faster rate than the blast radius. In 1962 Gerard Piel published "The Illusion of Civil Defense" (a title that made his own views on fallout shelters obvious). Piel claimed that a twenty-megaton bomb had a blast radius of ten miles and an incendiary radius of thirty miles. In the case of the fifty-megaton monster that the Soviets tested in late October 1961 (this was the largest nuclear device ever tested), Piel estimated that it would have a thirteen-mile blast radius but a fifty-mile incendiary radius. "The conclusion to be drawn," said Piel, "is that the bigger the weapon is, the more preponderantly it becomes an incendiary weapon." A twenty-megaton burst, according to Piel, would "produce a gigantic single fire, a conflagration so huge that it must be reckoned as a meteorological event—a firestorm." Blast would destroy the city center, but "the firestorm would incinerate the metropolitan area."[104] *Consumer Reports* also claimed that Americans would have more to fear from fire than fallout in a nuclear attack, and that thermal protection was expensive and "beyond the purchasing power of the great majority of U.S. families."[105]

As might be expected, advocates of fallout shelters ridiculed the massive firestorm model. Herman Kahn claimed that of all the objections offered to the administration's civil defense program, "none has given rise to more palpable nonsense than the question of firestorm." Kahn believed that predictions of "metropolitan area-wide firestorms are in all probability wrong," and that firestorms would be restricted to "heavily built up downtown areas and especially dense forests."[106] W. E. Strope, head of the Military Evaluations Group, claimed that firestorms would occur only in areas where the roof to ground area exceeded 20 percent (20 percent of an area under roof), and where such a concentration exceeded a square mile.[107]

Eugene Wigner also had his doubts. Wigner observed that the ability of nuclear weapons to start fires depended on both the quantity of combustible material and the "transparency of the atmosphere." "Smoke and fog," according to Wigner, "decrease the fire hazard by interfering with the propagation of the heat pulse." Wigner acknowledged the fear that fires "may coalesce and convert the community to an inferno," but referred to experiments under simulated conditions that "appear to show that isolated fires do not coalesce."[108] Edward Teller was one of those who advocated a national shelter system (he once referred to "this little, gentle contribution of civilian defense"), but he also cautioned that larger nuclear weapons would make for "greater damage from the firestorm," and advocated outfitting urban shelters with "heat insulation and sufficient air supply."[109]

Despite the lack of hard data on this phenomenon, the firestorm scenario was nearly irresistible to opponents of civil defense. Unmistakably, there was something primordial and savage, even biblical, in the image of a roiling wall of flame devastating everything in its path. The firestorm stimulated the apocalyptic imagination. Bentley Glass, for instance, believed it possible that a single ten-megaton bomb "could spread searing heat over 5000 square miles, which is about the area of the state of Connecticut."[110] In an era in which the fifty-megaton bomb was the largest ever exploded, a student group that marched on Washington in 1962 claimed that a hundred-megaton bomb could "start simultaneous fires over sixteen thousand square miles, an area larger than the state of Vermont."[111] Escalating the firestorm race to even more impressive proportions, Gerard Piel speculated that one of the effects of a thousand-megaton bomb "exploded at satellite altitude" could be to "set six of America's western states afire."[112]

Doctors

Among the scientific community, no profession more clearly illustrated the shifting attitudes toward civil defense and nuclear war than American physicians. As Paul Boyer has noted, in the early years after Hiroshima, doctors expressed confidence that with proper preparation and training they would be able to cope with a nuclear emergency. Doctors participated in FCDA-sponsored courses on the medical aspects of atomic attack, and at medical gatherings listened to speakers who insisted that an effective civil defense could make a difference. Morton D. Willcutts of the Naval Medical Center told doctors in 1950 that misleading reports had "excited too much respect and fear of the radiation hazards in the wake of an atomic explosion," and that "there is a defense. We do not need to hide or to become frightened out of our wits into hysteria."[113] As in the case of school professionals, doctors were told that one of their most important tasks would be to exude a calmness and competence that would soothe public fears. Dr. Harold C. Lueth claimed that the medical profession must "reassure the population that steps can be taken to minimize the effect of the atomic bomb."[114]

For much of the decade after Hiroshima doctors followed the party line promulgated by the Atomic Energy Commission (AEC) and its chairman, Lewis Strauss. The AEC insisted that nuclear tests did not pose a health risk, and in a 1953 report claimed that "the radioactivity released by fall-out has proved not to be hazardous." When a nuclear researcher at the University of Utah discovered in the same year that his children had absorbed as much radiation from the air as he had in eighteen years of nuclear research, the AEC's John Bugher replied that "atomic tests are conducted in the interests of national welfare, a circumstance which certainly warrants deviation from normal laboratory practices."[115] Strauss took the same line, first claiming that the health hazards of radiation had been "greatly exaggerated," then observing, "in any event, it is a calculated risk that we must take in order that our freedom may be preserved."[116] In a 1955 *U.S. News* article, Strauss played down the radioactive fallout produced by the 1954 Bravo test, and claimed that taking shelter "in an old-fashioned cyclone cellar" after a nuclear attack would reduce radiation "to a level completely safe, in even the most heavily contaminated area." Strauss further claimed that the radiation received by Americans from all nuclear testing was "about the same as the exposure received from one chest X ray."[117]

U.S. News proved to be extremely obliging to the AEC. A month after it printed Strauss's piece it published an article in response to what it called "scare stories of the most sensational type" concerning radioactive fallout. As the editor put it, "To get the facts of what really is going on, *U.S. News & World Report* went to official sources."[118] In other words, the AEC. *U.S. News* disputed Linus Pauling's claim that the increasing number of nuclear materials in the atmosphere might lead to genetic abnormalities and cause harmful mutations, and the magazine even cited a study in which fruit flies raised in a radioactive environment produced "a race of fruit flies with more vigor, hardiness, resistance to disease, [and] better reproductive capacity."[119] Arguing that "an H-bomb explosion could be conducted every week for an indefinite period without raising the level of this substance to dangerous heights," *U.S. News* concluded that there was no evidence that radiation from tests posed any threat to Americans.[120]

But as the decade of the 1950s wore on, physicians as well as the general public became increasingly disturbed by indications that radioactivity *did* pose a threat. There was mounting evidence of an accumulation of radioactive particles in the environment, and physicians were becoming progressively less willing to accept the AEC's benign assurances. The destructive power of nuclear weapons had also grown exponentially in a little over a decade, and many physicians now began to express doubts about the efficacy of civil defense and about the medical community's ability to do anything about the disaster of a nuclear war. In 1959 Walter Schneir, editor of a doctors' news magazine called *MD*, published an article in the *Nation* describing the alarming increase in the presence of strontium-90 in the bones of schoolchildren. Schneir stated flatly that "people throughout the world will suffer death and illness from the nuclear tests conducted to date—and the effects of these tests will still be felt by mankind 10,000 years from now."[121]

By 1961, doctors concerned with the growing threat of nuclear weapons had formed Physicians for Social Responsibility. The group's statement of purpose makes clear its views on a fallout shelter program ("a vast and scientifically unsupportable gamble with human life") and suggests that physicians explore "a new area of preventive medicine, the prevention of thermonuclear war."[122] The following year this group put together a series of articles on doctors and nuclear war that was published in the *New England Journal of Medicine*, and in 1963 these articles were collected and published in book form under the title *The Fallen Sky*. Overwhelmingly these articles emphasize the medical catastrophe that would be the result of nuclear war, and the powerlessness of medical professionals to deal with such an event. A persistent subtheme in these articles is the worthlessness of the fallout shelter program being promoted in Washington.

The Fallen Sky's leadoff article, "Human and Ecologic Effects in Massachusetts of an Assumed Thermonuclear Attack on the United States," is based on the 1959 Holifield committee's estimate of a "limited" attack on the United States totaling 1,446 megatons, with a 20-megaton attack on the city of Boston.[123] Throughout this article, the authors emphasize the relative futility of fallout shelters, claiming that Boston would be engulfed by a firestorm sixteen miles in radius, and that "huddling in a home shelter, particularly one without a self-contained air supply, might well be fatal if a fire storm developed overhead."[124] Beyond the range of blast and thermal damage (deaths from these effects in the Boston area were estimated at about 2,240,000), there was the danger of fallout. Even here, those staying in fallout shelters for the recommended two weeks might survive, but they would still be faced with "long-term genetic and somatic effects."[125] As Hudson Hoagland, president of the American Academy of Arts and Sciences, put it in a separate paper, "for the first time we have a weapon to smash up our genetic material."[126]

What part would the physician play after a nuclear attack? In "The Physician's Role in the Postattack Period," Victor W. Sidel et al. also used the Holifield committee's figures, and concluded that there would be about a thousand acutely injured persons for every one surviving physician after a nuclear attack on Boston. This would mean that it would take sixteen days for a doctor to see every patient if the doctor worked a sixteen-hour day and saw each patient for only fifteen minutes.[127] Ironically, if the physicians of Boston took shelter prior to the attack, the patient-to-physician ratio would be even worse in the immediate post-attack period. Doctors would be expected to stay in their shelters for at least two weeks because any physician leaving his shelter for longer than a few hours in the immediate aftermath of an attack "may himself suffer radiation injury."[128]

Once on the scene the doctor would immediately have grim ethical decisions to make. First, there would be a shortage of hospital beds, and about half of the available beds would be in psychiatric hospitals. To accommodate attack victims, doctors would have to displace occupants of psychiatric beds, and as Sidel et al. observe, "there is no medical or scientific basis for reaching a decision about whether a patient with schizophrenia or the victim of a third-degree burn 'deserves' or should be assigned an available bed."[129] In addition, patients with nearly fatal injuries would have to be neglected so that doctors could concentrate on more "salvageable" patients, a scenario that "would represent a profound and difficult reversal in the attitudes and performance of the physician."[130] Other ethical questions raised by Sidel et al. include

Does the physician remain at his post and neglect his family?
If the physician finds himself in an area high in radiation, does he leave the injured to secure his own safety?
How does he choose between saving the lives of the few and easing the pain of the many?
How does he allocate limited supplies of narcotics and analgesics?

And because many embryos exposed to radiation would be born malformed, "is there a place for mass abortion in the postattack period?" The authors note that neither the Hippocratic Oath, the American Medical Association's code of ethics, nor ordinary personal moral codes provided easy answers to these questions, and that in the context of thermonuclear war, these ethical guides "seem curiously and sadly obsolete, as if they reflected the human innocence of an earlier era."[131]

There would also be the medical problem of disposing of some two million corpses in the Boston area. Not only would many of these bodies be radioactive, but mounds of decomposing corpses would pose an overwhelming threat to public health. Faced with such an insurmountable problem, the survivors might have to abandon the city, and in the end, "the Boston area may thus become a mausoleum."[132] In the conclusion to this very bleak article, the authors condemn as "deeply misleading" many current analyses of the impact of nuclear war, and suggest that physicians must turn their efforts toward preventing nuclear war.[133]

In his contribution to *The Fallen Sky*, geneticist Bentley Glass observes that there had been such an increase in the number and size of nuclear weapons since the 1959 Holifield hearings that a 10,000-megaton attack on the United States was much more likely than a 1,500-megaton attack.[134] A nuclear war, according to Glass, would be fought without limits; and nuclear weapons would be aimed both at American military installations and at the civilian populations of American cities. Glass quotes NATO commander Lauris Norstad, who insisted that a nuclear war would be an all-out war because it was impossible to control "the size of this fire, the size of this blast, neatly, cold-bloodedly, once it starts."[135] The toll of a 10,000-megaton attack on the United States was estimated at 130 million dead within sixty days, overwhelmingly from blast and heat; as Glass put it, "fallout is simply not the problem in the primary target areas." Effective shelters, therefore, except in areas well removed from urban or military centers, would have to be blastproof, heatproof, and sealable, with oxygen supplies sufficient to survive a firestorm.[136] The expense of providing oxygen for shelter inhabitants would be considerable—about $300-$400 per person per day—and the bulky oxygen tanks would take up a large amount of storage space.[137]

The fallout shelter issue captured the attention of other scientists as well and dominated discussions at the 1961 annual meeting of the American Association for the Advancement of Science. The *AAAS Bulletin* claimed that not even a massive government-funded shelter program would enable

America to survive a nuclear war except as a "primitive, barbaric society."[138] Bentley Glass participated at this meeting, and described in what the *Bulletin* called "awesome detail" the world that would be awaiting survivors as they crawled from their shelters: "All domesticated and wild animals will be killed....The cultivated seed plants will be killed or made sterile.... Floods and erosion will be largely unchecked because of the loss of the forests.... The insects may be expected to survive, as will bacterial mutants that are radiation resistant." Cochairing the AAAS symposium on "Problems of Survival" were Barry Commoner and Margaret Mead. Commoner urged scientists to make a commitment to human survival, noting, "it is time to recognize that we cannot preserve our way of life by committing suicide." Margaret Mead made what was undoubtedly the most astonishing suggestion of the meeting. In order to assure the survival of the species, Mead proposed that an international shelter system be created that would house on a rotating basis a sampling of society's most productive members. Also placed in these shelters would be a contingent of society's most *re*productive members—a cross-section of the newly married.[139]

While much of the scientific community was hostile to the idea that shelters could be effective against a nuclear attack, the Stanford Research Institute was not only advocating the building of shelters, but by 1960 had built one in the basement of its Menlo Park facility for 1,600 staff members and their families. In 1962 an institute staff member, Rogers S. Cannell, published *Live: A Handbook of Survival in Nuclear Attack*, in which he described the shelter at Menlo Park, as well as individual shelters that readers could construct at a low cost. Throughout this work Cannell premised his suppositions on the effects of a five-megaton bomb—a much smaller weapon than the twenty-megaton bomb that Ervin et al. had used to destroy Boston. Consequently, Cannell was much more sanguine on the survivability of nuclear war. He described the possibility of a firestorm as "unlikely, except under rather exceptional circumstances," and in contrast to the Physicians for Social Responsibility claimed that "the nuclear weapon effect which poses the greatest threat to the greatest number of people is radioactive fallout."[140] Even if weapons bigger than five megatons were used, Cannell insisted (in a somewhat dubious analogy) that "the steps you take to avoid being killed by a Volkswagen are for the most part just as effective against a Mack truck."[141]

Perhaps most controversial, especially to critics of fallout shelters, were Cannell's suggestions for low-cost shelters and for what he called "quickfix" shelters (shelters that could be built with a one-hour warning time).

These included the "door over hole" shelter (dig a hole, put a door over it) and a "sandbag basement shelter" (stack a hundred sandbags around a table).[142] Those with a little more lead time might consider the "car body shelter" ("from junkyard to backyard . . . a simple and economical shelter!"). In this design a car is buried in the backyard and a plywood entry is built into one of the car's windows. Cannell suggested that this shelter would have sufficient room "for 2 adults and up to 3 children," a suggestion sure to produce horror among parents who had experienced long car trips with their children.[143]

Atomic Scientists

Of the many experts who engaged in this debate, the ones who spoke with perhaps the most authority were the ones most responsible for creating the terms of the debate: physicists and atomic scientists. As Lawrence Wittner emphasizes in his works on the nuclear disarmament movement, many atomic scientists had voiced anxieties about nuclear weapons from an early date. Leo Szilard, the émigré physicist who had played a key role in the development of the first atomic bomb, spoke for many when he called his work on such an awesomely destructive weapon the "lesser of two evils," and preferable to a world dominated by Nazi Germany. As early as 1942, however, Szilard had expressed his fears about a postwar world where nations possessed atomic weapons ("safeguard us from such a 'peace'"), and by late 1943 Niels Bohr was making the argument that the Allied leaders must come to an agreement on international control of atomic energy.[144]

Such reservations did not stop development of the bomb, but the actual use of atomic weapons on Japan was a sobering event, especially for physicists. "Physicists have known sin," said J. Robert Oppenheimer. Albert Einstein, drawing a parallel between physicists who had worked on the bomb and Alfred Nobel, inventor of dynamite, observed that physicists were "harassed by a similar feeling of responsibility, not to say guilt."[145] Even more common than guilt among atomic scientists was fear. Five months after the atomic bomb was dropped on Hiroshima Harold Urey, himself a Nobel laureate, penned an article for *Collier's* that began, "I write this to frighten you. I'm a frightened man, myself. All the scientists I know are frightened—frightened for their lives—and frightened for *your* life." Urey stressed the unprecedented destructiveness of the atomic bomb and the fact that there was no scientific defense against such a weapon. But what Urey was most afraid of was "what politicians and diplomats may do with the atomic bomb." "As a scientist," said Urey, "I tell you *there must never be another war*."[146] The solution? "As the scientists see it—and they are remarkably near unanimity—there is only one answer: *World Control*."[147] Albert Einstein had much the same perspective. In a letter published in the *Bulletin of the Atomic Scientists* in 1948, Einstein advocated world government because "there is no other possible way of eliminating the most terrible danger in which man has ever found himself."[148]

While Urey, Einstein, and other scientists began calling for international control and even world government to address the issue of nuclear weapons, public concern increased only slowly.[149] As the world entered the thermonuclear era in the mid-1950s, however, both public and scientific alarm began to rise. J. Robert Oppenheimer, who had led the atomic research at Los Alamos during the war, had publicly opposed development of the hydrogen bomb, and in 1953 he was stripped of his security clearance by the AEC. In 1955 a group of fifty-two Nobel laureates called attention to the great dangers posed by modern weapons, and asked the nations of the world "to renounce force as a final resort of policy."[150] The Federation of American Scientists went on record as favoring "a worldwide ban on further tests of nuclear weapons" in 1956, and in 1957 Albert Schweitzer attracted a lot of publicity by claiming that radiation from previous nuclear tests "represents a danger to the human race" and that additional tests would "increase this danger to an alarming extent."[151] By 1961 the chemist Linus Pauling had submitted an appeal to the United Nations calling for a test-ban treaty and for an end to the proliferation of nuclear weapons. The appeal was eventually signed by 200,000 people from forty-five countries.[152]

Often these scientists did not agree. Einstein claimed that the use of nuclear weapons on Japan may have been a "fatal error" because "men accustom themselves to thinking that a weapon which was used once can be used again," while the fifty-two Nobel laureates acknowledged that "perhaps peace is being preserved precisely by the fear of these weapons."[153] There was also considerable disagreement about the necessity of creating a world state. But with a few important exceptions, notably Edward Teller, Willard F. Libby, and Herman Kahn, most scientists believed that the buildup of radiation levels during the 1950s and 1960s represented a serious health threat, and that a nuclear war was not "survivable" in any real sense of the word.

Because of the formidable credentials of scientists such as Einstein, Szilard, and Pauling, AEC officials had an extremely difficult time discrediting this group of critics. Unable to challenge the expertise of these dissenting scientists, AEC officials often resorted to dark hints that conspiratorial forces were at work. For instance, in his 1958 response to the warnings of Linus Pauling and others that accumulations of radioactive fallout were reaching alarming levels, Lewis Strauss claimed that behind this "disturbance" was "a kernel of very intelligent, deliberate propaganda . . . we see that a great deal of money is being spent on it."[154] The *Wall Street Journal* also argued that the protests against increasing fallout concealed a "fringe of unreason" and perhaps a "devious propaganda." "Far worse than fallout," opined the *Journal*, "would be a fall-off in the United States' military power to preserve peace."[155]

Especially irritating to the AEC and its defenders was that the premier journal of these scientists, the *Bulletin of the Atomic Scientists*, had become a forum for mostly negative views on nuclear weapons and testing. This critique of American nuclear policies began at the top with the *Bulletin's* editor and cofounder, Eugene Rabinowitch. Rabinowitch had been one of the original participants in the "Pugwash" conferences, a series of forums held for scientists concerned about nuclear weapons.[156] To a great extent, the *Bulletin* would reflect the concerns of Rabinowitch and like-minded individuals, and along the way would become the AEC's *bête noire*. As early as 1953, AEC chairman Lewis Strauss had complained that the *Bulletin* had "not been objective." In 1957 Strauss again criticized both the *Bulletin* and Rabinowitch for attacking U.S. nuclear policy while "pretending to be objective."[157] Such criticism had little effect, and articles on every aspect of nuclear arms—including the shelter issue—continued to appear in the *Bulletin*. In a paper that was delivered at the third Pugwash conference in 1959 and reprinted in the *Bulletin*, Rabinowitch alerted scientists to their "peculiar responsibility," claiming that "more clearly than anybody else, scientists see the senselessness and the tragedy of the present situation of mankind." In a pointed reference to Strauss, Rabinowitch observed that "the basic cause of the predicament, into which the discovery of atomic energy has brought the world, lies not in the inadequate ethical standards of scientists," but in "the low ethical standards of national governments."[158] The solution, as outlined by Rabinowitch in a 1954 *Bulletin* editorial, was a "supra-national authority capable of enforcing world law."[159]

To show its concern for the nuclear peril facing humanity, the *Bulletin* created the "Bulletin Clock," and in the process produced one of the most enduring icons of the Atomic Age. Often featured on the cover of the *Bulletin*, the clock was established as a "symbol of the threat of doomsday hovering over humanity" (fig. 37). In 1954, for instance, the hands of the clock stood perilously close to midnight (with midnight being nuclear holocaust), and the *Bulletin* editors observed that

> The hands of the clock on the *Bulletin's* cover now stand at two minutes to midnight. Not to terrify, certainly, but to warn and to awaken, the clock is intended to be symbolic. Wishing will not stop the clock. The *Bulletin* may be wrong. It may actually be one minute—perhaps seconds—to midnight. The specter of atomic peril hovers constantly near.[160]

The shelter issue had been debated in the *Bulletin* from an early date, and two issues were devoted to the subject in October 1951 and September 1953. In the latter edition the architect Ellery Husted penned an article called "Shelter in the Atomic Age." Husted drew the same conclusions that many others would adopt over the next ten years—that the shelter problem was "extremely complex" and "possibly insoluble." "At every turn," according to Husted, "political and economic realities conflict with rational solutions."[161] Looking at the shelter issue a few years later, *Bulletin* contributor James W. Deer, a civil defense coordinator in the Portland, Oregon, area, expressed fears that an "international shelter race" might develop with many of the same characteristics of the arms race: "The more shelter one side builds, the more alarmed the other side becomes and considers this activity a warlike move, and so increases its own shelter program, and so on." Pushed to its logical extreme, the end result would be entire nations interred underground.[162] While clearly viewing such a prospect with horror, the fatalistic Deer believed that a shelter race was inevitable, and that "within the framework of fusion bombs, guided missiles, and shelters, there is nothing we can do but go ahead and play out our part in the preordained ritual."[163]

The Holifield hearings of 1956 and 1957 received considerable attention in the *Bulletin*. Mary Simpson wrote a lengthy review of the 1956 hearings ("A Long Hard Look at Civil Defense") that drew on the administration's most caustic civil defense critics. Simpson noted that almost all Holifield witnesses agreed that "we have no civil defense worthy of the name, but opinions differed as to whether it was reasonable to expect any."[164] Simpson believed that it was an open question whether or not a shelter program could buy protection from nuclear attack and create "firmer

FIG. 37. The "Bulletin Clock." *Bulletin of the Atomic Scientists*, May 1955. © 1999 by the Educational Foundation for Nuclear Science, 6042 South Kimbark, Chicago, Illinois 60637, USA. Reprinted by permission of the *Bulletin of the Atomic Scientists*. A one-year subscription is $28.

prospects for peace," or if "radioactive fall-out and further advances in weaponry would make it ineffective."[165]

As the *Bulletin*'s civil defense editor, Ralph Lapp was also a frequent contributor. Lapp had wide access to the media, penning articles for influential newspapers and periodicals such as the *New York Times*, and appearing on radio and television shows. Highly critical of American nuclear policies, Lapp was among the first to call attention to the unexpectedly high quantities of radioactive fallout produced by the 1954 Bravo test.[166] Lapp would go on to become a leading critic of civil defense policies in general and fallout shelters in particular. In May 1955 he called into question the AEC's optimistic estimates that thirty-six hours would be a sufficient length of time to remain sheltered from radioactive fallout after a nuclear blast (Lapp insisted that radioactive fallout would be a danger "for many weeks and even months"), and criticized the Atomic Energy Commission for its delay in informing the public about the results of the Bravo blast.[167] When he appeared on *Face the Nation* in June 1955, Lapp said that the civil defense program was flawed because it had not adequately considered fallout, and accused the AEC of adopting a "Father knows best" policy of secrecy that had been "terribly damaging."[168] On the same program in the following year Lapp continued the attack, calling for an end to nuclear testing and referring to AEC statements on radiation dangers as a "mishmash of facts" and "too little too late."[169] Lapp's contributions also included important *Bulletin* interviews with key civil defense figures such as Val Peterson and Chet Holifield. Lapp was perhaps even more unpopular with AEC director Lewis Strauss than Eugene Rabinowitch. According to Lawrence Wittner, "Lapp's activities obsessed Strauss, who—apparently with the assistance of FBI surveillance operations—even read the physicist's private mail."[170] Strauss's attempts to derail Lapp's career were not a success, and Lapp continued to speak out against civil defense policy, especially through the *Bulletin*.

In 1960 Lapp reviewed New York governor Nelson Rockefeller's proposed state civil defense program, noting that while the proposal recognized that "nuclear hazards pose a tremendous challenge to human survival," it also seemed to be writing off New York City as impossible to defend. Lapp also took the report to task for not acknowledging the problem of nuclear firestorm, which would render all but the most elaborate—and expensive—shelters useless.[171] It should be emphasized, however, that Lapp, unlike many of his contemporaries, was not anti-shelter per se. Lapp opposed the Kennedy fallout shelter program because he believed that it did not adequately address the problems of nuclear blast and thermal effects. Indeed, as a practical demonstration of what might constitute an effective shelter, Lapp and some of his neighbors built a three-family shelter with blast and thermal protection, an oxygen system, a built-in well, and a six-month food supply.[172]

One of the most extraordinary articles to appear in the *Bulletin* was Leo

Szilard's "The Mined Cities," published in 1961. In this fictional piece the narrative is developed through the perspective of a cryogenically frozen cancer patient who is awakened in 1980 after an eighteen-year slumber. "Dr. Jones" informs the patient that a cure for his cancer has been found, that the patient's family is fine, and that the patient's brother has become extremely wealthy because he "sold his construction company six months before people stopped building fallout shelters." The reason that there are large sums of money for cancer research and that nobody is building fallout shelters is that an accommodation has been reached with the Russians in which fifteen American and fifteen Russian cities have been "mined" with large hydrogen bombs buried beneath them. The bombs are maintained by crews from the opposite nation, with orders to detonate the bombs if the enemy attacks the homeland of the crews.[173] Since the crews themselves would be killed in any such detonation, "it gives Russia reasonable assurance that no American crew would blow up a Russian city, except in retaliation against the blowing up of an American city. This holds, of course, in the reverse, also."[174] The economic benefits of such an arrangement are, according to Dr. Jones, considerable:

> All atomic and hydrogen bombs, except those located below the mined cities, have now been destroyed. All submarines capable of firing rockets have been scrapped. The shelter construction program, which has cost us five billion dollars per year has been abandoned, and we save another 10 billion dollars a year because we do not have to maintain strategic striking forces any longer.[175]

Jones contrasts the mined cities era with the bad old days when both the United States and the Soviet Union staggered under huge defense expenditures. It had been a time, said Jones, when apprehensive wealthy Americans "built luxurious homes equipped with air-conditioned shelters, capable of storing a year's food supply, and with attics complete with machine guns mounted in the windows."[176] Dr. Jones acknowledges that while there was a certain apprehension connected to having a hydrogen bomb sitting underneath one's city, the government offered by way of compensation $3,000 per year to each family living in a mined city.[177]

At a minimum, the extraordinary suggestions put forward in "The Mined Cities" indicates how frightening nuclear tensions with the Soviet Union had become. Was Szilard serious? Szilard anticipates this question and engages it in "The Mined Cities" itself:

A: Who thought up these mined cities?

B: Szilard had proposed it in an article published in the *Bulletin of the Atomic Scientists* in 1961, but the idea may not have been original with him. His proposal was presented in the form of fiction and it was not taken seriously.

A: If he meant his proposal seriously, why didn't he publish it in serious form?

B: He may have tried and found that no magazine would print it in a serious form.[178]

Strategists and scientists proved to be as split on the issues of nuclear war as social critics and the American religious community. The form that such a war would take and the ultimate physical effects of nuclear war were bitterly debated. For scientists especially, the source of these divisions lay in the revolutionary nature of the weapons themselves. Nuclear weapons *are* radically different from other weapons because of their enormous destructiveness, and it is understandable that this quantum leap in military technology, coupled with nuclear data that were either lacking or inconclusive, produced widely different interpretations among scientists. Thus the firestorm issue or the impact of radioactivity on the environment could never be resolved scientifically in a definitive way.

The divisions among strategists, however, were of a different quality. Here the essentials had more to do with human nature than with weapons systems, and while there was only limited information on nuclear weapons effects, human history is replete with examples of population behavior during wartime. Counterforce advocates argued that nuclear war could, and would, be limited to military targets because it was rationally in the best interest of both warring parties to impose such a limitation. Indeed, the argument can be made that no war is "total," and that the combatants in every war impose limitations on the conduct of the war (such as the outlawing of dumdum bullets or the basic proposition that civilians have a different status from military personnel). The law and order of warfare, however, has come under extreme strain in modern times, and if the major wars of the twentieth century have produced a single trend, it is clearly toward war without limits. Certainly, few technological limits were placed on the conduct of warfare during World War I, and the prohibition against making war on civilians all but disappeared during World War II. While the argument can be made that the execution of six million Jews was not a "military" operation in the strictest sense (as if this somehow makes a difference to the horrific end result), there are a depressingly large number of other examples in which civilian and noncombatant populations were targeted by the military during this war. These include the Rape of Nanking, V-1 and V-2 rocket attacks against Britain, the Bataan Death March, Allied terror bombing of Germany, and nuclear attacks against Hiroshima and Nagasaki.

The counterforce argument that the civilian population would largely be excluded from the effects of nuclear war is certainly not validated by the results of the two world wars, where excesses that would have been unthinkable at the beginning of these wars became political necessities as casualties mounted and vast sums of money were spent. One of the obvious flaws of the counterforce argument is that, even more so than in the case of World War II, it would be virtually impossible to isolate the civilian population from attacks against the military. Even if directed at counterforce targets, the power of nuclear weapons, and the errors that are invariably made in the fog of war, would virtually guarantee large numbers of civilian casualties. There is also a curious assumption underlying the counterforce argument that somehow military personnel are not part of the larger society, that they do not have husbands and wives and parents and children and friends who would call for escalation and vengeance rather than rationally accept huge numbers of military casualties. Human beings frequently act out of irrational motives, and nothing brings out that irrationality more than the death of a loved one.

Once the counterforce argument has been eliminated and the likelihood established that a nuclear war would be a total war against both military and civilian populations, the assumptions of civil defense fall like a house of cards. Evacuation in the face of an enemy intent on destroying the civilian population would be futile, even ludicrous. Perhaps even more pathetic is the notion that an individual could assure the survival of his family from an all-out nuclear war by building a fallout shelter. The forces arrayed against such an individual were simply too great, and a realization of this Nuclear Age fact of life would play an important role in the American rejection of fallout shelters.

CHAPTER 6

The Shelters That Were Not Built, the Nuclear War That Did Not Start

Americans had excellent reasons to retreat underground. The day-to-day tensions of the Cold War, the occasional full-blown crises, the ubiquitous reminders in the press of the consequences of nuclear war, and the obvious fact that nuclear weapons were going to be around for a long time should theoretically have provided ample motivation for Americans to become a sheltered nation. Yet the United States did not build a system of community shelters, nor were private shelters built in the numbers expected. As Thomas Hine has observed, the fallout shelter issue "prompted far more introspection than excavation," and for complex reasons Americans simply did not respond as many thought they would.[1]

Certainly, entrepreneurs calculated that selling home fallout shelters was a can't-miss proposition. One illustration of the perils of a sure thing, and ultimately the public's ambivalence about fallout shelters, could be found in the experiences of James J. Byrne, a plywood salesman from Royal Oak, Michigan. Byrne believed that there was a great business opportunity in fallout shelters, and obtained a regional dealership for Kelsey-Hayes prefabricated fallout shelters in 1961. Byrne ordered fourteen unassembled shelters, sold thirteen to dealers around the state, and kept one to use as a display model. Kelsey-Hayes had assured Byrne that it would take two people two to four hours to assemble the shelter, but Byrne discovered that it took four of his men ten hours to assemble the display model. Even more discouraging was the public's reluctance to buy. Byrne put his shelter on display in shopping centers, parking lots, and veterans' halls. Thousands of people walked through, but nobody bought.

Next, Byrne attempted to drum up business by sending a corps of salesmen into the suburbs to sell shelters door-to-door.[2] Byrne's salesmen reported that people would take the literature, ask questions, and finally explain that they couldn't afford a shelter, or that they were going to see how things turned out in Berlin. Dealers to whom Byrne sold shelters fared no better. James Cline, manager of a lumber company in Royal Oak, reported that some 2,500 people visited his display shelter in a period of eight weeks. But Cline sold only one shelter, and was castigated by his fellow citizens: "People were confused, frightened, angry. I was accused of profiteering, war-mongering—you name it."[3]

Despite the discussions of nuclear war that pervaded society, surveys consistently reported that very few Americans—about .4 percent according to one study—were taking steps to build shelters.[4] In 1962 Peter I. Rose and his students at Smith College surveyed the citizens of Northampton, Massachusetts, on the threat posed by nuclear war and what those citizens were prepared to do about it. The study found a curious demographic pattern: Democrats, veterans, and Catholics or highly religious persons were the groups most likely to build or consider building a shelter, as were parents of school-age children, people with high school educations or less, and those with incomes under $5,000. "Considering" building a shelter and actually building one are two very different things, however, and only one person interviewed had actually constructed a fallout shelter. By far, the largest proportion of those surveyed indicated confusion (37 percent) or indecision (24 percent) about the shelter issue.[5]

Another 1962 study that compared eighty shelter owners with eighty non–shelter owners indicated that the two groups held fundamentally different worldviews. Non–shelter owners were generally more optimistic about the prospects for world peace, while shelter owners expressed a corresponding pessimism. Paradoxically, shelter owners believed that shelters reduced the chance of war, but were more convinced than non–shelter owners that war would occur.[6]

FIG. 38. The spartan interior of a $1,000 shelter built by Louis Severance of Akron, Michigan. OCD photograph. RG 397-MA 2-S-160 (box 18), Still Pictures Branch (NNSP), National Archives at College Park, MD.

The reluctance of Americans to purchase shelters was certainly not related to a lack of awareness of the issues. A *U.S. News* national survey conducted in 1961 at the height of Cold War tensions found that "everybody in this country, it seems, is thinking or talking about what to do in case war starts and nuclear bombs fall on the U.S." Yet paradoxically, *U.S. News* found "no mass movement toward preparedness." Instead, surveyors described the prevailing attitude as "fatalism," and characterized Americans as "more pessimistic about the chances of survival" than scientists and government officials. The *U.S. News* survey was not unique in its findings. The journal *Social Problems* also took note of the "widespread sense of futility on the part of most Americans who feel that nuclear war is not something *they* can help avert. . . . they tend to retreat into fatalistic lethargy."[7]

While fatalism certainly played a role in the American rejection of fallout shelters, it was only one element in a number of complicated, interlocking factors. Cost was undoubtedly a consideration, and the class as-

FIG. 39. The roomy interior of a $10,000 shelter built by Earl W. Reichert of Battle Creek, Michigan. *Battle Creek Enquirer & News*. RG 397-MA 14-S-8 (box 18), Still Pictures Branch (NNSP), National Archives at College Park, MD.

pects of shelters were obvious and troubling. Americans read about the Alfred Gwynne Vanderbilts and the Cortright Wetherills adding fallout shelters to their country estates, and about such denizens of Hollywood as Groucho Marx, Dinah Shore, and Pat Boone putting shelters in their homes, but for most homeowners the price of a shelter was simply out of reach.[8] Arthur Krock of the *New York Times* described the 1961 government pamphlet *Fallout Protection* as a "guide for the more fortunate—'fortunate' in having the money to build the private shelters so elaborately described, or in being sufficiently remote from a blast area to survive."[9] Even Rogers S. Cannell, who had written an upbeat book on surviving a nuclear war, observed, "you should buy as much protection as you can afford."[10] In his critique of the home shelter, James Reston claimed that it "favored the rich over the poor, the single-house dweller over the apartment dweller, the home owner over the renter."[11] Reston also called attention to the differences in wealth among various states and their abilities to provide fallout protection, and questioned a system that would "protect the citizens of rich states like New York but not the citizens of poor states like Mississippi."[12] The Society of Friends extended this observation to the international realm, noting that millions of people in other countries would also be exposed to the fallout from a nuclear war, but would not have access to any shelter "because of their limited resources."[13]

One St. Louis contractor estimated that 80 percent of his shelter orders were to homes of the well-to-do. The contractor noted that his firm received many calls from people building their own shelters and that "we give them all the help they want. There's no profit in that for us, but this isn't just a business. It's a moral thing, too."[14] Such moral concerns seemed to be lacking at the government level. An indignant William L. Shirer concluded that legislators had "passed the buck to the individual citizen. They have said in effect: every American family for itself and the devil take the hindmost."[15]

Among those who insisted that fallout shelters could be built inexpensively was former Atomic Energy Commission chairman Willard Libby. Libby, who was opposed to public funding for shelters, was once quoted as saying, "If I were President, I would declare martial law and force everyone to prepare his own shelter."[16] Libby wrote a fifteen-part newspaper series titled "You Can Survive Atomic Attack" in which he featured his own "poor man's shelter" that he had built in West Los Angeles. Libby claimed that his shelter, constructed of railroad ties and bags of dirt, had cost less than thirty dollars.[17] Libby's argument for the viability of the poor man's shelter was undercut somewhat when this structure was subsequently destroyed in a brushfire. Leo Szilard observed that this incident "proves not only that there is a God but that he has a sense of humor."[18] Most experts acknowledged that even a bare-bones shelter would cost in the vicinity of $2,500, and since the median family income was $5,315 in 1961, it was simply not realistic to expect most Americans to make such a huge financial sacrifice in the name of civil defense.[19]

Even those who could afford a suburban shelter often experienced an unease at installing these brooding, forbidding structures in their backyards. The relaxed, carefree life promised by the suburbs was clearly compromised by fallout shelters, which served as constant reminders of the possibility of nuclear war. John Cheever identifies this problem in his fictional account of the Pasterns, a suburban couple who have built a shelter in their backyard, but who cannot help but be reminded of the shelter's ultimate grim purpose:

Mrs. Pastern had bought the plaster-of-Paris ducks, the birdbath, and the gnomes in an attempt to give the lump in her garden a look of innocence; to make it acceptable—at least to herself. For, bulking as it did in so pretty and domestic a scene and signifying as it must the death of at least half the world's population, she had found it, with its grassy cover, impossible to reconcile with the blue sky and the white clouds.[20]

Civil defense officials in Washington also understood that shelters cast a pall over suburban life, and tried to make shelter designs more attractive by hiring the services of interior decorators. Model shelters were set up in shopping centers, trade shows, and other venues to promote interest in shelters while at the same time trying to deflect attention from their ghastly function. Shelters could be "more trim and less grim," enthused the Office of Civil Defense, but this policy of sugarcoating what fallout shelters were about sometimes backfired.[21] For instance, there were angry reactions at a trade show in Chicago when federal civil defense officials and the interior decorator Mark T. Nielsen displayed a model shelter labeled the "Family Room of Tomorrow" (fig. 40). This seemed like a tasteless joke to many, and one visitor responded, "If they want to invent a name for it, why not call it a mausoleum?"[22] Putting a more positive spin on the same shelter was *Life* magazine, which reassured readers that "if war never comes, children can claim it for a hideaway, father can use it for poker games and mother can count on it as a guest room."[23]

Such enticements left most Americans unmoved. When asked by Gallup pollsters in September 1961, "Have you made any plans or given any serious thought to preparing your home in case of a nuclear attack?" a resounding 93 percent said no.[24] With interest in fallout shelters clearly on the decline, Hammacher Schlemmer, the upscale gift store, began advertising "Shelters for *Living*," emphasizing multipurpose shelters that "can also be used and enjoyed day-by-day" as a "Family-Library-Music room."[25] By early 1962, the fallout shelter business was faltering badly as the possibility of nuclear war seemed to recede and the troubling moral and class questions associated with shelters began to accumulate. By May Frank Norton had lost $100,000 and proclaimed, "the market is dead—the manufacturers have had it. . . . if we had another international crisis, I don't know of a manufacturer who would make a move of his own until we got an explicit national plan endorsing home shelters." Leo Hoegh's Wonder Building Corporation was now selling only ten shelters a week, and with three thousand shelters crated in storage, Hoegh lamented, "I am bleeding rather profusely." Norton estimated that

FIG. 40. The family room of tomorrow? Shelter created by the American Institute of Decorators and shown at the Merchandise Mart, Chicago, January 1960. OCDM photograph. RG 397-MA 2-S-270 (box 18), Still Pictures Branch (NNSP), National Archives at College Park, MD.

between the fall of 1961 and the spring of 1962, six hundred firms had failed.[26] Some shelter manufacturers now began offering shelters on the installment plan, with ten years to pay.[27]

Cuba

By the fall of 1962 the home fallout shelter business was in a shambles and political support for a national system was quickly evaporating.[28] Then came the Cuban Missile Crisis, and if any event could have produced a permanent commitment to fallout shelters and civil defense, this was surely it. After all, the 1961 Berlin crisis had precipitated the initial enthusiasm for shelters, and the crisis in Cuba was far more serious. In fact, the Cuban crisis and the Berlin crisis have often been linked, but the dynamics of these crises were very different. The Berlin crisis unfolded at a relatively leisurely pace, developing over a period of several months and allowing sufficient time for a national examination of the implications of nuclear war and its survivability. The Berlin crisis was also punctuated by a number of climaxes, including the building of the Berlin Wall and the testing by the Soviets of the largest nuclear weapon ever detonated. In contrast to the Berlin crisis, the Cuban Missile Crisis reached its climax in a very short span of time, and ended almost before anyone had time to absorb what had happened.

Lasting from October 16, 1962, when unmistakable evidence of Soviet missiles in Cuba was revealed, to October 28, when Khrushchev acceded to American demands that the missiles be removed, the Cuban Missile Crisis is rightly considered the Cold War's most frightening confrontation. The Soviet Union's determination that missiles be installed in Cuba and the equal determination on the part of the United States that they *not* be installed produced a conflict that came close to escalating into thermonuclear war. Secretary of state Dean Rusk described this as "the most dangerous crisis the world has ever seen," and Robert Kennedy said that the Cuban crisis "brought the world to the abyss of nuclear destruction and the end of mankind."[29] This was a view that was generally shared by both sides. Khrushchev confirmed that "the two most powerful nations of the world had been squared off against each other, each with its finger on the button. You'd have thought that war was inevitable."[30] The Soviet diplomat Vassily Kuznetsov observed that "Khrushchev shit his pants" during the Cuban crisis, and surely he was not the only one.[31]

One of the salient features of the Cuban crisis is the degree to which the American leadership connected it to the situation in Berlin. In its assessment of how the Soviets would respond should the United States confront Khrushchev over the Cuban missiles, the Central Intelligence Agency predicted that "They would probably link Cuba with the Berlin situation and emphasize their patience and preference for negotiations, implying that Berlin was held hostage to U.S. actions in Cuba."[32] Dean Rusk concluded that "Khrushchev had more than Cuba on his mind—probably Berlin."[33] Kennedy secretly taped White House meetings of the Executive Committee (ExComm) that was advising him during the Cuban crisis, and these tapes also reveal a preoccupation with how the Cuban situation might impact Berlin. In one of these meetings on October 19 Kennedy ruminated on the chilling possibility that a U.S. airstrike on Cuban missile installations might push the Soviets into retaliating by "going in and taking Berlin by force. Which leaves me only one alternative, which is to fire nuclear weapons—which is a hell of an alternative—and begin a nuclear exchange."[34]

Fig. 41. Public shelters were to be marked with this symbol, which would become ubiquitous across the country. RG 397-MA 5-F-27 (box 10), Still Pictures Branch (NNSP), National Archives at College Park, MD.

The Cuban crisis almost immediately revealed how little progress had been made in a year's time in actually creating public fallout shelters or a viable civil defense.[35] When Kennedy asked for a civil defense status report on October 20, he learned that the shelter program was far behind schedule. To be fair, it was an enormous job to identify and analyze shelter space around the country, and many owners of buildings were reluctant to grant permission to use their facilities as shelters because they feared losing control of their property. There was also the problem of stocking and marking shelter spaces. The stocking had begun only three weeks before the Cuban crisis. Kennedy was informed that very few of the needed supplies had made their way into federal warehouses, and even fewer into public shelters. Kennedy ordered the immediate distribution to shelters of the supplies that existed, but clearly they were inadequate to the task at hand. (It would not be until 1963 that the shelter survey was completed and there were a significant number of stocked shelter spaces—too late for the Cuban Missile Crisis.)[36]

FIG. 42. Civil defense shelter supplies for fifty persons, 1962. Includes ten water drums, one sanitation kit, one medical kit, one shelter radiation kit, and ten cases of survival biscuits. U.S. army photograph. RG 397-MA 29-S-13 (box 19), Still Pictures Branch (NNSP), National Archives at College Park, MD.

The immediate danger, and a consideration that colored much of the decision making during the crisis, was that action against Cuba might provoke the firing of the Cuban missiles against the United States. There were some forty-eight operational medium-range ballistic missiles (MRBMs) in Cuba at the time of the crisis.[37] A number of Kennedy's advisers, including Maxwell Taylor and Paul Nitze, called for an airstrike against the missile sites, and when Kennedy met with a congressional delegation on October 22, most of the delegates seemed to share Senator Richard Russell's view that the sites should be attacked and an invasion of Cuba mounted. Kennedy observed at the time that if the United States invaded Cuba, "there is a chance these weapons will be fired at the United States," which Kennedy called "one hell of a gamble."[38]

While the consequences of an American invasion can never be known, Aleksandr Fursenko and Timothy Naftali believe that the Soviet commander in Cuba, Issa Pliyev, would have been authorized to use tactical, if not strategic, nuclear weapons, and that "Kennedy might well have discovered to his horror on October 23 that he had ordered thousands of American soldiers, marines, and sailors onto the first nuclear battlefield of the Cold War."[39] In an October 26 letter to Khrushchev, Castro insisted that the Soviet Union must never allow a situation "in which the imperialist could launch the first nuclear strike against it," and suggested that if the United States invaded Cuba, "that would be the moment to eliminate such danger forever through an act of clear legitimate defense, however harsh and terrible the solution would be." In responding to Castro, Khrushchev adopted the unaccustomed role of the voice of reason, noting that a nuclear strike against the United States "would have been the start of a thermonuclear world war. . . . the United States would have sustained huge losses, but the Soviet Union and the whole socialist camp would have also suffered greatly."[40]

In his memoirs, however, a less conciliatory tone emerges. Khrushchev bragged that while the Soviets had not delivered all the missiles they wanted to Cuba, "we had installed enough missiles already to destroy New York, Chicago, and the other huge industrial cities, not to mention a little village like Washington." Khrushchev also implied that if Soviet installations in Cuba had been attacked by the United States, the surviving missiles would have been unleashed on American targets. Khrushchev argued that "even if only one or two big ones were left—we could still hit New York, and there wouldn't be much of New York left."[41] Instead of an airstrike, Kennedy opted for what he considered to be the less provocative measure of a blockade of Cuba (euphemistically referred to as a "quarantine" by the administration) to take effect on October 23.

OCD director Steuart Pittman briefed Kennedy on October 23 on the damage that the Cuban missiles could do in the United States. Like other important meetings at the White House, this one was taped. Pittman estimated that with a range of some 1,100 miles, the missiles in Cuba could hit some fifty-eight major American cities, affecting a population of 92 million. Pittman observed that the stocking of shelters could be accelerated, but the protection factor of many shelter accommodations might have to be lowered from 100 to 40. Kennedy then asked Pittman whether evacuation was a possibility: "Can we, maybe before we invade, evacuate these cities?" Then the following exchange takes place:

PITTMAN: Well, if we knew that there would be no nuclear response, it might make some sense. If there will be fallout, the only protection that exists today is in the cities, and there's little or no protection in the rural areas.

PRESIDENT KENNEDY: Well, we have to assume that there isn't going to be very much, and on the assumption of that, we're not going to have an all-out nuclear exchange. If we were going to have an all-out nuclear exchange, then we'd have a different problem.[42]

Unfortunately, at this point the tape becomes virtually inaudible for eleven minutes, but in notes taken of the Pittman-Kennedy conversation by CIA director John McCone, McCone states, "I got the conclusion that not very much could or would be done; that whatever was done would involve a great deal of publicity and public alarm."[43]

October 27 marked the climax of the Cuban Missile Crisis. U.S. forces had been put on DEFCON 2 alert (the highest alert status short of war) for the first and only time during the Cold War. One-eighth of SAC's B-52 bombers were in the air at all times, refueled by aerial tankers and cruising toward their fail-safe points until others took their places. For the first time in history every SAC bomber was armed with nuclear weapons. Later that day an American U-2 reconnaissance aircraft was shot down over Cuba and the pilot was killed. This was the most serious incident of the crisis.[44] As these events were taking place, the Civil Defense Committee of the Governors' Conference was being briefed by John McCone at the Pentagon. Eleven governors or their representatives were in attendance, including Nelson Rockefeller of New York, Edmund Brown of

California, John A. Volpe of Massachusetts, Elmer L. Anderson of Minnesota, and Ferris Bryant of Florida. The group was shown aerial photographs of the missile installations, and Governor Anderson remembered being shocked at seeing "the missiles in place, pointed toward the United States."[45] Next, the governors were addressed by Steuart Pittman, who proposed a new civil defense program that would accelerate the marking and stocking of shelters. Some states had barely begun this process and were nearly totally unprepared.[46] Then the governors met with Kennedy at the White House. In response to a question from Governor Brown on whether Kennedy was showing sufficient resolve, Kennedy responded, "I chose the quarantine because I wondered if our people are ready for the bomb." Kennedy urged the governors to speed up their civil defense programs.[47]

In Miami, where the military was assembling the largest invasion force since World War II, fears ran high that that city might be subject to attack. Because of its proximity to Cuba, southern Florida was vulnerable to both nuclear attack and conventional attack, a point stressed by Maxwell Taylor in White House discussions with Kennedy.[48] Miami residents quickly discovered that their city had no officially designated shelters. Instead, Miami's civil defense director recommended that Miamians "go into the strongest building you can find nearest you," or "in your own home, go into a closet or inside room or hallway."[49] Miami builders were inundated with inquiries about fallout shelters. In one case, four prefabricated shelters that had been moldering in a warehouse for months were immediately sold, while another builder reported receiving fifteen firm orders for shelters. Only a relatively protracted crisis in Cuba would have benefited these customers, however, as the estimated time to complete a shelter was eight to ten weeks.[50] For the most part, Miamians seemed tense but calm, halting all conversations when the news came on, but otherwise going about their daily lives.[51] Across the peninsula the city of Tampa was equally unprepared: there were no public shelters and no stockpiles of food. Instead, Tampa residents created their own stockpiles, snapping up arms, ammunition, and foodstuffs as Mayor Julian Lane urged calm, and Tampa's civil defense director advised Tampans to "take cover as best you can."[52]

Not only the residents of Florida, but Americans throughout the country were anxiously focused on the Cuban crisis. In Boston residents bombarded local civil defense offices for the location of the nearest fallout shelter.[53] They learned that not a single public shelter was marked or was stocked with survival supplies.[54] Massachusetts governor Volpe predicted a long, drawn-out crisis in Cuba, issued an urgent plea to accelerate the public fallout shelter program, and appealed to every family "to provide some type of fallout shelter—even if it's a shelter in the basement corner made out of bookcases and sandbags."[55] In Dallas, military recruiters were inundated with inquiries about enlisting, and the A-OK Fallout Shelter Company reported some three hundred phone calls asking about shelters.[56] Civil defense offices were likewise busy fielding inquiries, and there was a rush on Dallas grocery stores as buyers snapped up bottled water, canned goods, and powdered milk.[57] City-county civil defense director B. B. Smith chided Dallas shoppers for their "panic buying," and somewhat inappropriately suggested that "this should be no more a task than buying goods for a picnic." Meanwhile, residents learned that Dallas had only one building marked as a public shelter—the Southland Life building—but that it had not yet been stocked.[58]

In Los Angeles there were enough supplies for some forty thousand persons sitting in a federal warehouse, but only two buildings in that city had actually been stocked with survival supplies.[59] In the nearby San Fernando Valley the situation was much the same. Three hospitals had been marked as public shelters, but none had been stocked. In Sherman Oaks a brief power failure produced phone calls asking whether the United States was under attack.[60] As in other parts of the country, volunteers for the military were running far above normal (the head of air force recruiting for southern California reported that enlistments were running at two to three times their normal rate).[61] In West Covina the civil defense office was receiving an average of one call a minute, and elsewhere in the San Gabriel Valley officials announced that school civil defense drills would be held, and that children would be kept in schools in the event of a "red alert."[62] Lack of preparedness was nearly universal in the Los Angeles area. On the west side there was not a single marked and stocked shelter in either Santa Monica or Beverly Hills. Deputy civil defense director R. M. Howell observed, "There are plenty of buildings along Wilshire Blvd. which would provide good shelter but the people would have to provide their own food and water."[63] By October 26 the Army Corps of Engineers was frantically marking public shelters in Los Angeles at the rate of six to eight a day, but the supplies for these shelters continued to sit in a Long Beach warehouse.[64]

In the Washington, D.C., area there were also increased calls to local civil defense offices (the District civil defense office received more than one thousand calls in twenty-four hours), and callers received the same information that they were receiving elsewhere: shelter space was virtually nonexistent. District civil defense director George Roderick immediately ordered the stocking and marking of one hundred fallout shelters in the District of Columbia.[65] By October 26 there were five shelters in the District that had been stocked and marked. In nearby Fairfax County not a single shelter had been stocked.[66] The columnist Bill Henry reported that residents of Washington did not seem especially alarmed, and were enduring the Cuban crisis with "magnificent aplomb." Henry also observed that the Soviets stationed in Washington did not seem overly worried either, and that "the Russians had a big party at their embassy Tuesday night at which a Soviet general was loudly belligerent, without apparently interfering with anybody's drinking."[67]

Meanwhile, the elaborate contingency plans that officials around the country had made for an emergency such as the Cuban Missile Crisis proved to have feet of clay when the crisis actually materialized. Don Oberdorfer, who wrote an article on the Cuban crisis for the *Saturday Evening Post* some five months after the event, noted that "half a dozen communities discovered that their CD directors had resigned weeks, months, even years earlier and had never been replaced." In Wukesha, Wisconsin, officials found that the city's civil defense survival plan had been lost for several years and "had never even been missed." Chicago was operating under an antiquated survival plan that called for massive evacuation, and when asked what to do in the event of an attack, the chief civil defense administrator advised, "Take cover and pray." When federal agencies in Washington were ordered to go on DEFCON alert, "many officials, including cabinet officers, did not even know what this meant."

Had the situation deteriorated, government officials would have been ordered to disperse to secret locations. It is debatable, however, how many would actually have gone where they were supposed to go. As one government employee put it, "If a serious war threat comes, you're going to find me getting home to my wife and kids."[68] Even Dean Rusk declared, "Having lived through the missile crisis, I am convinced that government leaders, if called upon to evacuate, are simply not going to say good-bye to their colleagues and possibly their own families and then board a helicopter and whirl away to some cave."[69]

Finally the crisis ended when Khrushchev agreed to remove the missiles from Cuba (in return for American assurances that the United States would not invade Cuba). There would be many consequences of this event, most notably a humiliating loss of face for the Soviet Union.

Khrushchev tried to put the best spin he could on it, calling the Cuban crisis a "great victory for us" because of the U.S. no-invasion-of-Cuba pledge. But the Cubans themselves were furious, and relations between the Soviet Union and Cuba would never be restored to previous levels of congeniality. (Making matters worse was that Kennedy never made public his pledge of nonaggression against Cuba as he had promised to do.)[70] Certainly the Soviet political elite did not view the results of the Cuban crisis as a "great victory," and this event would be a key element in Khrushchev's removal from power in 1964, and in the Soviet Union's determination to avoid similar Cold War embarrassments in the future by building up its missile forces to achieve rough parity with the United States by the 1970s.

What followed after the Cuban crisis was the "taming of the Cold War," as some historians have put it, or, in John Lewis Gaddis's words, the "long peace."[71] There would be more nuclear weapons than ever, but henceforward competition between the United States and the Soviet Union would be more carefully stage-managed to avoid the dangerous excesses that had produced the Berlin and Cuban crises. West Berlin mayor Willy Brandt believed that the world had contemplated "the suicide of mankind" during the Cuban crisis, and was convinced that this event was the "turning point as far as Berlin was concerned. . . . Since then everyone has been rather cautious about developments in Berlin."[72]

What did *not* follow after the Cuban Missile Crisis was renewed public enthusiasm for fallout shelters, even though, as Chet Holifield pointed out in a 1963 letter to Kennedy, the Cuban unpleasantness had "brought vividly to mind the fact that the United States has no effective civil defense."[73] While polls after the Cuban crisis show that Americans continued to believe that fallout shelters could be useful in the event of a nuclear attack, relatively few had actually built a shelter. In a study made for the Office of Emergency Planning in 1964, Hudson Institute researchers concluded that the public "supports the belief that war is a not-inconceivable possibility, supports the idea of shelter or other civil defense programs as a form of protection, but is little inclined to do anything about it." The researchers wryly observed, "It seems plain that most of the public would accept a cost-less, effort-less civil defense program if it were given to them."[74]

How many shelters were actually built? This is a difficult question to answer because many shelter owners were not anxious to advertise the fact that they had a shelter. But in June 1961, a month before the Kennedy speech that began the fallout shelter boom, governors from forty states reported that more than sixty thousand family fallout shelters had been built or were under construction.[75] By 1965, as many as 200,000 may have been in place.[76] If we accept the 200,000 number with the proviso that figures on shelter building are highly speculative, what does this number mean? Certainly the argument can be made that 200,000 is a lot of shelters, and in 1961 it would mean about one shelter for every 900 persons or one shelter for every 266 households.[77] But in an era in which most Americans (53 percent in 1961) believed that a nuclear war with the Soviet Union was likely to occur, an even more forceful argument can be made that 200,000 is a small number.[78] Given the fears of nuclear war, it is also significant that a political consensus never developed for an expensive, national shelter system funded by the federal government. Shelter building clearly peaked during the early 1960s. By 1967 there were few shelters under construction, and the Department of Defense was emphasizing "dual purpose fallout shelter space."[79]

What is clear is that at the height of Cold War tensions Americans *talked* a great deal about fallout shelters, but relatively few Americans actually *built* fallout shelters. The reasons for this are many. One of the most common suggestions for explaining the end of the fallout shelter debate and America's preoccupation with the nuclear issue is the test ban treaty signed by the United States and the USSR in 1963.[80] It should also be noted that shelters ran afoul of determined political opposition, especially in the person of Congressman Albert Thomas of Texas. One of the linchpins of the Kennedy civil defense plan was the Shelter Incentive Program, which would have provided up to 66.5 percent of the cost of fallout shelter construction in public places (mostly schools). This program depended on funding from the Independent Offices Subcommittee, of which Thomas was chairman. In 1962 one of the members of the Thomas subcommittee declared that "no one has been able to convince me that this fallout shelter program is worth a damn."[81] This was a bad omen for civil defense, and while the House would eventually authorize the Shelter Incentive Bill in the fall of 1963, it would get no funding from the Thomas subcommittee. Thomas proclaimed, "We're not building any fallout shelters, period."[82]

By this time the shelter program had also become entangled with the proposed Nike X antiballistic missile (ABM) program. Work on an ABM system had begun in 1956 with the Nike Zeus, but this program had been plagued from the beginning by the slow speed of its interceptor and the slow tracking abilities of its mechanical radar. To address its many deficiencies, planners proposed to arm the Nike Zeus with a nuclear warhead—a strategy that was also being extended to more conventional interceptors. Still the problems remained. Eisenhower vetoed deployment of the Nike Zeus in 1959, and Kennedy reaffirmed this decision in 1962.[83]

By the time development began on the Nike X in 1963, a number of technological advances had been made that addressed the limitations of the Nike Zeus, including phased-array radar and two interceptors, one for high altitude and one for low altitude.[84] In some circles, there was optimism that an effective ABM system would rekindle enthusiasm for a national fallout shelter program because the two would operate symbiotically. The Project Harbor study, for instance, noted that it would be "easier and less expensive" to establish an ABM system that intercepted incoming missiles at fifteen thousand feet rather than outside the atmosphere, but that such a system would have to include shelter for those in the target path and "close coordination of civil defense planning and the planning of active defense." In the end, the Project Harbor study promised that this combination of passive and active civil defense could "provide protection for a very large fraction of the population, even against extreme forms of attack."[85]

Robert McNamara was less convinced as to the utility of an ABM program, and believed that a shelter system should be given priority over ABMs because shelters represented the most cost-effective way of protecting the population. A related argument was that a shelter program without ABMs could be effective, but not vice versa, because an enemy seeking to avoid ABM sites could detonate missiles away from such sites and still kill the population with fallout.[86] In a 1964 news conference McNamara proclaimed that a fallout shelter program could stand alone without an ABM system, but "an anti-ballistic system cannot stand alone without a fallout shelter system."[87]

As McNamara no doubt knew, once into the realm of missile defenses, with countermeasures against missile defenses, and countermeasures against the countermeasures, the permutations become increasingly baroque and the cost of developing such systems virtually limitless. In one study produced for the army under the auspices of the Stanford Research Institute, it was anticipated that an enemy might seek to avoid missile or aircraft defenses by resorting to high-altitude "standoff thermal attacks" that would set cities on fire. As a countermeasure to such a strategy, cities under nuclear attack could activate smoke generators, which this study claimed might reduce thermal radiation to a tenth of its unattenuated value. Total cost of a fifteen-city smoke-generating system was estimated at $7.65 billion.[88] Whether the enemy was at work producing missiles armed with giant fans to defeat the smoke generators is not known, but at a fairly early date at least one magazine, *Mad*, had explored the rich possibilities of missile defense. *Mad* posited that an attack by a Russian missile might be intercepted by an American "Big Snip" missile (a rocket-propelled giant pair of scissors). As a countermeasure to the Big Snip, the Russians would launch a rocket-powered hacksaw, which would be countered by an American "Flying Nailfile," and so on.[89]

Congress did not see matters in the same light. When the already gutted Shelter Incentive Bill arrived in the Senate in March 1964, it was the influential Senator Henry Jackson, chairman of the Armed Services Subcommittee, who shelved the bill with the explanation that "the ballistic missile defense and the shelter program have been closely related and it is believed that a decision as to both should be similarly related."[90] This statement exasperated civil defense officials, who had "related" ABM and shelter programs in a way that was fundamentally different from Jackson's interpretation, but the deed had been done. The killing of the Shelter Incentive Program, in the words of Harry Yoshpe, "marked the great divide in the fortunes of OCD" in terms of both funding and stature.[91] By 1967 Congress had given McNamara more money than he wanted for ABMs, and had rejected his modest request for shelter subsidies.[92] Once again, despite the daunting problems associated with ABM development, sex appeal seemingly played a role in the preference for ABMs over shelters, just as it had in producing generous funding for the "active" Strategic Air Command, and little or no funding for "passive" defensive systems such as fallout shelters.

There was also the increasing American absorption with Vietnam.[93] In 1968 Robert McNamara, normally a stalwart supporter of civil defense, requested a civil defense budget of only $77.4 million—the lowest request since civil defense was placed in the Department of Defense in 1961. McNamara explained that "we have held the fiscal year 1969 program to the lowest possible sustaining rate, pending the end of the Vietnam conflict."[94]

Writing in the same year, an embittered Steuart Pittman claimed that McNamara himself must shoulder much of the blame for the decline of civil defense because McNamara was "the chief main architect and advocate of the argument against nuclear defense."[95] As we have seen, McNamara had endorsed both the idea of counterforce strategy and the need for a fallout shelter system in 1961. But in the wake of intense public criticism

McNamara retreated from his counterforce advocacy and the idea of limited nuclear war, and returned to an emphasis on "assured destruction," a strategic philosophy in which fallout shelters would hold little value. Variously described as countervalue, balance of terror, or mutual vulnerability, assured destruction meant that both the United States and the Soviet Union would maintain a preponderance of nuclear weapons that would guarantee the destruction of the population of the other.[96]

While critical of McNamara, Pittman seemed to reserve most of his bitterness for the American people themselves. A genuinely perplexed Pittman observed, "The question remains as to why this nation, unlike the Soviets, finds civil defense—protection of people at home and at work—a controversial and unappetizing undertaking." Answering his own question, Pittman claimed that as Americans, we are unable to "discipline our minds to consider the importance to national recovery of the difference between over half of the population surviving and one-quarter surviving. . . . We have gone overboard in exaggerating the concept of total destruction in order to persuade ourselves and our adversaries and our allies that nuclear war is impossible."[97] Herman Kahn made much the same point in his writings, and McGeorge Bundy, Kennedy's assistant for national security affairs, likewise concluded that the subject of nuclear war "may be too dreadful for rational discussion," and that "the risk of public misunderstanding was grossly neglected by all of us."[98]

The *Saturday Evening Post* editorialized that because the Kennedy administration had "failed to answer some fundamental questions" about underground shelters, Americans reacted "with commendable skepticism and common sense. They refused to buy."[99] Ralph Lapp was also critical of Kennedy, especially for initiating a program that was not well thought out. In Lapp's words, "It appeared that the new President thought he could pull a lever and the machinery of a civil-defense apparatus would start up." Lapp believed that a national shelter system failed to materialize because the public was resistant to making itself "part of the nuclear deterrent system." If the United States hardened its cities, said Lapp, "the weapons culture would see a complete envelopment of the civilian sector in a Fortress America."[100]

Another reason Americans rejected fallout shelters was that they understood that a fallout shelter program was essentially anti-urban, and that without blast and thermal protection only rural and suburban residents would survive a nuclear war. As the *Bulletin of the Atomic Scientists* asked in 1961, "What would people in cities do, even if their city were spared a direct hit? In most cases, they would die."[101] Bernard Brodie, a counterforce theorist and shelter advocate, also admitted that obtaining funding for elaborate urban shelters was problematic because of "the ever-recurrent suspicion that they would probably be of no use. . . . the case for the shelter against radioactive fallout in the country is much easier to make."[102]

Still, the extremely limited shelter program initiated in 1961 (in which existing buildings were stocked with survival supplies) continued to move forward, and by 1967 the National Fallout Shelter Survey had identified 160 million spaces with a protection factor of 40 or more. Ironically, a major portion of the fallout shelter space that had been inventoried was in downtown urban areas. Thus, despite the widespread discussion on the special requirements of urban shelters (and the relative worthlessness of ordinary fallout shelters against blast and fire), most shelter space by the late 1960s was to be found in precisely those areas where they would be the least effective. Representative Martha Griffiths (D–Mich.) had anticipated this situation in 1961, and had observed somewhat uncharitably that "if the bombs fell at night, you would save nobody but skid row characters, drunks, a few people in hospitals and maybe the night shift on the local newspapers."[103] Indeed, large "shelter deficit areas" remained, especially in American suburbs, and the OCD continued to promote the installation of shelters in suburban schools, even though it admitted that the success of this program had "varied substantially throughout the country."[104] In an effort to avoid the increasingly intractable problem of shelters in schools, the OCD sponsored an architectural competition in 1964 with the goal of placing fallout shelters in the very symbol of the suburban beast, the shopping center. The OCD compared the shopping center to the traditional town hall, noting that it served "the civic needs and activities of suburban neighborhoods" and that it would require "minimum conversion to meet emergency needs." The winning designs had dual-purpose spaces capable of providing shelter for at least four thousand shoppers during a nuclear attack.[105]

While the Kennedy administration was criticized for its failure to produce a coherent civil defense program, it can be argued that the incoherence of federal civil defense programs merely reflected the public's own ambivalence.[106] Writing on the Holifield hearings for the *Bulletin of the Atomic Scientists* in 1956, Mary Simpson found that the hearings "brought out how little, as a nation, we seem concerned about survival on the home front. . . . We appear to prefer not to listen to unpleasant facts about the peril we live under."[107] Ralph Lapp agreed, referring to the "enigma of civil defense" and taking note of the

> reluctance of Americans to accept responsibility for the bomb. The bomb is something they would prefer not to think about, and the shelter proposal hits not so much at the pocket books as at the conscience. The American people are dimly aware that the U.S. deterrent has as its real target Russian homes and Russian people, but as yet they have not really associated themselves with the bomb.[108]

While Americans *were* often reluctant to fully face up to the realities of nuclear holocaust (it is not an easy subject to keep constantly in mind), they were less passively fatalistic than they were often accused of being. Americans actively took part in the debate over shelters, and their rejection of fallout shelters was a conscious decision based on the social, moral, and economic implications of building those shelters. The physicist Freeman Dyson believes that at the root of the rejection of shelters by Americans was the cultural tradition of "freedom under the open sky. Americans seem to acquire from their native landscape an aesthetic revulsion against the whole idea of burrowing underground in pursuit of safety."[109] As early as 1946, long before the shelter debate, Albert Einstein argued that reasonable human beings would "refuse to contemplate a future in which our culture would attempt to survive in ribbons or in underground tombs," and Robert Moses echoed these sentiments in 1957, predicting that "sane" Americans would never support a national fallout shelter program: "We are not going underground. We shall not evacuate and disperse. We shall not change our way of life. The sane people of the country will not take this threat seriously enough to support a fantastic national underground escapist program."[110] Even Dwight D. Eisenhower proclaimed that if he found himself in a shelter without his family, he "would just walk out. I would not want to face that kind of a world and the loss of my family."[111]

Some suburbanites, of course, did build shelters, and it is tempting to try to draw some parallel between the suburban shelter building impulse of the 1960s and the suburban life of our own era. The contemporary image of gated suburban communities with tank-like sport utility vehicles issuing forth to do battle on the mean streets of America could be held up as evidence that suburbanites now, as in the 1960s, are obsessed with "security" and avoidance of contact with the outside world. Indeed, there has been a long-standing intellectual bias in the United States against the suburbs, and attacking the suburban straw man has proven to be both cheap and easy. In 1961, the year of the Berlin crisis, two notable academics published works on urban planning and history in which hostility toward suburban communities is palpable. In *The Death and Life of Great American Cities*, Jane Jacobs refers to an "insipid, standardized, suburbanized shadow of nature."[112] But Jacobs is the voice of moderation itself compared to Lewis Mumford, who in *The City in History* described the suburbs as a "multitude of uniform, unidentifiable houses, lined up inflexibly, at uniform distances, on uniform roads, in a treeless communal waste." The suburbs, said Mumford, promoted a "self-centered life" where residents hoped to "overcome the chronic defects of civilization while still commanding at will the privileges and benefits of urban society." Here life "was not even a cheap counterfeit, but rather the grim antithesis."[113]

In a 1961 *New York Times* article, Margaret Mead claimed that because of anxieties about nuclear attacks on cities, overpopulation, and urban crime Americans had retreated to the suburbs, where they were "hiding from the future and the rest of the world" and idealizing the individual family. "The armed, individual shelter," said Mead, "is the logical end of this retreat from trust in and responsibility for others."[114] Writing in the same year, Episcopal bishop James A. Pike argued that shelter owners were refusing to engage the enemy on the global battlefield, and that "with the building of back-yard bomb shelters, the last of our courage would seem to have fled."[115]

But it's all a bit too pat to condemn the selfish, soulless suburbs as opposed to the vital authenticity of inner-city communities, especially when a majority of inner-city residents would probably leave their authentic communities for the suburbs if given the faintest opportunity. As Kenneth Jackson has observed, those who moved to the suburbs during the 1950s and 1960s were not especially concerned with the problems of the inner city or the "snobbish views of Lewis Mumford and other social critics." What they were looking for were "good schools, private space, and personal safety," and they found them in the suburbs. It was the single-family tract home that "offered growing families a private haven in a heartless world."[116] Suburbanites who built fallout shelters in the two decades following World War II, like those who now live in gated communities and drive SUVs, stand accused of the heinous crime of trying to provide for the safety of their families.[117] In a letter to *Good Housekeeping*, one anxious reader asked, "Since when is it hysterical, inhuman and degrading to want to stay alive?" There can be little doubt that civil defense advocates were exploiting this natural, human instinct in their promotion of home fallout shelters.[118] The significance of the shelter issue in the 1950s and 1960s, however, is much like the significance of the dog that did not bark in the Sherlock Holmes story: it is to be found not in the number of suburbanites who built such shelters, but in the far greater number who, despite concerns over the vulnerability of their families to nuclear weapons, chose *not* to build because they were disturbed by the troubling moral aspects of shelters.[119]

The Critics

Cultural critics have interpreted this era in a number of ways. In *Nuclear Fear*, Spencer R. Weart concludes that the debate over shelters "drove home the idea of nuclear war as an indescribable catastrophe, while reinforcing murky associations with fantasies of victimization and survival, but it did little to bring the vague imagery into focus."[120] Allan Winkler contends that "the public proved to be an even greater source of pressure on the government" on civil defense matters than scientists, but more often than not public officials simply orchestrated such pressures to their own goals.[121]

Less skeptical as to the accomplishments of nuclear critics is Margot A. Henriksen, who emphasizes America's "atomic age culture of dissent" and the "revolutionary cultural awakening that had taken place on America's 'eve of destruction.'" Henriksen goes on to claim that "when American authorities risked the survival of civilization as Kennedy did in the early 1960s, the dissenting culture awakened to the threat and prevented the complete failure of the 'human element' in American society."[122] While it is difficult to divine what Henriksen might mean by the "human element" (surely Herman Kahn is no less "human" than Joan Baez), there is little evidence then (or now) that Americans were ready to unilaterally abandon their nuclear weapons. Public opinion polls taken during the worst crises of the Cold War, Berlin and Cuba, provide evidence not of a resurgent "dissenting culture," but of overwhelming public support for the moves taken by the Kennedy administration (a Gallup poll taken during the Cuban Missile Crisis gave Kennedy an 84 percent approval rating).[123] Kennedy also received bipartisan political support. In the midst of the Cuban crisis Richard Nixon, who certainly harbored no great love for the Kennedy administration, declared that "this is not a subject for partisan debate," and called on Americans to support the president and to "speak as one voice."[124] In addition, the press was nearly unanimous in its approval of the strong stands taken by Kennedy. And if one is seeking evidence of a genuine grassroots reaction to these crises emanating from the culture, perhaps the best example is the sharply increased numbers of volunteers for the armed forces.

The public's support for tough stands on both Berlin and Cuba—even to the extreme of nuclear war—also reveals a flaw in the argument that civil defense was a palliative designed to get the public to accept America's nuclear deterrent strategy. In *The Imaginary War* Guy Oakes asks, "If the price of freedom proved to be nuclear war, would Americans be willing to pay?" Oakes concludes that "the instrument chosen to convince the American people to pay the price for the failure of deterrence was civil defense. Americans would accept the risks of nuclear war only if they could be assured that a nuclear attack on their own cities would not be too costly."[125] In fact, as we have seen, Americans rejected civil defense programs (the most salient of which was the fallout shelter program) for a multitude of reasons (not least of which was the dubious effectiveness of any civil defense preparation in the face of nuclear attack). They did *not* reject America's nuclear deterrent, even though they were well aware of the consequences of deterrence's failure, nor did the overwhelming majority of Americans shrink from confronting the Soviets in the international arena, despite the risks of war.

The degree to which Americans were "militarized" during the Cold War is an obvious question, but the evidence for such a militarization is ambiguous. Certainly the American military establishment was huge during these years, but the greater society's endorsement of the military imperatives ebbed and flowed according to complicated social, economic, and political factors. In Michael Sherry's formulation, American militarization was "quixotic, capricious, and contingent," and never approached the totalitarian levels established by the Soviet Union, Imperial Japan, or Nazi Germany.[126] Individual home fallout shelters and a national fallout shelter system were widely perceived by Americans as steps toward a more militarized society, and Americans by and large turned away from this path. Laura McEnaney is correct in her observation that while Americans generally supported anticommunist initiatives and military expenditures, they "repudiated a level of militarization that required them to finance their own security, and they rejected the idea of living with a physical reminder of nuclear war inside or immediately outside their homes."[127]

After the passing of the Cold War's great crises, what we see is not Henriksen's "awakening" to nuclear issues, but rather an era that Paul Boyer has called the "Big Sleep."[128] "The sudden fading of the nuclear weapons issue after September 1963," notes Boyer, "whether as an activist cause, a cultural motif, or a topic of public discourse, is astonishing." Organizations devoted to nuclear test bans and disarmament vanished overnight. In one example, the Student Peace Union disbanded itself when only twenty-five delegates showed up at its convention in 1964.[129] Certainly nuclear weapons continued to be terrible instruments of war, and as Americans fretted about them the "spirit of doubt," as Tom Engelhardt has put it, did seep into the American consciousness at many points.[130] But on the most basic premise of the Cold War, that the Soviet Union *did* pose a real threat to the freedom and security of the world, most Americans were in agreement, despite the propagandistic excesses produced by their own government. In the realpolitik of the Cold War world there seemed to be no genuine alternative to maintaining a nuclear arsenal, despite the nightmarish potential of such weapons, and no real alternative to taking a firm stand against Soviet belligerence, despite the risks. It is not that Americans were ignorant of the possible consequences of nuclear war. As I have tried to show, there was no escaping the subject during these years. But there is a great difference between understanding the danger of something and conceiving of a way to live without it. Pat Watters, a writer for the *Atlanta Journal*, identified the conundrum in which many found themselves in 1961. Watters counted himself among those "who cry out instinctively against the death-wish ultimate of the possibility of nuclear war," but also found himself in the "paradoxical position" of supporting the buildup of the American military machine "because this is really the only hope to deter war, now and for a long time in the future."[131]

The threat of annihilation produced some serious strains on the American psyche. But such stresses can be endured for only so long, after which the individual must crack under the pressure or get on with his or her life. Throughout the history of civil defense in this country Americans have been excoriated for their supposed apathy. Early in the process (in 1951), a frustrated FCDA administrator, Millard Caldwell, complained that "the most vicious menace in America was the shocking apathy of the American people to their danger from enemy attack."[132] Eleven years later, Thomas Merton had much the same observation, noting that "after a season of brisk speculation, men seem to be fatigued by the whole question" of nuclear weapons.[133] These characterizations may have held a great deal of truth, but they miss the point about what people must do to live in a world that can be annihilated in a heartbeat. Clearly, Americans were anxious about such a world, but they were forced to learn to live with their anxieties about the bomb in the same way people live with the other traumas of life. In a 1961 sermon the Boston Unitarian minister Jack Mendelsohn admitted that he had accepted "the probability of nuclear holocaust, the literal cremation of hundreds of millions of people, including myself and my family, within the next five or ten years." But Mendelsohn also noted that he was "ignoring and dismissing what is simply too painful for me to perceive. To some extent we are all part of this retreat from reality, and a degree of it is essential to our ability to rise up in the morning and go about our normal duties."[134] Such complex mental accommodations had to be negotiated by most other Americans during this era.

The subtitle of *Dr. Strangelove*, the famous 1964 black comedy about the start of a nuclear war, is *How I Learned to Stop Worrying and Love the Bomb*. Americans did not stop worrying, and they did not learn to love the bomb. But seemingly they did learn to at least *live* with the bomb, and what followed the Cuban Missile Crisis was not heightened concern with nuclear weapons but a numbness to the issue as American political concerns became focused on other matters.

Today, the fallout shelter is indulgently viewed as a relic of the Cold War.[135] Fallout shelters no longer create the controversy that they once did, perhaps because most of the population has made up its mind that nuclear war is not survivable. Indeed, fallout shelters today, both public and private, are now quietly deteriorating or are being readapted to other uses. Robert Ruark, commenting on the fate of the fallout shelter, observed as early as the fall of 1962 that "whiskey once again replaced the iron rations on the fallout shelter shelves. Junior parked his busted bicycle in the first-aid room which rapidly became overstuffed with sister's decapitated doll babies."[136] School duck-and-cover drills also proved to have a short shelf life. One commentator remembers that by 1967 one of his high school classrooms was prominently displaying a set of civil defense instructions that was the usual Cold War fare except for the last line: "Put your head between your knees, and kiss your ass goodbye."[137] This mildly profane rejoinder has become the standard response to the suggestion that nuclear war is survivable, and the drills that are held in schools today are mostly concerned with surviving natural disasters—earthquakes, tornadoes, hurricanes—rather than the ultimate man-made disaster of nuclear war. Chillingly, in the wake of the Columbine High School shootings of 1999, increasing numbers of schools are also holding "intruder drills," a development that makes one almost wistful for the relatively impersonal threat of nuclear war.

While the fallout shelter is still with us, it no longer carries the huge, symbolic weight that it did during the 1960s, when it represented the garrison state or the Maginot Line, a "nation of moles" or a gun-thy-neighbor morality. Like few other icons of the Cold War, the fallout shelter was a conundrum, a riddle whose meaning was always just beyond reach. It was emblematic of human selfishness and savagery, or, as some saw it, a wise and prudent precaution in a dangerous world. The fallout shelter would bring the nation closer to war, or it would discourage the Soviets from waging war. The fallout shelter would foster the belief that there was life after nuclear holocaust, or alternatively, shelters would be America's pyramids, what remained of this civilization when the world had been reduced to a smoldering cinder.

At the very least, the fallout shelter prompted a debate on all levels of society over nuclear war and survival. This debate was engaged with an intensity that had never been seen before or subsequently during the Cold War. The overall rejection by Americans of fallout shelters and a subtopian life represented, I believe, a maturity that was often lacking in their political leadership. Roger Hagan claimed that this was evidence that Americans had "reverted to their traditional good sense—that is, to their salutary neglect" of civil defense, but there were stronger emotions at work here than mere absentminded neglect.[138] In the end Americans viewed fallout shelters with something close to revulsion, even horror, and they were wise enough to understand that if they let the bomb dictate the terms under which they lived, life would not be worth living. In the next war nuclear weapons would exact a fearsome toll, but putting the nation underground also came with an extremely high price. It would be costly materially and costly morally, and Americans finally accepted that living with the threat of nuclear war was preferable to the entombment of their nation and their souls.

Postscript

After 1964, interest in civil defense would languish for well over a decade, although there continued to be support for an ABM program as fears grew over China's missile capability. In March 1969 Richard Nixon authorized deployment of the Safeguard ABM, a relatively modest system that was installed near the Minuteman ICBM site in Grand Forks, North Dakota, in 1974. The Safeguard would become the only ABM to be deployed in the United States, but was removed in 1976 due to problems with cost and effectiveness.[1] During the Carter years the state of American civil defense briefly resurfaced as an issue because of the perception that the Soviets had strengthened *their* civil defense. As in the 1960s, a debate ensued over whether Soviet civil defense improvements were real and substantial or merely paper programs, and what enhancements in Soviet civil defense meant strategically.[2]

Also resuscitated in the late 1970s was the idea of population relocation. The notion that urban populations could be evacuated out of target areas before the commencement of a nuclear war had seemingly been refuted as early as the mid-1950s. The massive logistical problems associated with this strategy had certainly not disappeared, nor had the basic problem of knowing when, exactly, such an evacuation should take place. But the alternative of expending millions on in-place fallout or blast shelters did not appeal to the Carter administration because of fears that a shelter system would threaten ongoing negotiations for a new Strategic Arms Limitation Treaty (SALT II). Under such constraints, the relocation idea was all civil defense planners had to work with during the Carter years—a situation similar to the one in which Val Peterson found himself during the 1950s. Seeking to avoid costs and controversies, the Carter administration, like other administrations before it, adopted what Thomas Kerr has called "a posture of calculated ambivalence" toward civil defense.[3]

No such ambivalence would haunt the Reagan presidency. Strangely, the same issues that had been fought over in the 1950s and 1960s would be revived during the Reagan administration of the 1980s. Arguments about evacuation, fallout shelters, missile defense systems, and the survivability of nuclear war would flourish once again. It was Ronald Reagan who helped lead the successful attack against Carter's SALT II agreement (a pact widely denounced by the American Right as a sellout to the Soviets), and when Reagan became president in 1980, it was immediately apparent that a radical shift in relations with the Soviet Union was about to take place. The détente that had been established between the United States and the Soviet Union with the 1972 signing of the SALT I treaty was denounced by Reagan at his first press conference as "a one-way street the Soviet Union has used to pursue its own aims." A heated anticommunist rhetoric would be characteristic of the Reagan years. Reagan famously described the Soviet Union as "an evil empire" and promised to deposit communism on the "ash heap of history."[4]

Reagan had joined the critics who claimed that American military power had greatly deteriorated during the 1970s, and the most influential of these critics were members of the Committee on the Present Danger (CPD).[5] The CPD was a bipartisan group with an impressive membership that included Reagan, Kenneth Adelman, Richard Allen, William Casey, Paul Nitze, Jeane Kirkpatrick, Eugene Rostow, Clare Boothe Luce, and many others. The committee's declared purpose was to alert America "to the ominous Soviet military buildup and its implications, and to the unfavorable trends in the U.S.-Soviet military balance."[6] According to the CPD, much of the damage had been done under détente, which Eugene V. Rostow described as "a figment of political imagination."[7] While the committee's main concern was the decline of American military strength, the CPD also expressed concerns that the Soviets had embarked on a massive civil defense program and that the United States was badly lagging in this area. In an assertion that would be repeated with mantra-like frequency by civil defense proponents during the 1980s, the CPD claimed that the Soviets had been spending $2 billion annually for several years on civil defense, and that this program was "designed to ensure Soviet nuclear war-survival, recovery, and emergence as the dominant post-war global power."[8] According to the CPD the Soviet civil defense program would assure that the Soviets would suffer only one-tenth the casualties of the United States during a nuclear war.[9] Adding urgency to the CPD's pronouncements on civil defense was its disturbing vision of the future. In a chilling reprise of the rhetoric that dominated the early 1960s, the CPD observed that "the tides are once again rushing the world toward general war."[10] The CPD would wield considerable clout in Washington, with some thirty-three of its members serving in the Reagan administration.[11]

Another prophet of decline was Samuel P. Huntington, a professor of government at Harvard and consultant to the Kennedy, Johnson, and Nixon administrations. Writing in *The Strategic Imperative* in 1982, Huntington claimed that "the most important change of the 1970s was the relative decline in American military power compared to that of the Soviet Union." Huntington also believed that the Soviets were pouring money into a huge civil defense program, and he called not only for a U.S. military buildup, but also for "the enhancement of U.S. survivability" through civil defense and active defense. Like the CPD, Huntington declared that "the probability is high that the United States will go to war sometime in the 1980s."[12]

In 1982 the Reagan administration asked Congress for an increase of $100 million for civil defense for the coming fiscal year. This would be part of a huge program projected to cost $4.2 billion over seven years, with most of it spent on preparing American cities for mass evacuations to "host areas" in the countryside when nuclear war seemed imminent. The plan operated on the assumption that there would be at least a week's warning time in which to relocate urban residents, and that these transplanted urbanites could then help build their own fallout shelters. This proposal was immediately embroiled in controversy. The *Washington Post* declared that "both sides of the debate are offering variations on the themes they have sounded for 25 years."[13]

While Congress would prove to be more than obliging in giving Reagan the weapons systems he wanted, it would ultimately balk at providing funding for an invigorated civil defense. Many still remembered the fallout shelter controversy of the early 1960s, and while the arguments both for and against a more elaborate civil defense system remained much the same, the prospects for surviving a nuclear war, shelters or no shelters, had diminished in the intervening years because both the United States and the Soviet Union had greatly increased the number and megatonnage of their nuclear weapons. By 1982 the two nations between them would have some 17,500 nuclear warheads with over 11,000 megatons. By the end of the Cold War the United States and Soviet Union would together have at least 40,000 nuclear warheads.[14]

The energetic reporting of a single writer, Robert Scheer of the *Los Angeles Times*, would prove to be a key factor in derailing the Reagan civil defense program, and much of the damage was self-inflicted by Reagan officials. Indeed, in his 1982 newspaper series on civil defense and in his subsequent book, *With Enough Shovels: Reagan, Bush and Nuclear War*, Scheer managed to extract some remarkable quotes from members of the Reagan administration. In one interview, Reagan told Scheer of his belief that the Soviets "had come to the conclusion that there could be a nuclear war and that it would be winnable—by them." Reagan also expressed concerns that the Soviets had developed a highly effective civil defense program, and that the Soviets had at one point held an exercise in which twenty million urban residents had been evacuated out of the cities into the countryside. Scheer observes, "It is unknown where Reagan learned this; the CIA says there is no evidence the Russians have ever practiced evacuating their cities."[15] The efficacy of the Soviet civil defense effort, however, and the threat that this presented to American defense posture were gospel among civil defense proponents of the 1980s. Administration officials once again brought forward the $2 billion figure, with solemn assurances that this is what the Soviets were spending annually on civil defense (compared to $125 million for the United States). FEMA spokesman Russell Clanahan claimed that America's neglect of civil defense had created "a different sort of 'window of vulnerability.'"

Others had their doubts, including Henry Shapiro, a United Press International reporter who had spent forty years in Moscow and had never seen a single civil defense drill in that city after World War II. The idea that Moscow could be quickly evacuated was dismissed by Shapiro as "science fiction." Other problems with Soviet civil defense included the lack of paved roads and inadequately stocked and ventilated shelters.[16] As for the billions that the Soviets were supposedly spending on civil defense, Scheer and others cited a 1978 CIA report that pointed out that the $2 billion figure was based on what the Soviet Union would pay its civil defense workers (mostly soldiers) if those workers were paid on a U.S. wage scale (which they were not).[17]

Scheer would glean his most revealing insights into the administration's civil defense thinking in his discussions with deputy under secretary of defense Thomas K. Jones. Jones had worked for Boeing evaluating the Soviet civil defense program before joining the Reagan administration, and was convinced that if the United States had a similar program it could recover from an all-out nuclear war in two to four years. Jones defended the administration's civil defense proposals, claiming that it would be possible to evacuate the urban population in a relatively short period of time, and that constructing adequate shelter for these refugees would pose no great problem. As Jones put it, "Dig a hole, cover it with a couple of doors and then throw three feet of dirt on top. It's the dirt that does it." In a statement widely quoted in the media, Jones expressed his confidence that nuclear war or not, "Everybody's going to make it if there are enough shovels to go around."[18] Like Jones, FEMA publications exuded a sunny optimism as to the impact of nuclear war. FEMA dismissed predictions of rampant pestilence and disease in the aftermath of nuclear devastation as "a specter, not a realistic probability," and estimated that the United States "could survive nuclear attack and go on to recover within a relatively few years."[19] As FEMA put it, "Everyone agrees that a nuclear war could be an unparalleled disaster. But it need not be an *unmitigated* disaster."[20]

As Jones's "enough shovels" comments were quoted in columns around the country, this obscure administration official quickly acquired an unwelcome notoriety.[21] When Jones was asked to appear before a Senate civil defense hearing in March, two substitutes were sent to testify in his place. Jones had apparently been muzzled by the administration. An angry Senator Larry Pressler (R–S.D.) dismissed Jones's substitutes and alleged that the Reagan administration was "afraid to expose Mr. Jones to a wider audience" and "afraid to expose (its) civil defense plan to the light of day."[22]

This was only the beginning of Reagan's civil defense woes. The claim that 150 million American urban dwellers could be smoothly and quickly evacuated, then fed and housed for an indeterminate amount of time, was greeted with incredulity across the country. Marin County decided to make no civil defense plans at all; Marin supervisor Barbara Boxer noted, "The bottom line is that there's no way we can evacuate skeletons."[23] The city of Boulder also decided not to participate in any evacuation planning after residents denounced the idea in public hearings. In Memphis, civil defense director Billy Ray Schilling predicted that suburban residents south of Memphis would probably depart from the official evacuation plan and move south into Mississippi rather than north into Tennessee.

"But I don't know what they'd do if they got to the Mississippi host areas and nobody wanted them," said Schilling. In California, Governor Edmund G. Brown, Jr., pointed out that "Los Angeles cannot even evacuate itself on a Friday afternoon."[24] Supervisor Kenneth Hahn of Los Angeles County agreed, insisting, "This is colossal. Virtually impossible to do. You just can't evacuate Los Angeles County in any reasonable time." Hahn also called attention to what he called the "staggering" logistical problem of caring for the 7.2 million residents of the county once they had been evacuated.[25] The evacuation plan for Washington, D.C., was especially quixotic, calling for those with even-numbered license plates to leave the city first, while those with odd-numbered plates stayed off the highways and patiently waited their turn.[26] As for the nation's largest city, FEMA believed that it was possible to move the 6.5 million residents of New York in 3.3 days to areas two hundred to four hundred miles away. "Difficult?" asked *New York Times* columnist Tom Wicker. "Not if multilane divided highways, with all lanes made one-way outbound, carry 1,500 cars per hour per lane at 40 miles per hour for 20 hours a day for 3.3 days, with no 'flow interruptions' from accidents, breakdowns, running out of gas, poor traffic control and the like. No panic, of course."[27] Evacuation plans also called for a prohibition on evacuees taking along alcoholic beverages and firearms, a ban that would no doubt be as widely ignored as other civil defense provisions. The problem, as *Newsweek* expressed it, was that "there must be not only adequate warning time but also decent weather, docile evacuees and hospitable hosts."[28]

The claim that the United States could recover relatively quickly from a nuclear war was also attacked. Helping to lead the assault, as they had done twenty years previously, were physicians, as well as writers associated with the *Bulletin of the Atomic Scientists*. John Hiatt, dean of the Harvard School of Public Health, testified before a Senate committee in 1981 that "recent talk by public figures about winning or even surviving a nuclear war must reflect a widespread failure to appreciate a medical reality: Any nuclear war would inevitably cause death, disease and suffering of epidemic proportions and effective medical intervention on any realistic scale would be impossible." Herbert L. Abrams, also of Harvard, suggested that in a post–nuclear war environment insects "would thrive on the unburied corpses, infest surviving animals and, eventually, man."[29] An international physicians group, meeting in Amsterdam in June 1983, declared bluntly that "there is no effective civil defense for nuclear war," and that "a nuclear war would be the final epidemic for humankind."[30] When Helen Caldicott, president of the 10,000-member

Physicians for Social Responsibility, was asked why government officials persisted in promoting civil defense programs, she replied, "Because they're mad. In my experience, they are uniformly ignorant about the medical, scientific and ecological consequences of a nuclear war." Caldicott claimed that nuclear war would create "the last epidemic; it's an incurable disease."[31]

The *Bulletin of the Atomic Scientists* created a special supplement for its June-July issue in 1983 called "Programs for Surviving Nuclear War: A Critique." One of the articles described a curious document that was sent out by the Department of Defense to American hospitals in 1981. In this letter the DOD proposed creating what it called a Civilian-Military Contingency Hospital System, and it requested that large and medium-sized American hospitals commit a minimum of fifty beds each to this system (for a national total of fifty thousand). The commitment of extra beds was needed, said the DOD, for the treatment of the wounded resulting from "a future large-scale war overseas" between the United States and the Soviet Union—a war that would "produce casualties at a higher rate than any other war in history." The controversy produced by this letter was considerable, and at the center of the turmoil was whether a positive response was tantamount to "tacit approval for the planning of a nuclear war." Hospitals, like medical professional organizations, were hopelessly split on this issue. Many refused to cooperate, while others endorsed the plan (the plan was supported by the American Medical Association but condemned by the American Public Health Association).[32]

In 1982 Jonathan Schell published *The Fate of the Earth*, an influential book on the impact of nuclear war that ran originally as a series in the *New Yorker*. The titles of Schell's three chapters indicated his grim conclusions: "A Republic of Insects and Grass," "The Second Death," "The Choice." Schell was convinced of the uselessness of shelters, and called an evacuation before attack "an exercise in transporting people from one death to another." As Schell points out, in the months following a nuclear war there would be a reversal of the normal order in which "the dead would lie on the surface and the living, if there were any, would be buried underground." The shelter dweller who survived "would emerge into a dying natural environment. The vulnerability of the environment," said Schell, "is the last word in the argument against the usefulness of shelters: there is no hole big enough to hide all of nature in."[33] Even William F. Buckley, Jr., who was critical of Schell's stand on civil defense, confessed, "For what it matters, my personal position in the matter is that I pray I would be a victim, not a survivor, of any massive nuclear attack."[34]

Also arguing against the prospect of quick recovery from nuclear war was the recently developed theory of "nuclear winter." Evolving out of observations Carl Sagan had made of how Martian duststorms lowered the surface temperature of the planet, this theory predicted that nuclear weapons would ignite thousands of fires, and that the smoke from these fires would block out the sun and significantly cool the earth's surface.[35] This nuclear winter would, in the words of Thomas Powers, "threaten many plant and animal species, including man, with extinction."[36]

As the broad outlines of the Reagan political philosophy became clear—the hard-line stance against the Soviet Union, the calls for a massive military buildup and plans for an invigorated civil defense initiative—a pervasive fear of nuclear war resurfaced once again in the culture. There was a revival of the nuclear apocalyptic, and depictions of nuclear war and its aftermath were so numerous during this era that Paul Brians has concluded that "*the* classic age of nuclear war in fiction was the eighties."[37] Easily the most influential of the apocalyptic writers was Hal Lindsey, an evangelist and traveling speaker for the Campus Crusade for Christ. During the 1970s and 1980s Lindsey published a series of books predicting the forthcoming apocalypse based on biblical "prophecies." Such publications have certainly been common enough during the Nuclear Age, but what separated Lindsey from the rest of the pack was his incredible popularity. Lindsey's book *The Late Great Planet Earth* was published in 1970 and continued to be a best-seller for twenty years. There were nine million copies in print by 1978, and an astonishing twenty-eight million by 1990.[38] A bizarre mixture of the biblical, political, and scientific, *Late Great* predicts that those under the protection of the Antichrist (especially Russia) "will have fire fall on them." How, exactly, this would happen is not clear, but Lindsey notes that "God could allow the various countries to launch a nuclear exchange of ballistic missiles upon each other."[39] And lest readers in the West become complacent, Lindsey reminds them that they too will be scorched by fire. "Imagine," enthuses Lindsey, "cities like London, Paris, Tokyo, New York, Los Angeles, Chicago—obliterated!"[40] Lindsey also enjoyed success with *There's a New World Coming* (1973) and *The 1980s: Countdown to Armageddon* (1981). The latter work expressed the same concerns as the CPD, especially over the supposed decline of American military power. Lindsey also claimed that while the United States had been neglecting civil defense, "the Soviets have made major expenditures to develop underground shelter, population evacuation and industrial survival procedures." With the Soviets now poised "to fulfill their predicted dreadful role in history," observed Lindsey, "the pages of Ezekiel's and Daniel's prophecies are beginning to look like today's headlines."[41]

Another example of popular anxiety over the threat of nuclear war was the reaction to *The Day After*, a 1983 drama about the impact of a nuclear strike on two midwestern towns.[42] One of the most widely anticipated "events" in television history, *The Day After* was the subject of a *Newsweek* cover story that gushed that "the very idea of what television can do may never be the same" and that this program would "detonate a thermonuclear apocalypse in our communal psyche."[43] While few films could live up to such a billing, much less a made-for-TV movie, an estimated 100 million people tuned in to *The Day After*, and it was widely discussed for weeks afterward. A prominent point made by this film was the futility of civil defense planning.[44]

The renewal of tensions with the Soviets and the talk of nuclear war prompted a renewal of survivalist thinking in the 1980s, and some individuals once again built and stocked fallout shelters.[45] Niche businesses such as the New World Survival Company of Dalton, Georgia, which sold a line of $10,000 shelters as well as other survival gear, were prospering once again. *Survive* magazine was also reportedly doing well, with a circulation of eighty thousand. Kevin E. Steele, managing editor of *Survive*, maintained that "if the U.S. had a workable civil defense network and plan, I don't think you'd see any type of [private] survival publications."[46]

By far the most significant expression of anxiety over the administration's overall nuclear policies was the nuclear freeze movement. Beginning in 1980, freeze advocates called for a bilateral halt to the testing and development of nuclear weapons, and for a reduction of nuclear stockpiles. The initial success of this movement was impressive. By the end of 1982 a freeze petition had garnered 2.5 million signatures, and by early 1983, 348 city and 64 county councils and almost a dozen state legislatures had adopted freeze resolutions.[47] Opinion polls showed overwhelming public support for the freeze idea, and in June 1982, 700,000 people demonstrated outside United Nations headquarters in New York against the arms race.[48] In the spring of 1983 the House adopted a freeze resolution by a two-to-one margin.[49] This would be the high-water mark of the nuclear freeze movement, however, which would collapse under the weight of Reagan's overwhelming victory in the 1984 elections. While Americans and their representatives clearly supported the *idea* of a nuclear freeze, it seems they were unwilling to abandon a strong military or nuclear deterrents. Indeed, twenty days after the House adopted the freeze resolution, it approved funding for the MX missile.[50] The administration's request for civil defense funding, however, was cut in half.[51]

As in the 1960s, broad support for nuclear deterrents did not translate into broad support for civil defense, and by the mid-1980s Democrats realized that attacking the administration's civil defense proposals was a less risky strategy than questioning America's overall defensive posture. Democratic civil defense critics included New York governor Mario Cuomo, who insisted that "in a nuclear war, you're not going to evacuate, and I don't want people to think that you can."[52] The Democratic vice presidential candidate Geraldine Ferraro also blasted the administration's civil defense plans for creating the impression that "nuclear war would be a survivable, tolerable experience." Ferraro declared that "making plans to run away from bombs after they've gone off is not my way of assuring safety."[53] Public concerns that the United States was preparing for nuclear war prodded administration officials to quietly drop the purchase from Turkey of 10,000 pounds of morphine sulfate that were to be stockpiled against a possible nuclear war.[54]

By March 1985, the New York Times was reporting that due to budget cuts and stiff resistance around the country, FEMA had shelved its civil defense evacuation plans.[55] By this time the Reagan administration had already shifted away from civil defense to an emphasis on the Strategic Defense Initiative (SDI). Almost immediately this program was nicknamed "Star Wars." An "active" defensive system that would supposedly destroy enemy missiles before they reached the United States, SDI would assure that American security would no longer have to "rest upon the threat of instant U.S. retaliation to deter a Soviet attack," Reagan claimed. "Wouldn't it be better," asked Reagan, "to save lives than to avenge them?"[56] A host of critics, however, saw SDI in much less benign terms, calling into question the technological feasibility of the project and its potential to escalate the arms race. Mikhail Gorbachev called SDI a "very dangerous" innovation that would "whip up the arms race," while New Republic editor Charles Krauthammer saw in SDI an opportunity to pour "vast national resources into a black hole."[57]

The end of the Cold War in 1989 and the signing of the START I treaty in 1991 dampened enthusiasm for an expensive and technologically unproven SDI, but concerns about missile attacks from "rogue states" have revived the SDI concept in the early twenty-first century under what is now called National Missile Defense. Test results thus far have been underwhelming, and in fact there is little evidence that the proposed National Missile

Defense would be able to address the problems of decoys and other countermeasures that have plagued missile defenses since the 1960s.[58]

In the months leading to the new millennium there was a brief renewal of interest in shelters associated with "Y2K" (year 2000) anxieties. Alarmists feared that the Y2K computer rollover would "topple this electronic pack of cards, sending planes crashing to the ground, nukes leaping from their silos, electricity to a standstill." For apocalypse buffs, Y2K was a disappointing non-event. The *Time* writer Joel Stein advised those who had taken shelter during the millennium changeover to "emerge from your Y2K bunker as your father did from his bomb shelter after the Cuban missile crisis and as your forefather did from his cave when the first eclipse passed."[59] The one place where there has been a more permanent revival of shelter building is in Russia. While the Soviet-era shelters that were built for ordinary citizens are being now rented out to businesses that include karate studios, weightlifting clubs, and Japanese car dealerships, there is evidence of new shelter construction in Russia for political elites.[60] Fearing the consequences of NATO expansion, the Russian government is building two new underground shelters designed to house high-ranking officials under the villages of Sharapovo and Voronovo near Moscow. In addition, the network of tunnels and bunkers that was built under the Moscow suburb of Ramenki in the early 1970s for important Communist Party officials is being overhauled.[61]

Without the Cold War to justify its existence, and weighed down by a history of controversy and failure, civil defense in America has returned to the realm of neglect that it has traditionally occupied. Indeed, the very notion of civil defense has radically changed since the early 1960s. In one example, the *San Francisco Chronicle* reported in February 1999 that San Francisco and twenty-six other cities were "quietly building a civil defense network for the post–Cold War era—a time when lunatics and fanatical bands are to be feared more than nuclear annihilation." With a $158 million grant from the federal government, these cities were stocking up on nerve gas antidotes and biological warfare equipment against possible terrorist attacks.[62]

As for the fallout shelter, it is now almost universally viewed as a grim Cold War relic. Seemingly, even FEMA has grown weary of encouraging Americans to build shelters against the possibility of nuclear war. The latest FEMA publication on shelter building, for instance, contains elaborate plans for various shelters and a discussion of the hazards that might make such shelters necessary, including tornadoes and hurricanes. No mention is made of nuclear attack.[63]

Notes

NOTES TO THE INTRODUCTION

1. "Company Shelters Are Ready," *Business Week*, 21 October 1961, 137.

2. See "Fallout Protection: Here Are Case Histories of Family Shelters Recently Built in the West," *Sunset* 127, no. 5 (November 1961): 107–14.

3. "Civil Defense: The Sheltered Life," *Time*, 20 October 1961, 21.

4. Earl Pomeroy, "Fallout Shelter for Whole Town," *Denver Post*, 6 November 1961.

5. Arthur I. Waskow and Stanley L. Newman, *America in Hiding* (New York: Ballantine, 1962), 23.

6. Khrushchev's stand on Berlin was motivated by the huge numbers of East Germans who were fleeing the German Democratic Republic for the West—mostly through the open city of Berlin. In 1959, 144,000 left; in 1960, 200,000. Between 1949 and 1961 a total of 2.8 million—one-sixth of the population—crossed into the West. Jeremy Isaacs and Taylor Downing, *Cold War: An Illustrated History, 1945–1991* (Boston: Little, Brown, 1998), 172, 170.

7. Khrushchev and Kennedy quoted in Dean Rusk, *As I Saw It* (New York: Norton, 1990), 221. In August 1963, after the signing of the Limited Test Ban Treaty, Rusk gives the following account of a private conversation with Khrushchev that Rusk claims "still chills my blood":

"Mr. Rusk," said Khrushchev, "Konrad Adenauer has told me that Germany will not fight a nuclear war over Berlin. Charles de Gaulle has told me that

France will not fight a nuclear war over Berlin. Harold Macmillan has told me that England will not fight a nuclear war over Berlin. Why should I believe that you Americans would fight a nuclear war over Berlin?"

That was quite a question, with Khrushchev staring at me with his little pig eyes. I couldn't call Kennedy and ask, "What do I tell the son of a bitch now?" So I stared back at him and said, "Mr. Chairman, you will have to take into account the possibility that we Americans are just goddamn fools." We glared at each other, unblinking, and then he changed the subject and gave me three gold watches to take home to my children. (227–28)

8. "Radio and Television Report to the American People on the Berlin Crisis," 25 July 1961, in *Public Papers of the Presidents of the United States: John F. Kennedy, 1961* (Washington, D.C.: GPO, 1962), 533–40.

9. See Gordon Wright, *The Ordeal of Total War, 1939–1945* (New York: Harper and Row, 1968), 263–64. Wright notes that "there are no accepted casualty figures" for either of the world wars, and that "civilian casualties are especially controversial."

10. Quoted in Gerard Piel, "The Illusion of Civil Defense," *Bulletin of the Atomic Scientists* 17, no. 2 (February 1962): 5.

11. House Subcommittee of the Committee on Government Operations, *New Civil Defense Legislation*, 85th Cong., 1st. sess., 1957, 266.

12. Arnold quoted in Gregg Herken, *The Winning Weapon: The Atomic Bomb in the Cold War, 1945–1950* (New York: Knopf, 1980), 211–12.

13. C. Vann Woodward, "The Age of Reinterpretation," *American Historical Review* 66 (October 1960): 2.

14. Eugene P. Wigner, "Nuclear War and Civil Defense," in *Who Speaks for Civil Defense?* ed. Eugene P. Wigner (New York: Scribner's, 1968), 26.

15. "If H-Bomb Comes—What You Can Do about It" (interview with Val Peterson), *U.S. News and World Report*, 8 April 1955, 126.

16. Howard Simons, "Backyard Front Lines," *Science News Letter*, 16 April 1955, 250. Nelson Rockefeller emphasized in 1958 that "no longer do we have a chance in this country to do what we have done in previous wars, which is to mobilize after war starts somewhere else. In an all out war, the war is going to start here. It's going to start on this country and we are going to fight with what we have in being." "Nelson A. Rockefeller, January 12, 1958," in *Face the Nation, 1958: The Collected Transcripts from the CBS Radio and Television Broadcasts* (New York: Holt Information Systems, 1972), 14.

17. House Subcommittee No. 3 of the Committee on Armed Services, *Civil Defense—Fallout Shelter Program*, pt. 1, 88th Cong., 1st. sess., 1963, 3129.

18. "What You Should Know about Fallout," *Successful Farming*, January 1962, 36.

19. W. F. Byrne and M. C. Bell, *Livestock, Fallout and a Plan for Survival* (Oakridge, TN: Agricultural Extension Service, University of Tennessee, 1973), 4, 1. Collection of the FEMA Library, Washington, D.C.

20. Richard Rutter, "Ways to Survive Nuclear Strike," *New York Times*, 1 Octo-

ber 1961; U.S. Department of Agriculture, *Bunker-Type Fallout Shelter for Beef Cattle*, Miscellaneous Publication no. 947 (Washington, D.C.: GPO, 1964). This government publication notes that "this shelter provides low-cost and adequate radiation protection for unattended farm animals. Although designed primarily for beef cattle, the shelter could be modified for use by sheep, hogs, or poultry."

21. Norman Cousins, "Shelters, Survival, and Common Sense," part 1, *Saturday Review*, 21 October 1961, 66.

22. Piel believed that because neither side would be able to knock out the "hardened" military striking force of the other, "the target against which such forces would be directed and against which they could expect to deliver an attack with success" was the civilian population. Piel noted that "the enemy would have to deliver a salvo totaling 300 megatons in order to knock out the 18 hardened Titan missile bases that surround the city of Tucson. By contrast a single 20-megaton bomb, burst in the air over Chicago, would suffice to destroy the entire metropolis." Gerard Piel, "On the Feasibility of Peace," *Science*, 23 February 1962, 648–49.

23. Lewis Mumford, "The Morals of Extermination," *Atlantic* 204, no. 4 (October 1959): 39.

24. Foreign policy experts also had to make difficult adjustments. Campbell Craig has argued that "the existence of military technology capable of traversing the oceans, and of a regime potentially interested in using such technology" against the United States forced the American government "to develop, for the first time, a basic national security policy. This phenomenon distinguishes United States foreign policy during the years 1945–1989 from eras before and since." Campbell Craig, *Destroying the Village: Eisenhower and Thermonuclear War* (New York: Columbia University Press, 1998), 3–4.

25. Herman Kahn, *Thinking about the Unthinkable* (New York: Avon, 1962), 87.

26. Hannah Arendt, *On Revolution* (1963; New York: Viking, 1969), 5. Michael Walzer claims that the doctrine of nuclear deterrence "turned American and Russian civilians into mere means for the prevention of war." Michael Walzer, *Just and Unjust Wars: A Moral Argument with Historical Illustrations* (New York: Basic Books, 1977), 271.

27. Bernard Brodie, "Implications for Military Policy," in *The Absolute Weapon: Atomic Power and World Order*, ed. Bernard Brodie (New York: Harcourt, Brace, 1946), 76.

28. Eugene Rabinowitch, "The Realities of Atom Bomb Defense," *New Republic*, 25 September 1950, 21.

29. Julius Duscha, "Kennedy to Use A-Bomb if Needed, Brother Says," *Washington Post*, 25 September 1961.

30. *Washington Post*, 27 July 1961.

31. American Institute of Public Opinion, *The Gallup Poll: Public Opinion, 1935–1971* (New York: Random House, 1972), 1729. Support was bipartisan: 81

percent of Democrats polled were in favor of keeping troops in Berlin "even at the risk of war," and 82 percent of Republicans also responded in the affirmative. See George Gallup, "Voters in Both Parties Favor Risking War to Hold Berlin," *St. Louis Post-Dispatch*, 4 August 1961.

32. Fifty-three percent of Americans believed there would be war within five years, the highest percentage making this response since the early days of the Korean War. American Institute of Public Opinion, *The Gallup Poll*, 1738. See also George Gallup, "Fear of World War Is at 10-Year High," *Washington Post*, 8 October 1961.

33. Dean Pearson, "Kennedy Will Call for Shelters," *Washington Post*, 20 July 1961.

34. Richard C. Hottelet, "World Peace and America's Price," *PTA Magazine* 56, no. 1 (September 1961): 11. "The Power and the Honor," *Life*, 15 September 1961, 4.

35. Thomas R. Phillips, "Malinovsky Speech Gives West an Official Report on Soviet Military Power," *St. Louis Post-Dispatch*, 29 October 1961.

36. A RAND Corporation report released in 1958 observed that when faced with a serious Soviet challenge, Americans might "find even the risk of devastation preferable to the consequences of accepting defeat." House Subcommittee of the Committee on Government Operations, *Civil Defense*, 85th Cong., 2d sess., 1958, RAND Corporation, "Report on a Study of Nonmilitary Defense" (Exhibit B), 479.

37. American Institute of Public Opinion, *The Gallup Poll*, 1741.

38. "Playboy Interview: Bertrand Russell," *Playboy* 10, no. 3 (March 1963): 46.

39. Although the museum's most popular jewelry item, these earrings have been withdrawn from sale in response to protests from Gensuikyo, a Japanese antinuclear group. Said Gensuikyo spokeswoman Naomi Kishimoto, "It's not the sort of thing you should be hanging from your ears or using to decorate your desk." *Santa Rosa Press Democrat*, 7 August 1999.

40. Mark Ehrman, "The Cold War Southwest," *Travel and Leisure*, April 1999, 214.

41. See Ted Gup, "The Ultimate Congressional Hideaway," *Washington Post Magazine*, 31 May 1992.

42. *Sacramento Bee*, 12 November 1999.

43. Bruce Watson, "We Couldn't Run, So We Hoped We Could Hide," *Smithsonian*, April 1994, 47.

44. Henry A. Kissinger, *Nuclear Weapons and Foreign Policy* (New York: Harper and Brothers, 1957), xi.

45. Margaret Mead, "Science, Freedom and Survival," *American Association for the Advancement of Science Bulletin* 7, no. 2 (1962). P. Herbert Leiderman and Jack H. Mendelson observed that "the serious introduction of such a possibility by an eminent anthropologist points up the magnitude of some of the issues in even planning a defense shelter program." P. Herbert Leiderman and Jack H. Mendelson,

"Some Psychiatric Considerations in Planning for Defense Shelters," in *The Fallen Sky: Medical Consequences of Thermonuclear War*, ed. Saul Aronow (New York: Hill and Wang, 1963), 45.

NOTES TO CHAPTER I

1. Paul Fussell, *Thank God for the Atom Bomb and Other Essays* (New York: Ballantine, 1988), 15, 28. One young naval officer serving in the Pacific named John F. Kennedy complained in 1943 that "when I read that we will fight the Japs for years if necessary and will sacrifice hundreds of thousands if we must, I always like to check from where he's talking: it's seldom out here." Quoted in Fussell, *Thank God for the Atom Bomb*, 6.

2. Freeman Dyson, *Weapons and Hope* (New York: Harper and Row, 1984), 117, 121.

3. Gar Alpernovitz argues that if the Japanese could have been given assurances that the emperor would be maintained, and given time to absorb the shock of Russia declaring war against Japan, the war could have ended without invasion. Alpernovitz claims that "the notion that it [the bomb] was the only way to save large numbers of lives is clearly a myth," and that "the most that may be said is that the atomic bombs may have saved the lives which might have been lost in the time it would have taken to arrange the final surrender terms." Gar Alpernovitz, *The Decision to Use the Atomic Bomb* (New York: Vintage, 1996), 10, 13, 633–34.

Richard B. Frank, on the other hand, after sorting through the "Magic" summaries of Japanese diplomatic messages, has called "the image that Japan was near to capitulation" before the use of atomic weapons "illusory." Frank emphasizes that, "As the Magic interpreters underscored, not a single diplomatic message originating from Japanese authorities in Tokyo indicated any disposition for peace prior to mid-July." Not only does Frank find no movement toward ending the war on the part of the Japanese, he also believes that the Japanese military buildup on Kyushu would have made the cost of invasion "unacceptable," and that in a "non-nuclear arena" the Japanese had sufficient leverage to force a negotiated peace. Richard B. Frank, *Downfall: The End of the Imperial Japanese Empire* (New York: Random House, 1999), 238, 343.

Certainly, for those who were actually doing the fighting in the Pacific, the inevitability of Japanese surrender seemed much less than certain, which helps account for the great gap in opinion on the use of these weapons that exists between those who fought in the Pacific and many scholars who have subsequently written about it. At Okinawa, the last Pacific battle before the projected invasion of the Japanese home islands, the Japanese resistance had been fierce enough to turn this into the costliest naval campaign in American history, with twelve thousand American soldiers and sailors killed, and thirty-two thousand wounded. Over 107,000 Japanese soldiers died in the defense of Okinawa. At sea, Japanese Kamikazes sank thirty-four American ships. In addition, seventy-five thousand Okinawans were killed. The battle for Okinawa, according to John Costello, produced "the heaviest casualties inflicted by the Imperial Navy on the U.S. Navy in any battle of the entire war." John Costello, *The Pacific War, 1941–1945* (New York: Quill, 1982), 578. Ronald Spector believes that the total of Japanese dead at Okinawa was closer to seventy thousand, but concurs with Costello on the cost of this campaign. Spector notes that the casualties suffered by the U.S. navy were "far exceeding the losses suffered in any previous U.S. naval campaign." Ronald H. Spector, *Eagle against the Sun: The American War with Japan* (New York: Free Press, 1985), 540.

One might also meditate on the practical consequences of allowing the Japanese a few weeks' time to mull over whether to surrender. Allied casualties were running at seven thousand a week, and as Fussell observes, a few weeks would "mean the world if you're one of those thousands or related to one of them." Fussell, *Thank God for the Atom Bomb*, 18. Richard Frank also emphasizes the high cost that the victims of Japanese aggression in Asia would be paying if action against Japan were delayed. The Chinese by themselves were losing as many as 100,000 lives a month to the Japanese, and as Frank puts it, "arguments that alternative means could have ended the war without atomic weapons in 'only' three months need to be held against this reality." Frank, *Downfall*, 359.

4. Truman claimed that in an invasion of Japan, American forces would have sustained losses of 250,000 dead and 500,000 wounded, with similar casualties for Japan. "Truman Doesn't Regret A-Bombing of Japanese," *Los Angeles Times*, 15 September 1961.

5. In a project created by the Newseum, a museum of journalism in Arlington, Virginia, the judges were given a choice of five hundred news events. Placing first in the list of the top hundred stories was "United States drops atomic bombs on Hiroshima, Nagasaki: Japan surrenders to end World War II. 1945." "The Top 100 Stories of the 20th Century," *Sacramento Bee*, 14 March 1999.

6. Arthur Koestler, "Reflections on the Year 15 P.H.," *New York Times Magazine*, 20 March 1960, 29.

7. Wilson believed that increased East-West tensions made it imperative for Americans "to face realistically the almost overwhelming facts of the nuclear age." Vincent Wilson, Jr., "Surviving the Bomb," *Commonweal*, 26 May 1961, 222. Claude C. Bowman claimed that "in the post-war world the public and its leaders have been unable or unwilling to face the new realities ushered in by the attack on Hiroshima." Claude C. Bowman, "The Family and the Nuclear Arms Race," *Social Problems* 11, no. 1 (summer 1963): 30.

8. Quoted in Gregg Herken, *The Winning Weapon: The Atomic Bomb in the Cold War, 1945–1950* (New York: Knopf, 1980), 203.

9. Quoted in Herken, *The Winning Weapon*, 207. Among those expressing skepticism about the impact of atomic weapons was William Hessler, who concluded in

a 1949 article that "atom bombs and long-range aircraft will never win a war for us. The rightful place of the atom bomb in American military policy, therefore, is very restricted." William H. Hessler, "The A-Bomb Won't Do What You Think!" *Collier's*, 17 September 1949, 72.

10. Quoted in Herken, *The Winning Weapon*, 226; also quoted in Allan M. Winkler, *Life under a Cloud: American Anxiety about the Atom* (New York: Oxford University Press, 1993), 63.

11. Paul Boyer, *By the Bomb's Early Light: American Thought and Culture at the Dawn of the Atomic Age* (Chapel Hill: University of North Carolina Press, 1994), 22.

12. In his introduction to the study Frederick Osborn, deputy U.S. representative to the U.N. Atomic Energy Commission, observed that "the percentage is not large, but it seems hard to believe that after all the efforts to enlighten the public there may still be some two million people in this country who have never heard of the bomb." Leonard S. Cottrell, Jr., and Sylvia Eberhart, *American Opinion on World Affairs in the Atomic Age* (1948; New York: Green Press, 1969), x.

13. The authors of the study found pervasive evidence that "the government, its problems, and the measures it undertakes to solve them are remote and shadowy, not only among the poor and uneducated but also to a large extent among those who according to socio-economic norms must be classed as at least average Americans." Cottrell and Eberhart, *American Opinion on World Affairs in the Atomic Age*, 22, 24, 27, 57.

14. When asked, *If there should be another world war, do you think the hydrogen bomb (H-bomb) will be used against us?* 63 percent of the respondents in 1954 and 1956 answered in the affirmative. By 1957, 71 percent believed that hydrogen bombs would be used against the United States in another war, and by 1958 the number had risen to 75 percent. Hazel Gaudet Erskine, "The Polls: Atomic Weapons and Nuclear Energy," *Public Opinion Quarterly* 27, no. 2 (summer 1963): 157.

15. When Americans were asked in 1960 whether they had done anything to prepare for a war emergency, 89 percent said no. Asked, *Have you given any thought to building a home bomb shelter?* 79 percent said they had not. When asked, *Would you favor or oppose a law which would require each community to build public bomb ("fall-out") shelters?* 71 percent answered in the affirmative, and 62 percent said that they would "be willing to work a day or two on weekends or to give one or two days' pay to help build it." Erskine, "The Polls: Atomic Weapons and Nuclear Energy," 160.

16. McNamara quoted by Philip W. Kelleher in House Subcommittee No. 3 of the Committee on Armed Services, *Civil Defense—Fallout Shelter Program*, 88th Cong., 1st sess., 1963, 3039.

17. Office of Civil Defense Planning, *Civil Defense for National Security* (Washington, D.C.: GPO, 1948), 1, 13. Collection of the FEMA Library, Washington, D.C.

18. Thomas J. Kerr, *Civil Defense in the U.S.: Bandaid for a Holocaust?* (Boulder: Westview, 1983), 7.

19. David Alan Rosenberg, "The Origins of Overkill: Nuclear Weapons and American Strategy, 1945–1960," *International Security* 7, no. 4 (spring 1983): 11–12.

20. "NSC 68: United States Objectives and Programs for National Security (April 14, 1950): A Report to the President Pursuant to the President's Directive of January 31, 1950," in *American Cold War Strategy: Interpreting NSC 68*, ed. Ernest R. May (Boston: Bedford/St. Martin's, 1993), 81, 80.

21. "NSC 68," 64, 58. John Lewis Gaddis has called NSC 68

a deeply flawed document, in the sense that the measures it recommended undercut the goals it was trying to achieve. A military buildup might enhance American security if American interests remained stable, but NSC-68 expanded interests. Fragmentation of the communist world might be a desirable objective, but treating communists everywhere as equally dangerous was not the way to achieve it. A more moderate Soviet attitude toward the outside world was certainly to be welcomed, but a negotiating posture that required Soviet capitulation could hardly hasten it. . . . NSC-68's recommendations for action provided less than adequate guidance as to how objectives and capabilities were to be combined to produce coherent strategy.

John Lewis Gaddis, *Strategies of Containment: A Critical Appraisal of Postwar American National Security Policy* (New York: Oxford University Press, 1988), 106.

22. The contents of NSC 68 would remain secret until 1975, when it was declassified by Henry Kissinger. See May, *American Cold War Strategy*, 16.

23. The $31 billion defense budget Eisenhower submitted for fiscal year 1955, for instance, was $10 billion lower than what Truman had recommended in his last budget message. Samuel F. Wells, Jr., "The Origins of Massive Retaliation," *Political Science Quarterly* 96, no. 1 (spring 1981): 33.

24. Kurt Gottfried and Bruce G. Blair, eds., *Crisis Stability and Nuclear War* (New York: Oxford University Press, 1988), 48. Delivery vehicles for these weapons included 538 B-52s, 1,291 B-47s, 19 B-58s, and 12 Atlas ICBMs. In Europe there were 60 Thor IRBMs and 30 Jupiter IRBMs. Eisenhower had additionally approved constructing 780 additional Atlas, Titan, and Minuteman ICBMs, as well as 19 Polaris submarines, each capable of carrying 16 Polaris missiles. See Andreas Wenger, *Living with Peril: Eisenhower, Kennedy, and Nuclear Weapons* (Lanham, MD: Rowman and Littlefield, 1997), 175–76. The air force claimed the lion's share of defense funding during the Eisenhower years, receiving an average of 47 percent of total defense appropriations from fiscal years 1954 to 1957. See Rosenberg, "The Origins of Overkill," 29.

25. Wells, "The Origins of Massive Retaliation," 38.

26. See Gaddis, *Strategies of Containment*, 150, 151.

27. Lemay quoted in Thomas Powers, "Nuclear Winter and Nuclear Strategy," *Atlantic* 254, no. 5 (November 1984): 60.

28. Richard H. Kohn and Joseph P. Harahan, eds., *Strategic Air Warfare: An Inter-

view with Generals Curtis E. LeMay, Leon W. Johnson, David A. Burchinal, and Jack J. Catton (Washington, D.C.: Office of Air Force History, 1988), 90.

29. Rosenberg, "The Origins of Overkill," 37–38. Rosenberg also emphasizes the bureaucratic edge that SAC enjoyed:

SAC occupied a nearly unique position in U.S. operational war planning. It was both a separate major Air Force administrative command under the Air Force Chief of Staff and a specified command within the JCS national unified and specified command system. . . . All the services had a strong interest in attempting to influence the content and direction of SAC's nuclear targeting and attack plans through the JCS review process, but SAC's semi-autonomous stature gave the command and its leaders a tremendous advantage in achieving their objectives in Pentagon bureaucratic struggles. (10)

30. Kohn and Harahan, *Strategic Air Warfare*, 109.

31. Campbell Craig, *Destroying the Village: Eisenhower and Thermonuclear War* (New York: Columbia University Press, 1998), 69. Craig claims that "in 1956 and 1957 Eisenhower rearranged official American basic security policy so that a war with the Soviet Union would escalate, automatically, into general thermonuclear war. He made *a point* of eliminating strategies that could be used to moderate or prevent that escalation; he derided advisers, like his Secretary of State, who thought such moderation possible and desirable" (67).

32. Wells, "The Origins of Massive Retaliation," 38, 36. As early as 1954 Dulles had observed that "massive atomic and thermonuclear retaliation is not the kind of power which could most usefully be evoked under all circumstances" (36).

33. John Lewis Gaddis believes that "the Eisenhower administration was prepared to 'go nuclear' in any of several contingencies," and that "the most startling deficiency of the Eisenhower administration's strategy was its bland self-confidence that it could use nuclear weapons without setting off an all-out nuclear war." Gaddis, *Strategies of Containment*, 171, 173. Wells insists, however, that Eisenhower was "never as unsubtle as commonly believed," and that he was well aware of "the advantages of studied ambiguity." Wells, "The Origins of Massive Retaliation," 36.

34. Immediately after the war, in 1946, General Leslie Groves advocated a preventive nuclear strike against any "aggressor nation" about to acquire its own nuclear weapons, and as late as 1953 Eisenhower himself had entertained the notion of a preventive strike against Soviet thermonuclear facilities before finally abandoning this idea. See Herken, *The Winning Weapon*, 222; Craig, *Destroying the Village*, 48. In a 1953 memorandum to Dulles, Eisenhower mused that "if the contest to maintain this relative position should have to continue indefinitely, the cost would either drive us to war—or to some form of dictatorial government. In such circumstances, we would be forced to consider whether or not our duty to future generations did not require us to initiate war at the most propitious moment we

could designate." A year later Eisenhower declared that "the United States and its allies must reject the concept of preventive war or acts intended to provoke war." Eisenhower quoted in Rosenberg, "The Origins of Overkill," 33, 34. Politically there was not sufficient public support for a preventive attack. While the Joint Chiefs of Staff also found the preventive strike attractive in certain situations, they privately concluded that "it is not politically feasible under our system to do so or to state that we will do so." Herken, *The Winning Weapon*, 223. Even the authors of NSC 68, who had emphasized that striking the first blow had become "increasingly important with modern weapons," reluctantly concluded that a preventive nuclear strike against the Soviet Union would be "repugnant to many Americans" and that the "shock of responsibility for a surprise attack would be morally corrosive" to the nation." "NSC 68," 70.

Preemption was a different issue. As early as 1945 the Joint Chiefs had declared that the United States must "strike the first blow if necessary . . . when it becomes evident that the forces of aggression are being arrayed against us," and NSC 68, which ruled out preventive attack, did *not* rule out a preemption, which it defined as "a counter-attack to a blow which is on its way or about to be delivered." See Rosenberg, "Origins of Overkill," 17; "NSC 68," 70. Curtis LeMay also insisted that "if the U.S. is pushed in a corner far enough we would not hesitate to strike first," but the difficulty inherent in preemption was in establishing unambiguously that the United States was indeed about to be attacked. LeMay quoted in Rosenberg, "The Origins of Overkill," 35. A misinterpretation of intentions could obviously have fatal results. Nevertheless, by 1960 SAC had spent a decade preparing not only for massive retaliation, but also for what David Alan Rosenberg has called "massive preemption" against Soviet nuclear forces. Rosenberg, "The Origins of Overkill," 66. The preemptive strike, however, became increasingly less attractive as the Soviets built up their own nuclear capability, and by 1962 Robert McNamara had sent a memorandum to the president declaring that "we would not be able to achieve tactical surprise, especially in the kinds of crisis circumstances in which a first-strike capability might be relevant," and that "the Soviets would be able to launch some of their retaliatory forces before we had destroyed their bases." McNamara quoted in Scott D. Sagan, "SIOP-62: The Nuclear War Plan Briefing to President Kennedy," *International Security* 12, no. 1 (summer 1987): 31.

Another aspect of the first use of nuclear weapons concerned the NATO alliance in Europe. The Soviets enjoyed an overwhelming advantage in conventional forces in Europe, and U.S. nuclear weapons were meant to serve as a counterpoise to these forces. In the face of a Soviet attack against NATO forces, the United States might have to make first tactical—and if need be strategic—use of nuclear forces against the Soviets. NSC 68 rejected the suggestion that the United States should declare that it would not make any first use of nuclear weapons because "such a declaration would be interpreted by the USSR as an admission of great weakness and by our allies as a clear indication that we intended to abandon them." "NSC 68," 57. By December 1954 NATO had decided that rather than retreating to the Rhine in the face of a Soviet attack, NATO forces would stand and engage the Soviets in a "forward strategy." As *U.S. News and World Report* breathlessly put it, "As soon as Soviet invaders lift the Iron Curtain, they will be met and engaged with atomic weapons at the very 'threshold' of West Germany." "First Blueprint for Atomic War," *U.S. News and World Report*, 25 February 1955, 24. NSC 162/2 bluntly stated that "The major deterrent to aggression against Western Europe is the manifest determination of the United States to use its atomic capability and massive retaliatory striking power if the area is attacked." Quoted in Gaddis, *Strategies of Containment*, 167.

35. Later, a critic of assured destruction named Donald Brennan would add the word "mutual" to create the acronym MAD. See Eric Semler et al., *The Language of Nuclear War: An Intelligent Citizen's Dictionary*, s.v. "Mutual Assured Destruction (MAD)" (New York: Harper and Row, 1987). The third option, other than preemption and second strike retaliation, was launch on warning. Using this strategy, the military would launch aircraft and missiles immediately upon receiving word that an attack had begun. Bruce Blair claims that "the U.S. strategic posture gravitated to the launch-on-warning option—Midnight Express became the colloquial Strategic Air Command (SAC) term for it—between the late 1960s and early 1970s. Its feasibility under many Soviet attack scenarios grew after the United States deployed a constellation of early-warning satellites in the early 1970s." Bruce G. Blair, *The Logic of Accidental Nuclear War* (Washington, D.C.: Brookings Institute, 1993), 185–86.

36. Oppenheimer said, "We may anticipate a state of affairs in which two Great Powers will each be in a position to put an end to the civilization of the other, though not without risking its own. We may be likened to two scorpions in a bottle, each capable of killing the other, but only at the risk of his own life." See Richard Rhodes, *Dark Sun: The Making of the Hydrogen Bomb* (New York: Simon and Schuster, 1995), 409.

37. Quoted in Kerr, *Civil Defense in the U.S.*, 20.

38. U.S. National Security Resources Board, Civil Defense Office, *Survival under Atomic Attack* (Washington, D.C.: GPO, 1950), 1, 3, 4.

39. Civil Defense Office, *Survival under Atomic Attack*, 6, 8, 21.

40. Civil Defense Office, *Survival under Atomic Attack*, 14.

41. Robinson quoted in Harry B. Yoshpe, *Our Missing Shield: The U.S. Civil Defense Program in Historical Perspective* (Washington, D.C.: Federal Emergency Management Agency, 1981), 115.

42. House Military Operations Subcommittee of the Committee on Government Operations, *Civil Defense for National Survival*, 84th Cong., 2d sess., 1956, 23. According to Thomas J. Kerr, the reasons for these rejections were many. Presentations by the FCDA to congressional committees were often confused and contradictory—a situation that was not improved by the fact that the Atomic Energy

Commission, which had been directing all military and civilian nuclear research since 1946, refused to share sensitive nuclear test data with the FCDA. Also, the demands of the Korean War made funding scarce for many programs, and certain key legislators, most notably Clarence Cannon in the House and Albert Thomas in the Senate, contended that the best civil defense was a strong air defense. See Kerr, *Civil Defense in the U.S.*, 46–58.

43. Philip J. Funigiello, "Managing Armageddon: The Truman Administration, Atomic War, and the National Security Resources Board," *Journal of Policy History* 2, no. 4 (1990): 417, 404. Harry B. Yoshpe also notes that "In part at least, FCDA budgets were being slashed because of a feeling in Congress, generated by testimony and press reports, that the military could repel any attack upon the United States, thus obviating the need for civil defense." Yoshpe, *Our Missing Shield*, 174.

44. Husted added that "one may as well accept the fact that few if any federally supported shelters will be built." Ellery Husted, "Shelter in the Atomic Age," *Bulletin of the Atomic Scientists* 9, no. 7 (September 1953): 275.

45. Augustin M. Prentiss, *Civil Defense in Modern War* (New York: McGraw-Hill, 1951), 396.

46. Husted, "Shelter in the Atomic Age," 276.

47. Peterson quoted in Yoshpe, *Our Missing Shield*, 199.

48. Ralph E. Lapp, "Civil Defense Faces New Peril," *Bulletin of the Atomic Scientists* 10, no. 9 (November 1954): 351.

49. "An Interview with Governor Val Peterson," *Bulletin of the Atomic Scientists* 10, no. 10 (December 1954): 375–77.

50. See Kerr, *Civil Defense in the U.S.*, 75.

51. House Subcommittee, *Civil Defense for National Survival* (1956), 79. The committee's own report called the FCDA's reliance on evacuation "weak and ineffective" and "dangerously shortsighted," and the national civil defense program "aimless and ineffectual" (2, 18). Project East River was initiated by Associated Universities, a research group founded by nine universities. It issued its ten-volume report on civil defense in 1952. See Associated Universities, *Report of the Project East River*, 10 vols. (New York: Associated Universities, 1952).

52. House Subcommittee, *Civil Defense for National Survival* (1956), 81, 80.

53. House Subcommittee of the Committee on Government Operations, *New Civil Defense Legislation*, 85th Cong., 1st sess., 1957, 267.

54. *New York Times*, 19 February 1957.

55. House Subcommittee, *Civil Defense for National Survival* (1956), 26.

56. In his analysis of Operation Alert, Guy Oakes observes that the "outcome of the exercise and the resolution of the dramatic ordeal were a foregone conclusion, preordained by the constraints of nuclear crisis mastery as well as the public-relations requirements of the FCDA." Guy Oakes, *The Imaginary War: Civil Defense and American Cold War Culture* (New York: Oxford University Press, 1994), 85.

57. The public was so indifferent to Operation Alert that only a handful of

Quakers, anarchists, Catholic Workers, and members of the War Resisters League could be induced to protest the yearly exercises. The Operation Alert protests reached their lowest ebb in 1958, when only twelve protesters turned out in New York. In 1961, the last year for Operation Alert, there was a turnout of some 2,500. While Dee Garrison claims that the difference is attributable to the involvement of a group of young mothers who "transformed the American peace movement," the evidence for such a broad claim is not compelling. The likeliest explanation is the simplest, which is that nuclear issues had acquired more urgency with the general public by 1961 because of deteriorating relations between the United States and the Soviet Union. See Dee Garrison, "'Our Skirts Gave Them Courage': The Civil Defense Protest Movement in New York City, 1955–1961," in *Not June Cleaver: Women and Gender in Postwar America, 1945–1960*, ed. Joanne Meyerowitz (Philadelphia: Temple University Press, 1994), 209–10, 217, 202.

58. "Civil Defense: Best Defense? Prayer," *Time*, 27 June 1955, 17.

59. "Civil Defense: So Much to Be Done," *Time*, 27 June 1955, 21.

60. "Ralph E. Lapp, June 19, 1955," in *Face the Nation, 1954–1955: The Collected Transcripts from the CBS Radio and Television Broadcasts* (New York: Holt Information Systems, 1972), 266, 265; see Kerr, *Civil Defense in the U.S.*, 80, 81, 82.

61. *New York Times*, 24 March 1957.

62. Robert Moses, "The Civil Defense Fiasco," *Harper's* 214, no. 1290 (November 1957): 32.

63. See David H. Morrissey, "A Blast from the Past," *Progressive* 47, no. 2 (February 1983): 32.

64. House Subcommittee, *New Civil Defense Legislation* (1957), 289.

65. E. W. Kenworthy, "Civil Defense Cuts by House Indicate Doubts on Program," *New York Times*, 24 March 1957.

66. Yoshpe, *Our Missing Shield*, 165.

67. *New York Times*, 14 February 1957.

68. Richard Wayne Dyke, *Mr. Atomic Energy: Congressman Chet Holifield and Atomic Energy Affairs, 1945–1974* (New York: Greenwood, 1989), 193.

69. See Kerr, *Civil Defense in the U.S.*, 105–6.

70. *New York Times*, 12 March 1957.

71. House Subcommittee, *New Civil Defense Legislation* (1957), 258.

72. Kerr, *Civil Defense in the U.S.*, 108.

73. *Deterrence and Survival in the Nuclear Age (The "Gaither Report" of 1957)* (Washington, D.C.: GPO, 1976), 31. David Sarnoff, chairman of the board of RCA, was even more sanguine on the subject of civil defense. Sarnoff believed that with nuclear warfare, "civil defense has become as important as military defense," that military victories could be undermined by "the collapse of morale and organized civil life at home," and that the "penalty for failure" in both civil and military defense was "defeat." Sarnoff quoted in House Subcommittee, *New Civil Defense Legislation* (1957), 255.

With the deployment of Soviet ICBMs expected in the near future, the Gaither Report also emphasized the increasing vulnerability of SAC facilities. Indeed, the situation seemed so perilous that three Gaither committee members privately urged Eisenhower to reconsider the option of preventive war. See David L. Snead, *The Gaither Committee, Eisenhower, and the Cold War* (Columbus: Ohio State University Press, 1999), 125; Rosenberg, "The Origins of Overkill," 47. Former secretary of defense Robert Lovett observed of the Gaither Report that "it was like looking into the abyss and seeing Hell at the bottom." Lovett quoted in Winkler, *Life under a Cloud*, 119.

74. The physicist Leonard Reiffel has recently revealed that in 1958, in the demoralizing days after the Sputnik launch, he headed a secret air force study that was developing a plan to launch a rocket to the moon and detonate a nuclear weapon on the moon's surface. The blast would have been easily visible from the Earth. The purpose of the explosion, according to Reiffel, "was to impress the world with the prowess of the United States. It was a PR device, without question, in the minds of the people from the Air Force." Among those who worked on this project was a young Carl Sagan. The project was abandoned after Reiffel and others argued that "there was no point in ruining the pristine environment of the moon." William J. Broad, "Physicist: U.S. Mulled Nuclear Explosion on Moon," *Sacramento Bee*, 16 May 2000.

75. *International Security: The Military Aspect (Report of Panel II of the Special Studies Project* (Garden City, NY: Doubleday, 1958), 6, 46. The Rockefeller Report, it should be noted, claimed that most Americans would have a warning time of forty-five minutes before an attack. But with the advent of ICBMs and submarine-launched ballistic missiles (SLBMs), many observers believed that forty-five minutes would be relatively luxurious, and that the actual warning time would be much less. *International Security*, 48. Commenting on the complications posed by nuclear missiles, the *Nation* concluded, "civil defense is dead, as of right now." "Civil Defense Is Dead," *Nation* 185, no. 9 (28 September 1957): 186.

76. "Nelson A. Rockefeller, January 12, 1958," in *Face the Nation, 1958: The Collected Transcripts from the CBS Radio and Television Broadcasts* (New York: Holt Information Systems, 1972), 12.

77. RAND Corporation, *Report on a Study of Non-Military Defense* (R-322-RC) (Santa Monica, CA: RAND Corporation, 1958), 7, 8, 36.

78. House Subcommittee of the Committee on Government Operations, *Civil Defense*, 85th Cong., 2d sess., 1958, 174, 177.

79. "Willard F. Libby, November 16, 1958," in *Face the Nation, 1958*, 359. Libby claimed that individuals could construct effective and cheap fallout shelters by "using shovels and brooms and firehoses and going into cellars." Quoted in Kerr, *Civil Defense in the U.S.*, 75.

80. See Kenworthy, "Civil Defense Cuts by House Indicate Doubts on Program." See also Kerr, *Civil Defense in the U.S.*, 77.

81. "If H-Bomb Comes—What You Can Do about It," *U.S. News and World Report*, 8 April 1955, 129–30.

82. House Subcommittee, *New Civil Defense Legislation* (1957), 212. See Stanley A. Blumberg and Gwinn Owens, *Energy and Conflict: The Life and Times of Edward Teller* (New York: Putnam's, 1976); *New York Times*, 15 February 1957.

83. Kerr, *Civil Defense in the U.S.*, 90–91.

84. Donald W. Mitchell, *Civil Defense: Planning for Survival and Recovery* (Washington, D.C.: Industrial College of the Armed Forces, 1963), 46. Mitchell notes that in Houston, Texas, only 1 percent of the houses had basements.

85. Paul G. Steinbicker, "Shelter or Evacuation?" *Bulletin of the Atomic Scientists* 13, no. 5 (May 1957): 167.

86. When he briefed Kennedy during the Cuban Missile Crisis on the consequences of Cuban missiles being launched against the United States, OCD director Steuart Pittman stated that "for a light, relatively light, nuclear attack of this type, we would lower the protection factors we use in deciding what existing buildings would serve as adequate protection [against blast, heat, and direct exposure to radiation from the nuclear detonation]. We'd be up against going down to a 40-protection factor. We now set a limit of a 100-protection factor." Pittman quoted in Ernest R. May and Philip D. Zelikow, eds., *The Kennedy Tapes: Inside the White House during the Cuban Missile Crisis* (Cambridge, MA: Belknap, 1997), 338.

87. L. V. Spencer, A. B. Chilton, and C. M. Eisenhauer, *Structure Shielding against Fallout Gamma Rays from Nuclear Detonations* (Washington, D.C.: U.S. Department of Commerce, National Bureau of Standards, 1980), 25–26.

88. Moses, "The Civil Defense Fiasco," 30.

89. *Life* magazine had been especially enthusiastic, publishing a 1957 article that included detailed drawings of elaborate urban and suburban shelters. "Scientific Blueprint for Atomic Survival," *Life* 42, no. 11 (18 March 1957): 146–48. The same issue also featured an article by the engineer and civil defense expert Willard Bascom. Emphasizing the deterrent aspects of a strong civil defense, Bascom claimed that

> Civil defense could also be of great value in preventing a war. Our policy in foreign affairs is to take a strong stand against Soviet intimidation of our allies and the neutral nations. But a strong stand, with the threat of war it implies, may be meaningless if the enemy knows that our civilian population is virtually naked before an attack. Protective arrangements for the public would greatly strengthen the hand of our President in a crisis by increasing his bargaining capacity at the international conference table.

Willard Bascom, "'Difference between Victory and Defeat,'" *Life* 42, no. 11 (18 March 1957): 150. Even in the unlikely event that a national shelter program were approved, the time it would take to complete such a program would, according to Robert Moses, be "nearer twenty years" than five or six. Moses, "The Civil Defense Fiasco," 34. Donald W. Mitchell of the Industrial College of the Armed Forces believed that there would be a two-year lag time between congressional appropriations and the actual building of shelters, and that "the construction industry would probably need up to a decade to handle a large shelter program." Mitchell, *Civil Defense: Planning for Survival and Recovery*, 49.

90. Dwight D. Eisenhower, *Waging Peace, 1956–1961* (Garden City, NY: Doubleday, 1965), 222. Eisenhower expressed his fears of a garrison state on a number of occasions. In 1958 he resisted calls for increased defense spending because he believed that larger expenditures on the military would lead to "what is euphemistically called a controlled economy, but which in effect would be a garrison state." Quoted in Rosenberg, "The Origins of Overkill," 54.

91. Eisenhower, *Waging Peace, 1956–1961*, 222–23.

92. Eisenhower, *Waging Peace, 1956–1961*, 223. Although the contents of the Gaither Report were widely leaked, it was officially classified until 1973, and not published until 1976. Assessing the suggestions made by the Gaither Report versus Eisenhower's caution, David Snead concludes that "in retrospect it seems clear that Eisenhower's more cautious approach was the most appropriate one." Snead, *The Gaither Committee, Eisenhower, and the Cold War*, 192–93.

93. House Military Operations Subcommittee of the Committee on Government Operations, *New Civil Defense Program: Ninth Report by the Committee on Government Operations* (Washington, D.C.: GPO, 1961), 44.

94. Hoegh quoted in Oakes, *The Imaginary War*, 131. Vincent Wilson, Jr., also drew a pioneer analogy, claiming that for the individual American citizen the fallout shelter was "no more than the nuclear age's equivalent of keeping his powder dry." Wilson, "Surviving the Bomb," 224.

95. William K. Chipman commented that the "'do-it-yourself' shelter, especially if hurriedly improvised, is not likely to produce impressive results on a national basis." See Mitchell, *Civil Defense: Planning for Survival and Recovery*, 52.

96. House Subcommittee, *Civil Defense* (1958), 403.

97. "Civil Defense Shelters: An Interview with Congressman Chet Holifield," *Bulletin of the Atomic Scientists* 14, no. 4 (April 1958): 131–34.

98. According to the committee's summary report, the most significant finding presented during the hearings was that "civil defense preparedness" could reduce the fatalities of a nuclear attack on the United States "from approximately 25 percent of the population to about 3 percent," and that provisions for "shielding against radiation effects would at the same time protect against blast and thermal effects for the vast majority of the population." Joint Committee on Atomic Energy, Summary-Analysis of Hearings, June 22–26, 1959, *Biological and Environmental Effects of Nuclear War* (Washington, D.C.: GPO, 1959), 8, 52, 53. The original text read "30 percent of the population" and was amended to "25 percent" in a following erratum page.

99. In one example, William E. Minshall of Ohio, who had served with Holifield on several congressional committees on civil defense, revealed in 1958 that

he had polled the residents of Cleveland on the shelter issue, and that they had opposed shelter building by four or five to one. See House Subcommittee, *Civil Defense* (1958), 179, 405.

100. House Subcommittee, *New Civil Defense Program* (1961), 44. In his study on the Gaither Committee, David Snead concludes that despite the recommendations of numerous committees and individuals that a shelter system be built, "neither the public nor Congress showed a strong willingness to support expanded expenditures for shelters," and that as a consequence "Eisenhower felt no concerted pressure to expand his civil defense policies." Snead, *The Gaither Committee, Eisenhower, and the Cold War*, 168–69.

101. The plan was referred to as SIOP-62—the Single Integrated Operational Plan for Fiscal Year 1962. Briefing the Kennedy administration on SIOP-62 was General Lyman L. Lemnitzer, chairman of the Joint Chiefs of Staff. Lemnitzer argued against withholding a portion of America's strategic assets from the initial attack because he feared that these would not survive a Soviet attack. Lemnitzer also opposed a strictly counterforce strategy because the proximity of many Soviet military targets to urban centers would make it virtually impossible for the Soviets to distinguish a counterforce attack from a total attack. Sagan, "SIOP-62: The Nuclear War Plan Briefing to President Kennedy," 37.

102. Gottfried and Blair, *Crisis Stability and Nuclear War*, 53.

103. See Albert Wohlstetter, "The Delicate Balance of Terror," *Foreign Affairs* 37 (January 1959); Maxwell D. Taylor, *The Uncertain Trumpet* (New York: Harper and Row, 1959).

104. Curtis LeMay, who took a dim view of the Kennedy administration's nuclear strategy, believed that the "flexible response" phrase had been created

to counter the "immorality" of the massive retaliation that everybody thought meant we would dump all the atomic weapons we had automatically on a poor helpless foe. That was immoral; flexible response was, "No, we don't have to do that. We are just going to use what force is necessary to do the job." Of course, this violates the principles of war, and over the centuries we have found that it doesn't work. But we couldn't convince anybody in the Pentagon at the time it wouldn't work.

Kohn and Harahan, *Strategic Air Warfare*, 121–22.

105. On the debate over the possible use of nuclear weapons during the Quemoy-Matsu crisis, see Craig, *Destroying the Village*, 78–85. On Eisenhower and Dien Bien Phu, see Stephen E. Ambrose, *Eisenhower*, vol. 2, *The President* (New York: Simon and Schuster, 1984), 184.

106. W. W. Rostow, *View from the Seventh Floor* (New York: Harper and Row, 1964), 48, 43. Michael Sherry comments that the Kennedy administration outlook "might entail the very brinkmanship Democrats had excoriated when Dulles employed it; but *their* brinkmanship, they assumed, would be rationally exercised and counterbalanced by diplomatic flexibility, displays of American vitality in space

and technology, and aid to struggling nations." Michael S. Sherry, *In the Shadow of War: The United States since the 1930s* (New Haven: Yale University Press, 1995), 243–44.

107. "Special Message to the Congress on Urgent National Needs," 25 May 1961, in *Public Papers of the Presidents of the United States: John F. Kennedy, 1961* (Washington, D.C.: GPO, 1962), 402.

108. See Spencer, Chilton, and Eisenhauer, *Structure Shielding against Fallout Gamma Rays*, 36–37. Fitzsimons added, however, that Kennedy apparently "did not realize that the OCDM was in no position to respond to the public's clamor for civil defense action." Neal Fitzsimons, "Brief History of American Civil Defense," in *Who Speaks for Civil Defense?* ed. Eugene P. Wigner (New York: Scribner's, 1968), 42.

109. The Office of Civil Defense was under the Department of Defense from 1961 to 1964, and under the Department of the Army from 1964 to 1972. It became the Defense Civil Preparedness Agency again under the Department of Defense from 1972 to 1979, and was merged with emergency preparedness and natural disaster programs into the Federal Emergency Management Agency in 1979.

110. Neal Stanford, "Civil Defense Comes of Budget Age," *Christian Science Monitor*, 3 October 1961.

111. After the large appropriations for fiscal year 1962, what followed for the OCD was, in the words of Harry B. Yoshpe, "years of lowered prestige, declining budgets, and erosion of basic programs." Annual appropriations averaged about $91 million between 1963 and 1972. Yoshpe, *Our Missing Shield*, 321.

NOTES TO CHAPTER 2

1. Karl Jaspers, *The Future of Mankind* (Chicago: University of Chicago Press, 1958), 3. Jaspers noted that "the atom bomb, as the problem of mankind's very existence, is equaled by only one other problem: the threat of totalitarian rule (not simply dictatorship, Marxism, or racial theory), with its terroristic structure that obliterates all liberty and human dignity. By one, we lose life; by the other, a life that is worth living" (4).

2. Quoted in Ronald W. Clark, *The Life of Bertrand Russell* (New York: Knopf, 1976), 518.

3. "Playboy Interview: Bertrand Russell," *Playboy* 10, no. 3 (March 1963): 42. Russell believed that the only solution to such a grim situation was world government: "There's only one way that I can see and that is the establishment of a world government with a monopoly of all the important weapons of war." *Bertrand Russell Speaks His Mind* (Cleveland: World Publishing Company, 1960), 154, 160.

4. C. Wright Mills, *The Causes of World War Three* (1958; Westport, CT: Greenwood, 1976), 6. Erich Fromm, *May Man Prevail? An Inquiry into the Facts and Fictions of Foreign Policy* (Garden City, NY: Doubleday, 1961), 30, 248.

5. Reinhold Niebuhr, foreword to *Community of Fear* by Harrison Brown and James Real (Santa Barbara, CA: Center for the Study of Democratic Institutions, 1960), 5.

6. Urey quoted in Lawrence S. Wittner, *Rebels against War: The American Peace Movement, 1941–1960* (New York: Columbia University Press, 1969), 149. Leo Szilard, "Are We on the Road to War?" *Bulletin of the Atomic Scientists* 18, no. 4 (April 1962): 23. Szilard calculated that humanity had "a ten per cent chance" of avoiding nuclear war. See Joseph Roddy, "The Big March for Peace," *Look* 26, no. 14 (3 July 1962): 15.

7. W. Warran Wagar, *The City of Man: Prophecies of a World Civilization in Twentieth-Century Thought* (Boston: Houghton Mifflin, 1963), 3, 9.

8. Stan Lee, *Origins of Marvel Comics* (New York: Simon and Schuster, 1974), 142, 143.

9. Lee, *Origins of Marvel Comics*, 83, 84.

10. *Them!* was one of the biggest grossing films of the year for Warner Brothers. See Michael Paul Rogin, "Kiss Me Deadly: Communism, Motherhood, and Cold War Movies," in *Ronald Reagan, the Movie, and Other Episodes in Political Demonology* (Berkeley: University of California Press, 1987), 263.

11. Paul Brians, *Nuclear Holocausts: Atomic War in Fiction, 1895–1984* (Kent, OH: Kent State University Press, 1987), 356–59.

12. Paul A. Carter notes that when John W. Campbell, editor of *Astounding* magazine, was asked by a reporter what he was doing now that science fact had seemingly overtaken science fiction in the wake of Hiroshima, Campbell replied that most of the stories he was now publishing took place "after the end of the world." Paul A. Carter, *Another Part of the Fifties* (New York: Columbia University Press, 1983), 247.

13. The prescience of H. G. Wells is on full display in his little-known novel *The World Set Free*, published in 1914. Wells predicts the development of atomic weapons, and his description of the effects of such a weapon is eerily similar to descriptions made by crew members of the *Enola Gay* over Hiroshima. The following is Wells's description of the first use of this new weapon:

> The bomb flashed blinding scarlet in mid-air and fell, a descending column of blaze eddying spirally in the midst of a whirlwind. Both the aeroplanes were tossed like shuttlecocks, hurled high and sideways; and the steersman with gleaming eyes and set teeth fought in great banking curves for a balance. The gaunt man clung tight with hands and knees; his nostrils dilated, his teeth biting his lips. He was firmly strapped. . . .
>
> When he could look down again it was like looking down upon the crater of a small volcano. In the open garden before the Imperial castle a shuddering star of evil splendour spurted and poured up smoke and flame towards them like an accusation. They were too high to distinguish people clearly, or mark the bomb's effect upon the building until suddenly the façade tottered and crumbled before the flare as sugar dissolves in water.

H. G. Wells, *The World Set Free: A Story of Mankind* (New York: Dutton, 1914), 113.

14. Robert A. Heinlein, *Farnham's Freehold* (New York: Berkeley Medallion, 1964), 35.

15. This scene includes the following dialogue:

"Barbara, Barbara!"

"Hugh darling! I love you. Oh!"

"I love you, Barbara."

"Yes. Yes! Oh, please! *Now!*"

"*Right now!*"

Heinlein, *Farnham's Freehold*, 39–40.

16. Heinlein, *Farnham's Freehold*, 59.

17. Nevil Shute, *On the Beach* (New York: Ballantine, 1974), 78. Interestingly, Shute was an aviation engineer who worked on the development of secret weapons for the British during World War II. "About the Author" in Shute, *On the Beach*, 279.

18. *On the Beach* sold 100,000 copies in its first six weeks of publication, and was serialized by forty newspapers with a total of eight million readers. See Robert A. Divine, *Blowing on the Wind: The Nuclear Test Ban Debate, 1954–1960* (New York: Oxford University Press, 1978), 162.

19. Carter, *Another Part of the Fifties*, 254.

20. Bosley Crowther, "Top Films of 1959," in *The New York Times Film Reviews, 1959–1968* (New York: New York Times and Arno Press, 1970), 3167.

21. House Subcommittee of the Committee on Government Operations, *Civil Defense*, 86th Cong., 2d sess., 1960, 115. In 1959 Frank Shelton, technical director of the Defense Atomic Support Agency, called *On the Beach* "pure fiction from a worldwide fallout point of view." Quoted in Dean Brelis, *Run, Dig or Stay? A Search for an Answer to the Shelter Question* (Boston: Beacon, 1962), 47–48. The urban planner Robert Moses, on the other hand, observed that while Shute "may or may not be a major prophet," he was "certainly right in ignoring the possibilities of a shelter program." Robert Moses, "The Civil Defense Fiasco," *Harper's* 214, no. 1290 (November 1957): 30.

22. Allan W. Winkler, *Life under a Cloud: American Anxiety about the Atom* (New York: Oxford University Press, 1993), 105. Clarence R. Huebner, director of the New York state civil defense office, called *On the Beach* a "fantasy," and claimed that defense against fallout was "not only possible, but relatively simple." *New York Times*, 18 December 1959. In his work on the apocalyptic novel, Joseph Dewey dismisses the early "glut of forgettable speculative fiction that embraced atomic devastation" and lamented that "the most direct treatments of the day of nuclear wrath itself come off as labored and as artificial as Michael Wigglesworth's 1661 attempt to create the Christian day of judgment. These fictions—*On the Beach* and *Alas, Babylon* come to mind—seem unconvincing, didactic to the point of accusative, and oddly (even serenely) cinematic." Joseph Dewey, *In a Dark Time: The Apocalyptic Temper in the American Novel of the Nuclear Age* (West Lafayette, IN: Purdue University Press, 1990), 8, 9.

23. Walter M. Miller, Jr., *A Canticle for Leibowitz* (New York: Bantam, 1960), 52.

24. Miller, *A Canticle for Leibowitz*, 14.

25. Pat Frank, *Alas, Babylon* (New York: Bantam, 1964), 30.

26. Frank, *Alas, Babylon*, 69, 77.

27. Frank, *Alas, Babylon*, 82–83.

28. Frank, *Alas, Babylon*, 278–79.

29. Quoted in Spencer R. Weart, *Nuclear Fear: A History of Images* (Cambridge: Harvard University Press, 1988), 132.

30. Philip Wylie, "A Better Way to Beat the Bomb," *Atlantic Monthly* 187, no. 2 (February 1951): 40, 41.

31. Philip Wylie, *Tomorrow!* (New York: Rinehart, 1954), 58–59.

32. Wylie, *Tomorrow!* 236–37.

33. Wylie, *Tomorrow!* 269, 272–73.

34. Wylie, *Tomorrow!* 350.

35. Wylie, *Tomorrow!* 351, 354.

36. Wylie, *Tomorrow!* 367.

37. Philip Wylie, *Triumph* (Garden City, NY: Doubleday, 1963), 134.

38. Wylie, *Triumph*, 137–38.

39. Wylie, *Triumph*, 95.

40. Wylie, *Triumph*, 42.

41. Wylie, *Triumph*, 122.

42. Wylie, *Triumph*, 124–25.

43. Wylie quoted in Walter Goodman, "The Truth about Fallout Shelters," *Redbook* 118, no. 3 (January 1962): 43.

44. Eugene Burdick and Harvey Wheeler, *Fail-Safe* (New York: McGraw-Hill, 1962), 117–18.

45. Burdick and Wheeler, *Fail-Safe*, 122.

46. Burdick and Wheeler, *Fail-Safe*, 121.

47. Burdick and Wheeler, *Fail-Safe*, 94, 97.

48. Burdick and Wheeler, *Fail-Safe*, 97, 98.

49. Burdick and Wheeler, *Fail-Safe*, 99.

50. The fail-safe system of the novel was based on a set of procedures that had been installed by the air force in 1958. Called the "fail safe" or "positive control" system, it was designed, according to David Alan Rosenberg, to "permit rapid response without the risk of initiating war through miscalculation. Bombers would take off at the first sign of a Soviet strike, and proceed along Emergency War Plan routes toward their targets, but their missions would be aborted at a pre-specified point unless they received the 'go' to continue." David Alan Rosenberg, "The Origins of Overkill," *International Security* 7, no. 4 (spring 1983): 49. In 1972 John R. Raser published an article in which he demonstrates how even a "relatively foolproof" Polaris submarine could cross over the fail-safe line, launch its missiles, and plunge the planet into World War III. John R. Raser, "The Failure of Fail-

Safe," in *Beyond Conflict and Containment: Critical Studies of Military and Foreign Policy*, ed. Milton J. Rosenberg (New Brunswick, NJ: Transaction, 1972), 142–43.

51. Burdick and Wheeler, *Fail-Safe*, 262.

52. Burdick and Wheeler, *Fail-Safe*, 279.

53. Brians, *Nuclear Holocausts*, 150.

54. Mordecai Roshwald, *Level 7* (New York: McGraw-Hill, 1959), 12, 13.

55. Roshwald, *Level 7*, 122, 123.

56. Roshwald, *Level 7*, 125. One science fiction novel that lies slightly outside our time frame but is nevertheless worthy of note is Philip K. Dick's *Do Androids Dream of Electric Sheep?*, published in 1968. In this tale a nuclear war, called "World War Terminus," has covered the globe with a radioactive cloud, killing much of the planet's human life and most of its animal life. Owning a real, organic pet has become an incredible luxury, and most residents must content themselves with artificial "electric" pets. The world's population is being further depleted by massive immigration to Mars. Huge strides have been made in artificial intelligence, and the main plot of this novel concerns the activities of Rick Deckard, a bounty hunter whose job it is to hunt down and kill rogue androids posing as human beings. *Do Androids Dream of Electric Sheep* was adapted to the screen as *Blade Runner*, Ridley Scott's enormously influential film, which was released in 1982. Philip K. Dick, *Do Androids Dream of Electric Sheep?* (1968; New York: Ballantine, 1982). Dick manages to get in a dig at the RAND Corporation in this novel, noting, "it had been a costly war despite the valiant predictions of the Pentagon and its smug scientific vassal, the Rand Corporation" (12).

57. Asimov quoted in David Dowling, *Fictions of Nuclear Disaster* (Iowa City: University of Iowa Press, 1987), 5.

58. Robert Del Tredici, *At Work in the Fields of the Bomb* (New York: Perennial, 1987), 188. Observing the Hiroshima blast from above, crew members of the *Enola Gay* were awestruck by the giant mushroom cloud. Tail gunner George Caron said, "The mushroom itself was a spectacular sight, a bubbling mass of purplish-gray smoke and you could see it had a red core to it, and everything was burning inside." Bombardier Thomas W. Ferrebee claimed, "you could actually see parts of things moving up in the cloud, parts of buildings or just rubbish of all kinds." "15 Years Later: The Men Who Bombed Hiroshima," *Coronet* 48, no. 4 (August 1960): 87. Paul Tibbets, pilot of the *Enola Gay*, said, "down below it the thing reminded me more of a boiling pot of tar than any other description I can give it. It was black and boiling underneath with a steam haze on top of it." Tibbets quoted in John Costello, *The Pacific War, 1941–1945* (New York: Quill, 1982), 591.

59. John Hersey, *Hiroshima* (New York: Bantam, 1985), 38. In his recent book on postwar Japan, John Dower has concluded that

> Despite widespread denunciations of the "cruel" and "inhuman" American bombings, however, no abiding strain of virulent anti-American hatred carried over into the postwar period. Even before censorship was imposed, the

tone of most commentary about the nuclear devastation had turned philosophical. The weapon itself, rather than those who deployed it, largely absorbed the characteristics of being cruel and inhuman; and from this, what came to be indicted was the cruelty of war in general. Defeat, victimization, an overwhelming sense of powerlessness in the face of undreamed-of weapons of destruction soon coalesced to become the basis of a new kind of anti-military nationalism.

John W. Dower, *Embracing Defeat: Japan in the Wake of World War II* (New York: Norton, 1999), 493.

60. R. E. Lapp, "Atomic Bomb Explosions—Effects on an American City," *Bulletin of the Atomic Scientists* 4, no. 2 (February 1948): 50.

61. "Civil Defense: The City under the Bomb," *Time*, 2 October 1950, 12, 14.

62. The editors claimed that the purpose of this issue was

(1) to warn the evil masters of the Russian people that *their* vast conspiracy to enslave humanity is the dark, downhill road to World War III; (2) to sound a powerful call for reason and understanding between the peoples of the West and East—before it's too late; (3) to demonstrate that if The War We Do Not Want is forced upon us, we will win.

"Operation Eggnog," *Collier's* 128, no. 17 (27 October 1951): 6.

63. "The Unwanted War," *Collier's* 128, no. 17 (27 October 1951): 17.

64. See Edward R. Murrow, "A-Bomb Mission to Moscow," *Collier's* 128, no. 17 (27 October 1951): 19; Walter Winchell, "Walter Winchell in Moscow," *Collier's* 128, no. 17 (27 October 1951): 39.

65. Robert E. Sherwood, "The Third World War," *Collier's* 128, no. 17 (27 October 1951): 27. In his contribution, Hanson W. Baldwin also emphasizes the limited nature of U.S. nuclear bombing, noting that "the atomic bomb was used extensively by both sides but our war was primarily against Communism and the Soviet rulers rather than the Russian people, and the unlimited atomic holocaust did not occur." Hanson W. Baldwin, "How the War Was Fought," *Collier's* 128, no. 17 (27 October 1951): 22.

66. Sherwood, "The Third World War," 30, 31. Sherwood adds that "the American people had not bothered to learn that civil defense involves the active, instantaneous participation of every able-bodied man, woman and child" (30).

67. Hal Boyle, "Washington under the Bomb," *Collier's* 128, no. 17 (27 October 1951): 21, 20.

68. Sherwood, "The Third World War," 70.

69. See Philip Wylie, "Philadelphia Phase," *Collier's* 128, no. 17 (27 October 1951): 42.

70. "Operation Eggnog," 6.

71. Even the CBS news broadcaster Walter Cronkite had a post–nuclear war scenario: "If there are enough of us left after a nuclear war to carry on our government, one can safely forecast that the first order of business of the first post-war Congress

will be the gosh-darndest investigation this nation has ever witnessed. Subject? What Ever Happened to Civil Defense?" Walter Cronkite, Introduction to *Who Speaks for Civil Defense?* ed. Eugene P. Wigner (New York: Scribner's, 1968), 11.

72. "A Frightening Message for a Thanksgiving Issue," *Good Housekeeping*, November 1958, 61.

73. CNI is probably best known for its 1962 "baby tooth survey," in which scientists studied 67,500 baby teeth and found that the strontium-90 level had increased by a factor of 14 between 1951 and 1954. See Louise Reiss, "Baby Tooth Survey—First Results," *Nuclear Information* 4, no. 1 (November 1961).

74. Florence Moog, "Nuclear War in St. Louis: One Year Later," *Nuclear Information* 2, no. 1 (September 1959): 1–4.

75. Los Angeles was the focus of the cheesy novel by Robert Moore Williams, *The Day They H-Bombed Los Angeles* (New York: Ace, 1961).

76. "Red Alert! What if H-Bomb Hits Los Angeles?" *Los Angeles Times*, 12 March 1961.

77. Brown and Real, *Community of Fear*, 15.

78. Brown and Real, *Community of Fear*, 16.

79. The *New York Times* noted that while the fifty-megaton bomb was 2,500 times more powerful than the bomb dropped on Hiroshima,

> the ranges of the various degrees of destruction that would be caused by the fifty-megaton bomb do not extend proportionately further than those of a twenty-megaton weapon. . . . These facts on the effects of atomic weapons—known as well by Soviet weapons scientists as by American scientists—have given rise to the prevailing argument that the fifty-megaton bomb and its promised successor, the 100-megaton weapon, are principally weapons of terror.

New York Times, 31 October 1961.

80. "Home Shelters—'False Security'?" *Science Digest*, February 1962, 79–80. *Science Digest* was quoting from a description provided by the Scientists' Committee for Radiation Information.

81. Wilson quoted in Weart, *Nuclear Fear*, 131.

82. *Buffalo Evening News*, 20 July 1956.

83. *Grand Rapids Herald*, 21 July 1956.

84. Charles Walter Clarke, "VD Control in Atom-Bombed Areas," *Journal of Social Hygiene* 37, no. 1 (January 1951): 4. See also Elaine Tyler May, "Explosive Issues: Sex, Women, and the Bomb," in *Recasting America: Culture and Politics in the Age of Cold War*, ed. Lary May (Chicago: University of Chicago Press, 1998), 154.

85. Clarke, "VD Control in Atom-Bombed Areas," 5.

86. Clarke, "VD Control in Atom-Bombed Areas," 6, 7.

87. House Subcommittee No. 3 of the Committee on Armed Services, *Civil Defense—Fallout Shelter Program*, 88th Cong., 1st sess., 1963, 4795, 4801.

88. Vance Aandahl, "Adam Frost," *Playboy* 9, no. 4 (April 1962): 134.

89. Aandahl, "Adam Frost," 141.

90. RAND Corporation, *Report on a Study of Non-Military Defense* (R-322-RC) (Santa Monica, CA: RAND Corporation, 1958), 24.

91. Sharon Mindel Helsel, "The Comic Reason of Herman Kahn: Conceiving the Limits to Uncertainty in 1960" (Ph.D. diss., University of California, Santa Cruz, 1993), 24.

92. Jessica Smith, review of *On Thermonuclear War*, by Herman Kahn, *New World Review* 31, no. 1 (January 1963): 46.

93. George G. Kirstein, review of *On Thermonuclear War*, by Herman Kahn, *Nation* 192, no. 2 (14 January 1961): 35.

94. James R. Newman, review of *On Thermonuclear War*, by Herman Kahn, *Scientific American* 204, no. 3 (March 1961): 197.

95. Herman Kahn, *On Thermonuclear War* (Princeton: Princeton University Press, 1960), 44.

96. Kahn, *On Thermonuclear War*, 20.

97. Kahn, *On Thermonuclear War*, 57, 311.

98. Kahn, *On Thermonuclear War*, 41–42.

99. Kahn, *On Thermonuclear War*, 21.

100. Kahn quoted in Goodman, "The Truth about Fallout Shelters," 76.

101. Herman Kahn, *Thinking about the Unthinkable* (New York: Avon, 1962), 91.

102. See Gilbert Burck, "The Economy Can Survive Nuclear Attack," *Fortune* 64, no. 5 (November 1961): 254–55. Marshall K. Wood, "The Economic Impact of a Nuclear Attack," in American Management Association, *Survival and Recovery: Industrial Preparedness in the Nuclear Age*, ed. Jerome W. Blood and Harley M. Clements, AMA Management Bulletin 15 (New York: AMA, 1962), 36.

103. John A. Osmundsen, "Faster Recovery in Atom War Seen," *New York Times*, 8 April 1960.

104. "Civil Defense: The Sheltered Life," *Time*, 20 October 1961, 25.

105. Richard F. Dempewolff, "Don't Let the Cries of Doomsday Panic You," *Popular Mechanics*, April 1962, 114.

106. Christiansen quoted in Brelis, *Run, Dig or Stay?* 145.

107. "If Bombs Do Fall on U.S.—What People Look For," *U.S. News and World Report*, 25 September 1961, 54.

108. Norman Cousins, "Shelters, Survival, and Common Sense," part 1, *Saturday Review*, 21 October 1961, 66.

109. Bentley Glass, "The Biology of Nuclear War," in *The Fallen Sky: Medical Consequences of Thermonuclear War*, ed. Saul Aronow (New York: Hill and Wang, 1963), 103, 104.

110. Dowling, *Fictions of Nuclear Disaster*, 116.

111. Dewey, *In a Dark Time*, 5, 7.

112. Barkun notes that "the apocalyptic myths of the last several decades have been cast on a global scale: world depression, world war, nuclear holocaust, over-

population, ecological disaster." Michael Barkun, *Disaster and the Millennium* (New Haven: Yale University Press, 1974), 200–202, 204.

113. Michael Barkun, "The Language of Apocalypse: Premillennialists and Nuclear War," in *The God Pumpers: Religion in the Electronic Age*, ed. Marshall Fishwick and Ray B. Browne (Bowling Green, OH: Bowling Green State University Popular Press, 1987), 166.

114. Klaus Koch, *The Rediscovery of Apocalyptic: A Polemical Work on a Neglected Area of Biblical Studies and Its Damaging Effects on Theology and Philosophy* (Naperville, IL: Alec R. Allenson, ca. 1970), 119. Koch quotes Luther's view of the Book of Revelations as "every mob-leader's bag of tricks" (121).

115. Paul Boyer, *When Time Shall Be No More: Prophecy Belief in Modern American Culture* (Cambridge, MA: Belknap Press, 1995), 117.

116. Quoted in Boyer, *When Time Shall Be No More*, 125.

117. Michael Barkun cites a national survey taken in 1984 in which 39 percent of the respondents believed that "When the Bible predicts that the earth will be destroyed by fire, it's telling us that a nuclear war is inevitable." Barkun, "The Language of Apocalypse," 167.

118. Boyer, *When Time Shall Be No More*, 119.

119. Kurt Vonnegut, *Cat's Cradle* (1963; New York: Delta, 1998), 9–10.

120. Quoted in Boyer, *When Time Shall Be No More*, 125.

121. In August Harrell had given shelter to an AWOL marine, refusing to give him up because God had told Harrell to protect him. Harrell threatened to use force against any attempts to apprehend the marine. Some hundred law enforcement officers (and a half-track armored vehicle) became involved, but when Harrell's estate was raided Harrell and his followers did not resist. They were charged with harboring a deserter and were jailed. J. Harry Jones, Jr., *The Minutemen* (Garden City, NY: Doubleday, 1968), 100–101. For an examination of popular apocalyptic beliefs at the end of the twentieth century, see Alex Heard, *Apocalypse Pretty Soon: Travels in End-Time America* (New York: Norton, 1999).

122. Arthur I. Waskow, "The Shelter-Centered Society," *Scientific American* 206, no. 5 (May 1962): 47.

123. Weart, *Nuclear Fear*, 138–39. Wylie's virulent anticommunism was in part related to a visit to Russia that he made with his half brother in the 1930s. Wylie contracted cholera shortly after his visit, and blamed the Russians both for his illness and for his brother's fatal fall from a window. See Rogin, "Kiss Me Deadly: Communism, Motherhood, and Cold War Movies," 243.

By the time he published *Triumph* in 1963, however, Wylie had clearly moved to the position that *both* sides were culpable. At the end of this novel one of Wylie's characters, trying to come to grips with the nuclear cataclysm that is the subject of the book, observes,

> They came to love *things* more than one another. They were, on one side, godly by assertion. On the other, atheist. But above and beyond that, on *both*

sides, they were materialists. Marx established his materialism as a substitute worship. Our own was established by ourselves and its voice was not Marx but a nonexistent slot in rubble once called Madison Avenue, where we wrote a new theology of things also. We can remember that, and help the world, perhaps, to remember it forever. The *use* of things can lead to man's salvation, as it has led, in our small, pitiful cases. But things as man's *end* become—became—the end of man.

Wylie, *Triumph*, 275.

124. Russell tried to claim that he had never made such a suggestion, telling the Cambridge University Labor Club in 1950, "I have never advocated a preventive war, as your members would know if they took any trouble to ascertain facts." When interviewed by John Freeman in 1959, however, Russell was asked, "Is it true or untrue that in recent years you advocated that a preventive war might be made against communism, against Soviet Russia?" Russell replied, "It's entirely true, and I don't repent of it." Quoted in Clark, *The Life of Bertrand Russell*, 527, 528. The Strategic Air Command's Curtis LeMay was convinced that there was a period in the 1950s when the United States could have attacked the Soviet Union with virtually no losses to American aircraft:

There was a time in the 1950s when we could have won a war against Russia. It would have cost us essentially the accident rate of the flying time, because their defenses were pretty weak. One time in the 1950s we flew all of the reconnaissance aircraft that SAC possessed over Vladivostok at high noon. Two reconnaissance airplanes saw Migs, but there were no interceptions made. It was well planned too—crisscrossing paths of all the reconnaissance airplanes. Each target was hit by at least two, and usually three, reconnaissance airplanes to make sure we got pictures of it. We practically mapped the place up there with no resistance at all. We could have launched bombing attacks, planned and executed just as well, at that time. So I don't think I am exaggerating when I say we could have delivered the stockpile had we wanted to do it, with practically no losses. Of course that has changed now, but that was the condition that existed in the 1950s.

Richard H. Kohn and Joseph P. Harahan, eds., *Strategic Air Warfare: An Interview with Generals Curtis E. LeMay, Leon W. Johnson, David A. Burchinal, and Jack J. Catton* (Washington, D.C.: Office of Air Force History, 1988), 95–96.

125. Robert Lee Arnett, "Soviet Attitudes towards Nuclear War Survival (1962–1977): Has There Been a Change?" (Ph.D. diss., Ohio State University, 1979), 112, 114.

126. Brians, *Nuclear Holocausts*, 54.

127. Paul Tillich, "The Power of Self-Destruction," in *God and the H-Bomb*, ed. Donald Keys (New York: Bellmeadows Press, 1961), 35. Writing in the same collection Harold E. Fey, editor of the *Christian Century*, said that "the central question of the nuclear age" was "What did God intend by permitting man to learn

how to release the energy of the atom at this moment in history?" Harold E. Fey, "Fifteen Years in Hell Is Enough," in Keys, *God and the H-Bomb*, 89.

128. House Subcommittee, *Civil Defense—Fallout Shelter Program* (1963), 4938. One scientific paper noted that cockroaches "are not appreciably damaged" by gamma radiation of 400,000 r—ten times the lethal dose for humans. Frank R. Ervin et al., "Human and Ecologic Effects in Massachusetts of an Assumed Thermonuclear Attack on the United States," in Aronow, *The Fallen Sky: Medical Consequences of Thermonuclear War*, 18.

129. Arthur Koestler, "Reflections on the Year 15 P.H.," *New York Times Magazine*, 20 March 1960, 29.

130. Thomas Merton, "Nuclear War and Christian Responsibility," *Commonweal*, 9 February 1962, 509.

131. Merton, "Nuclear War and Christian Responsibility," 510–11.

132. Merton, "Nuclear War and Christian Responsibility," 510–12.

133. Merton's conclusion was that "war must be abolished. A world government must be established. We have still time to do something about it, but the time is rapidly running out." Merton, "Nuclear War and Christian Responsibility," 513.

134. Kahn, *On Thermonuclear War*, 145.

135. Kahn, *On Thermonuclear War*, 146, 147.

136. Kahn, *On Thermonuclear War*, 145.

137. Kahn, *On Thermonuclear War*, 523.

138. Kahn noted, "it is my belief that neither the U.S. nor the Soviet Union will manufacture any Doomsday Machines, but this will be a political, economic, and moral choice and not one dictated by technology." Kahn, *On Thermonuclear War*, 510. Appallingly, it was revealed in 1996 that Russia had installed an automated, "doomsday" system. In response to the installation of Pershing II missiles in Europe in 1983, which could reach Soviet targets in twenty minutes, the Soviet Union began work on a system that would automatically launch missiles even if the Russian leadership had been killed. Run by computers, Russia's doomsday system will launch "radio rockets" into space if the computers detect an attack. The rockets will send back coded messages to Russian missile sites, and the missiles will be launched without orders from any human being. The system became operational in 1996. James Adams, "Russia's Doomsday Missiles," *Sunday Times* (London), 25 February 1996.

139. Merritt Abrash has noted that while the air force general in *Dr. Strangelove* is clearly a lunatic, the novel from which this film was derived, *Red Alert*, features an air force general who launches a nuclear attack on the basis of "cool, replicable logic." *Red Alert* was written by Peter Bryant, a pseudonym for Peter George, and was published in 1958. Merritt Abrash, "Through Logic to Apocalypse: Science-Fiction Scenarios of Nuclear Deterrence Breakdown," *Science-Fiction Studies* 13 (July 1986): 130.

140. Peter George, *Dr. Strangelove, or How I Learned to Stop Worrying and Love the*

Bomb (New York: Barnes and Noble Books, 1998), 16–17. George's novel is based on the screenplay by Stanley Kubrick, Peter George, and Terry Southern.

141. George, *Dr. Strangelove*, 96.

142. George, *Dr. Strangelove*, 108, 109.

143. George, *Dr. Strangelove*, 157, 158.

144. George, *Dr. Strangelove*, 161.

145. George, *Dr. Strangelove*, 161, 162.

146. George, *Dr. Strangelove*, 161.

147. For *Dr. Strangelove's* cultural significance, see Margot A. Henriksen, *Dr. Strangelove's America: Society and Culture in the Atomic Age* (Berkeley: University of California Press, 1997).

148. Richard Slotkin, *Regeneration through Violence: The Mythology of the American Frontier, 1600–1860* (Middletown, CT: Wesleyan University Press, 1973), 5. See also Richard Slotkin, *Gunfighter Nation: The Myth of the Frontier in Twentieth-Century America* (New York: Atheneum, 1992).

149. Authors who did offer a political solution often came from the far-right fringes. Lydia R. Strother and Claude L. Strother decried "the increasing empathy extended to pot, porn and homos by establishment society." As a step toward halting the progress of "the international Red wolf pack," the authors recommended an ABM system and the passage of legislation "to control internal subversion, 'student' rioting, and tutorial propagandizing by college professors." Lydia R. Strother and Claude L. Strother, *Prepare for Armageddon: Survival in the Nuclear Age* (1968; Glendale, CA: Lee Press, 1973), 242, 245.

150. Brians, *Nuclear Holocausts*, 55.

151. Winkler, *Life under a Cloud*, 7.

152. Thomas Mann, *The Magic Mountain*, trans. H. T. Lowe-Porter (New York: Modern Library, 1992), 207.

153. Arthur Waskow expressed concerns that

the image of a world of death and destruction might act as a kind of "pornography of violence" to attract people to civil defense work who "want to get it over with"—who see nuclear war as a relief of intolerable tensions and as a way of "ending" international conflict—or who see themselves as survivors and rulers in a world where affluence and internal bickering had given way to pioneer exertions and tightly controlled order.

Waskow, "The Shelter-Centered Society," 49.

NOTES TO CHAPTER 3

1. Department of Defense, Office of Civil Defense, *Fallout Protection: What to Know and Do about Nuclear Attack* (Washington, D.C.: GPO, 1961), 6–7.

2. Department of Defense, Office of Civil Defense, *Fallout Protection: What to Know and Do about Nuclear Attack*, 9, 6.

3. "Civil Defense Booklet Hit," *Science News Letter*, 3 February 1962, 78.

4. "A Falling Out on Fallout," *Commonweal*, 2 February 1962, 482.

5. "Coffins or Shields?" *Time*, 2 February 1962, 15.

6. House Subcommittee of the Committee on Government Operations, *Civil Defense*, 86th Cong., 2d sess., 1960, 20.

7. "Enter the Survival Merchants," *Consumer Reports* 27, no. 1 (January 1962): 47.

8. "Survival: Are Shelters the Answer?" *Newsweek*, 6 November 1961, 19.

9. "All Out against Fallout," *Time*, 4 August 1961, 11.

10. "Boom to Bust," *Time*, 18 May 1962, 20.

11. Hoegh quoted in James Reston, "U.S. Shelter Policy Badly Needed," *Denver Post*, 14 November 1961; "Boom to Bust," 20.

12. "Shelter Boom," *Newsweek*, 18 September 1961, 32.

13. An interesting regional variation on the fallout shelter could be found in New Orleans, where shelter builders were counseled to build watertight shelters equipped with periscopes because a nuclear blast would almost certainly destroy the levees on the Mississippi and flood the city. "Civil Defense: The Sheltered Life," *Time*, 20 October 1961, 22, 23.

14. James Reston, "Those Sweet and Kindly Shelter Builders," *New York Times*, 12 November 1961.

15. "Dig We Must?" *Newsweek*, 2 October 1961, 24.

16. "Enter the Survival Merchants," 47.

17. Raisin quoted in Dean Brelis, *Run, Dig or Stay?* (Boston: Beacon, 1962), 55.

18. "Enter the Survival Merchants," 48; "Shelter Boom," 32.

19. *New York Times*, 15 November 1961.

20. "A New Urgency, Big Things to Do—and What You Must Learn," *Life* 51, no. 11 (15 September 1961): 97, 96.

21. "Use and Limit of Shelters," *Life* 52, no. 2 (12 January 1962): 4.

22. "Survival: Are Shelters the Answer?" 20.

23. "Life in Shelters Foreseen for U.S.," *New York Times*, 8 January 1959.

24. *New York Times*, 17 October 1960.

25. "Coffins or Shields?" 15. The Nobel laureate biochemist Albert Szent-Gyorgyi predicted that America as "an idea of democracy" could not survive the next war because "after a nuclear war we will have here only a crude, barbaric dictatorship of a nation of half cripples." Szent-Gyorgyi quoted in Joseph Roddy, "The Big March for Peace," *Look* 26, no. 14 (3 July 1962): 14.

26. Charles Newman, "Reflections on Protection," *Yale Review*, March 1963, 405.

27. Ronald E. Sleeth, "Urgently Needed: An Ethic for Moles," *Christian Century* 78, no. 4 (23 August 1961): 1006.

28. House Subcommittee No. 3 of the Committee on Armed Services, *Civil Defense—Fallout Shelter Program*, 88th Cong., 1st sess., 1963, Murray and Kennan quoted in statement of Philip W. Kelleher, counsel to Committee on Armed Services, 3040.

29. Gerard Piel, "The Illusion of Civil Defense," *Bulletin of the Atomic Scientists*

17, no. 2 (February 1962): 7–8. Piel also noted that "the extrapolation of thermonuclear violence and of countermeasures to that violence speedily leads us into a realm of underground subeconomies and subtopias that appear no more plausible and no less challenging to human ingenuity than a world without war. One may take as much heart from this observation as one can." Gerard Piel, "On the Feasibility of Peace," *Science* 135 (23 February 1962): 650.

30. Hurt quoted in Brelis, *Run, Dig or Stay?* 61.

31. House Subcommittee of the Committee on Government Operations, *Civil Defense*, 85th Cong., 2d sess., 1958, 260.

32. House Subcommittee, *Civil Defense—Fallout Shelter Program* (1963), 3059.

33. Rogers S. Cannell, *Live: A Handbook of Survival in Nuclear Attack* (Englewood Cliffs, NJ: Prentice-Hall, 1962), n.p.

34. House Subcommittee of the Committee on Government Operations, *New Civil Defense Legislation*, 85th Cong., 1st sess., 1957, 217.

35. *New York Times*, 10 November 1961.

36. Bentley Glass, "The Biology of Nuclear War," in *The Fallen Sky: Medical Consequences of Thermonuclear War*, ed. Saul Aronow (New York: Hill and Wang, 1963), 104.

37. Ralph E. Lapp, *The Weapons Culture* (New York: Norton, 1968), 140.

38. Robert Moses, "The Civil Defense Fiasco," *Harper's* 214, no. 1290 (November 1957): 33.

39. William L. Shirer, "Let's Stop the Fall-Out Shelter Folly!" *Good Housekeeping*, February 1962, 151, 152.

40. "Civil Defense: The Sheltered Life," 21. Newman, "Reflections on Protection," 410. Eisendrath, in somewhat overwrought prose, declared,

Even amid this dance macabre of world-wide incineration there will be no decency, no democracy, unless the voice and force of religion repel this vile and vicious "do-it-yourself, dig-your-own hole" individualism which will doom the poor, the weak, the ailing to scream and scratch at the sealed and sinister doors of the shelters of the still privileged few.

New York Times, 13 November 1961.

41. Erich Fromm and Michael Maccoby, "The Case against Shelters," in *No Place to Hide: Fact and Fiction about Fallout Shelters*, ed. Seymour Melman (New York: Grove Press, 1962), 78. Brown quoted in "The Moral Dilemma of Fallout Shelters," *Senior Scholastic*, 29 November 1961, 16.

42. P. Herbert Leiderman and Jack H. Mendelson, "Some Psychiatric Considerations in Planning for Defense Shelters," in Aronow, *The Fallen Sky: Medical Consequences of Thermonuclear War*, 52.

43. Harrison Brown and James Real, *Community of Fear* (Santa Barbara, CA: Center for the Study of Democratic Institutions, 1960), 38–39.

44. Robert B. Meyner, "Bomb Shelters Will Not Save Us!" *Coronet* 48, no. 5 (September 1960): 64.

45. Meyner, "Bomb Shelters Will Not Save Us!" 68.

46. Hanson W. Baldwin, "The Case against Fallout Shelters," *Saturday Evening Post*, 31 March 1962, 9.

47. LeMay insisted that such money would be better spent on strategic weapons—"something to fight with that will add to our deterrent force." House Subcommittee, *Civil Defense* (1960), 157, 156. LeMay generally took a dim view of civil defense, declaring, "I don't think civil defense as set up now has an organization capable of carrying out the job," and "I favor militarizing the civil defense" (141, 142). See also Gilbert Burck, "The Economy Can Survive Nuclear Attack," *Fortune* 64, no. 5 (November 1961): 115.

48. House Subcommittee, *Civil Defense* (1960), 159.

49. Kenneth Boulding, introduction to *Conflict and Defense*, ed. Kenneth Boulding (New York: Harper and Row, 1962), v.

50. House Subcommittee, *Civil Defense—Fallout Shelter Program* (1963), 4936; "Fallout Shelters—The Word," *National Review*, 16 December 1961, 405. Writing in 1970, some ten years after the fallout shelter controversy, Roy Bongartz in *Esquire* observed, "somehow it all seems very far away from us, as remote as the French Maginot Line of the Thirties." Roy Bongartz, "Remember Bomb Shelters?" *Esquire*, May 1970, 130.

51. Dwight D. Eisenhower, *Waging Peace, 1956–1961* (Garden City, NY: Doubleday, 1965), 222.

52. Baldwin, "The Case against Fallout Shelters," 9.

53. Piel, "The Illusion of Civil Defense," 8. The perennial socialist presidential candidate Norman Thomas claimed that "liberty cannot be preserved in a fall-out shelter," and that even if the nation survived a nuclear war, "we will have to live under the worst form of dictatorship afterwards." *New York Times*, 12 November 1961.

54. Richard Wayne Dyke, *Mr. Atomic Energy* (New York: Greenwood, 1989), 189.

55. Arthur I. Waskow, "The Shelter-Centered Society," *Scientific American* 206, no. 5 (May 1962): 46, 47.

56. David R. Inglis, "Shelters and the Chance of War," *Bulletin of the Atomic Scientists* 18, no. 4 (April 1962): 21. The increasing role of the military in American life also led some observers to fear the possibility of a military coup attempt. In 1960 Harrison Brown and James Real theorized that this might happen "in the event of a disarmament agreement which the military does not consider foolproof." Brown and Real, *Community of Fear*, 28. This was exactly the scenario of the 1964 John Frankenheimer film *Seven Days in May*, in which a rogue air force general, played by Burt Lancaster, plots to overthrow an American president who has signed an unpopular disarmament treaty with the Soviets.

57. "Civil Defense Shelters: An Interview with Congressman Chet Holifield," *Bulletin of the Atomic Scientists* 14, no. 4 (April 1958): 133.

58. House Subcommittee, *Civil Defense—Fallout Shelter Program* (1963), 3681.

59. Roger Hagan, "Community Shelters," in Melman, *No Place to Hide*, 179–80.

60. Quoted in Herman Kahn, "The Case for Shelters," in *No Place to Hide*, 60.

61. House Subcommittee, *Civil Defense* (1960), 47.

62. Gifford H. Albright, ed., *Planning Atomic Shelters: A Guidebook for Architects and Engineers* (University Park: Pennsylvania State University Press, 1961), 31. Collection of the FEMA Library, Washington, D.C.

63. "Gun Thy Neighbor?" *Time*, 18 August 1961, 58.

64. Bongartz, "Remember Bomb Shelters?" 130.

65. "Gun Thy Neighbor?" 58.

66. Norman Cousins, "Shelters, Survival, and Common Sense," part 2, *Saturday Review*, 28 October 1961, 26.

67. Quoted in Victor W. Sidel, H. Jack Geiger, and Bernard Lown, "The Physician's Role in the Postattack Period," in Aronow, *The Fallen Sky: Medical Consequences of Thermonuclear War*, 36.

68. "Gun Thy Neighbor?" 58.

69. McHugh conceded that "in the Christian view, there is great merit in turning the other cheek and bearing evils patiently out of the love of God," but called this an "exalted brand of supernatural motivation" and referred to persons thusly motivated as "heroic Christians." L. C. McHugh, "Ethics at the Shelter Doorway," *America*, 30 September 1961, 824–26.

70. "Gun Thy Neighbor?" 58.

71. Quoted in "Says Morality Requires Community Shelters," *Christian Century*, 25 October 1961, 1262. See also *New York Times*, 14 October 1961.

72. "Incivility in Civil Defense," *Christian Century*, 23 August 1961, 995. The Rabbinical Council of America endorsed the building of community shelters throughout the country, and suggested that Jewish congregations contemplating new construction make provisions for fallout shelters that would be open to everyone. "Civil Defense: Survival (Contd.)," *Time*, 3 November 1961, 19.

73. Graham quoted in Peter Braestrup, "The Shelter Dilemma: Great Confusion Exists over What to Do," *New York Times*, 19 November 1961. Elson quoted in Bongartz, "Remember Bomb Shelters?" 130.

74. Jessett quoted in Thomas Hine, *Populuxe* (New York: MJF Books, 1999), 137. Jessett suggested that "if we really want to be safe, we'd better start shooting our neighbors now, to be sure we get them all" (138).

75. Theodore Shabad, "Soviet Twits U.S. on Civil Defense," *New York Times*, 26 August 1961.

76. Cousins, "Shelters, Survival, and Common Sense," part 2, 26. Cousins's statement reads,

People speculate on the horrors that would be let loose by nuclear war. It is not necessary to speculate on such horrors. Some of the worst horrors are already here. The transformation today of otherwise decent people into death-calculating machines; the psychological preconditioning for an age of cannibalism; the wholesale premeditation of murder and the acceptable conditions thereof; the moral insolence of those who presume to prescribe the circumstances under which it is spiritually permissible to kill one's neighbors; the desensitization of human response to pain; the acquiescence in the inevitability of disaster; the cheapening of human personality with its concomitant of irresponsible fatalism—all these are part of an already existing, fast-swelling chamber of horrors.

77. "Home Shelters—'False Security'?" *Science Digest*, February 1962, 79.

78. Richard Horchler, "A Falling Out on Fallout," *Commonweal*, 2 February 1962, 482. Others taking this line included Elizabeth H. Farquhar of the Women's International League for Peace and Freedom. Farquhar noted that when a large portion of the citizenry accepted the necessity of "stocking a sawed-off shotgun in private shelters for use against one's neighbors," the "moral fibre of that nation is already being undermined." House Subcommittee, *Civil Defense—Fallout Shelter Program* (1963), 4164–65.

79. Kolko added that "we can only deeply regret that our democratic civilization has absorbed an aspect of barbarism so casually, and without hesitation." Gabriel Kolko, "On the Value of a Shelter Program," in Melman, *No Place to Hide*, 124.

80. Kennedy quoted in Allan M. Winkler, *Life under a Cloud: American Anxiety about the Atom* (New York: Oxford University Press, 1993), 130.

81. Robert Kennedy quoted in Arthur M. Schlesinger, Jr., *A Thousand Days: John F. Kennedy in the White House* (Boston: Houghton Mifflin, 1965), 749.

82. Seymour Chwast and Edward Sorel, "How to Stop Worrying about the Bomb," *Playboy* 9, no. 3 (March 1962): 81.

83. The critic David Segal said that for Feiffer the bomb was "both representative symbol and an appalling apotheosis." *Contemporary Authors: A Bio-Bibliographical Guide to Current Authors and Their Works*, ed. Clare D. Kinsman, vols. 17–20, s.v. Jules Feiffer (Detroit: Gale Research Company, 1976).

84. "If H-Bomb Comes—What You Can Do about It," *U.S. News and World Report*, 8 April 1955, 75.

85. Cousins, "Shelters, Survival, and Common Sense," part 2, 26; *Los Angeles Times*, 1 August 1961. Adair was reprimanded by his superiors for his statement, and J. B. Colegrove of the Los Angeles civil defense office observed that a nuclear attack on Los Angeles would be disruptive to Las Vegas not because of fleeing Angelenos, but because "Southern Nevada is dependent 100% on the Los Angeles market for its food supply." Las Vegas civil defense officials were meeting in Los Angeles to discuss ways to insure the flow of food supplies from Los Angeles to Las Vegas during an emergency. *Los Angeles Times*, 1 August 1961.

86. *Los Angeles Times*, 5 August 1961.

87. In the previous month, Los Angeles mayor Samuel Yorty had expressed his gratitude to Bakersfield's city manager Leland Gunn for leaving that city's doors

open to possible victims of nuclear attack. *San Francisco Chronicle*, 23 September 1961.

88. Walter H. Waggoner, "Concern over Civil Defense Increases throughout the Nation," *New York Times*, 5 September 1961.

89. See Peter Braestrup, "Civil Defense Stirs New Debate," *New York Times*, 22 October 1961; Braestrup, "The Shelter Dilemma: Great Confusion Exists over What to Do"; James T. Rogers, "Report from the Nation: Reaction to Fall-Out Shelters," *New York Times*, 19 November 1961.

90. James Reston, "How to Be Evaporated in Style," *New York Times*, 15 October 1961.

91. Reston, "Those Sweet and Kindly Shelter Builders."

92. James Reston, "Kennedy's Shelter Policy Re-Examined," *New York Times*, 26 November 1961.

93. Meyner observed that even if people happened to survive in their shelters, "What kind of world would they come up to? What would they use for air? What would they use for food? What would they use for hospitals? What would they use for streets? What would they use for people?" *New York Times*, 20 March 1960. See also *New York Times*, 27 March 1960; and Ralph E. Lapp, "Rockefeller's Civil Defense Program," *Bulletin of the Atomic Scientists* 16, no. 4 (April 1960): 134.

94. *New York Times*, 24 March 1960.

95. Rockefeller also presided over the civil defense committee of the 1961 Governors' Conference, which drafted a statement calling fallout protection "imperative if our people are to survive in case of war." Peter Kihss, "Governor Builds 4 Bomb Shelters," *New York Times*, 23 July 1961. Meyner continued to be unimpressed, and in a television interview called the claim that fallout shelters could insure the survival of large numbers of people a "delusion." *New York Times*, 10 August 1961.

96. See *Los Angeles Times*, 14 September 1961; Braestrup, "Civil Defense Stirs New Debate."

97. Braestrup, "The Shelter Dilemma: Great Confusion Exists over What to Do."

98. "What 50 Megatons Could Do Here," *New York Times*, 31 October 1961.

99. John Wicklein, "12 Families Moving to Find Atom Haven," *New York Times*, 16 September 1961.

100. *Denver Post*, 20 August 1961.

101. *Denver Post*, 14 August 1961.

102. *Denver Post*, 21 October 1961.

103. *Denver Post*, 6 November 1961.

104. "New Life for Civil Defense Program," *Denver Post*, 6 August 1961.

105. "Civil Defense: To Each His Own?" *Denver Post*, 11 September 1961.

106. *Denver Post*, 11 September 1961.

107. *Denver Post*, 3 November 1961.

108. Lawrence G. Weiss, "Moral Dilemma at the Shelter Door," *Denver Post*, 15 October 1961.

109. Marquis W. Childs, "Question on Fallout Shelters: What Happens on Emergence?" *St. Louis Post-Dispatch*, 5 October 1961.

110. Raymond P. Brandt, "Protection against Nuclear Attack Is Subject of Confusion and Apathy," *St. Louis Post-Dispatch*, 3 December 1961; Richard Dudman, "Ability of Individual Shelters to Protect Families Questioned; Definite Building Guide Lacking," *St. Louis Post-Dispatch*, 4 December 1961.

111. "The Shelter Illusion," *St. Louis Post-Dispatch*, 8 November 1961. The *Post-Dispatch* also reprinted a speech by Gerard Piel in which Piel referred to the "hoax on public opinion" perpetrated by game theorists that nuclear war is survivable. See "Fallout Shelters—A Hoax on the Public," *St. Louis Post-Dispatch*, 8 December 1961.

112. On the fallout shelter debate Mauldin observed, "The government provided plans for do-it-yourselfers, and speculators got rich selling family-size sections of sawed-off highway drainage pipe. Even pets were provided for in the mass interment program." From Bill Mauldin, *I've Decided I Want My Seat Back* (New York: Harper and Row, 1965), 2.

113. Howard James, "City's Plight a Dread One if Bomb Drops," *Chicago Tribune*, 22 August 1961.

114. Howard James, "Chicago Lags in Civil Defense," *Chicago Tribune*, 20 August 1961.

115. *Chicago Tribune*, 19 August 1961. A reporter for the *Christian Science Monitor* who attended this meeting observed that,

> When some majority aldermen were not harassing the discussion they clipped fingernails or yawned toward the ceiling, for the most part paying little attention to the government shelter documents handed them at the beginning of the meeting. Few of those asked to vote for the significant ordinance had ever seen the pertinent data previously, further indication of the perfunctory action apparently expected of the meeting.

Robert Colby Nelson, "Chicago Shelter Plan Voted," *Christian Science Monitor*, 24 August 1961.

116. Howard James, "Grim Picture of Bomb Hit in Loop Is Given," *Chicago Tribune*, 23 August 1961.

117. Pat Watters, "Is Self-Preservation Last Law of Nature as Well as the First?" *Atlanta Journal*, 4 August 1961.

118. Donovan Bess, "Shelter Builder Needs a Big Pipe," *San Francisco Chronicle*, 15 September 1961.

119. A number of Angelenos suggested that Los Angeles County's storm drains be employed as makeshift fallout shelters. Civil defense officials were taking storm drains seriously, if nothing else as a way to move people out of contaminated areas. *Los Angeles Times*, 7 August 1961.

120. "Red Alert! What if H-Bomb Hits Los Angeles?" *Los Angeles Times*, 12 March 1961.

121. John Cheever, "The Brigadier and the Golf Widow," in *The Stories of John Cheever* (New York: Knopf, 1979), 505.

122. Cheever, "The Brigadier and the Golf Widow," 508.

123. Cheever, "The Brigadier and the Gold Widow," 505.

124. Cheever, "The Brigadier and the Golf Widow," 507.

125. John Cheever, *The Journals of John Cheever* (New York: Ballantine, 1991), 153.

136. Jules Feiffer, *Crawling Arnold, Horizon* 4, no. 2 (November 1961): 49.

127. Feiffer, *Crawling Arnold*, 50.

128. Feiffer, *Crawling Arnold*, 50, 52.

129. Feiffer, *Crawling Arnold*, 54, 56.

130. Hughes quoted by Arnold Rampersad, introduction to *The Return of Simple*, by Langston Hughes (New York: Hill and Wang, 1994), xx.

131. Langston Hughes, "Serious Talk about the Atom Bomb," in *The Return of Simple*, 113.

132. Langston Hughes, "Bones, Bombs, Chicken Necks," in *The Best of Simple* (New York: Hill and Wang, 1997), 201.

133. Langston Hughes, "Radioactive Red Caps," in *The Best of Simple*, 211.

134. See Donald Robinson, "If H-Bombs Fall," *Saturday Evening Post*, 25 May 1957, 110. Roger Hagan asked in 1962, "Then too, who will go to the CD training schools to become the absolute leaders in the crisis and post-attack world? Policemen and retired military officers, to judge from the local civil defense cadres of some states. The Southern Negro may well wonder what fallout can do to him that the local police chief cannot." Hagan, "Community Shelters," 188.

135. The show was in its third season in 1961, and Serling's biographer Gordon F. Sander notes that "the most striking quality about the scripts he [Serling] wrote for the third season was the way they closely reflected current events and personalities about which the creator felt strongly." In this respect, according to Sander, *The Twilight Zone* became "a script for the liberal conscience of the early 1960s." Gordon F. Sander, *Serling: The Rise and Twilight of Television's Last Angry Man* (New York: Dutton, 1992), 181.

136. Rod Serling, "The Shelter," in *From the Twilight Zone* (Garden City, NY: Doubleday, 1962), 303–4.

137. Serling, "The Shelter," 309.

138. Serling, "The Shelter," 313–14. At the end of the show Serling comments, "No moral, no message, no prophetic tract. Just a simple statement of fact: for civilization to survive, the human race has to remain civilized. Tonight's very small exercise in logic from the Twilight Zone." Sander, *Serling*, 181.

139. Bob Dylan, "Let Me Die in My Footsteps," in *Bob Dylan: The Bootleg Series*, vol. 1 (1991) (Columbia 47382). Dylan quoted by John Bauldie in liner notes to *Bob Dylan: The Bootleg Series*, 10.

140. Walter Lippmann, "Mistaken Fallout Shelter Scare," *St. Louis Post-Dispatch*, 15 November 1961.

141. Waskow, "The Shelter-Centered Society," 47.

NOTES TO CHAPTER 4

1. See Daniel Lang, "Search for a Hideout," in *From Hiroshima to the Moon: Chronicles of Life in the Atomic Age* (New York: Simon and Schuster, 1959), 112.

2. Philip J. Funigiello, "Managing Armageddon," *Journal of Policy History* 2, no. 4 (1990): 408.

3. Quoted in Funigiello, "Managing Armageddon," 411.

4. "If Bombs Do Fall—Who'll Run Things," *U.S. News and World Report*, 16 October 1961, 45–47.

5. Ted Gup, "The Ultimate Congressional Hideaway," *Washington Post Magazine*, 31 May 1992, 11; Mike Allen, "Congress' Cold War Fallout Shelter Takes on New Role," *San Francisco Chronicle*, 13 August 1997.

6. Gup, "The Ultimate Congressional Hideaway," 11, 15.

7. Gup, "The Ultimate Congressional Hideaway," 13, 26.

8. See *Washington Post*, 3 June 1992.

9. Allen, "Congress' Cold War Fallout Shelter Takes on New Role."

10. During World War II German, Italian, and Japanese diplomats were kept at Greenbrier until they could be exchanged for American diplomats. The army would later turn the hotel into a hospital for twenty thousand wounded. Sandra Fleishman, "Resort's Post-Nuclear Future," *Washington Post*, 13 April 2000.

11. Ted Gup, "Underground Government: A Guide to America's Doomsday Bunkers," *Washington Post Magazine*, 31 May 1992, 14.

12. Richard Amper, "2 Million Briefed on Skills in War," *New York Times*, 28 December 1957.

13. *New York Times*, 14 May 1961. See also the testimony of Leo Hoegh in House Subcommittee of the Committee on Government Operations, *Civil Defense*, 86th Cong., 2d sess., 1960, 105.

14. *U.S. News* noted that "both industry and labor have taken to the idea of formal contracts. They are used to doing business that way. Also, they realize they would be commandeered anyway, in case of war, and welcome the protection of a contract negotiated in advance." "If Bombs Do Fall—Who'll Run Things," 49.

15. Richard F. Dempewolff, "Don't Let the Cries of Doomsday Panic You," *Popular Mechanics*, April 1962, 222.

16. "If Bombs Do Fall on U.S.—What People Look For," *U.S. News and World Report*, 25 September 1961, 55.

17. See Guy Oakes, *The Imaginary War* (New York: Oxford University Press, 1994), 154–55.

18. Gup, "Underground Government," 15. Donald W. Mitchell, *Civil Defense:*

Planning for Survival and Recovery (Washington, D.C.: Industrial College of the Armed Forces, 1963), 60.

19. James L. Robertson, "Assuring the Continuity of Money and Credit," in American Management Association, *Survival and Recovery: Industrial Preparedness in the Nuclear Age*, ed. Jerome W. Blood and Harley M. Clements, AMA Management Bulletin 15 (New York: AMA, 1962), 10. Robertson warned businesses not to "hoard currency in periods of grave international tension" (12).

20. Kurt Gottfried and Bruce G. Blair, eds., *Crisis Stability and Nuclear War* (New York: Oxford University Press, 1988), 51. Gup, "Underground Government," 14–15.

21. "If Bombs Do Fall—Who'll Run Things," 48–49.

22. Cheyenne Mountain is the most elaborate of the government underground installations. Its fifteen buildings are each covered in half-inch thick steel, and sit atop 1,300 metal coils, each about five feet tall, designed to absorb the shock from a nuclear explosion. It has an elaborate ventilation system, its own six-million-gallon reservoir, and a half-million-gallon reservoir for diesel fuel. There are six 1,750-kilowatt generators, and enough food and supplies to support eight hundred people for a month. Michael Taylor, "Built to Survive Bombs, Budget Cuts," *San Francisco Chronicle*, 16 November 1998.

23. Edward W. Ziegler, "$8 Billion Stockpile Fiasco: The Cold War in Storage," *Nation* 189, no. 20 (12 December 1959): 434–36.

24. Marjorie Hunter, "Medical Supplies Being Stockpiled," *New York Times*, 3 December 1961. To insure that enough medical supplies would survive a nuclear war, the Johnson and Johnson company proposed splitting the cost with the federal government of constructing an underground medical storage facility in Texas. See William H. Baumer, "Restoring Production after Attack," in American Management Association, *Survival and Recovery*, 17.

25. "If an H-Bomb Hits—A Report by Top Scientists," *U.S. News and World Report*, 2 March 1956, 43. Philip Wylie was among those who were dubious about Teller's cave idea. While Wylie's novel *Tomorrow!* had expressed confidence that civil defense efforts could assure a rapid recovery after nuclear attack, by 1957 much of his optimism had been replaced with skepticism, including skepticism about Teller's cave idea. "I doubt that the American people will spend the awesome billions for the caverns and the gear," noted Wylie, nor would they "train themselves for a period as technological troglodytes." Wylie believed that Americans would conclude that by the time their "giant caves and gigantic gadgets were ready," there would be weapons available that "could blast them out of the earth's crust as readily as current weapons can blast, burn, and ray them off it." Philip Wylie, letter, *Bulletin of the Atomic Scientists* 13, no. 4 (April 1957): 146.

26. Oskar Morgenstern, *The Question of National Defense* (New York: Random House, 1959), 127–28.

27. *International Security: The Military Aspect (Report of Panel II of the Special Studies Project)* (Garden City, NY: Doubleday, 1958), 48.

28. RAND Corporation, *Report on a Study of Non-Military Defense* (R-322-RC) (Santa Monica, CA: RAND Corporation, 1958), 28–29, 30.

29. RAND Corporation, *Report on a Study of Non-Military Defense*, 48.

30. The Moreel Report was named after Ben Moreel, chairman of the board of the Jones and Laughlin Steel Corporation. "Dispersal of American Industry," *Bulletin of the Atomic Scientists* 10, no. 6 (June 1954): 196, 205. See also Ben Moreel, "What the H-Bomb Can Do to U.S. Industries," *U.S. News and World Report*, 7 May 1954, 58.

31. Eugene Rabinowitch, "Must Millions March?" *Bulletin of the Atomic Scientists* 10, no. 6 (June 1954): 195.

32. The Defense Production Act of 1956 read, "it is the policy of the Congress to promote the geographical dispersal of the industrial facilities of the United States in the interest of the national defense." Mary M. Simpson, "A Long Hard Look at Civil Defense," *Bulletin of the Atomic Scientists* 11, no. 9 (November 1956): 348.

33. House Military Operations Subcommittee of the Committee on Government Operations, *Civil Defense for National Survival*, 84th Cong., 2d sess., 1956, 33. As early as 1951 Augustin Prentiss had concluded that there was "little prospect" for significant industrial dispersal "unless the Federal government steps in and compels the proper strategic relocation of vital industries by legislation." Augustin M. Prentiss, *Civil Defense in Modern War* (New York: McGraw-Hill, 1951), 173.

34. Bernard Brodie, *Strategy in the Missile Age* (Princeton: Princeton University Press, 1959), 206, 207. John H. Redmond of Koppers Company observed that "if we believe attack is imminent then stronger incentives [to disperse] are needed than exist at the present." But if attack is not imminent, and lay twenty or twenty-five years in the future, then "natural growth and relocation" would accomplish the goal of industrial dispersion. See House Subcommittee of the Committee on Government Operations, *New Civil Defense Legislation*, 85th Cong., 1st sess., 1957, 453.

35. House Subcommittee, *Civil Defense* (1960), 101.

36. Cited in Joseph J. Corn and Brian Horrigan, *Yesterday's Tomorrows: Past Visions of the American Future* (New York: Summit, 1984), 118.

37. Richard Rutter, "Ways to Survive Nuclear Strike," *New York Times*, 1 October 1961.

38. House Subcommittee No. 3 of the Committee on Armed Services, *Civil Defense—Fallout Shelter Program*, 88th Cong., 1st sess., 1963, 4134, 4142.

39. John H. Fenton, "Bank Constructs a Bomb Shelter," *New York Times*, 2 December 1960.

40. House Subcommittee, *Civil Defense—Fallout Shelter Program* (1963), 3813, 3877, 3883.

41. Standard Oil Company, "Blueprint for Industrial Security" in House Subcommittee, *Civil Defense—Fallout Shelter Program* (1963), 4175, 4177. By 1962 some 31 million microfilm images had been stored at Morristown in a specially pre-

pared underground vault. See Kenneth E. Yandell, "Protecting Headquarters Operations," in American Management Association, *Survival and Recovery*, 23, 22.

42. Rutter, "Ways to Survive Nuclear Strike"; House Subcommittee, *Civil Defense—Fallout Shelter Program* (1963), 4244. There was at least one suggestion that industrial *personnel* be dispersed. John I. Snyder, Jr., president of U.S. Industries, recommended a "Noah's Ark" policy in which executives would be sent to foreign branch offices where they would likely "survive to fight and work another day in case front-line men are lost" in a nuclear attack. John I. Snyder, Jr., "A Positive Attitude toward Survival," in American Management Association, *Survival and Recovery*, 6.

43. House Subcommittee, *Civil Defense—Fallout Shelter Program* (1963), 4670.

44. "Civil Defense: Survival (Contd.)," *Time*, 3 November 1961, 19.

45. Notes and Comment, *New Yorker*, 2 December 1961, 51. As the *New Yorker* observed, the "opportunities for litigation at the end of the world would not appear to be great, and the need for estate planning at first blush negligible. . . . But those twenty—*twenty!*—municipal officers, and those civil-defense officials, who would seem to have their responsibilities behind them! Here is some excess fat."

46. Snyder, "A Positive Attitude toward Survival," 4. A survey of 205 large manufacturers that was conducted by the National Industrial Conference Board and released in November 1961 showed that only 5 percent had installed fallout shelters, but that 40 percent had made some provision for safekeeping of important records. Mitchell, *Civil Defense: Planning for Survival and Recovery*, 60. At least one obnoxious feature of modern life would, it seems, survive a nuclear war. The Outdoor Advertising Association announced that it would stockpile twelve thousand posters containing emergency instructions that it would put up on billboards after a nuclear war. *New York Times*, 17 January 1961.

47. Hirshleifer observed that "destroyed firms will be unable to pay debts upon which undestroyed firms have been relying for funds to pay their creditors, [and] the second-order defaults will create third-order ones, and so forth." Hirshleifer quoted in Mitchell, *Civil Defense: Planning for Survival and Recovery*, 61.

48. See Gilbert Burck, "The Economy Can Survive Nuclear Attack," *Fortune* 64, no. 5 (November 1961): 264. Civil defense administrator Leo Hoegh testified in 1960 that the United States had some seventy-five items in its strategic stockpile with a total value of about $7 billion. House Subcommittee, *Civil Defense* (1960), 109. Donald Robinson, "If H-Bombs Fall," *Saturday Evening Post*, 25 May 1957, 25.

49. John George and Laird Wilcox, *Nazis, Communists, Klansmen, and Others on the Fringe: Political Extremism in America* (Buffalo, NY: Prometheus, 1992), 274–75.

50. J. Harry Jones, Jr., *The Minutemen* (Garden City, NY: Doubleday, 1968), 50–51.

51. Lauchli's previous arrest record included a conviction for possession of machine guns in 1955, and stealing bazookas and selling them to South American

revolutionaries in 1959. Kenneth Jacobson, "Rightist Group Holds School on Guerrilla War," *St. Louis Post-Dispatch*, 22 October 1961.

52. *St. Louis Post-Dispatch*, 23 October 1961.

53. J. Edgar Hoover testified before Congress that "there is little real evidence that the Minutemen are anything more than essentially a paper organization, with just enough followers over the country so they can occasionally attract a headline." See George and Wilcox, *Nazis, Communists, Klansmen, and Others on the Fringe*, 277.

54. Jones, *The Minutemen*, 97.

55. Jacobson, "Rightist Group Holds School on Guerrilla War." The emphasis on gun ownership is another similarity with militia groups. Robert DePugh declared that one of the purposes of the Minutemen was to "resist by all legal means the passage of laws which regulate the private ownership of firearms." *St. Louis Post-Dispatch*, 23 October 1961.

56. "Organizations: The Minutemen," *Time*, 3 November 1961, 19. Such fantasies of fighting a guerrilla war after the breakdown of civil order were not the exclusive province of right-wing paranoiacs. Arthur I. Waskow, writer, strategic analyst, and congressional staffer, called for the establishment of the very world government that the Minutemen feared. But Waskow also advocated the creation of a "civilian resistance force" to address the possibility that such a peaceful world order might break down, and that the United States might be invaded by a hostile army. Eerily mirroring the Minutemen's own ideas, Waskow's civilian force would perfect the arts of guerrilla warfare. In Waskow's words, "the entire population of the United States would learn how to resist an aggressor." Skills acquired by this force would include "how to broadcast from clandestine radio stations in the face of enemy prohibitions, how to sabotage industrial plants that were making goods for the enemy's use, how to use ordinary civilian materials to make weapons with which to attack enemy occupation troops." Arthur I. Waskow, *The Limits of Defense* (Garden City, NY: Doubleday, 1962), 94.

57. R. E. Lapp, *Must We Hide?* (Cambridge, MA: Addison-Wesley, 1949), 162–64. Lapp rejected the building of a shelter system because "the psychological effects of going underground would be at least as serious as the economic disruption" (159).

58. "How U.S. Cities Can Prepare for Atomic War," *Life* 29, no. 25 (18 December 1950): 78–79. The *Life* article acknowledged that "the cost of constructing the belts in terms of dollars and man-power would be huge—right-of-way for the tracks alone can run to $1 million per mile—and probably will bring the greatest opposition to the plan" (81).

59. Sylvian G. Kindall, *Total Atomic Defense* (New York: Richard R. Smith, 1952), 118–19, 196.

60. "If an H-Bomb Hits—A Report by Top Scientists," 43.

61. Philip Wylie, *Tomorrow!* (New York: Rinehart, 1954), 367, 366.

62. "Sweden: The Cavemen," *Time*, 23 June 1958, 22.

63. F. W. Edmondson, Jr., "Design of a Nuclear City," in *Design for the Nuclear Age* (Washington, D.C.: National Academy of Sciences–National Research Council, 1962), 89, 83–84. Collection of the FEMA Library, Washington, D.C.

64. "Nuclear Cities Coming," *Science News Letter*, 23 December 1961, 412. According to Edmondson, present-day cities had been

on the firing line too long. Born by geography but grown by the technology of Eli Whitney, they are reacting weakly to the surgical concept of renewal. The prognosis is poor. The old arteries are collapsed, the organs of social and mechanical functions are diseased and intravenous feeding of Federal, State, and private finance simply extends disability payments for a few more years.

65. Harold C. Urey, "I'm a Frightened Man," *Collier's*, 5 January 1946, 19.

66. *Bulletin of the Atomic Scientists* 10, no. 9 (November 1954): n.p.

67. Heinz Haber, *The Walt Disney Story of Our Friend the Atom* (New York: Simon and Schuster, 1956), 134.

68. Haber, *The Walt Disney Story of Our Friend the Atom*, 137, 152. In the prologue to *Our Friend*, author Heinz Haber notes,

We all know of the story of the military atom, and we all wish that it weren't true. . . . It does have all the earmarks of a drama: a frightful terror which everyone knows exists, a sinister threat, mystery and secrecy. . . . So far, the atom is a superb villain. Its power of destruction is foremost in our minds. But the same power can be put to use for creation, for the welfare of all mankind.

"It is up to us," says Haber, "to give the story a happy ending" by using atomic energy wisely (13).

69. JoAnne Brown, "'A Is for Atom, B Is for Bomb': Civil Defense in American Public Education, 1948–1963," *Journal of American History* 75, no. 1 (June 1988): 71.

70. Brown, "'A Is for Atom,'" 73–74.

71. Michael J. Carey, "The Schools and Civil Defense: The Fifties Revisited," *Teachers College Record* 84, no. 1 (fall 1982): 114.

72. Brown, "'A Is for Atom,'" 70.

73. Quoted in Carey, "The Schools and Civil Defense," 117. Offering a different perspective was Lewis Mumford, who condemned the participation of children in air raid drills as a "sadistic mummery." Lewis Mumford, "The Morals of Extermination," *Atlantic* 204, no. 4 (October 1959): 42.

74. Federal Civil Defense Administration, *Bert the Turtle Says Duck and Cover* (Washington, D.C.: GPO, [1951]), n.p. Responding to parents who worried that children might find *Duck and Cover* unsettling, the New York City Board of Education praised the film's "mental hygiene approach, its underlying qualities of cheerfulness and optimism." Quoted in Carey, "The Schools and Civil Defense," 118. In what may have been an oblique swipe at Bert's qualifications as a leader in the field of civil defense, Arthur Waskow declared that "human beings have always had before them the object lesson of the turtle, which adopted a civil defense policy millennia ago and

has been unable to progress since. The price for the one-turtle blast shelter has been stagnation in an evolutionary backwater." Arthur Waskow, "Civil Defense: Both Red and Dead," in *No Place to Hide: Fact and Fiction about Fallout Shelters*, ed. Seymour Melman (New York: Grove Press, 1962), 46.

75. Janice M. Johnson, *Skit for Planning a Home Shelter Area*. Classroom Practices no. 2, March 28, 1957 (Washington, D.C.: Department of Education, U.S. Department of Health, Education and Welfare, 1957).

76. L. J. Mauth, "Prevention of Panic in Elementary-School Children," *Journal of Education* 137, no. 2 (November 1954): 10–11.

77. Quoted in Brown, "'A Is for Atom,'" 76.

78. One school psychologist in New York City told the following story:
The mother of a bright twelve-year-old boy who is a happy, well-adjusted youngster tells of their hearing an explosion one evening. As the father rushed down to the furnace, the boy went to the window, looked out, remarked casually, "No mushroom cloud," and returned to his homework with a pleasant, reassuring smile at his mother.
Quoted in Brown, "'A Is for Atom,'" 77–78.

79. An excellent collection of clips from nuclear propaganda films can be found in *The Atomic Cafe*, a documentary produced in 1990.

80. Carey, "The Schools and Civil Defense," 115.

81. Todd Gitlin, *The Sixties: Years of Hope, Days of Rage* (New York: Bantam, 1987), 23.

82. Annie Dillard, *An American Childhood* (New York: Harper and Row, 1987), 181.

83. Tim O'Brien, *The Nuclear Age* (New York: Delta, 1989), 9.

84. Ron Kovic, *Born on the Fourth of July* (New York: McGraw-Hill, 1976), 45.

85. Doris Kearns Goodwin, *Wait till Next Year* (New York: Touchstone, 1997), 157.

86. Goodwin, *Wait till Next Year*, 158. Goodwin remembers viewing a civil defense film in school that emphasized the importance of a stocked fallout shelter and civil defense volunteers, and soon makes the important discovery that the local shops in her neighborhood were connected underground through their basements. Goodwin now becomes obsessed with the idea that her family—indeed, her entire neighborhood—could not only survive a nuclear war, but positively thrive by taking shelter in these facilities:
Everything was there. With Doc Schimmenti as our resident physician, we could use the supplies in the drugstore to set up a makeshift infirmary, complete with Band-Aids, Ace bandages, and all sorts of drugs and medicines. The rack of best-sellers would provide reading material, supplemented by the magazines and comic books from both the drugstore and the soda shop. Canned peas, string beans, tuna fish, peanut butter, and soups would be available from the delicatessen. In a pinch, the huge burlap bags filled with sawdust beneath the butcher shop could provide bedding.

As Goodwin describes it, "This was too big an idea to keep to myself," and subsequently takes it upon herself to inform the bemused merchants of her great brainstorm for surviving the nuclear holocaust (160, 161).

87. Vladislav Zubok and Constantine Pleshakov, *Inside the Kremlin's Cold War: From Stalin to Khrushchev* (Cambridge: Harvard University Press, 1996), ix.

88. See Brown, "'A Is for Atom,'" 80–83.

89. "Civil Defense in Schools," *Scholastic Teacher* edition of *Senior Scholastic* 80, no. 5 (7 March 1962): 1.

90. W. Gayle Starnes, "Schools and Civil Defense," *American School Board Journal* 135, no. 1 (July 1957): 22.

91. "Civil Defense in Schools," 1–3.

92. Eberle M. Smith Associates, *School Shelter: An Approach to Fallout Protection* (1960; Washington, D.C.: Department of Defense, Office of Civil Defense, 1962), 2–3.

93. Walter Rein, "Double Duty for School Plants," *American School Board Journal* 133, no. 2 (1956): 24.

94. House Subcommittee, *New Civil Defense Legislation* (1957), 54.

95. "Planning a School Fallout Shelter," *American School Board Journal* 143, no. 5 (November 1961): 29.

96. Jim Dutton and Richard Pearce, "A Study of a School Fallout Shelter," *American School Board Journal* 147, no. 4 (October 1963): 32.

97. See Brown, "'A Is for Atom,'" 88.

98. Lyndon Welch, "Architectural Design of Protected Areas," *Design for the Nuclear Age* (Washington, D.C.: National Academy of Sciences–National Research Council, 1962), 53. Collection of the FEMA Library, Washington, D.C.

99. House Subcommittee, *Civil Defense* (1960), 50.

100. Cavers also found the incentive money offered by the federal government to schools to be insufficient and claimed that financially strapped schools were being asked "to aid the affluent Department of Defense, which I think might be called the 'Daddy Warbucks' of Federal Government." House Subcommittee, *Civil Defense—Fallout Shelter Program* (1963), 3679–80.

101. "The Question of Fallout Shelter-Schools," *American School Board Journal* 144, no. 3 (March 1962): 26–27.

102. This was "the recommended minimum protection factor," according to Dutton and Pearce, "A Study of a School Fallout Shelter," 32.

103. "The Question of Fallout Shelter-Schools," 27.

104. President Gideonse of Brooklyn College quoted in Roger Hagan, "Community Shelters," in Melman, *No Place to Hide*, 183.

105. Eberle M. Smith Associates, *Technical Guide Manual: Fallout-Radiation Protection in Schools* (interim draft), ca. 1960. Collection of the FEMA Library, Washington, D.C.

106. Office of Civil Defense, *A Realistic Approach to Civil Defense: A Handbook for School Administrators* (Washington, D.C.: GPO, 1966), 4.

107. Shepoiser also argued that children faced a greater danger from "the commitment of a nation to irresponsible fatalism" and "adults speculating on the inevitability and horrors of thermonuclear war." "Civil Defense in Schools," 1–3.

108. "Fallout Shelters and the Schools," *NEA Journal*, February 1962, 23. "We're sitting on a powder keg today," said Heap. "In some measure, whether our children live through the night depends on whether Khrushchev pushes a button. The all-sword, no-shield policy of national defense is gambling with the lives of everyone, and this is callous and negligent." Richard P. Hunt, "One Town's 'Great Debate' over Shelters," *New York Times Magazine*, 4 February 1962, 57.

109. Hunt, "One Town's 'Great Debate' over Shelters," 58.

110. John M. Fowler, a professor at Washington University, objected to the Norwalk Plan mainly on psychological grounds: "Your whole town will think and talk war; your children will know that someone is going to bomb them and force them to live in those things under the playground." Fowler claimed that an effective fallout shelter program would "increase the chances of war" and "make us more daring in our power politics, and divert what little energy we have from peacemaking." Norman Cousins, the editor of *Saturday Review* and a consistent critic of the government's nuclear weapons program, maintained in his letter to the *NEA Journal* that in the event of a nuclear attack "the average city basement or shelter would be meaningless" and called it "an act of prime irresponsibility to lead the American people to believe that ninety-five per cent of them can be saved in their shelters." Hunt, "One Town's 'Great Debate' over Shelters," 24, 25.

111. Mary M. Grooms, "A Revolt against Shelters," *Nation* 192, no. 19 (13 May 1961): 412.

112. Grooms, "A Revolt against Shelters," 413. Quite aside from the psychological attributes of shelters, the forum also emphasized that civil defense plans for the region had become obsolete because upstate New York now contained a number of hardened ICBM sites, making the Rochester area a prime target. "If Russia would only be reasonable and drop no more than one bomb on Buffalo," the forum caustically observed, "fallout shelters in Rochester would be a definite help" (412).

113. David Nevin, "Nuclear-Age School," *Saturday Evening Post*, 26 January 1963, 64–66.

114. Nevin, "Nuclear-Age School," 66.

115. Nevin, "Nuclear-Age School," 66.

116. California's chief of school planning, Charles Gibson, reiterated the state's stand on the issue, calling "the expenditure of any educational funds for fallout protection ridiculous." Nevin, "Nuclear-Age School," 66.

117. Marquis Childs, "What Can We Tell Our Children about Today's Bewildering World?" *Parents Magazine*, April 1962, 36.

118. Childs, "What Can We Tell Our Children about Today's Bewildering World?" 74.

119. "Atom . . . Bomb . . . Children," *Newsweek*, 20 November 1961, 23.

120. House Subcommittee, *Civil Defense—Fallout Shelter Program* (1963), 3687.

121. House Subcommittee, *Civil Defense—Fallout Shelter Program* (1963), 3680.

122. Sibylle K. Escalona, "Children and the Threat of Nuclear War," in *Behavioral Science and Human Survival*, ed. Milton Schwebel (Palo Alto, CA: Science and Behavior Books, 1965), 201.

123. Escalona, "Children and the Threat of Nuclear War," 203. Escalona found a correlation between class and nuclear concerns, with 39 percent of underprivileged children expressing concerns about nuclear war, compared with 62 percent of the lower-middle-class, and 100 percent of the upper-middle-class children (203).

124. Escalona, "Children and the Threat of Nuclear War," 205.

125. Peter I. Rose, "The Public and the Threat of War," *Social Problems* 11, no. 1 (summer 1963): 75.

126. Zeldine Golden, letter, *Newsweek*, 20 November 1961, 4–6. In another *Newsweek* letter, M. Bigelow of Sainte Anne de Bellevue, Quebec, wrote that in the current era "our children's birthright is strontium 90 and an uncertain life." Parents, according to Bigelow, "are urged to make elaborate survival plans, but we feel that no plan is ambitious enough, no shelter deep enough." M. Bigelow, letter, *Newsweek*, 20 November 1961, 2–4.

127. Howard quoted in Oakes, *The Imaginary War*, 137, 140.

128. House Subcommittee, *Civil Defense* (1960), 15.

129. Janice M. Johnson, *Civil Defense Education Practices and References for Elementary School*, Classroom Practices no. 1, March 26, 1957 (Washington, D.C.: Department of Education, U.S. Department of Health, Education, and Welfare, 1957).

130. See Elaine Tyler May, "Explosive Issues: Sex, Women, and the Bomb," in *Recasting America: Culture and Politics in the Age of Cold War*, ed. Lary May (Chicago: University of Chicago Press, 1998), 160–61.

131. Federal Civil Defense Administration, *Grandma's Pantry Was Ready, Is Your "Pantry" Ready in Event of Emergency?* (Washington, D.C.: GPO, 1955).

132. "Your Cellar Could Mean Your Life," *Science News Letter*, 14 May 1960, 314.

133. Elaine Tyler May, *Homeward Bound: American Families in the Cold War Era* (New York: Basic Books, 1988), 105. It is indeed true that elements of patriarchal moralism inevitably seemed to emerge in the context of the home fallout shelter. Hugo Maria Kellner, writing in the *Catholic World* in 1962, condemned a national network of community shelters not only because of its immense costs, but also because it would mark "the greatest socialistic-communistic venture mankind has ever dreamt of.... In these community shelters, better called communist shelters, no privacy would exist. Morality, especially sexual morality, would collapse beyond description, as it did in European refugee camps." Instead, Kellner advocated the "family shelter," not only because it "allows for privacy and decency," but also because "it gives the head of the family his natural place in making decisions in fateful circumstances." Hugo Maria Kellner, "Community or Family Shelters," *Catholic World* 195, no. 1165 (April 1962): 272, 275.

134. Wylie, *Tomorrow!* 307–8. Wylie critiqued what he saw as a matriarchal dominance in America ("momism") in the 1942 *Generation of Vipers*.

135. Betty Friedan, *The Feminine Mystique* (1963; New York: Norton, 1983), 51.

136. "Fall-Out Shelters: The Great Controversy," *Good Housekeeping*, February 1962, 34.

137. Milton Mayer, "Mr. Babcock's Folly," *Better Homes and Gardens* 40, no. 1 (January 1962): 6. In the article, Mayer interviews Henry T. Babcock about the fallout shelter that Babcock has recently built. The interview turns into a painful cross-examination and a withering critique of the unknowables and inadequacies of the home fallout shelter. Mayer concludes that "Babcock's trouble is that he doesn't want to die, but he knows he's going to die and where he's going to die and where he's going to be buried" (18).

138. *Redbook* counseled that "new mothers can cut down the strontium in their babies' milk by breast feeding," but that for the calcium needs of older children, whether it be from milk, grains, or vegetables, "they would be getting strontium along with it whatever the source." Walter Goodman, "Fallout and Your Family's Health," *Redbook* 114, no. 1 (November 1959): 105.

139. Ruth Brecher and Edward Brecher, "What We Are Not Being Told about Fallout Hazards," *Redbook* 119, no. 5 (September 1962).

140. William Peters, "The Testing of a Family," *Redbook* 115, no. 1 (May 1960): 91, 92.

141. Peters, "The Testing of a Family," 94.

142. Peters, "The Testing of a Family," 95. When the Powners were preparing a list of the things they would need, researchers suggested a bottle of whiskey for the adults, and tranquilizing pills for the children (91, 93).

143. "On the Beach," *Redbook* 114, no. 2 (December 1959): 6; Robert Jungk, "The Survivors of Hiroshima," *Redbook* 117, no. 4 (August 1961): 44.

144. Robert Bendiner, "Are We Powerless to Prevent War?" *Redbook* 119, no. 3 (July 1962): 48.

145. Margaret Mead, "Must Our Children Fear the Future?" *Redbook* 118, no. 5 (March 1962): 6.

146. Walter Goodman, "The Truth about Fallout Shelters," *Redbook* 118, no. 3 (January 1962): 73.

147. Goodman, "The Truth about Fallout Shelters," 76.

148. Goodman, "The Truth about Fallout Shelters," 42, 76.

149. "A Frightening Message for a Thanksgiving Issue," *Good Housekeeping*, November 1958, 61.

150. William L. Shirer, "Let's Stop the Fall-Out Shelter Folly!" *Good Housekeeping*, February 1962, 151, 152.

151. Rada Adzhubei, "A Remarkable Letter from Khrushchev's Daughter," *Good Housekeeping*, July 1962, 55.

152. Adzhubei, "A Remarkable Letter from Khrushchev's Daughter," 164.

153. Ray Robinson, "President Kennedy Talks about You, Your Children and Peace," *Good Housekeeping*, November 1963, 178.

NOTES TO CHAPTER 5

1. Vladislav Zubok and Constantine Pleshakov, *Inside the Kremlin's Cold War: From Stalin to Khrushchev* (Cambridge: Harvard University Press, 1996), 166.

2. Zubok and Pleshakov, *Inside the Kremlin's Cold War*, 167.

3. Zubok and Pleshakov, *Inside the Kremlin's Cold War*, 166.

4. Khrushchev and Molotov quoted in Lawrence S. Wittner, *Resisting the Bomb: A History of the World Nuclear Disarmament Movement, 1954–1970* (Stanford: Stanford University Press, 1997), 102.

5. Zubok and Pleshakov, *Inside the Kremlin's Cold War*, 167, 140.

6. Robert Lee Arnett, "Soviet Attitudes towards Nuclear War Survival (1962–1977): Has There Been a Change?" (Ph.D. diss., Ohio State University, 1979), 54.

7. Thomas R. Phillips, "Malinovsky Speech Gives West an Official Report on Soviet Military Power," *St. Louis Post-Dispatch*, 29 October 1961.

8. Arnett, "Soviet Attitudes towards Nuclear War Survival (1962–1977)," 110, 70. In a 1957 *Face the Nation* interview, Khrushchev said that nuclear war "would be a tremendous calamity both for capitalist and socialist countries." Khrushchev added, however, that the destruction would not be total, that "mankind would not be destroyed, and since mankind would continue to live, that means that the ideas would continue to live, and the immortal idea of mankind is that of communism." "Nikita S. Khrushchev, June 2, 1957," in *Face the Nation, 1957: The Collected Transcripts from the CBS Radio and Television Broadcasts* (New York: Holt Information Systems, 1972), 169.

9. Arnett, "Soviet Attitudes towards Nuclear War Survival (1962–1977)," 69.

10. Arnett, "Soviet Attitudes towards Nuclear War Survival (1962–1977)," 97, 98.

11. Malinovsky quoted in Phillips, "Malinovsky Speech."

12. Henry A. Kissinger, *Nuclear Weapons and Foreign Policy* (New York: Harper and Brothers, 1957), 231–32.

13. "Henry A. Kissinger, November 10, 1957," in *Face the Nation, 1957*, 365, 367.

14. Gene Marine, "'Think Factory' De Luxe," *Nation* 188, no. 7 (14 February 1959): 131.

15. Marine, "'Think Factory' De Luxe," 133, 132. Gaither was also chairman of the board of the Ford Foundation.

16. Bernard Brodie, "War in the Atomic Age," in *The Absolute Weapon: Atomic Power and World Order*, ed. Bernard Brodie (New York: Harcourt, Brace, 1946), 22.

17. Brodie, "War in the Atomic Age," 46. Brodie noted that "no belligerent would be stupid enough, in opening itself to reprisals in kind, to use only a few bombs." Bernard Brodie, "Implications for Military Policy," in Brodie, *The Absolute Weapon: Atomic Power and World Order*, 88.

18. Brodie, "Implications for Military Policy," 71.

19. Brodie, "War in the Atomic Age," 63; Brodie, "Implications for Military Policy," 80, 91, 84.

20. Bernard Brodie, *Strategy in the Missile Age* (Princeton: Princeton University Press, 1959), 214.

21. Brodie, *Strategy in the Missile Age*, 310.

22. Brodie, *Strategy in the Missile Age*, 296.

23. Oskar Morgenstern, *The Question of National Defense* (New York: Random House, 1959), 296.

24. Morgenstern, *The Question of National Defense*, 147, 134–35.

25. Morgenstern, *The Question of National Defense*, 153.

26. Morgenstern, *The Question of National Defense*, 153–54.

27. Morgenstern, *The Question of National Defense*, 113, 121, 122.

28. Morgenstern, *The Question of National Defense*, 113.

29. Morgenstern, *The Question of National Defense*, 132, 120.

30. Morgenstern, *The Question of National Defense*, 133.

31. Herman Kahn, "Some Comments on Controlled War," in *Conflict and Defense*, ed. Kenneth Boulding (New York: Harper and Row, 1962), 18.

32. Herman Kahn, *Thinking about the Unthinkable* (New York: Avon, 1962), 89.

33. Kahn, *Thinking about the Unthinkable*, 86.

34. Kahn, *Thinking about the Unthinkable*, 88.

35. "Lauris Norstad, April 5, 1959," in *Face the Nation, 1959: The Collected Transcripts from the CBS Radio and Television Broadcasts* (New York: Holt Information Systems, 1972), 110. On the same show two years earlier, Norstad had stated that "we must always assume that if a war or incident, that we can call a limited war of that magnitude, would develop, and if atomic weapons or any other weapons on that scale would be used, we must count on this developing into something larger, and larger weapons being used." "Lauris Norstad, May 12, 1957," in *Face the Nation, 1957*, 144.

36. House Subcommittee of the Committee on Government Operations, *Civil Defense*, 86th Cong., 2d sess., 1960, 230.

37. Burke believed that a small, mobile force based on the Polaris would frustrate any Soviet ideas of a surprise attack because the location of the force would be unknown. Burke quoted in David Alan Rosenberg, "The Origins of Overkill: Nuclear Weapons and American Strategy, 1945–1960," *International Security* 7, no. 4 (spring 1983): 57. Rosenberg notes that "the emergence of 'finite deterrence,' and the implicit corollary that Polaris could and should eventually replace SAC, was perceived as a serious threat by the Air Force. . . . In November 1958, SAC Chief Power publicly proposed that SAC should be given control of the Polaris force, in the interests of coordination" (57, 60).

38. McNamara quoted in Scott D. Sagan, "SIOP-62: The Nuclear War Plan Briefing to President Kennedy," *International Security* 12, no. 1 (summer 1987): 38.

39. "Robert McNamara and Counterforce 'No Cities' Doctrine, 1962," in *The American Atom: A Documentary History of Nuclear Policies from the Discovery of Fission to the Present*, ed. Philip L. Cantelon, Richard G. Hewlett, and Robert C. Williams (Philadelphia: University of Pennsylvania Press, 1991), 208. SAC commanders complained that McNamara did not give them the weapons they needed for effective counterforce strategy. "Don't ever use 'counterforce targeting' and 'McNamara' in the same paragraph," said David Burchinal. "He gutted any capability we had for counterforce targeting." The basis for Burchinal's complaint was McNamara's rejection of Burchinal's plan to put one Minuteman missile on every Soviet ICBM silo. McGeorge Bundy, on the other hand, believes that McNamara actually gave the air force more Minuteman missiles than he personally preferred, and that "when he chose to have 1,000 Minuteman missiles, he was choosing a number that Congress would find acceptably large, not a number that he himself could demonstrate as strategically necessary." Richard H. Kohn and Joseph P. Harahan, eds., *Strategic Air Warfare: An Interview with Generals Curtis E. LeMay, Leon W. Johnson, David A. Burchinal, and Jack J. Catton* (Washington, D.C.: Office of Air Force History, 1988), 122, 123. McGeorge Bundy, *Danger and Survival: Choices about the Bomb in the First Fifty Years* (New York: Random House, 1988), 547. By 1963 McNamara was referring to the "damage-limiting strategy." McNamara noted that while America's nuclear arsenal was an effective deterrent to "aggression in the high end of the spectrum" (such as a full-scale nuclear attack or a Soviet invasion of Europe), "at the very low end of the spectrum a nuclear response may not be fully credible." The use of smaller, tactical nuclear weapons would not be, as McNamara put it, "an easy first choice," and McNamara called for "strong and ready conventional forces" to respond to those events at the lower end of the spectrum. Robert S. McNamara, "The Damage-Limiting Strategy," in *The Debate over Thermonuclear Strategy*, ed. Arthur I. Waskow (Boston: D. C. Heath, 1965), 49, 50.

40. Bundy, *Danger and Survival*, 548. According to Bundy, "on the official list of 1,860 Soviet-bloc targets projected for 1969 (as one guide to force planning), 1,650 were military and only 210 urban-industrial." Bundy also emphasized that "no one could guarantee that cities would be spared by the other side" (548).

41. Edward Teller, for instance, believed that it was possible to use nuclear weapons in a "limited" way, and that "we need nuclear weapons among other things to be used in limited war." Teller added that "we must never spread such a war beyond the territory in which the Russian aggression has been committed. If we can act according to these principles, we will have made another important step toward lasting peace." Edward Teller, "Peace through Civil Defence," *Vital Speeches of the Day*, 1 February 1962, 246.

42. Harrison Brown and James Real, *Community of Fear* (Santa Barbara, CA: Center for the Study of Democratic Institutions, 1960), 9.

43. Gerard Piel, "The Illusion of Civil Defense," *Bulletin of the Atomic Scientists* 17, no. 2 (February 1962): 7.

44. Arthur I. Waskow, *The Limits of Defense* (Garden City, NY: Doubleday, 1962), 15.

45. Waskow, *The Limits of Defense*, 26, 27.

46. Waskow, *The Limits of Defense*, 23.

47. Waskow, *The Limits of Defense*, 24–25.

48. Waskow, *The Limits of Defense*, 29.

49. Herman Kahn, *On Thermonuclear War* (Princeton: Princeton University Press, 1960), 516. Mario G. Salvadori, a professor of civil engineering and architecture at Columbia University, estimated that "a bare shelter structure designed to withstand the blast effect of a 20-megaton nuclear bomb at the rim of the ball of fire would cost $290 per person sheltered." Mario G. Salvadori, "Cost of Blast Resistant Structures," in *No Place to Hide: Fact and Fiction about Fallout Shelters*, ed. Seymour Melman (New York: Grove Press, 1962), 141.

50. Waskow, *The Limits of Defense*, 29.

51. Waskow, *The Limits of Defense*, 92. While Waskow's critiques of counterforce and other Cold War strategies are often insightful, his powers desert him when it comes to devising an alternate system. The quixotic Waskow suggests, for example, that the goal of American foreign policy should be the adoption of a law signed by all the nations of the world "against the making, possession, or use by any individual of any weapon above the level of small arms." Waskow's recommendations for achieving what he calls "disarmament-plus" include an invitation to Soviet military officials to sit in at Distant Early Warning (DEW) Line stations. (The DEW Line was designed to warn the United States of the approach of Soviet missiles and bombers.) In return, Waskow suggests that the Soviets might reciprocate by "inviting Western observers into their army camps in East Germany." The final step would be international arms control agreements leading to total disarmament and "an effective police force to enforce such laws" (105, 78–79). Gerard Piel claimed that if the civilian population came under attack, "the elaborate studies of the fallout hazard can be set aside entirely" because the destruction of such soft targets as people and cities could be achieved with relative ease. Piel, "The Illusion of Civil Defense," 7.

52. Schelling refers to "the deliberate creation of a recognizable risk of war, a risk that one does not completely control. It is the tactic of deliberately letting the situation get somewhat out of hand, just because its being out of hand may be intolerable to the other party and force his accommodation." Thomas C. Schelling, *The Strategy of Conflict* (Cambridge: Harvard University Press, 1963), 200.

53. Schelling, *The Strategy of Conflict*, 260.

54. Blast protection for city residents would cost about $200 per shelter occupant for protection against blast pressures of 25–35 psi (pounds per square inch). The cost would be doubled for protection against a blast pressure of 100 psi, and a shelter built to withstand 500 psi would run about $700 per occupant. See Donald W. Mitchell, *Civil Defense: Planning for Survival and Recovery* (Washington, D.C.: Industrial College of the Armed Forces, 1963), 42.

55. House Subcommittee of the Committee on Government Operations, *Civil Defense*, 85th Cong., 2d sess., 1958, 254–55. Oskar Morgenstern also noted that shrinking warning times "hardly would make it possible to take an elevator to a deep shelter after the alarm sounds." Morgenstern, *The Question of National Defense*, 121.

56. See Gabriel Kolko, "On the Value of a Shelter Program," in Melman, *No Place to Hide*, 123–24.

57. Mitchell, *Civil Defense: Planning for Survival and Recovery*, 43.

58. Ralph Lapp, "A Blast, Fire, and Fallout Shelter," *Consumer Reports* 27, no. 1 (January 1962): 15.

59. "The Fallout Shelter," *Consumer Reports* 27, no. 1 (January 1962): 8.

60. Morgenstern, *The Question of National Defense*, 118.

61. Galbraith quoted in Spencer R. Weart, *Nuclear Fear* (Cambridge: Harvard University Press, 1988), 256. Referring to a draft of Kennedy's civil defense pamphlet, Galbraith proclaimed, "I am not at all attracted by a pamphlet which seeks to save the better elements of the population, but in the main writes off those who voted for you. I think it particularly injudicious, in fact it is absolutely incredible, to have a picture of a family with a cabin cruiser saving itself by going out to sea. Very few members of the UAW can go with them." Galbraith quoted in Arthur M. Schlesinger, Jr., *A Thousand Days: John F. Kennedy in the White House* (Boston: Houghton Mifflin, 1965), 748.

62. Khrushchev comments, "I was delighted. Stalin showed great wisdom and boldness. He had taken into account the long-range factor of civil defense, and he decided on that basis that tunnels merited the extra expense." Nikita Khrushchev, *Khrushchev Remembers*, trans. and ed. Strobe Talbott (Boston: Little, Brown, 1970), 70.

63. Leon Gouré, *Civil Defense in the Soviet Union* (Berkeley: University of California Press, 1962), 139.

64. Gouré, *Civil Defense in the Soviet Union*, 52, 55, 56.

65. Gouré, *Civil Defense in the Soviet Union*, 80, 86, 87.

66. Gouré, *Civil Defense in the Soviet Union*, 59, 60.

67. Malinovsky quoted in "Coffins or Shields?" *Time*, 2 February 1962, 15. See also "Russia: Shelters on the Other Side," *Time*, 10 November 1961, 31–32.

68. J. David Singer, "Deterrence and Shelters," *Bulletin of the Atomic Scientists* 17, no. 8 (October 1961): 314.

69. See Theodore Shabad, "Soviet Twits U.S. on Civil Defense," *New York Times*, 26 August 1961; Preston Grover, "Russians Get Fallout Advice But No Shelters Are Found," *Washington Post*, 29 October 1961.

70. See Carey Scott, "Kremlin Refurbishes Nuclear Bunkers as Fear of NATO Grows," *Sunday Times* (London), 13 April 1997.

71. Sidney E. Cleveland, Ina Boyd, Diana Sheer, and E. Edward Reitman, "Effects of Fallout Shelter Confinement on Family Adjustment," *Archives of General Psychiatry* 8, no. 1 (January 1963): 45.

72. Cleveland et al., "Effects of Fallout Shelter Confinement on Family Adjustment," 43.

73. Cleveland et al., "Effects of Fallout Shelter Confinement on Family Adjustment," 45–46.

74. Cleveland et al., "Effects of Fallout Shelter Confinement on Family Adjustment," 43, 44.

75. Mary P. Beussee, John A. Hammes, and Thomas A. Ahearn, "Effects of Fallout Shelter Confinement on Mental Health," *Mental Hygiene* 55, no. 1 (January 1971): 121.

76. Beussee et al., "Effects of Fallout Shelter Confinement on Mental Health," 122–23. Also adding considerably to the stress level was dealing with small children in a shelter. Citing studies of the effect of shelter life on children, Rogers S. Cannell was perhaps damning shelters with faint praise when he noted, "Children were no more restless in shelter than they normally are on long automobile trips." Rogers S. Cannell, *Live: A Handbook of Survival in Nuclear Attack* (Englewood Cliffs, NJ: Prentice-Hall, 1962), 96.

77. P. Herbert Leiderman and Jack H. Mendelson, "Some Psychiatric Considerations in Planning for Defense Shelters," in *The Fallen Sky: Medical Consequences of Thermonuclear War*, ed. Saul Aronow (New York: Hill and Wang, 1963), 49.

78. House Subcommittee, *Civil Defense* (1960), 115, 116, 55.

79. "Civil Defense: Sheltered Life," *Time*, 9 March 1962, 26.

80. James S. Murakoa, a project scientist with the U.S. Naval Civil Engineering Laboratory, argued that foul odors in fallout shelters "may affect the health of occupants by causing a lessening of food and water intake, disturbing sleeping, promoting nausea and vomiting, and by creating mental disturbance." "Foul Odors of Shelters," *Science News Letter*, 20 January 1962, 38.

81. "Civil Defense: Sheltered Life," 26.

82. Otto Friedrich, *The End of the World: A History* (New York: Fromm International, 1986), 349.

83. House Subcommittee No. 3 of the Committee on Armed Services, *Civil Defense—Fallout Shelter Program*, 88th Cong., 1st sess., 1963, 3689.

84. House Subcommittee, *Civil Defense* (1960), 137.

85. House Subcommittee, *Civil Defense* (1960), 79.

86. House Subcommittee, *Civil Defense* (1960), 150.

87. House Subcommittee, *Civil Defense* (1960), 169.

88. House Subcommittee, *Civil Defense* (1960), 171. In truth, this debate was a continuation of interservice sniping from the mid-1950s, when air force officials had criticized the navy's new Forrestal class aircraft carrier as a "sitting duck" to missile and aircraft attacks. Burke replied that the aircraft carrier was "not nearly so fast as a plane but is quite a bit faster than a fixed base." See "Arleigh A. Burke, June 10, 1956," in *Face the Nation, 1956: The Collected Transcripts from the CBS Radio and Television Broadcasts* (New York: Holt Information Systems, 1972), 182, 183.

89. Piel, "The Illusion of Civil Defense," 7.

90. Roger Hagan, "Community Shelters," in Melman, *No Place to Hide*, 181–82.

91. Ralph E. Lapp, "Rockefeller's Civil Defense Program," *Bulletin of the Atomic Scientists* 16, no. 2 (April 1960): 135.

92. House Subcommittee, *Civil Defense* (1960), 234.

93. LeMay quoted in House Subcommittee, *Civil Defense* (1960), 157. Lapp, "Rockefeller's Civil Defense Program," 135.

94. House Subcommittee, *Civil Defense* (1960), 155.

95. House Subcommittee, *Civil Defense* (1960), 233.

96. Freeman Dyson, *Weapons and Hope* (New York: Harper and Row, 1984), 117.

97. Frank R. Ervin et al., "Human and Ecologic Effects in Massachusetts of an Assumed Thermonuclear Attack on the United States," in Aronow, *The Fallen Sky*, 7. Temperatures near the center of the firestorm were probably hotter. In some shelters glass melted, which requires a temperature between 2000 and 2300°F. See Victor Paschkis, "A New Look at Thermal Conditions in Shelters," in Melman, *No Place to Hide*, 144.

98. Arthur Harris, *Bomber Offensive* (New York: Macmillan, 1947), 173, 174.

99. Michael S. Sherry, *The Rise of American Air Power: The Creation of Armageddon* (New Haven: Yale University Press, 1987), 153. Doctors attending patients in cities where firestorms occurred estimated that 70 percent of deaths occurred due to carbon monoxide poisoning, and only 15 percent due to burns and inhalation of hot gases. Charles Webster and Noble Frankland, *The Strategic Air Offensive against Germany, 1939–1945*, vol. 2 (London: Her Majesty's Stationery Office, 1961), 236.

100. Ervin et al., "Human and Ecologic Effects in Massachusetts of an Assumed Thermonuclear Attack," 7.

101. Other cities in which firestorms were created included Tokyo and Dresden. Hidezo Tsuchikura, a Japanese factory worker who survived the firestorm at Tokyo, remembered that

> Fire winds with burning particles ran up and down the streets. I watched people, adults and children, running for their lives, dashing madly about like rats. The flames raced after them like living things, striking them down. They died by the hundreds right in front of me. . . . The whole spectacle with its blinding lights and thundering noise reminded me of the paintings of purgatory—a real inferno out of the depths of hell itself.

Quoted in John Costello, *The Pacific War, 1941–1945* (New York: Quill, 1982), 550–51. Kurt Vonnegut witnessed the firestorm at Dresden, and describes it in *Slaughterhouse-Five, or The Children's Crusade: A Duty-Dance with Death* (New York: Delacorte Press, 1969).

102. Eugene P. Wigner, "Nuclear War and Civil Defense," in *Who Speaks for Civil Defense?* ed. Eugene P. Wigner (New York: Scribner's, 1968), 16.

103. The total megatonnage in the U.S. nuclear arsenal had increased from about 5,000 in 1955 to 20,000 by 1960. See Bundy, *Danger and Survival*, 320.

104. Piel, "The Illusion of Civil Defense," 5, 6. When he discussed the Soviet fifty-megaton test, Linus Pauling claimed with a touch of hyperbole that "This act was the most horrifying and immoral in the history of the world." Linus Pauling, "Recent Developments, 1958–1962," in Linus Pauling, *No More War* (Westport, CT: Greenwood, 1962), ix.

105. "The Fallout Shelter," 8.

106. Kahn, *Thinking about the Unthinkable*, 89.

107. House Subcommittee of the Committee on Government Operations, *New Civil Defense Legislation*, 85th Cong., 1st sess., 1957, 32.

108. Wigner, "Nuclear War and Civil Defense," 16.

109. Teller, "Peace through Civil Defence," 246. House Subcommittee, *New Civil Defense Legislation* (1957), 214.

110. Bentley Glass, "The Biology of Nuclear War," in Aronow, *The Fallen Sky: Medical Consequences of Thermonuclear War*, 103.

111. Arthur I. Waskow and Stanley L. Newman, *America in Hiding* (New York: Ballantine, 1962), 106.

112. Piel, "The Illusion of Civil Defense," 6.

113. Quoted in Paul Boyer, "The American Medical Profession and the Threat of Nuclear War," in *Fallout: A Historian Reflects on America's Half-Century Encounter with Nuclear Weapons* (Columbus: Ohio State University Press, 1998), 77–78.

114. New York City hospital administrator Marcus D. Kogel recommended the training of mobile medical squads based on the army model that would be "capable of going into high gear the moment the disaster strikes." Kogel and Leuth quoted in Boyer, "The American Medical Profession and the Threat of Nuclear War," 79.

115. Quoted in Allan M. Winkler, *Life under a Cloud: American Anxiety about the Atom* (New York: Oxford University Press, 1993), 103.

116. "Lewis L. Strauss, February 26, 1956," in *Face the Nation, 1956*, 66.

117. Lewis L. Strauss, "The Truth about Radioactive Fall-Out," *U.S. News and World Report*, 25 February 1955, 36, 38. Nuclear tests conducted by the AEC included Greenhouse and Buster-Jangle (1951), Tumbler-Snapper and Ivy (1952), Upshot-Knothole (1953), Castle (1954), Teapot (1955), Redwing (1956), Plumbbob (1957), and Hardtack (1958). The FCDA participated in these tests to gain information on fallout shelter design. See Harry B. Yoshpe, *Our Missing Shield* (Washington, D.C.: Federal Emergency Management Agency, 1981), 247.

118. "The Facts about A-Bomb 'Fall-Out,'" *U.S. News and World Report*, 25 March 1955, 21.

119. "The Facts about A-Bomb 'Fall-Out,'" 26.

120. *U.S. News* claimed that "there is no evidence that 'fall-out' from test explosions now being carried out by U.S. will be hazardous either to people now, to future generations, to food crops, or even to the weather." "The Facts about A-Bomb 'Fall-Out,'" 25, 26.

121. Walter Schneir, "Strontium-90 in U.S. Children," *Nation* 188, no. 17 (25 April 1959): 355.

122. Introduction to Aronow, *The Fallen Sky: Medical Consequences of Thermonuclear War*, xiv.

123. Ervin et al., "Human and Ecologic Effects in Massachusetts of an Assumed Thermonuclear Attack," 2.

124. Ervin et al., "Human and Ecologic Effects in Massachusetts of an Assumed Thermonuclear Attack," 7–8.

125. Ervin et al., "Human and Ecologic Effects in Massachusetts of an Assumed Thermonuclear Attack," 8, 9.

126. Hoagland quoted in Kolko, "On the Value of a Shelter Program," 128.

127. Victor W. Sidel, H. Jack Geiger, and Bernard Lown, "The Physician's Role in the Postattack Period," in Aronow, *The Fallen Sky*, 24, 26.

128. Sidel et al., "The Physician's Role in the Postattack Period," 29.

129. Sidel et al., "The Physician's Role in the Postattack Period," 28.

130. Sidel et al., "The Physician's Role in the Postattack Period," 32.

131. Sidel et al., "The Physician's Role in the Postattack Period," 36, 37.

132. Sidel et al., "The Physician's Role in the Postattack Period," 34.

133. Sidel et al., "The Physician's Role in the Postattack Period," 38. Sidel et al. note,

It is deeply misleading, therefore, to speak of any single disaster plan as a secure answer to the hazards of thermonuclear war. It is deeply misleading to focus on radiation shelters while ignoring the problems of blast and fire storm. And it is deeply misleading to propose patterns of medical treatment without examining the magnitude of the task or the availability of resources in sufficient detail to reveal the nature of the anticipated problems.

134. Glass, "The Biology of Nuclear War," 77.

135. Glass, "The Biology of Nuclear War," 77.

136. Glass, "The Biology of Nuclear War," 78, 79.

137. See Kolko, "On the Value of a Shelter Program," 122.

138. "Science, Freedom and Survival," *AAAS Bulletin* 7, no. 1 (January 1962): 1.

139. "Science, Freedom and Survival," 2. Mead was not the only one to raise such a possibility. Reverend Jack Mendelsohn of the Arlington Street Church (Unitarian) of Boston gave a sermon on September 17, 1961, in which he took issue with what he called the *Life* magazine "snow job" on fallout shelters. Mendelsohn insisted he was not opposed to a real civil defense effort, only

let it be real, like stockpiling populations deep, deep underground in remote areas, carefully chosen sets of people with all the necessary skills, physically and mentally strong people, with all the factories, schools, machinery and equipment that would be necessary to carry life on underground, not for

two weeks, or two months, but perhaps for as much as ten years, until the surface of the earth was once again safe for human habitation.
Mendelsohn quoted in Dean Brelis, *Run, Dig or Stay?*(Boston: Beacon, 1962), 178.

140. Cannell, *Live*, 8, 14.

141. Cannell, *Live*, 11.

142. Cannell, *Live*, 40–49.

143. Cannell, *Live*, 48–49.

144. Lawrence S. Wittner, *One World or None: A History of the World Nuclear Disarmament Movement through 1953* (Stanford: Stanford University Press, 1993), 8, 20, 21.

145. Oppenheimer and Einstein quoted in Lawrence S. Wittner, *Rebels against War: The American Peace Movement, 1941–1960* (New York: Columbia University Press, 1969), 149, 148.

146. Harold C. Urey, "I'm a Frightened Man," *Collier's*, 5 January 1946, 18.

147. Urey, "I'm a Frightened Man," 19.

148. Albert Einstein, "A Reply to the Soviet Scientists," *Bulletin of the Atomic Scientists* 4, no. 2 (February 1948): 37.

149. After World War II, the Emergency Committee of Atomic Scientists was created. Members included Harold Urey, Hans Berthe, Linus Pauling, Leo Szilard, and Victor Weisskopf. Albert Einstein, as chairman of the committee, declared in 1946 that "a world authority and an eventual world state are not just *desirable* in the name of brotherhood, they are *necessary* for survival." Albert Einstein, "Only Then Shall We Find Courage," in Pauling, *No More War!* 213. See also Wittner, *Rebels against War*, 165, 166. Sumner Welles, former under secretary of state, described as "wholly impossible" Einstein's idea that "the secret of the bomb should be committed to a world government." Sumner Welles, "The Atomic Bomb and World Government," *Atlantic* 177, no. 1 (January 1946): 40, 39.

150. "The Mainau Declaration of Nobel Laureates," in Pauling, *No More War!* 222–24.

151. See Wittner, *Resisting the Bomb*, 135, 11, 32; Albert Schweitzer, "A Declaration of Conscience," in Pauling, *No More War!* 226.

152. "An Appeal to Stop the Spread of Nuclear Weapons," in Pauling, *No More War!* 245–49.

153. Einstein, "Only Then Shall We Find Courage," 218; "The Mainau Declaration of Nobel Laureates," 222.

154. "Lewis L. Strauss, May 4, 1958," in *Face the Nation, 1958: The Collected Transcripts from the CBS Radio and Television Broadcasts* (New York: Holt Information Systems, 1972), 138.

155. *Wall Street Journal*, 10 April 1958.

156. The Pugwash conferences were named after the site of the first meeting in Pugwash, Nova Scotia, in 1957.

157. Wittner, *Resisting the Bomb*, 33–37, 134.

158. Eugene Rabinowitch, "Responsibilities of Scientists in the Atomic Age," *Bulletin of the Atomic Scientists* 15, no. 1 (January 1959): 2, 3.

159. Eugene Rabinowitch, "Must Millions March?" *Bulletin of the Atomic Scientists* 10, no. 6 (June 1954): 194.

160. *Bulletin of the Atomic Scientists* 10, no. 9 (November 1954): n.p.

161. Ellery Husted, "Shelter in the Atomic Age," *Bulletin of the Atomic Scientists* 9, no. 7 (September 1953): 273.

162. Deer cites a National Radiological Defense Laboratory (NRDL) study that suggests the creation of some one hundred underground city-states, each self-sufficient, with its own power supply, air filtration systems, and even hydroponic farming operations. Because of the constant threat of surprise attack, a substantial portion of the population of each city-state would remain underground. James W. Deer, "The Unavoidable International Shelter Race," *Bulletin of the Atomic Scientists* 13, no. 2 (February 1957): 66.

163. Deer, "The Unavoidable International Shelter Race," 67. Deer advocated funding for a national shelter program equal to appropriations for developing and stockpiling fusion bombs and guided missiles.

164. Mary M. Simpson, "A Long Hard Look at Civil Defense," *Bulletin of the Atomic Scientists* 11, no. 9 (November 1956): 346.

165. Simpson, "A Long Hard Look at Civil Defense," 348.

166. Ralph E. Lapp, "Civil Defense Faces New Peril," *Bulletin of the Atomic Scientists* 10, no. 9 (November 1954): 349.

167. Ralph E. Lapp, "Fall-Out and Candor," *Bulletin of the Atomic Scientists* 11, no. 5 (May 1955): 170.

168. "Ralph E. Lapp, June 19, 1955," in *Face the Nation, 1954–1955: The Collected Transcripts from the CBS Radio and Television Broadcasts* (New York: Holt Information Systems, 1972), 265, 264.

169. "Ralph E. Lapp, October 7, 1956," in *Face the Nation, 1956,* 326, 327, 328.

170. Wittner, *Resisting the Bomb,* 137.

171. Lapp, "Rockefeller's Civil Defense Program," 134. Lapp noted, "To date the Office of Civil and Defense Mobilization has not faced up to this vexing dilemma of shelter design. It is understandable that the problem remains unresolved at the State level" (134).

172. See Lapp, "A Blast, Fire, and Fallout Shelter," 15.

173. Leo Szilard, "The Mined Cities," *Bulletin of the Atomic Scientists* 17, no. 10 (December 1961): 407.

174. Szilard, "The Mined Cities," 408.

175. Szilard, "The Mined Cities," 407.

176. Szilard, "The Mined Cities," 411–12.

177. Szilard, "The Mined Cities," 407–8.

178. Szilard, "The Mined Cities," 409.

NOTES TO CHAPTER 6

1. Thomas Hine, *Populuxe* (New York: MJF Books, 1999), 138.

2. One aid for shelter salesmen was reportedly a booklet called *Mr. Atom and His Sinister Blanket*. See Roy Bongartz, "Remember Bomb Shelters?" *Esquire*, May 1970, 130.

3. Alfred Balk, "Anyone for Survival?" *Saturday Evening Post*, 27 March 1965, 74.

4. See Stephen B. Whithey, *The U.S. and the U.S.S.R.* (Ann Arbor: Survey Research Center, University of Michigan, 1962).

5. Peter I. Rose, "The Public and the Threat of War," *Social Problems* 11, no. 1 (summer 1963): 68, 66.

6. F. Kenneth Berrien, the author of the study, pointed to an obvious inconsistency in the views of shelter owners: "If shelter owners endorse military means to preserve the peace, and also believe our military strength is increasing, why build a shelter, and why be more certain the war will come—at some delayed point in time?" The answer, according to Berrien, was to be found in "cognitive dissonance," in which an individual's action (in this case, building a fallout shelter) is not validated by subsequent events, prompting the individual to hold even more firmly to his original belief while trying to convince others to adopt the same belief. The nagging suspicion of the shelter owner that he may have incurred an unnecessary expense is reduced "by an enhanced perception of threat." F. Kenneth Berrien, "Shelter Owners, Dissonance and the Arms Race," *Social Problems* 11, no. 1 (summer 1963): 90. See also "Shelter Owners Pro-War," *Science News Letter*, 20 April 1963, 246. Berrien referred to a "self-generating spiral" in which "a predisposition for military action leads to action designed to deter conflict; this action leads to a perception of enhanced strength and an increased expectation of war, which adds to the need for additional deterrence, etc." See F. K. Berrien, Carol Schulman, and Marianne Amarel, "The Fallout-Shelter Owners: A Study of Attitude Formation," *Public Opinion Quarterly* 27, no. 2 (summer 1963): 216.

7. "If Bombs Do Fall on U.S.—What People Look For," *U.S. News and World Report*, 25 September 1961, 51, 52; Peter I. Rose and Jerome Laulicht, "Editorial Foreword," *Social Problems* 11, no. 1 (summer 1963): 3.

8. "Survival: Are Shelters the Answer?" *Newsweek*, 6 November 1961, 19.

9. Krock quoted in P. Herbert Leiderman and Jack H. Mendelson, "Some Psychiatric Considerations in Planning for Defense Shelters," in *The Fallen Sky: Medical Consequences of Thermonuclear War*, ed. Saul Aronow (New York: Hill and Wang, 1963), 44.

10. Rogers S. Cannell, *Live: A Handbook of Survival in Nuclear Attack* (Englewood Cliffs, NJ: Prentice-Hall, 1962), 31.

11. James Reston, "Kennedy's Shelter Policy Re-Examined," *New York Times*, 26 November 1961.

12. James Reston, "Those Sweet and Kindly Shelter Builders," *New York Times*, 12 November 1961.

13. House Subcommittee of the Committee on Government Operations, *New Civil Defense Legislation*, 85th Cong., 1st sess., 1957, 447.

14. "Civil Defense: The Sheltered Life," *Time*, 20 October 1961.

15. Shirer added that the "vast majority of Americans are to be sacrificed so that the financially more fortunate may have a chance to live." William L. Shirer, "Let's Stop the Fall-Out Shelter Folly!" *Good Housekeeping*, February 1962, 151. In Sylvan Shores, Florida, a large private shelter was built under an orange grove that could accommodate twenty-five families. Rooms were sold to families at $1,500 per room, and occupants were sworn to keep the location of the shelter secret. Bongartz, "Remember Bomb Shelters?" 130.

16. See Norman Cousins, "Shelters, Survival and Common Sense," part 4, *Saturday Review*, 25 November 1961, 31.

17. See Richard Dudman, "Ability of Individual Shelters to Protect Families Questioned; Definite Building Guide Lacking," *St. Louis Post-Dispatch*, 4 December 1961; "All Out against Fallout," *Time*, 4 August 1961, 11. R. M. Stephenson, professor of nuclear engineering at the University of Connecticut, also submitted a design for a thirty-dollar shelter to *Science* magazine. "You *Can* Build a Low-Cost Shelter *Quickly*," *Science*, December 1961, 87.

18. Szilard quoted in Edward Zuckerman, *The Day after World War III* (New York: Viking, 1984), 138.

19. *Historical Statistics of the United States, Colonial Times to 1970*, pt. 1 (Washington, D.C.: U.S. Department of Commerce, Bureau of the Census, 1975), 303.

20. John Cheever, "The Brigadier and the Golf Widow," in *The Stories of John Cheever* (New York: Knopf, 1979), 505.

21. "Fallout Shelters' 'Lived-In' Look," *Science News Letter*, 14 October 1961, 258. Laura McEnaney has observed that "by focusing on what family shelters represented—individualism, moral courage, family values, patriotism—civil defense officials could avoid talking about their true function." Laura McEnaney, *"Civil Defense Begins at Home": Militarization Meets Everyday Life in the Fifties* (Princeton: Princeton University Press, forthcoming).

22. Cynthia Kellogg, "Reactions Are Angry or Resigned to Model of Tiny Survival Shelter," *New York Times*, 5 January 1960. Working toward the same end was an individual in Salt Lake City who suggested, "Make the best of a shelter world; paint outdoor scenes on the walls, a sort of picture window for your shelter." Quoted in Dean Brelis, *Run Dig or Stay?* (Boston: Beacon, 1962), 56.

23. "A Spare Room Fallout Shelter," *Life* 48, no. 3 (25 January 1960): 46.

24. American Institute of Public Opinion, *The Gallup Poll: Public Opinion, 1935–1971* (New York: Random House, 1972), 1741.

25. See Hammacher Schlemmer advertisement, *New York Times*, 12 November

1961. The store offered models ranging from $695 to $20,000. See *New York Times*, 17 November 1961.

26. "Boom to Bust," *Time*, 18 May 1962, 20.

27. See Rose, "The Public and the Threat of War," 64.

28. Polls taken of their constituents by representatives to Congress revealed widespread apathy or hostility toward civil defense and fallout shelters. Representative Harold C. Ostertag of New York reported a 58.3 percent negative response to the question "Do you approve of federal aid for construction of public fallout shelters in schools, hospitals, and other public centers?" There were 6,700 replies. Also responding negatively to civil defense: Representative Walter Norblad of Oregon received 15,000 replies, of which 87 percent were negative. Representative William E. Minshall of Ohio received 20,000 replies, of which 69.4 percent were negative. Representative James G. O'Hara of Michigan had a 52.4 percent negative response. D. H. Greenberg, "Fallout Shelters: Administration's Program Is Facing Difficulty on Capitol Hill," *Science* 136 (4 May 1962): 377.

29. Dean Rusk, *As I Saw It* (New York: Norton, 1990), 229; Robert F. Kennedy, *Thirteen Days: A Memoir of the Cuban Missile Crisis* (New York: Mentor, 1969), 23. Ernest May and Philip Zelikow called the Cuban Missile Crisis "the Pearl Harbor *and* Midway of the Cold War." Ernest R. May and Philip D. Zelikow, conclusion to *The Kennedy Tapes: Inside the White House during the Cuban Missile Crisis*, ed. Ernest R. May and Philip D. Zelikow (Cambridge, MA: Belknap, 1997), 691.

30. Nikita Khrushchev, *Khrushchev Remembers*, trans. and ed. Strobe Talbott (Boston: Little, Brown, 1970), 500.

31. Kuznetsov quoted in Vladislav Zubok and Constantine Pleshakov, *Inside the Kremlin's Cold War: From Stalin to Khrushchev* (Cambridge: Harvard University Press, 1996), 266.

32. Central Intelligence Agency, *The Secret Cuban Missile Crisis Documents* (Washington, D.C.: Brassey's [US], 1994), 199.

33. Rusk, *As I Saw It*, 242.

34. May and Zelikow, *The Kennedy Tapes*, 176. The following exchange, also concerning Berlin, was taped on October 18:

BUNDY: If we could trade off Berlin, and not have it our fault . . .

DILLON: Well, that's the danger. The whole reaction in Cuba . . .

MCNAMARA: Well, when we're talking about taking Berlin, what do we mean exactly? That they take it with Soviet troops?

PRESIDENT KENNEDY?: That's what I would think.

MCNAMARA: I think there's a real possibility there. We have U.S. troops there where they do.

BALL: I think it's perfectly clear. They get overrun. They get overrun.

UNIDENTIFIED: [Unclear] then what do we do?

BALL: Go to general war.

BUNDY: It's then general war.

PRESIDENT KENNEDY: You mean a nuclear exchange?

UNIDENTIFIED: Mmm-hmm.

UNIDENTIFIED: That's right.

May and Zelikow, *The Kennedy Tapes*, 144.

The evidence for a Soviet linkage between Berlin and Cuba is ambiguous. In his memoirs Khrushchev reveals himself to be concerned with the possibility of an American invasion of Cuba, and with U.S. attempts to "force Cuba away from the path of socialism and make it drag behind American policy." The purpose of installing missiles in Cuba, according to Khrushchev, was "not to wage war against the US, but to prevent the US from invading Cuba and thus starting the war." Nikita Khrushchev, *Khrushchev Remembers: The Last Testament*, trans. and ed. Strobe Talbott (Boston: Little, Brown, 1974), 510, 511. In the first volume of his memoirs Khrushchev said that "The main thing was that the installation of our missiles in Cuba would, I thought, restrain the United States from precipitous military action against Castro's government." Khrushchev, *Khrushchev Remembers* (1970), 494. But Khrushchev himself also creates a link to Berlin, proclaiming that "the Americans knew that if Russian blood were shed in Cuba, American blood would surely be shed in Germany." Khrushchev, *Khrushchev Remembers* (1970), 500. Scholars have also struggled with the Berlin-Cuba connection. Recently Vladislav Zubok and Constantine Pleshakov have argued that

> Khrushchev believed that because the Americans had extended their influ-
> ence into Europe, the Soviets had the right to extend theirs into the zone of
> the Monroe Doctrine. Despite the firm belief of an entire generation of
> American policymakers and some prominent historians that Khrushchev's
> gamble in Cuba was actually aimed at West Berlin, there is little evidence of
> that on the Soviet side.

But Zubok and Pleshakov acknowledge that Khrushchev precipitated the Cuban crisis because of his "revolutionary commitment and his sense of rivalry with the United States. From this perspective, the Cuban adventure was linked to the Berlin crisis." Zubok and Pleshakov, *Inside the Kremlin's Cold War*, 260, 261. Another Soviet Cold Warrior making the Cuba-Berlin connection was Aleksandr Feklisov, KGB chief in Washington. When Feklisov met an American journalist named John Scali to confer on the Cuban crisis on October 26, Feklisov declared that if Americans attack Cuba, "at the very least, the Soviet Union would occupy West Berlin." Feklisov quoted in Aleksandr Fursenko and Timothy Naftali, "*One Hell of a Gamble": Khrushchev, Castro and Kennedy, 1958–1964* (New York: Norton, 1997), 265.

35. In the fall of 1962 the General Accounting Office released a study that found dozens of instances in which government surplus equipment turned over to local governments for civil defense purposes had disappeared, was abandoned, or was adopted for purposes other than civil defense. James McCartney, "Much CD Equipment Abused, Misused," *Miami Herald*, 5 November 1962.

36. Dino A. Brugioni, *Eyeball to Eyeball: The Inside Story of the Cuban Missile Crisis* (New York: Random House, 1991), 323; Thomas J. Kerr, *Civil Defense in the U.S.: Bandaid for a Holocaust?* (Boulder: Westview, 1983), 125–26.

37. Brugioni, *Eyeball to Eyeball*, 452.

38. Fursenko and Naftali, "*One Hell of a Gamble*," 243–45.

39. Fursenko and Naftali, "*One Hell of a Gamble*," 242, 245. Zubok and Pleshakov note that when the Cubans shot down an American U-2 on October 27, Khrushchev sent a message to Pliyev forbidding any use of nuclear weapons. Zubok and Pleshakov, *Inside the Kremlin's Cold War*, 267.

40. The Castro-Khrushchev letters are reprinted in James G. Blight, Bruce J. Allyn, and David A. Welch, *Cuba on the Brink: Castro, the Missile Crisis and the Soviet Collapse* (New York: Pantheon, 1993), 481, 486.

41. Khrushchev, *Khrushchev Remembers* (1970), 496, 494.

42. May and Zelikow, *The Kennedy Tapes*, 338–39.

43. May and Zelikow, *The Kennedy Tapes*, 339–40.

44. Jeremy Isaacs and Taylor Downing, *Cold War: An Illustrated History, 1945–1991* (Boston: Little, Brown, 1998), 198, 194, 201.

45. The others in attendance were Albert D. Rosellini of Washington, William W. Barron of West Virginia, and Ernest Vandiver of Georgia. General Frances A. Woofley represented Jimmie H. Davis of Louisiana and General John McGreedy represented Governor John H. Notte, Jr., of Rhode Island. Brugioni, *Eyeball to Eyeball*, 454. What nonexperts could actually discern from such photographs is debatable. Robert Kennedy remembered that

> experts arrived with their charts and their pointers and told us that if we looked carefully, we could see there was a missile base being constructed in a field near San Cristobal, Cuba. I, for one, had to take their word for it. I examined the pictures carefully, and what I saw appeared to be no more than the clearing of a field for a farm or the basement of a house. I was relieved to hear later that this was the same reaction of virtually everyone at the meeting, including President Kennedy.

Kennedy, *Thirteen Days*, 23–24.

46. Brugioni, *Eyeball to Eyeball*, 455.

47. Brugioni, *Eyeball to Eyeball*, 456.

48. On October 16 Taylor said, "I'd like to stress this last point, Mr. President. We are very vulnerable to conventional bombing attack, low-level bombing attacks, in the Florida area." May and Zelikow, *The Kennedy Tapes*, 88–89.

49. Jean Wardlow, "Civil Defense Phone Busy as Citizens Ask Questions," *Miami Herald*, 24 October 1962.

50. Juanita Greene, "Shelter Builders Busy—Answering Telephone," *Miami Herald*, 27 October 1962.

51. Juanita Greene, "Tense Talk of War—without Panic," *Miami Herald*, 24 October 1962.

52. Tom O'Connor, "Mayor Urges Calm; Tampa Mostly Is," *Tampa Tribune*, 25 October 1962. See also Peter B. Greenough, "Crisis Gave Tampa Case of Jitters," *Boston Globe*, 30 October 1962.

53. William J. Lewis, "Volpe Convenes State Agencies to Assess CD Capabilities," *Boston Globe*, 25 October 1962.

54. Robert A. McLean, "4306 Fallout Shelters in State—but Most Are Unmarked, Unstocked," *Boston Globe*, 28 October 1962.

55. William J. Lewis, "Volpe on CD," *Boston Globe*, 26 October 1962.

56. Don Millsap, "CD, Shelter Firms, Military Bases Busy," *Dallas Morning News*, 24 October 1962.

57. Kent Biffle, "Run on Emergency Supplies Reported by Dallas Stores," *Dallas Morning News*, 25 October 1962.

58. Eddie Hughes, "Avoid Panic Buying, CD Leaders Warn," *Dallas Morning News*, 27 October 1962.

59. Gene Hunter, "Stock Fallout Shelters, City Council Urged," *Los Angeles Times*, 24 October 1962.

60. *Los Angeles Times*, 24 October 1962.

61. *Los Angeles Times*, 25 October 1962.

62. *Los Angeles Times*, 25 October 1962.

63. *Los Angeles Times*, 25 October 1962. See also Jack Goulding, "Fallout Shelter Survey Gives Alarming Picture," *Los Angeles Times*, 27 October 1962.

64. Jack Smith, "Most Shelters Found Unmarked, Unusable," *Los Angeles Times*, 26 October 1962.

65. John M. Goshko, "Civil Defense Queries Rise in D.C. Area," *Washington Post*, 24 October 1962; *Washington Post*, 25 October 1962.

66. Kim Willenson, "103 Shelters Licensed, Five Are Ready to Use," *Washington Post*, 26 October 1962.

67. Bill Henry, "Capital Refuses to Be Panicked," *Los Angeles Times*, 26 October 1962.

68. Don Oberdorfer, "Survival of the Fewest," *Saturday Evening Post*, 23 March 1963, 17.

69. Rusk, *As I Saw It*, 244.

70. Khrushchev, *Khrushchev Remembers* (1970), 500. Zubok and Pleshakov, *Inside the Kremlin's Cold War*, 268.

71. Zubok and Pleshakov, *Inside the Kremlin's Cold War*, 271; see John Lewis Gaddis, *The Long Peace: Inquiries into the History of the Cold War* (New York: Oxford University Press, 1987), 215–45.

72. "Willy Brandt, May 17, 1964," in *Face the Nation, 1963–64: The Collected Transcripts from the CBS Radio and Television Broadcasts* (New York: Holt Information Systems, 1972), 213, 212.

73. Quoted in Richard Wayne Dyke, *Mr. Atomic Energy* (New York: Greenwood, 1989), 210.

74. Anthony J. Wiener and Paul C. Berry, "The Public Response to Civil Defense," unpublished report prepared by the Hudson Institute for the Office of Emergency Planning, 30 September 1964, 131. Collection of the FEMA Library, Washington, D.C.

75. See Peter Kihss, "Governor Builds 4 Bomb Shelters," *New York Times*, 23 July 1961.

76. Balk, "Anyone for Survival?" 74. When OCDM director Leo Hoegh tendered his resignation to President Eisenhower in 1960, his accompanying report claimed that more than one million family fallout shelters had been built. See Dwight D. Eisenhower, "Letter Accepting Resignation of Leo A. Hoegh as Director, Office of Civil and Defense Mobilization. December 30, 1960," in *Public Papers of the Presidents of the United States: Dwight D. Eisenhower, 1960–61, Containing the Public Messages, Speeches, and Statements of the President* (Washington, D.C.: GPO, 1961), 384.

77. The population in 1961 was 183,691,000, with 53,291,000 households. *Historical Statistics of the United States*, 10, 42.

78. See American Institute of Public Opinion, *The Gallup Poll*, 1738. See also George Gallup, "Fear of World War Is at 10-Year High," *Washington Post*, 8 October 1961.

79. The Department of Defense and the American Institute of Architects sponsored a competition "for the design of a community educational and recreational center incorporating dual purpose fallout shelter space." See Notes and Comments, *New Yorker*, 14 October 1967, 47.

80. Chet Holifield had concluded by 1963 that "the recent test ban treaty will have a psychological effect on some of the Members and will militate against them being willing to vote appropriations for civil defense." Quoted in Dyke, *Mr. Atomic Energy*, 212. Roger Hagan claimed that as early as 1962 Kennedy recognized "that he got involved in CD merely by reacting too precipitately to the political thunder of Rockefeller and by listening to the croonings of Chet Holifield, and is now trying to find a way to reverse the process he started." Hagan believed that Kennedy welcomed the congressional move to put funding decisions for civil defense under Congressman Albert Thomas, a staunch opponent of the shelter program. Roger Hagan, "Community Shelters," in *No Place to Hide: Fact and Fiction about Fallout Shelters*, ed. Seymour Melman (New York: Grove Press, 1962), 176.

81. Greenberg, "Fallout Shelters: Administration's Program is Facing Difficulty on Capitol Hill," 376.

82. Thomas quoted in Kerr, *Civil Defense in the U.S.*, 131.

83. See Ralph E. Lapp, *Kill and Overkill: The Strategy of Annihilation* (New York: Basic Books, 1962), 112–15. Because of its limitations, the Nike Zeus would have had to intercept incoming missiles above the atmosphere, where enemy missiles could employ decoys and defeat the system relatively easily. Designers hoped to overcome the deficiencies of the Nike Zeus by arming the interceptors with nu-

clear warheads, but the detonation of such warheads creates its own problems for the defense in the form of "radar blackout." Charles M. Herzfeld, "Missile Defense: Can It Work?" in *Why ABM? Policy Issues in the Missile Defense Controversy*, ed. Johan J. Holst and William Schneider, Jr. (New York: Pergamon, 1969), 18. In a 1956 interview on *Face the Nation*, AEC chairman Lewis Strauss alluded to tests of nuclear "defensive weapons" that would include "smaller weapons against incoming planes, let us say, or against incoming missiles." When pressed by Raymond Brandt of the *St. Louis Post-Dispatch* as to what exactly this meant ("Do you mean to say we are going to have ground-to-air defensive weapons, with atomics?"), Strauss replied, "I would hope that atomic weapons will be available for all kinds of defensive purposes—except hand grenades." "Lewis L. Strauss, February 26, 1956," in *Face the Nation, 1956: The Collected Transcripts from the CBS Radio and Television Broadcasts* (New York: Holt Information Systems, 1972), 65, 66, 67. On the same program in 1958, the AEC's Willard Libby claimed that much of the nuclear testing that was then being done by the United States was "in the direction of defensive weapons" and other small nuclear devices. "Willard F. Libby, November 16, 1958," in *Face the Nation, 1958: The Collected Transcripts from the CBS Radio and Television Broadcasts* (New York: Holt Information Systems, 1972), 354. One result of this research was the nuclear-armed Nike-Hercules surface-to-air missile. By 1958 this missile had been deployed to defend both Europe and the continental United States. David Alan Rosenberg, "Origins of Overkill," *International Security* 7, no. 4 (spring 1983): 43. See also Eric Semler et al., *The Language of Nuclear War*, s.v. "Surface-to-Air Missile (SAM)" (New York: Harper and Row, 1987); Abram Chayes, Jerome B. Wiesner, George W. Rathjens, and Steven Weinberg, "An Overview," in *ABM: An Evaluation of the Decision to Deploy an Antiballistic Missile System*, ed. Abram Chayes and Jerome B. Wiesner (New York: Harper and Row, 1969), 3–4; see also Oran R. Young, "Active Defense and International Order," *Bulletin of the Atomic Scientists* 23, no. 5 (May 1967): 35; Laurence W. Martin, "Ballistic Missile Defense and Europe," *Bulletin of the Atomic Scientists* 23, no. 5 (May 1967): 42.

84. Phased-array radar tracks targets electronically rather than mechanically. The two interceptors employed by the Nike X system were the Spartan, a nuclear-armed missile that operated above the atmosphere, and the Sprint, a high-speed vehicle designed to intercept missiles at lower altitudes, where the atmosphere could filter out decoys, chaff, and other light objects. William Schneider, Jr., "Missile Defense Systems: Past, Present, and Future," in Holst and Schneider, *Why ABM? Policy Issues in the Missile Defense Controversy*, 5–6.

85. *Civil Defense: Project Harbor Summary Report* (Washington, D.C.: National Academy of Sciences–National Research Council, 1964), 20. Collection of the FEMA Library, Washington, D.C. The Project Harbor study was a report produced by a group assembled by the National Academy of Sciences in the summer of 1963 under the directorship of Eugene Wigner. The Project Harbor report addressed a wide variety of civil defense issues, including ABMs. Generally upbeat

about the utility of civil defense and the survivability of nuclear war, the study insisted that "general nuclear war is unlikely to occur except after a build-up of tensions," and that this relatively lengthy warning time would make it possible to accomplish "strategic evacuation and improvised shelter construction" (10, 11). As for the post-attack environment, "large-scale primary fires, totally destructive insect plagues, and ecological imbalances that would make normal life impossible are not to be expected" (25). The study also advocated the creation of a professional civil defense cadre, whose size "might approximate the Coast Guard or the Public Health Service, i.e., have about 30,000 full-time employees" (16).

86. Raymond D. Gastil, "Civil Defense and Missile Defense," in Holst and Schneider, *Why ABM? Policy Issues in the Missile Defense Controversy*, 235–36.

87. McNamara quoted in Kerr, *Civil Defense in the U.S.*, 132.

88. Floyd I. John, "Protection against Standoff Thermal Attacks," Stanford Research Institute, February 1967, 1, 2. Collection of the FEMA Library, Washington, D.C.

89. "The Race Is On for the Super Guided Missile," *Mad*, July 1956, 10.

90. See Kerr, *Civil Defense in the U.S.*, 132, 131. See also Harry B. Yoshpe, *Our Missing Shield* (Washington, D.C.: Federal Emergency Management Agency, 1981), 374, 373.

91. Yoshpe, *Our Missing Shield*, 374, 376.

92. Herbert Roback, "Civil Defense and National Defense," in *Who Speaks for Civil Defense?* ed. Eugene P. Wigner (New York: Scribner's, 1968), 92, 100. In 1967 McNamara announced that while he was in favor of a "thin" ABM system (the Sentinel program) costing in the vicinity of $5 billion, he was opposed to a large-scale "heavy" system costing some $40 billion. McNamara insisted that "the $40 billion is not the issue. If we could build and deploy a genuinely impenetrable shield over the United States, we would be willing to spend not only $40 billion, but any reasonable multiple of that amount that was necessary. The money in itself is not the problem; the penetrability of the proposed shield is the problem." McNamara worried that an ABM system could be easily defeated by enemy countermeasures, and that ABMs could precipitate a new arms race, with both sides spending more money to protect their offensive capabilities. The proposed Sentinel system was not deployed. Robert S. McNamara, *The Essence of Security: Reflections in Office* (New York: Harper and Row, 1968), 63–66.

93. Paul Boyer lists "the illusion of diminished risk," the "loss of immediacy," the "promise of a world transformed by atomic energy," the "complexity and comfort of deterrence theory," and the Vietnam War as factors underlying the public's lack of interest in the issues of nuclear war after 1963. Paul Boyer, *By the Bomb's Early Light* (Chapel Hill: University of North Carolina Press, 1994), 357–58.

94. McNamara quoted in Steuart L. Pittman, Afterword to Wigner, *Who Speaks for Civil Defense?* 112. In 1971 the General Accounting Office completed a survey of civil defense efforts in the United States and found that between fiscal years 1962 and 1970

civil defense funding as a percentage of Department of Defense funding averaged .19 percent. Its lowest point was in 1969, when it stood at .08 percent. The GAO conclusion was that civil defense "does not seem to be regarded as a primary element of national defense." See Yoshpe, *Our Missing Shield*, 389–90.

95. Steuart L. Pittman, "Government and Civil Defense," in Wigner, *Who Speaks for Civil Defense?* 51–52.

96. Thomas J. Kerr notes that "the Soviets had quickly denounced the whole [counterforce] idea as 'monstrous' and announced they would have nothing to do with it. Although McNamara never formally repudiated the doctrine, he stopped emphasizing it and, in fact, complained that 'in some ways the press overplayed that part of the speech.'" Kerr, *Civil Defense in the U.S.*, 138.

97. Pittman, "Government and Civil Defense," 53–54.

98. As Bundy put it, "But when our leaders talk of shelters, are they telling us that we are going to need them? What do they have up their sleeves, then? Why should we *plan* for what we *must* avoid?" McGeorge Bundy, *Danger and Survival* (New York: Random House, 1988), 356. Bundy claimed that Kennedy's shelter proposal "was put forward with inadequate preparation, and Kennedy's most important statement about it was unwisely placed in a speech about decisions on the Berlin crisis, with the result that it was wrongly perceived as a means of response to imminent danger." Bundy believed that Kennedy felt as Bundy did, that "in a world of real nuclear danger civil defense is indeed a prudent form of insurance" (355).

99. These unanswered questions, according to the *Post*, were, "Do underground shelters really protect us or simply provide a false sense of security? Should such decisions be left to the whims and resources of individual homeowners? And finally, would the survivors of underground life find a habitable world remaining aboveground?" "The Bomb-Shelter Mania," *Saturday Evening Post*, 27 March 1965, 88.

100. Ralph E. Lapp, *The Weapons Culture* (New York: Norton, 1968), 50, 163.

101. "Civil Defense Developments," *Bulletin of the Atomic Scientists* 17, no. 8 (October 1961): 347. Even the civil defense promoters Walter H. Murphey and Bjorn Klinge acknowledged the grim outlook for urban dwellers, describing American civil defense as "a good *rural* program." Walter H. Murphey and Bjorn Klinge, "Civil Defense Abroad," in Wigner, *Who Speaks for Civil Defense?* 85.

102. Brodie also notes, "Part of that apathy in the city dweller unquestionably stems from the realization that though with heroic measures the statistical chances for his bare survival could be somewhat increased, the city with which his life is identified would inevitably be a charred and dismal waste after an attack. It would be hard to convince him otherwise." Bernard Brodie, *Strategy in the Missile Age* (Princeton: Princeton University Press, 1959), 212, 213.

103. Griffiths went further, claiming that the emphasis on shelters in urban areas was basically antiwoman because most women would be at home in the suburbs. "If you are going to survive after a nuclear war," said Griffiths, "we've got to save women of child-bearing age." *Los Angeles Times*, 3 August 1961.

104. See Yoshpe, *Our Missing Shield*, 354–55. The shelter space that had actually been *marked* by 1967 was enough for 92.7 million persons, with sufficient supplies for 47.1 million persons for two weeks (350). See Office of Civil Defense, *Existing Schools: Their Future, Upgraded Schoolhouses with Fallout Protection* (1968). Collection of the FEMA Library, Washington, D.C.

105. Department of Defense, Office of Civil Defense, *Winning Designs for Fallout Shelters in Shopping Centers*, H-13 (1965), 1, 2. Collection of Robert Harris.

106. Allan Winkler argues that at no time "did a coherent national policy fully take hold and become a permanent part of American life." Allan M. Winkler, *Life under a Cloud: American Anxiety about the Atom* (New York: Oxford University Press, 1993), 110.

107. Mary M. Simpson, "A Long Hard Look at Civil Defense," *Bulletin of the Atomic Scientists* 11, no. 9 (November 1956): 348.

108. Ralph E. Lapp, "Rockefeller's Civil Defense Program," *Bulletin of the Atomic Scientists* 16, no. 4 (April 1960): 136, 135.

109. Freeman Dyson, *Weapons and Hope* (New York: Harper and Row, 1984), 88, 92.

110. Einstein maintained that "our defense is not in armaments, nor in science, nor in going underground. Our defense is in law and order." Albert Einstein, "Only Then Shall We Find Courage," in Linus Pauling, *No More War!* (Westport, CT: Greenwood, 1962), 214–15. Robert Moses, "The Civil Defense Fiasco," *Harper's* 214, no. 1290 (November 1957): 34.

111. Eisenhower quoted in Walter Goodman, "The Truth about Fallout Shelters," *Redbook* 18, no. 3 (January 1962): 74.

112. Jane Jacobs, *The Death and Life of Great American Cities* (New York: Vintage, 1961), 445.

113. Lewis Mumford, *The City in History* (New York: Harcourt, Brace and World, 1961), 486.

114. Mead believed that the shelter controversy "was an expression of a much wider ethical conflict" that began when the first bomb was dropped on Hiroshima. According to Mead, Americans realized that in future wars all combatants would be risking "suicide and the destruction of their own civilization," and that now there was no nation safe from the threat of annihilation. Americans reacted to this new state of affairs by both expanding and drawing in among themselves. Expansionism was reflected in the extension of American defenses around the world and in the creation of "new frontiers" in space and in the ocean depths. Suburban shelter building represented the contrary impulse. Margaret Mead, "Are Shelters the Answer?" *New York Times*, 26 November 1961.

115. James A. Pike, "Survival by Shelter or Sanity?" in *God and the H-Bomb*, ed. Donald Keys (New York: Bellmeadows Press, 1961), 187. Pike claimed that "the cold war is a political, ideological and economic war; it is not a shooting war" (185).

116. Kenneth T. Jackson, *Crabgrass Frontier: The Suburbanization of the United States* (New York: Oxford University Press, 1985), 244.

117. In *Homeward Bound*, Elaine Tyler May claims that "family shelters symbolized family security and togetherness in the face of a frightening world," and that "civil defense merged with widespread popular wishes for family security." Elaine Tyler May, *Homeward Bound: American Families in the Cold War Era* (New York: Basic Books, 1988), 107.

118. Barbara Burr, letter, *Good Housekeeping*, April 1962, 18.

119. In Arthur Conan Doyle's "Silver Blaze," the following conversation takes place between Colonel Ross and Sherlock Holmes:

"Is there any point to which you would wish to draw my attention?"

"To the curious incident of the dog in the night-time."

"The dog did nothing in the night-time."

"That was the curious incident," remarked Sherlock Holmes.

Arthur Conan Doyle, "Silver Blaze," in *The Complete Sherlock Holmes* (New York: Barnes and Noble, 1992), 347.

120. Spencer R. Weart, *Nuclear Fear* (Cambridge: Harvard University Press, 1988), 257.

121. Winkler, *Life under a Cloud*, 110.

122. Margot A. Henriksen, *Dr. Strangelove's America: Society and Culture in the Atomic Age* (Berkeley: University of California Press, 1997), 387–88.

123. George Gallup, "Vast Majority Backs Kennedy Cuba Policy," *Washington Post*, 24 October 1962.

124. See Jerry Gillam, "Civil Defense Plans Sound, Brown Asserts," *Los Angeles Times*, 26 October 1962.

125. Guy Oakes, *The Imaginary War* (New York: Oxford University Press, 1994), 6. The *International Journal of Politics, Culture and Society* published an issue devoted to Oakes's book *The Imaginary War*. See Arthur J. Vidich, "Atomic Bombs and American Democracy," 499–506, John Lukacs, "Reason and Unreason in Civil Defense," 507–10, Franco Ferrarotti, "Gullible Leaders and Followers," 511–16, all in *International Journal of Politics, Culture and Society* 8, no. 3 (1995).

126. Michael S. Sherry, *In the Shadow of War* (New Haven: Yale University Press, 1995), 500, 499.

127. McEnaney, "Civil Defense Begins at Home."

128. Boyer, *By the Bomb's Early Light*, 355.

129. Paul Boyer, "From the Test Ban Treaty to Three Mile Island," in *Fallout: A Historian Reflects on America's Half-Century Encounter with Nuclear Weapons* (Columbus: Ohio State University Press, 1998), 110–11.

130. Engelhardt claimed that the presence of nuclear weapons created "a netherworld of consciousness where victory and defeat, enemy and self, threatened to merge," and led to an "un-American spirit of doubt" and "triumphalist

despair." Tom Engelhardt, *The End of Victory Culture: Cold War America and the Disillusioning of a Generation* (New York: Basic Books, 1995), 6, 9.

131. Pat Watters, "War Is for Continuation of Life, Not Annihilation, Super-Patrotism [*sic*]," *Atlanta Journal*, 7 August 1961.

132. Quoted in Philip J. Funigiello, "Managing Armageddon," *Journal of Policy History* 2, no. 4 (1990): 419.

133. Thomas Merton, *Original Child Bomb: Points for Meditation to Be Scratched on the Walls of a Cave* (New York: New Directions, 1962), n.p.

134. Mendelsohn quoted in Brelis, *Run, Dig or Stay?* 183, 182.

135. As early as 1958, Luke Vortman, an engineer with the Scandia corporation, had worried about fallout shelters "which a peaceful world might look back on as merely monuments to the current threat of war." House Subcommittee of the Committee on Government Operations, *Civil Defense*, 85th Cong., 2d sess., 1958, 55.

136. Robert C. Ruark, "Chips Were Down, Shelters Weren't," *Miami Herald*, 1 November 1962.

137. James Connolly, interview by author, Chico, CA, 20 May 2000. Connolly's school was St. John's College High School in Washington, D.C. Connolly is currently a professor of management information systems at California State University, Chico.

138. Hagan, "Community Shelters," 177.

NOTES TO THE POSTSCRIPT

1. See William R. Kintner, ed., *Safeguard: Why the ABM Makes Sense* (New York: Hawthorn, 1969); Marvin Kalkstein, "ABM and the Arms Race," in *Beyond Conflict and Containment: Critical Studies of Military and Foreign Policy*, ed. Milton J. Rosenberg (New Brunswick, NJ: Transaction, 1972); Eric Semler et al., *The Language of Nuclear War*, s.v. "Safeguard" (New York: Harper and Row, 1987).

2. See Harry B. Yoshpe, *Our Missing Shield* (Washington, D.C.: U.S. Federal Emergency Management Agency, 1981), 455–57. See also Thomas J. Kerr, *Civil Defense in the U.S.: Bandaid for a Holocaust?* (Boulder: Westview, 1983), 152–53.

3. See Kerr, *Civil Defense in the U.S.*, 157–61.

4. Jeremy Isaacs and Taylor Downing, *Cold War: An Illustrated History, 1945–1991* (Boston: Little, Brown, 1998), 333, 334.

5. Thanks to my colleague Jeff Livingston for introducing me to this material. Jeffrey Livingston, "Triumph, Decline and the Rapture: America at the Millennium" (paper presented at California State University, Chico, 2000).

6. Max M. Kampelman, introduction to *Alerting America: The Papers of the Committee on the Present Danger*, ed. Charles Tyroler II (Washington, D.C.: Pergamon-Brassey's, 1984), xv–xvi.

7. See "Peace with Freedom: A Discussion by the Committee on the Present

Danger before the Foreign Policy Association, 14 March 1978," in Tyroler, *Alerting America: The Papers of the Committee on the Present Danger*, 30.

8. Committee on the Present Danger, "Has America Become Number 2? The U.S.-Soviet Military Balance and American Defense Policies and Programs," in Tyroler, *Alerting America: The Papers of the Committee on the Present Danger*, 217; Committee on the Present Danger, "Is America Becoming Number 2? Current Trends in the U.S.-Soviet Military Balance," in Tyroler, *Alerting America: The Papers of the Committee on the Present Danger*, 90. The $2 billion claim is made in Department of Defense, *Soviet Military Power* (Washington, D.C.: GPO, 1981), 68.

9. The CPD did admit to the "unattractiveness of civil defense to an open society." Committee on the Present Danger, "Is America Becoming Number 2?" 58.

10. Committee on the Present Danger, "The 1980 Crisis and What We Should Do about It," in Tyroler, *Alerting America: The Papers of the Committee on the Present Danger*, 177.

11. Jerry W. Sanders, *Peddlers of Crisis: The Committee on the Present Danger and the Politics of Containment* (Boston: South End Press, 1983), 287–88.

12. Samuel P. Huntington, "The Renewal of Strategy," in *The Strategic Imperative: New Policies for American Security*, ed. Samuel P. Huntington (Cambridge, MA: Ballinger, 1982), 1, 39, 50. Also beating the drum for civil defense was Stephen Peter Rosen, who asserted that civil defense would "reduce the suffering if deterrence failed," and would have the strategic bonus of demonstrating to the Soviets that the United States would "take all steps necessary to stop Soviet advances." Stephen Peter Rosen, "Foreign Policy and Nuclear Weapons: The Case for Strategic Defenses," in Huntington, *The Strategic Imperative*, 149.

13. Felicity Barringer, "Civil Defense Evacuation Plan Stirs Anew," *Washington Post*, 29 January 1982; George C. Wilson, "Civil Defense Plan Rebuffed in Senate," *Washington Post*, 2 April 1982; "Fallout Shelters: Making a Comeback," *Newsweek*, 22 February 1982.

14. In 1972 the United States had 5,700 warheads in its arsenal, and 9,480 by 1982. The Soviets had 2,500 warheads in their arsenal in 1972, and 8,040 by 1982. By 1982 the total U.S. nuclear destructive force was 3,505 megatons, while the Soviets had 7,868 megatons of nuclear destructive power. See "Living with Mega-Death," *Time*, 29 March 1982, 22; Isaacs and Downing, *Cold War*, 245.

15. Reagan told Scheer, "And so, in addition to their great military buildup, they have practiced this, they have practiced evacuation, when we finally began to learn the facts, we learned that in one summer alone, they took over 20 million young people out of the cities into the country to give them training in just living off the countryside." Robert Scheer, *With Enough Shovels: Reagan, Bush and Nuclear War* (New York: Random House, 1982), 106.

16. David H. Morrissey, "A Blast from the Past," *Progressive* 47, no. 2 (February 1983): 37.

17. Barringer, "Civil Defense Evacuation Plan Stirs Anew"; Robert Scheer, "U.S. Will Revive Civil Defense," *Los Angeles Times*, 15 January 1982.

18. Scheer, "U.S. Will Revive Civil Defense."

19. See Robert Scheer, "U.S. Could Survive War in Administration's View," *Los Angeles Times*, 16 January 1982.

20. Quoted in Ed Zuckerman, "How Would the U.S. Survive a Nuclear War?" *Esquire* 97, no. 3 (March 1982): 38.

21. See, for instance, Ellen Goodman, "Civil Defense Follies," *Washington Post*, 3 February 1982.

22. Ellen Hume, "Senators Bar Pentagon Witnesses, Seek Silenced Official at Civil Defense Hearing," *Los Angeles Times*, 17 March 1982.

23. "Does Civil Defense Make Sense?" *Newsweek*, 26 April 1982, 31.

24. Jay Mathews, "Head-for-the-Hills Civil Defense Schemes Produce Mixed Reviews," *Washington Post*, 16 May 1982.

25. John Kendall, "Hahn Assails Civil Defense Planning," *Los Angeles Times*, 23 January 1982.

26. "Living with Mega-Death," 24.

27. Tom Wicker, "The Hardest Truth," *New York Times*, 16 December 1983.

28. "Does Civil Defense Make Sense?" 31.

29. Scheer, "U.S. Could Survive War in Administration's View."

30. Robert Scheer, "Soviet Doctors Join in Denouncing Nuclear Civil Defense as 'an Illusion,'" *Los Angeles Times*, 23 June 1983.

31. Richard Leakey, "Genes, War and Human Fate," *Science Digest* 90, no. 11 (November 1982): 71, 70. See Helen Caldicott, *Missile Envy: The Arms Race and Nuclear War* (New York: Bantam, 1985).

32. Herbert L. Abrams, "Preparing for 'the Highest Rate of Casualties in History,'" *Bulletin of the Atomic Scientists* 39, no. 6 (June–July 1983): 11S. Also included in the *Bulletin* supplement was a critique of FEMA that claimed that the agency's plans "take place within a reality bounded by good luck" and fail "to comprehend how nuclear war differs from previous disasters." Jennifer Leaning and Matthew Leighton, "The World according to FEMA," *Bulletin of the Atomic Scientists* 39, no. 6 (June–July 1983): 3S. In his contribution to the *Bulletin's* supplement, John Lamperti argued that even strictly defensive measures, such as civil defense, could have a destabilizing impact on the arms race, and he uses the development of ABMs in the early 1960s as an example. While ABMs were not weapons of offense, both sides viewed them as threats to their nuclear arsenals, and in response MIRVs—multiple independently targetable reentry vehicles—were developed to overwhelm an ABM defense. Lamperti concluded that the end result of ABM development of the 1960s was not greater security but an escalation of the arms race, and that in the 1980s "civil defense, like the ABM, could intensify the arms race and increase the threat of war." John Lamperti, "'What Harm Can It Do?'" *Bulletin of the Atomic Scientists* 39, no. 6 (June–July 1983): 9S.

33. Jonathan Schell, *The Fate of the Earth* (New York: Knopf, 1982), 59–61.

34. William F. Buckley, Jr., "Nuclear Nonthink," *National Review* 35, no. 2 (4 February 1983): 140.

35. Joseph P. Evans, "The Big Chill," *Commonweal* 111, no. 8 (20 April 1984): 231.

36. Thomas Powers, "Nuclear Winter and Nuclear Strategy," *Atlantic* 254, no. 5 (November 1984): 55.

37. Paul Brians, "Farewell to the First Atomic Age," *Nuclear Texts and Contexts*, no. 8 (fall 1992): 2.

38. See Paul Boyer, *When Time Shall Be No More* (Cambridge, MA: Belknap Press, 1995), 5. Taking note of the 1980s surge of interest in the apocalypse, William Martin observed that "millions of American evangelicals apparently believe that within the present generation, and probably sometime in the 1980s, Jesus will return to lay the groundwork for a glorious thousand-year reign here on earth." William Martin, "Waiting for the End," *Atlantic Monthly* 249, no. 6 (June 1982): 31.

39. Hal Lindsey, *The Late Great Planet Earth* (Grand Rapids, MI: Zondervan, 1970), 161.

40. Lindsey, *The Late Great Planet Earth*, 166.

41. Hal Lindsey, *The 1980s: Countdown to Armageddon* (New York: Bantam, 1981), 77, 76, 86.

42. Also shown on television in 1983 was *Testament*, which portrayed the struggles of a woman and her three children after a nuclear war has devastated nearby San Francisco. See Allan M. Winkler, *Life under a Cloud: American Anxiety about the Atom* (New York: Oxford University Press, 1993), 194–95.

43. "TV's Nuclear Nightmare," *Newsweek*, 21 November 1983, 66.

44. See J. Michael Hogan, *The Nuclear Freeze Campaign: Rhetoric and Foreign Policy in the Telepolitical Age* (East Lansing: Michigan State University Press, 1994), 49.

45. For an example of shelter building in the 1980s, see Phil McCombs, "Meet the Whitneys; They're Ready," *Washington Post*, 18 January 1984.

46. Phil McCombs, "Digging In for the Bomb," *Washington Post*, 19 January 1984.

47. Hogan, *The Nuclear Freeze Campaign*, 19. Some believed that the freeze movement was overly timid in its goals. Sidney Lens referred to "an excess of caution" among freeze organizers, and declared that "we should regard the freeze as only the first step toward our *real* goal . . . the abolition of all nuclear weapons on this planet." Sidney Lens, "How Deep a Freeze," *Progressive* 46, no. 5 (May 1982): 17.

48. Sanders, *Peddlers of Crisis*, 331–32, 334.

49. Hogan, *The Nuclear Freeze Campaign*, 20.

50. Hogan, *The Nuclear Freeze Campaign*, 3. Hogan calls the House nuclear freeze resolution "a strategically ambiguous affirmation, not of the freeze in particular, but of arms control in general" (189).

51. *Washington Post*, 29 April 1983.

52. Michael Oreskes, "Civil Defense Planning Futile, Cuomo Says," *New York Times*, 15 May 1984.

53. Maura Dolan, "Ferraro Raps Reagan Civil Defense Plan, Says It Implies Nuclear War Is 'Tolerable,'" *Los Angeles Times*, 31 August 1984.

54. Judith Miller, "U.S. Delays Buying Morphine to Avoid War-Ready Image," *New York Times*, 14 February 1983.

55. FEMA spokesperson Russell Clanahan said, "The crisis relocation planning has been abandoned, no question about it." *New York Times*, 4 March 1985.

56. Ronald Reagan, "Launching the SDI," in *Promise or Peril: The Strategic Defense Initiative*, ed. Zbigniew Brzezinski (Washington, D.C.: Ethics and Public Policy Center, 1986), 49, 48.

57. Mikhail Gorbachev, "SDI: A Threat to Peace," in Brzezinski, *Promise or Peril: The Strategic Defense Initiative*, 223. Charles Krauthammer, "The Illusion of Star Wars," in Brzezinski, *Promise or Peril: The Strategic Defense Initiative*, 140.

58. See John Isaacs, "A Political Decision," 23–25; Theodore A. Postol, "The Target Is Russia," 30–35; Richard L. Garwin, "The Wrong Plan," 36–41, all in *Bulletin of the Atomic Scientists* 56, no. 2 (March–April 2000). George N. Lewis et al. have noted, "Arms-control concerns, technological doubts, enormous price tags—these and other problems have dogged U.S. attempts to establish nationwide defenses for more than three decades. . . . Only a national defense that can reliably counter a real threat to U.S. security should be pursued: the system the U.S. is preparing to put in place will do neither." George N. Lewis, Theodore A. Postol, and John Pike, "Why National Missile Defense Won't Work," *Scientific American*, August 1999, 41.

59. Joel Stein, "Hey, You in That Bunker, You Can Come Out Now!" *Time*, 1 January 2000, 54, 60. See also Richard Lacayo, "The End of the World as We Know It?" *Time*, 18 January 1999, 60–70.

60. Fred Hiatt, "Commerce Goes Underground in Moscow," *Washington Post*, 27 November 1992.

61. Carey Scott, "Kremlin Refurbishes Nuclear Bunkers as Fear of Nato Grows," *Sunday Times* (London), 13 April 1997. In another indication of how strategy has shifted since the end of the Cold War, Russia carried out a large military exercise in July 1999 based on a scenario in which Russia is forced to respond with nuclear weapons to superior NATO conventional forces. See Michael R. Gordon, "Russia Confirms Mock Nuclear Strike," *Sacramento Bee*, 10 July 1999.

62. Sabin Russell, "S.F. Quietly Stockpiling Civil Defense Gear," *San Francisco Chronicle*, 26 February 1999.

63. See *Taking Shelter from the Storm: Building a Safe Room inside Your House*, Federal Emergency Management Agency no. 320 (1999).

Index

Index

National Academy of Sciences, 26, 291n. 85
National Atomic Museum, 11
National/community shelter systems, 2, 24, 28–32, 37, 81, 86–88, 98, 102, 105, 107, 186, 257n. 72
National Education Association, 137
National Fallout Shelter Survey, 206
National Missile Defense, 223, 300n. 58
National Museum of American History, 12
National Planning Association, 68
National Radiological Defense Laboratory, 283n. 162
National Review, 90
National Security Council, 19, 29
National Security Resources Board (NSRB), 23, 114
National Shelter Association, 80
National Stockpile, 117
Naval Medical Center, 171
NEA Journal, 137
Nelson, Otto L., 26
Nevins, Allan, 54
New England Journal of Medicine, 173
New Look, 19
New Orleans, Louisiana, 254
New Republic, 223
New York, New York, 48, 49, 50, 53, 54, 55, 61–62, 65, 81, 100–102, 147, 160, 182, 196, 219, 221, 222
New Yorker, 52, 220
New York State Civil Defense Commission, 86
New York Stock Exchange, 120
New York Times, 43, 80, 88, 100–102, 181, 189, 208, 219, 223
New World Review, 67
New World Survival Company, 222
Newman, Charles, 86
Newman, James R., 67
Newsweek, 80, 86, 140, 219, 222
Ney, Virgil, 122
Niebuhr, Reinhold, 39, 145
Nielsen, Mark T., 191
Nike Hercules missile, 291n. 83
Nike X missile, 202, 203
Nike Zeus missile, 44, 202–203
Nineteen-Eighties: Countdown to Armageddon (H. Lindsey), 221
Nitze, Paul, 19, 196, 215
Nixon, Richard M., 168, 209, 214, 216

No More War (L. Pauling), 280n. 104
Norborne, Missouri, 122
Norstad, Lauris, 156, 175, 274n. 35
North American Air Defense Command, 117
Northampton, Massachusetts, 140, 187
North Atlantic Treaty Organization (NATO), 156, 157, 175, 224, 234–235n. 34, 300n. 61
Norton, Frank F., 80, 191–192
Norwalk, Connecticut, 137
Norwalk Plan, 137
NSC 68, 19, 234n. 34
NSC 162/2, 19
Nuclear Age (T. O'Brien), 132
Nuclear Fear (S. Weart), 209
Nuclear freeze movement, 222–223
Nuclear Holocausts: Atomic War in Fiction, 1895–1984 (P. Brians), 40
Nuclear Information, 57–58
Nuclear-proof cities, 124–126, 255n. 29
"Nuclear War in St. Louis: One Year Later" (F. Moog), 57
Nuclear Weapons and Foreign Policy (H. Kissinger), 152–153
Nuclear winter, 221
Number of shelters, 79, 93, 201–202, 209, 290n. 76
Nutley, NJ, 91–92

Oakes, Guy, 210, 236n. 56
Oberdorfer, Don, 200
O'Brien, Tim, 132
Office of Civil and Defense Mobilization (OCDM), 32, 33, 34, 37, 141, 283n. 171, 290n. 76
Office of Civil Defense (OCD), 37, 78, 134, 137, 160, 191, 204, 206
Office of Civil Defense Planning, 18
Office of Defense Mobilization, 32, 115
Office of Emergency Planning, 201
O'Hare Inn, 121
Omaha, Nebraska, 167
O'Neill, Thomas P. "Tip," 115
On the Beach (N. Shute), 43, 76, 145
On Thermonuclear War (H. Kahn), 66–68, 155–156, 159
Operation Alert, 27–28, 62
Operation Kids, 28
Opinion polls, 18
Oppenheimer, J. Robert, 1, 22, 177, 178
Osborn, Frederick, 321n. 12

Index

Index

About the Author

Kenneth D. Rose teaches history at California State University, Chico, and is the author of *American Women and the Repeal of Prohibition,* also available from NYU Press.